Indian Names on
Wisconsin's Map

Indian Names on Wisconsin's Map

Virgil J. Vogel

The University of Wisconsin Press

The University of Wisconsin Press
114 North Murray Street
Madison, Wisconsin 53715

3 Henrietta Street
London WC2E 8LU, England

5   4   3   2   1

Printed in the United States of America

Library of Congress Cataloging-in-Publication Data
Vogel, Virgil J.
    Indian names on Wisconsin's map / Virgil J. Vogel.
    342 pp.   cm.
    Includes bibliographical references and index.
    ISBN 0-299-12980-2   ISBN 0-299-12984-5
        1. Indians of North America—Wisconsin—
    Names.   2. Names, Geographical—Wisconsin.
    3. Wisconsin—History—Miscellanea.
    I. Title.
    E78.W8V64   1991
    917.75'0014—dc20   91-7294

To Louise
who made it possible

Contents

vii

Illustrations

Preface

The definition of "place name" is not always self-evident. The geographical names used in this compilation are almost entirely from those listed in the *Alphabetical Finding List of Wisconsin Place Names*, prepared by the U.S. Geological Survey, National Mapping Division, Reston, Virginia. This list is based on names shown in U.S. topographic maps. However, certain kinds of names used in the USGS list are not considered here because they lack permanence, because their application is too insignificant to warrant attention, or because they are names of a private or commercial nature. Excluded are the names of structures (including buildings, dams, bridges, churches, hospitals, and schools), camps and resorts, cemeteries, industries, mines, farms, golf courses, airports, monuments, rail sidings, and real estate subdivisions.

I have undertaken to include all political toponyms. My usage of "city" and "village" follows official state practice. These designations are based on the local form of government rather than size. According to lists in the State of Wisconsin *1989–1990 Blue Book*, as of January 1, 1988, there were 188 cities and 395 villages in the state. In addition, I have also used "village" to refer to mapped unincorporated settlements. Civil towns, or towns, are the Wisconsin equivalent of townships elsewhere. In official state usage, a town is referred to by name and a survey township only by range and township number. For convenience, though, I have occasionally used "township" with a name, chiefly when locating a geographical place or feature within that area. All topographical names of land and water are also included. The generic names listed—"bay," "bluff," "marsh,"—are defined as in the USGS list.

Another matter of style should be mentioned here, relating to plural forms of tribal names. Publishers are not in agreement on this matter, but I prefer the recommendation of the U.S. Bureau of Ethnology in 1904, that the same form should be used for both the singular and plural if the tribal name was in an Indian language (e.g., Ojibwa) but that the standard plural form should be used for tribal names given in European languages (e.g., Foxes). In the same year, the Bureau of American Ethnology (BAE) adopted standard spellings for tribal names; these spellings have been followed here except in cases in which the map name is different.[1] Tribes that are known by several names are referred to first by the geographical names which honor them, and then by other recognized names. The orthography of personal names used herein is that which has been incorporated into geographical names or the form that is used in standard sources such as F. W. Hodge's *Handbook of American Indians North of Mexico*.[2]

In compiling a book such as this, a writer soon discovers that much of the information sought is not to be found in printed or known manuscript sources. It is necessary to probe the unpublished information in possession of local residents, including Indians, when possible. Therefore, I have relied heavily upon personal interviews and correspondence. Candor compels me to admit that information obtained by such means was not always reliable. However, it often contained clues leading to new ways of tracing a name. At times these contacts provided fragments of hitherto unrecorded folklore which, though not historical, has its own value as a body of knowledge deserving of preservation.

Numerous individuals contributed information in response to my inquiries, either through interviews, or by correspondence, or both. Foremost among them is Frances R. Perry of Black River Falls, a reliable scholar of the Winnebago language and friend of the Winnebago people, who remains active in her nineties. Not only was she my guide on a tour of nearby Winnebago communities, but she also was a valuable informant and took the trouble to write numerous letters in reply to my inquiries. Another who went out of his way to be helpful was Professor Frederic Cassidy, editor of the *Dictionary of American Regional English*. Among my Indian informants were several members of the St. Croix band of Chippewa Indians of Polk, Washburn, and Douglas counties, interviewed in September 1986. Among them was Eugene Taylor, chairman of the St. Croix band, of Webster, Wisconsin; his mother, Lolita Taylor, author of *The Native American*; and Bennie Skinaway, of Luck, Wisconsin, vice-chairman of the St. Croix Chippewa. Also helpful was Gene Conner, Historic Preservation Officer of the St. Croix Chippewa, of Webster. Larry Matrious, Potawatomi speaker and teacher at the Hannahville reservation of Wilson, Michigan, also answered questions in an interview. Another helpful informant was Father Luke Leiterman of Pickerel, Wisconsin, then (1980) president of the Langlade County Historical Society.

The numerous individuals who kindly answered written inquiries are listed in the bibliography in alphabetical order. Whether their contributions were large or small, all were useful, and this notice is their only reward.

The principal research libraries used in this study were the University of Chicago's Regenstein Library; the Newberry Library of Chicago, where John Aubrey was always particularly helpful; the Chicago Historical Society, where Archie Motley, curator of manuscripts, performed special favors; and the State Historical Society of Wisconsin, Madison.

My wife, Louise Vogel, has been a diligent research assistant, performing a number of mundane tasks, and has also been indispensable in view of my own limitations. She has also been my photographer and illustrator. My son John has been my driver, errand boy, and all-around helper.

Introduction

Robert Louis Stevenson wrote that "there is no part of the world where nomenclature is so rich, poetical, humourous and picturesque as in the United States of America."[1] Certainly part of this richness is due to the abundance of native American names that have survived the European conquest. However, these names do more than add a poetic and picturesque quality to the American map. Place names are cultural artifacts which tell us much about how people lived, as do the relics dug from the ground. They are historical records which can chart the location and migration of people, both native and European. Some names tell of topographic features which have changed or which disappeared long ago. Others record the former range of plant and animal species that have undergone drastic changes in their number and distribution. Place names may preserve fragments of ancient languages that disappeared before they were recorded anywhere else, or they may commemorate historic events of which there is no record except in oral tradition or archaeology. Names also tell us something about those people we have called Indians, including their cosmic views, their values, their understanding of their place in nature, and their ways of life.

Moreover, the native place names tell us much about the intruders from the Old World. The European newcomers adopted thousands of aboriginal names and carried them from one place to another in their migrations. Their poets, novelists, playwrights, and essayists adopted and popularized Indian names in their written works, and many of these were transferred to the map as names of settlements and physical features of land and water.

Toponomy is studied in order to trace the sequent occupation geography of particular regions.[2] Successive groups of occupants leave layers of names on the landscape, which may be only partly displaced by later arrivals, who add their own layers of names. Thus, names form a record of cultural succession similar to that of the layers of physical artifacts studied by archaeologists. Morris Swadesh, in arguing for the utilization of the methods and skills of various disciplines in studying prehistory, showed how linguistics is one key to the study of prehistory and cited place names as a useful tool in tracing the diffusion of cultures.[3]

Place names in particular demand the use of both linguistic and historical procedures. A place name can be erroneously analyzed by breaking it into supposed syllables of a language not native to the area. Although names can often indicate where a tribe lived, it is likewise necessary at times to use historical data on tribal movements in order to establish the linguistic origin of particular names.

Names, however, should not be the province of scholars only. Names brighten the countryside, speak of its history, and heighten the joy of travel. Once we cease to think of the names of places as mere labels and begin to see them as having cultural and historical meaning, we add a new dimension to our appreciation of the environment.

The geographical names left by the Indians are the oldest and perhaps the most neglected by scholars and least understood by the public. While they form but a small part of our total name heritage, it is still a prominent part. The larger rivers, lakes, mountain ranges, and other topographical features are likely to have Indian names. While most of our cities and towns have European names, fully half of the states have Indian names. Of Wisconsin's seventy-two counties, eighteen, or 25 percent, have Indian names. Eight more have French names that are translations from Indian names, or French names of individual Indians, or French names of Indian cultural phenomena.

What is not generally known is how many of our local names are translations of Indian names of those places. Sometimes the name of a place has gone through two language changes. The Indians called a certain river Kipikaoui. The French, translating the Indian name, called it Racine, and the Anglo-Americans named it Root River but kept the French name for the city at the river's mouth. Thus, the full effect of aboriginal influence on our map is not measured by native names only: the translated names, insofar as possible, also deserve mention. So also do the names that commemorate historical events relating to the Indians, most of which, unfortunately, recall warfare. In addition, there are personal names that became place names. Often, these names are translations of Indian names but obviously of Indian origin, such as Black Hawk; others are European names given to or adopted by Indians, such as Langlade. Indian personal names were not used as place names by unacculturated Indians. Their presence is a sign of white influence.

My aim in writing this book was to give the origin, language, and meaning of all Indian names in Wisconsin. This goal has not been fully achieved. Much of the information I sought is lost in the mists of time. Early records often fail to yield the desired information. Oral or traditional information is often unreliable. Indian names are frequently corrupted, abbreviated, or spelled in so many ways that identifying them becomes elusive. One example of this problem is the name of the state itself, the origin and meaning of which may never be established beyond a reasonable doubt.

Indian names were recorded by people who heard them in different ways. Milwaukee has been written in such diverse ways as Melleoki and Manawaki. Waushara was originally Daywaushara. Sac, Sauk, and Ozaukee, all on the Wisconsin map, represent variant spellings of the same tribal name. Another Indian tribe called themselves Mesquakie, but were called Outagamie by the Ojibwa, Renards by the French, and Foxes by the English. Only the last two names are synonymous, and they are unrelated to the first two.

The foregoing names have yielded to analysis, but others—such as Metonga, Wautoma, and Wiota—remain in doubt. Some of these mystery names may have literary origins. Two former mystery names, Monona and Waucousta, are among those of such origin. Some baffling names are found to be artificial, though aboriginal in appearance. Two such pseudo-Indian names, Irogami and Mohawksin, were formed by joining together syllables from unrelated languages. The story behind such a name can sometimes be learned only from living informants, who possess much useful, heretofore unrecorded information. However, it is evident that such data are often unreliable. Local mythmakers are numerous, and their stories, though remarkably long-lived, prove upon investigation to be without foundation. Their legends are categorized by scholars as folk etymology.

In the analysis of names, scholars sometimes come to conclusions that are in sharp contrast to the conclusions of their colleagues. Sometimes such divergence seems to result from using the methods of only one discipline to find answers. Sometimes it is due to incomplete or contradictory data. In some cases, it must be concluded that the correct solution is presently unattainable.

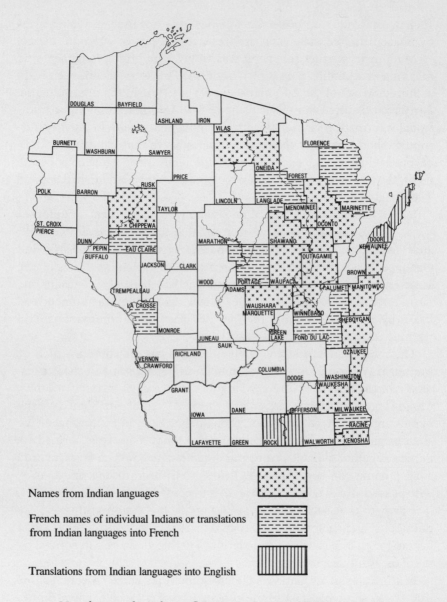

Names from Indian languages

French names of individual Indians or translations
from Indian languages into French

Translations from Indian languages into English

Map showing the Indian influences on names in Wisconsin counties

I am by training and career a historian, and my procedure here reflects that fact. Nevertheless, I have used the best available information on the Indian languages studied. Fortunately, dictionaries or vocabularies and other linguistic materials, published and unpublished, are available for each language spoken by Wisconsin tribes.

It has seemed best to omit the phonetic symbols, except in direct quotations. Early writers used a variety of systems to record sounds. In many cases, the correct pronunciation is not known. The present pronunciation of a name may vary from place to place and is often inconsistent with known aboriginal pronunciation. At best, the reproduction of pronunciation is a task for specialists, and usually it is of little interest to the general public.

I believe in the importance of visiting the places I am writing about, in order to get the "feel" of a locality, to pick up local information, and to observe whether descriptive names correctly describe places. I have visited sixty-eight of Wisconsin's seventy-two counties and all of its Indian reservations.

I have avoided an alphabetical dictionary-style listing of names. That is convenient for both author and reader, but my preference is to group names according to their cultural context and to let them convey historical and cultural information. Mere presentation of linguistic data would not accomplish this.

This book is intended to interest the average curious reader as well as to provide specialists with useful information. Pride of place is a common American trait, and interest in local names is widespread, although knowledge is often lacking. My aim is to enrich understanding of our environment and its past and to create a measure of appreciation of the cultural inheritance we have received from the first Americans.

Indian Names on

Wisconsin's Map

1

Wisconsin's Name

We were once a powerful but now a small nation. When
the white people first crossed the big water and landed
on this island, they were then small as we are now. I
remember when Wiskonsin was ours and it now has our
name. We sold it to you.

> Chief Wapello of the Mesquakie,
> October 16, 1841

O f all the states of the American union, none has a name that has
been spelled in more ways, or interpreted more variously, than
Wisconsin. Among the spellings listed are Mesconsin, Meskousing,
Mishkonsing, Ouisconsens, Ouisconsin, Ouisconsing, Ouiscousing,
Ouiskonsin, Owisconsing, Quisconsing, Weeskonsan, Wisconsan, Wisconsin, Wishkonsing, and Wiskonsin. The name has been attributed
to the French, Menominee, Ojibwa, Potawatomi, Sauk-Fox, and Winnebago languages.[1]

In early June 1673, Father Jacques Marquette spent three days at an
Indian village of mixed composition, which he called Maskoutens, near
present-day Portage, Wisconsin. Then, with two Miami guides, his
party portaged from the Fox River to another which would carry their
canoes to the Mississippi. "The river on which we embarked," wrote
Marquette, "is called Meskousing. It is very wide, it has a sandy bottom,
which forms various shoals that render its navigation very difficult."
Later, Marquette shortened the name to Meskous but gave no explanation of the meaning of the name or from whom it was obtained.[2]

The name belonged to the river, and its first recorded application to
the territory was probably when Wisconsan was shown as part of Michigan Territory on Stephen H. Long's map, published in 1823.[3] Caleb Atwater, in 1829, may have been the first to call it Wisconsin. The name
Wiskonsin was still applied to the territory (organized 1836) on George

3

F. Cram's map of 1839. In 1845 the territorial legislature adopted Wisconsin as the official spelling, and it became the name of the state in 1848.[4]

The definitions of Wisconsin include "stream of the Thousand Isles" (Capt. Frederick Marryat, 1838), "Gathering of the Waters" (Alfred Brunson, 1849), "small lodge of a beaver or muskrat" (Bishop Baraga, 1878), and "Gathering river," from Winnebago *Nee-koonts-sa-ra* (B. W. Brisbois, 1882). Father Chrysostom Verwyst (1892) said he was informed that *wisconsin* was a Chippewa term for "muskrat house," but added that "this is doubtful. I have not found two Indians to agree on the word." Alanson Skinner (1921) linked Wisconsin with Menominee *wiskos* or *wisko^ns*, "little muskrat house." Henry E. Legler (1902) listed several possible meanings, without endorsing any; they included "wild rushing channel," "beautiful little river" (from the Winnebago), and "great stone or rock." Huron H. Smith (1930) and Albert O. Barton (1945) proposed "hole in the bank of a stream, in which birds nest," from the Sauk language, as an explanation. Linguist Charles F. Hockett in 1948 suggested the name was from a Potawatomi phrase meaning "towards where it is cold." Phebe J. Nichols in the same year connected the name to Menominee words meaning "the river of flowery banks" or "a good place in which to live." John P. Harrington (1934) said "the name apparently means 'grassy place' in the Chippewa language." Edward Taube in 1967 added still one more explanation, "at the great point," referring to the promontory on the south side of the Wisconsin River's junction with the Mississippi.[5]

One source assumed that the name is of French origin. John H. Kinzie in 1831 wrote a manuscript called "Sketch of Hoo-wan-nee-kaw," which was annotated by his daughter, Nellie Kinzie Gordon. A note on it declares: "Ouiskonsin [Wisconsin] is a corruption of the French phrase 'Ou ce q'on descend,' or 'the place from which one comes down,' meaning the 'rapids,' or 'falls.'"[6] However, there are no rapids or falls in the river below Portage, the most heavily travelled part of the river.

None of the explanations that have been offered seems convincing. To explain this name, we must begin with Marquette's form, *Meskousing*. Despite a variety of spellings, the initial *M* in this name was used by Joliet, La Salle, Hennepin, Membre, and Thevenot—all writing or mapping before 1700. Without doubt, Marquette first learned the name from Indians at the village of Mascoutens, which he said was composed of "Miamis, Maskoutens, and Kikabous." The Mascouten or Mascoutin are of uncertain identity, but they may have been absorbed by the Sauk and Foxes (Mesquakie). St. Cosme wrote that in 1698 the Mascoutin and Foxes lived together with some Potawatomi at Milwaukee.[7]

A clue to the solution of the three-century-old mystery of Wisconsin's name may be found in the speech cited in the chapter epigraph. In the fall of 1841 the Sauk and Fox chiefs and headmen were gathered at their agency near Ottumwa, Iowa, to hear a proposal that they cede their Iowa lands. In the course of an eloquent speech against the treaty, chief Wapello of the Foxes declares, "I remember when Wiskonsin was ours and it now has our name."[8] There must have been a Fox tradition about the name Wisconsin in order for Wapello to say that Wisconsin was named for, or by, his tribe. The Foxes' tribal name is Mesquakie, also spelled Meskwaki, Miscoquis, Miskwkeeyuk, Muskwaki, Musquakie, etc. The name means "red earth," deriving from the Fox tradition that they were created of red earth by the Great Spirit. The French called them Renards (Foxes) because they mistook a clan name for the tribal name. There is a resemblance between Marquette's *Meskousing* and the name Mesquakie. The terminal -*akie* in the tribal name means "earth," and the terminal -*ing* in Meskousing means "place." It is possible that the original term was *Meskwa* ("red, inanimate") *aki* ("earth") *ing* ("place"). Marquette could have shortened it. Such contractions are common, but we have no proof that it happened in this instance.

It has been remarked by some that the banks of the Wisconsin at Portage are not red. There are other places where they are, but if the river was named for the tribe, the matter is irrelevant. The speech of Wapello is only a shred of evidence, insufficient for a final conclusion, but it should be considered with the other data.

In Wisconsin the name of the river and state appears in the city names of Wisconsin Dells in Columbia County and Wisconsin Rapids in Wood County, as well as in Lake Wisconsin in Columbia and Sauk counties.

2

Tribal Names

We will go. The peace of the foothills and the prairies
will be for the people who know no peace. Here in the
land where medicine whispers came from the grass and
herbs, here in the ground we thought would always keep
our tribes alive, will lie buried our hearts as we learn to
walk other ways, rip the sunlight from our deerskin,
forget the names we gave our rivers, forget the wild onion
smell. We will go. The rag-tag settlers will keep some of
our names. Ohio, Winnebago, Menominee. Ouray.
Kalispell. May they taste dust and feel cold winds each
time their tongues call the names that are ours.

Fred Red Cloud, Akwesasne Notes
(early autumn 1974)

From the beginning there were names. The earliest human beings migrating into Wisconsin as the last mountains of ice retreated northward about eleven thousand years ago marked the lakes, streams,
marshes, hills, regions, and villages with names. Those who came after
them gave new names, each tribe in its own language. When white men
came, they sometimes adopted the "savage" names; at other times they
substituted their own or translated the difficult Indian sounds into their
own words. Many of these names were placed on the Europeans' first
crude maps, and a great number survive to the present day.

In Europe, the inhabitants lived in areas with established boundaries,
and each of these areas, called nations, had a name, such as France,
Spain, and Portugal. In America, too, Europeans recorded on their maps
the names of the Indian nations which populated each region. Contrary
to common belief, these nations had established boundaries, most frequently demarcated by natural features. The boundaries might change,
just as they did in Europe, because of migrations and wars, and so the
names might also change. Some of these names, which recorded where

the Indian nations have lived at various times, survived to become the names of states: Alabama, Arkansas, the Dakotas, Illinois, Iowa, Kansas, Massachusetts, Missouri, Tennessee, and Utah. Many that did not become the names of the white man's conquered territories remained attached to lakes, streams, counties, and towns; and these, too, tell us where the people once lived, or still live.

The Indian tribes which have lived in Wisconsin since the white people came have all left their names affixed to the land and waters of Wisconsin. Sometimes the names are found in various languages and spellings, as for example, Fox-Outagamie, Chippewa-Ojibwa, and Dakota-Sioux. When the white people induced or forced eastern tribes to move to Wisconsin, their names, too, became affixed to the land: Oneida, Stockbridge, and Brothertown (the last two being our names for fragments of the storied Mohican and Delawares). Again, tribes which were forced to leave the state or which disappeared because of merger or extinction also left their names on the land. So the state is dotted with names such as Huron, Kickapoo, and Noquet.[1]

The whites also introduced native tribal names from the East and West into Wisconsin. The names from the East were adopted in nostalgic remembrance of the homes whites had left behind. Among these are the names of Iroquoian tribes of New York—Cayuga, Mohawk, and Seneca. Western names such as Cheyenne reveal an interest in Indians the local whites had never seen.

Tribal names, altogether, are but a fraction of the native names on the map. There are also personal names, descriptive names, commemorative names, and cultural names, each of which we will examine. But we begin with the names of the Indian nations because of their number and their importance as records of occupancy and movement.

The Three Fires

Most visible among Wisconsin tribal names are those of the Three Fires: the Chippewa (or Ojibwa), the Ottawa, and the Potawatomi. Many of the first and last named still live in Wisconsin; the Ottawa are now mainly in Michigan. The Three Fires were loosely allied, although not composing a formal confederacy. In the far past they were one people, as is suggested by the close identity of their languages, customs, and traditions.

The Chippewa

Largest of the Three Fires tribes, and the nation from which the other two arose, was the Chippewa, also called Ojibwa. About three thousand of them still occupy six major reservations in Wisconsin: Bad River near Ashland, Lac Courte Oreilles in Sawyer County, Lac du Flambeau in Iron and Vilas counties, Mole Lake (Sakaogan) in Forest County, Red Cliff near Bayfield, and St. Croix in separated tracts in Burnett, Douglas, and Polk counties. Other organized groups of Chippewa live in Michigan, Minnesota, Montana, North Dakota, Oklahoma, and Ontario, Canada.

The Chippewa were early allies of the French, and their language was the *lingua franca* of the upper Great Lakes. They lived along the north and south shores of Lake Superior, from one end of that lake to the other, embracing nearly all of Michigan's Upper Peninsula, westward through Wisconsin to the site of the city of Superior, and on into Minnesota, where their territories continued west nearly to Red River, south to Mille Lacs, and north into Canada. They also occupied, often with the Ottawa, large parts of the Lower Peninsula of Michigan. In Wisconsin they claimed dominion over the northern third of the state and beyond that in many places. Not surprisingly, the places named for them are in the regions where they lived, or now live.

On the present-day Lac Courte Oreilles Reservation in Sawyer County is the spiderlike expanse of Lake Chippewa and the Chippewa Flowage. In Namekagon Township of Bayfield County there is Chippewa Lake (with the position of the term "lake" in second place, opposite to that in the name of Lake Chippewa). From Lake Chippewa and the complex of connecting waters in Sawyer County the Chippewa River flows generally southward to join the Mississippi nearly opposite to Wabasha, Minnesota. This river was the war road for bands of Sioux moving north, or Chippewa moving south, each to attack the other. Two-thirds of the way from the sources of Chippewa River, just above Eau Claire, is the city of Chippewa Falls in Chippewa County. It very nearly marks the southern limit of the former territory of the Chippewa. Along Chippewa River in Dunn County just west of Eau Claire are Chippewa Bottoms and Chippewa Island.

The more nearly correct name of the Chippewa tribe is Ojibwa, although it is less common as a place name. In Wisconsin it is found in the small village of Ojibwa in Sawyer County, nearby Ojibwa State Park, and, surrounding these, Ojibwa Township.

Chippewa is a corruption from *Odjibway, Ojibwa, Ojibway,* or *Otchipwe,* to list but a few of the variant spellings of this name. The often fanciful and contradictory Henry R. Schoolcraft (1793–1864) remarked in one place that Chippewa was anglicized from a term signifying "the power of virility." Elsewhere he wrote that "Odjibwa" signified "sibilant or hissing voices."[2] Neither view has won acceptance. The most popular opinion is that of William Keating (1823), chronicler of Stephen Long's expedition to Minnesota, who held that Chippewa "signifies plaited shoes, from the fashion among these Indians of puckering their moccasins." The common short definition is "to roast till puckered up," referring to the moccasins, as Keating indicated.[3] A more gruesome explanation was given in the last century by Ojibwa historian William Warren, who held that an element of the original name, *Abboin-ug,* "roasters," arose from the Ojibwa custom of burning Dakota captives. Chippewa today prefer to describe themselves as *Anishinabe,* "original people" or "spontaneous people" (also *A-nish-in-au-bay, An-ish-in-au-bag,* etc.).[4]

The Ottawa

The Ottawa were temporary residents of Wisconsin. Originally occupying Manitoulin Island in Lake Huron, the Ottawa River of Ontario, and the north shore of Georgian Bay, they, like some of their Huron neighbors, were driven by the Iroquois into Upper Michigan after 1650. In the early 1660s most of them were settled about Chequamegon Bay of Lake Superior (on the present site of Ashland). At some point a band of them settled at Lac Courte Oreilles (French: "Short Ears"), which may have been named for them. The Chippewa once called this lake Ottawa Lake because of the tribe's residence there. Trade River, which joins the St. Croix in Polk County, was called Ottoway River on Keating's map (1825) and *Attanwa Sibi* in Nicollet's journal (August 4, 1837). It is not known whether there was an Ottawa presence there.

In 1670–71 the Ottawa and Huron abandoned Chequamegon and moved to Sault Ste. Marie. In the eighteenth century most of them moved into Lower Michigan and populated the region about Grand Traverse Bay, Little Traverse Bay, and the Lake Michigan shore north to Mackinaw and south to Grand River.[5]

When pressure for their removal to the West grew strong, many Ottawa returned to their ancient homeland on Manitoulin Island, while others successfully resisted forced migration and remain today in the Grand Traverse region.[6] Some who did migrate have given their name to Ottawa County, Kansas, and Ottawa County, Oklahoma. Other Ottawa intermingled and intermarried with the Chippewa and Potawatomi.

Because the Ottawa residence in Wisconsin was brief, their place-name legacy is small. Their tribal name is found on Ottawa Lake, the town of Ottawa, and Ottawa Recreation Area, all in Waukesha County west of Milwaukee. As a tribe, the Ottawa never occupied that area, although some were intermixed with the resident Potawatomi.

William Warren's account of the origin of the name Ottawa has been accepted by most writers:

> The Ottoways remaining about the spot of their final separation [from the Chippewa and Potawatomi] and being therefore the most easterly section, were first discovered by the white race, who bartered with them their merchandise for furs. They for many years acted as a medium between the white traders and their more removed western brethren, providing them in turn at advanced prices, with their much desired commodities. They thus obtained the name of Ot-tah-way, "traders," which they have retained as their tribal name to the present day.[7]

The Potawatomi

The remaining member of the Three Fires was the Potawatomi nation, first found by the French living about Green Bay and southward on or near the shore of Lake Michigan. They lived at Milwaukee and southwestward to Lake Geneva and beyond. They later spread around the southern end of Lake Michigan, westward to Rock River, and southward to Peoria and the Kankakee River. Their occupation of northern Indiana was above the Miami on the Wabash and extended into southern Michigan as far as Grand Haven and eastward to the fringes of Detroit.

Most of the Potawatomi were removed in the 1830s to western Iowa and northwestern Missouri; others were transported to eastern Kansas and finally to central Oklahoma. Some who left for Canada to avoid forced migration settled on Walpole Island near Detroit and above Georgian Bay. Small islands of Potawatomi remain in southwestern Lower Michigan, and reservations now exist in Menominee County, Michigan, and Forest County, Wisconsin.

The Potawatomi of Upper Michigan and Forest County, Wisconsin, are descendants of those from the Chicago area who either evaded transfer to the West or returned to Wisconsin after moving west. Several small, scattered bands established themselves in the northern woods and carried on a precarious existence hunting, fishing, and gathering. As early as 1883 a Methodist missionary assisted the Upper Michigan group in purchasing land, which was the core of the present Hannahville Reservation. In 1913 Congress purchased more land for the homeless Indians near Wilson, Michigan (Hannahville Reservation), and Crandon, Wisconsin.

Potawatomi began moving into Forest County in the 1890s to work in the logging industry. Some took up forty-acre homesteads under the Indian Homestead Act of 1875. The Reverend F. P. Morstad, a Lutheran missionary, persuaded Sen. Robert M. La Follette, Jr., to introduce into the U.S. Senate an act providing for the purchase of additional lands for the Indians. The Indians were settled in two areas, one near Wabeno, the other at Stone Lake near Crandon. The land was purchased in a checkerboard fashion in order to promote "assimilation" with whites. Eighty-acre allotments, held in trust by the government and protected from alienation, were provided for Indian families. Ownership of the land, totalling nearly 12,000 acres, is now invested mainly in the tribe, which incorporated under the Wheeler-Howard Act in 1937. The membership in 1980 was reported as 390 persons.[8]

There is little disagreement about the name Potawatomi. William Warren explained the tribal name as "those who keep the fire." The name came from a tradition that when the three associated "fires" separated, "the Potta-wat-um-ees moved up Lake Michigan, and by taking with them or for a time perpetuating the national fire, which according to tradition was sacredly kept alive in their more primitive days, they have obtained the name of 'those who make or keep the fire,' which is the literal meaning of the tribal cognomen."[9] William Keating, who met the Potawatomi in Fort Wayne, Indiana, in 1823, explained the name in almost the same manner—"we are making a fire"—but gave it a different origin. He was told that a Miami Indian met three Indians of a strange tongue and invited them into his cabin. He built a fire near the entrance, which upon being seen by the others, was understood to signify a council fire in token of peace between the tribes.[10]

Potawatomi names are attached to numerous places in Wisconsin, but the tribal name itself is limited to a few insignificant features. Potawatomi Island was an old name of Washington Island in Lake Michigan off the tip of the Door County peninsula. There are also Potawatomi Bay and Potawatomi State Park near Sturgeon Bay.[11]

The Foxes

The Foxes received their popular name by mistake. Maj. Morrell Marston in 1820 reported the following extract from an interview with the Fox chief Wapello at Fort Armstrong (Rock Island), Illinois:

Q. What is the name of your nation?
A. Mus-quak-ie or Mus-quak-kie-uck.
Q. What (is) the original name?
A. Since the Great Spirit made us we have had that name and no other.
Q. What (are) the names by which it has been known among Europeans?
A. The French called us Renards, and since, the white people have called us Foxes.[12]

According to William Jones, a Fox Indian scholar (1871–1909), the tradition was that members of the Fox clan met some Frenchmen, who asked who they were, and the Indians replied by naming their clan, and so the French took it to be the name of the entire tribe. The tribe's own name, Jones added, was *Mesh-kwa-ki-hugi,* "red earth people," so named "because of the kind of earth from which they are supposed to have been created." Finally, the Chippewa and other Algonquians called them *Utagamig*, "people of the other shore."[13] The two aboriginal names are variously spelled: *Meckwa-ki-hagi, Mesquakie, Mesquakiauck,* and *Odagamig, O-dug-am-eeg, Outagamie,* etc. From the last comes the name of Outagamie County, which retains French orthography but is pronounced *Utagami* in English. The name Foxes is given in Potawatomi as Wakusheg.[14]

The history of the Foxes before 1680 is hazy. By that time they were settled in the relatively crowded area along the Green Bay–Fox River–Lake Winnebago waterway. It was there that they forged the alliance with the Sauks which lasted until 1832. They were also allied with the Sioux and Iroquois against the neighboring Chippewa and Illinois, as well as the French. Wars with these tribes, and especially with the French, between 1730 and 1733, left them greatly depleted in numbers, but they recovered and were estimated to number 1,200 in 1805.

When Jonathan Carver visited them in 1766, the Foxes were mainly located about a day's journey down the Wisconsin River from Sauk Prairie (now the site of Sauk City and Prairie du Sac). Some, however, had already removed to Iowa about the sites of present Dubuque and Davenport, and to Illinois about Rock Island. The Sauks also removed to the Rock Island area before the American Revolution.

Although clearly allied, and having a common history until after 1850, the Sauk and Foxes retained their separate identity and their own villages. The Foxes on the Illinois side of the Mississippi yielded to government pressure to move across the river by 1830, and when Black Hawk led a force of Sauk back into Illinois in 1832, most Foxes did not join them. After this, the two tribes drew apart, but the government continued to treat them as virtually one. In 1842 they were pressured into signing a treaty to move from Iowa to Kansas within three years. In Kansas they were beset by disease and further agitated by government insistence on individual allotment of their land. In 1852 some Foxes drifted back to Iowa, joining some who had never left. In 1856 they purchased eighty acres of land on the Iowa River in Tama County, and nearly all Kansas Foxes moved there, with permission of the Iowa legislature. They continued to purchase land, using their annuities (after a temporary cutoff), until their holdings comprised 3,600 acres, which are now occupied by more than seven hundred Indians. The tribe clings strongly to its language and traditions.[15]

Besides the adoption of their Ojibwa name in Outagamie County (which is also the name of a yacht club in Oshkosh and of a state wild-life area in the county) both of Wisconsin's Fox Rivers are named for them: the Fox River which empties into Green Bay and the one which begins in Waukesha County and joins the Illinois at Ottawa, Illinois. The Illinois portion of the river was long called Pisticoui or Pistakee (with other variants), signifying "buffalo." By 1790 John Armstrong's map designated the river in Illinois also as the "Foxes River." In Wisconsin it was called Waukesha ("fox"), the Potawatomi name for the river, after which the city and county of Waukesha were named.[16] Joshua Hathaway (1849) sought to take credit for adopting the name Waukesha, claiming, "It is very probable that this name was never seen in English characters until 1846, when it was inscribed by the writer of this, upon an oak tree."[17] However, "Pashtic or Fox River" was the name for this river on Cram's map (1839) and several others before Hathaway's date, and it is evident that the city and county were named from the Potawatomi name for this river.

The Sauk

The Sauk, longtime allies of the Foxes, no longer live in Wisconsin, but their name is on ten places in the state. According to Black Hawk (1767–1838), the Sauk lived near Montreal in his great-grandfather's time. Many writers report that they later lived around Saginaw Bay in Michigan and that their name stems from that place; others say the bay was named for them. More probably, the name Saginaw means "the outlet" (of the Saginaw River) and was in place earlier. Black Hawk did not mention Sauk residence there, and no white observer reports seeing them there, although a tradition among both Indians and white claims it was once their home. Black Hawk says they removed from Montreal to Mackinaw, and the Jesuits reported them at Chequamegon on Lake Superior in 1666–67, but their presence there was transitory.[18] By 1721 they were at Green Bay, where they allied with the Foxes, soon to be embroiled in a devastating war with the French. In ensuing years they moved up the Fox River and down the Wisconsin, where Carver found them in 1766:

> On the 8th of October [1766] we got our canoes into the
> Ouisconsin River [at Portage] . . . and the next day arrived at

the Great Town of the Saukies. This is the largest and best built Indian town I ever saw. It contains about ninety houses, each large enough for several families. They are built of hewn planks neatly jointed, and covered with bark so completely as to keep out the most penetrating rains. Before their doors are placed comfortable sheds, in which the inhabitants sit, when the weather will permit, and smoak their pipes. The streets are regular and spacious, so that it appears more like a civilized town than the abode of savages. The land near the town is very good. In their plantations, which lie adjacent to their houses, and which are neatly laid out, they raise great quantities of Indian corn, beans, melons &c. so that this place is esteemed the best market for traders to furnish provisions of any within eight hundred miles of it.[19]

After only a day Carver moved down the river and came to the first village of the "Ottigaumies" (Foxes), containing about fifty houses. Most of the people had fled because of an epidemic.

The site of the Sauk town is now occupied by the twin villages of Sauk City and Prairie du Sac in Sauk County. At the time of Carver's visit, many Sauk apparently had already moved to the mouth of Rock River, in Illinois, for Black Hawk reports that he was born there in 1767.[20]

The Foxes settled on both sides of the Mississippi near the Sauk, some of whom settled in Missouri. In 1804 a Sauk delegation to St. Louis, seeking the release of a Sauk prisoner accused of murder, were inveigled by Gov. William H. Harrison into signing a treaty ceding all Sauk and Fox land east of the Mississippi, with the proviso that they might live on it until the land was needed.

The Sauk sided with the British in both the Revolutionary War and the War of 1812. In the 1820s they began to be surrounded by white settlers, and in 1831, under threat of military force, they crossed the Mississippi River. The following spring, about nine hundred of them, led by Black Hawk, returned to Illinois, setting off what is called the Black Hawk War. They were pursued by militia and regulars and on July 21 fought a battle at Wisconsin Heights just south of Sauk City. Most of them escaped, some going down the Wisconsin River on rafts, while others went overland, until they were overtaken south of Bad Axe River on August 1–2 and nearly destroyed. On September 21, 1832, the Sauk signed a treaty at Rock Island. Black Hawk and a few others were held prisoner for a time, and the remnant settled in Iowa. The Sauk and Foxes, closely allied until 1832, were thereafter alienated from each other.

In 1845 the Sauk and Foxes were removed to Kansas, but as noted above, a band of Foxes returned to Iowa during the 1850s and bought land near Tama, where their descendants still reside. The Sauk in Kansas were moved to Oklahoma in 1867 and their reservation was broken up in 1889. A small band of them now occupies a tiny reservation on the Kansas-Nebraska border.[21]

Sauk (sometimes written Sac) is a contraction of the original name of the tribe, which has been written as *Osaki-wug, Osawkee, Ozaukee, Sac, Sakie, Saukie, Saukie-uck, Sakewe,* etc. Cadillac, Schoolcraft, Quaife, and others believed that Saginaw ("river mouth"), Michigan, was named for them.[22] The Sauks, however, have always maintained that their name means "yellow-earth people," because they were created of yellow earth by the Great Spirit. According to Thomas Forsyth, Indian agent at Rock Island in 1827, "The original and present name of the Sauk Indians proceeds from the compound word Sakie, alias, A-saw-we-kee, literally Yellow Earth."[23] Further evidence against the theory of "outlet" or "river mouth" is the fact that the word for "outlet," *sagi*, has no initial *O-* sound, as the word for "yellow" does. The older form of the tribal name may be seen in the names of Ozaukee County, Wisconsin, and the towns of Osakis, Minnesota, and Ozawkie, Kansas.

Wisconsin places named for the Sauk, besides the two counties and two villages already mentioned (Sauk, Ozaukee; Sauk City, Prairie du Sac) are Sauk Creek and the village and town of Saukville in Ozaukee County, Sauk Hill, Sauk Point, Sauk Prairie, and the village and town of Prairie du Sac in Sauk County; and Sauk Rapids on the Rock River. On Cram's map of 1839, the site of Port Washington, in Ozaukee County, was called Sauk Harbor. Sauk Creek discharges there.

The Kickapoo

On May 1, 1670, Father Claude Allouez visited a village of "Kikabou" who "speak the same language as the Machkouteng" (Mascoutin). He reported that they "were eager to lavish on me all the best things they had" and were "kind beyond all power of belief."[24]

As place names suggest, the Kickapoo once lived in Vernon and Crawford counties in southwestern Wisconsin. Reportedly they were on the Kickapoo River before 1700. By 1750 some of them, with bands from other tribes, lived around the site of Milwaukee. During the eighteenth century, they moved into central and southeastern Illinois, and in the nineteenth, as a result of treaties, they moved in stages to Missouri, Kansas, and Oklahoma. Some of them even moved into Mexico in order to rid themselves of U.S. control, and most of their descendants remain today in the state of Coahuila. About two hundred from that group recently resettled at Eagle Pass, Texas. There is no organized group of Kickapoo in Wisconsin today.[25]

The most important memorial to the Kickapoo in Wisconsin is the Kickapoo River, which rises in Monroe County and joins the Wisconsin River at Wauzeka. Little Kickapoo Creek also joins the Wisconsin at Wauzeka, and just west of town is Kickapoo Caverns. In Vernon County to the north is the village of Kickapoo Center and the town of Kickapoo. Perhaps more ubiquitous than place names in memorializing the Kickapoo is the presence, only in Wisconsin, of Kickapoo gasoline stations.

James Mooney traced the tribal name to *Kiwigapawa,* meaning "he stands about" or "he moves about, standing now here, now there." This could perhaps be freely translated as "wanderers," a term which correctly describes the tribe's mobile ways. Schoolcraft's alternative derivation, from *Neg-ik-abo,* "otter's ghost," has not won acceptance.[26]

The Menominee

The Menominee Tribe, a member of the Algonquian language family, is the only group of Wisconsin Indians to have escaped exile or fragmentation. Twice they have stood on the brink of possible extinction as a tribe. The first time was in 1848 when twenty-eight of their leaders, including the venerable Oshkosh, were induced to sign a treaty ceding all their Wisconsin lands in exchange for a swampy reservation in Minnesota. After viewing their proposed new home, however, the chiefs had a change of heart and sought to have the treaty abrogated. With the help of white friends, including the missionary Florimond Bonduel (for whom the village of Bonduel in Shawano County is named), and the support of the legislature, the Menominee managed to get the treaty overturned. No such victory had ever been won by an Indian tribe. The second threat to their tribal survival came in 1961, when Congress abolished the Menominee reservation and terminated all federal support. The state legislature then turned the reservation into Menominee County. With the cessation of federal services, financial hardship followed, and the beleaguered tribe began selling long-term leases to resort developers. Soon, members of a movement called DRUMS (Determination of Rights and Unity for Menominee Shareholders) began a campaign to restore the reservation. Their drive won a victory when the Menominee Restoration Act became law on April 23, 1965.[27]

The densely forested Menominee land, now consisting of 233,000 acres, once extended from upper Michigan southward to the Fox River, westward to the Wisconsin and beyond, and along Lake Michigan to the site of Milwaukee. The Menominee River, which forms much of the boundary between Wisconsin and Upper Michigan, was already named for them when Father Claude Allouez traveled there on May 6, 1670. The priest then reported, "I paid a visit to Oumalouminek, eight leagues distant from our cabin, and found them at their river." Three years later, Father Jacques Marquette entered Green Bay on his way to the Mississippi and recorded that "the first nation that we came to was that of the Folle Avoine (Wild Oat). I entered their river." Explaining the name, he added that "the wild oat, whose name they bear because it is found in their country, is a sort of grass, which grows naturally in the small rivers with muddy bottoms and in swampy places." Following a detailed account of how the grain was harvested and prepared as food, he concluded, "Cooked in this fashion, the wild oats have almost as delicate a taste as rice when a better seasoning is added."[28]

Today we call the "wild oats" wild rice (*Zizania aquatica*), and it has become an expensive gourmet food. The tribe was known to its Algonquian neighbors for its association with this plant and so were called "*O-mun-o-min-eeg*, wild rice people" by the Ojibwa, *Man-o-min-ag* by the Potawatomi, and *Manome-inanni* by themselves.[29]

Several of the Menominee place names in Wisconsin are far from the tribe's territory, and may owe their names to the presence of wild rice (see Chapter 13). However, those names found in or near the areas now or formerly inhabited by the tribe are probably named for the tribe.

Besides the Menominee River and Rapids on the Michigan border in Marinette County, there is a Menomonee River (variant spelling) which joins Lake Michigan at Milwaukee. From it are named Menomonee

Falls, both the village and the cataract, in Waukesha County, and the Menomonee Parkway in Milwaukee. The river has a tributary, Little Menomonee, which is followed by Little Menomonee Parkway. Menominee County (note spelling), which is coterminous with the present reservation, contains Menominee Creek, and Menominee Park is in Oshkosh, Winnebago County.

In extreme southwestern Wisconsin the Menominee and Little Menominee rivers flow from Grant County into the Mississippi in Jo Daviess County, Illinois. The Menominee Indians did not live in this area, and wild rice does not grow in this hilly region. However, William Keating reported finding "Menomone, or wild rice eaters," camping in northern Illinois during his journey across the state in 1823. The name could commemorate either of two events: the slaughter, by Menominee and Sioux, of a party of Fox Indians who were on their way from Dubuque to Prairie du Chien in 1830, or the vengeance slaying of some twenty-five Menominee by Sauk and Foxes near Fort Crawford, Wisconsin, the following year.[30] Menomonie Lake in Marquette County is apparently named for the tribe. A cluster of "Menominie" names in Dunn County and Munnomin Lake in Iron County are probably named for the wild rice plant.

The Noquet

On September 25, 1698, the Jesuit missionary Jean François Buisson de St. Cosme wrote that upon approaching "The Bay of the Puants" (Green Bay), "one passes on the right hand another small bay called that of the Noquest. The bay of the Puants [Winnebago] is inhabited by several savage tribes: the Noquest, the Folles Avoines [Wild Oats, referring to the Menominee], the Renards [Foxes], the Poûtoûatamis, and the Saki." Jonathan Carver wrote (1766) that on the northwest part of Lake Michigan the waters branched into two bays, called Bay of Noquets and Green Bay.[31]

Earlier the Noquet had been reported on the shores of Lake Superior. They have not been positively identified. Augustin Grignon (1856), pointing to the early presence of the Menominee at "Bay de Noque," said that these were called by the early French Des Noques or Des Noquia. He reported, "They are represented as being at all times closely united to the Outchiboues or Ojibways, and apparently became eventually confounded with them." The Noquets are believed to have been absorbed by the Menominee or the Ojibwa, as their name disappears from the records in the eighteenth century. The possibility that they were never more than an Ojibwa clan is suggested by Warren's remark that "the No-ka or Bear family are more numerous than any of the other clans of the Ojibways, forming full one sixth of the entire tribe."[32] Today there are no Indians who are individually or collectively identified as Noquet.

The chief geographic memorials to the Noquet are Big and Little Bay de Noc and Bay de Noc Township in Delta County, Michigan. However, Wisconsin has Lake Noquebay and Lake Noquebay Wildlife Area in Marinette County. The name Noquet (or Noká) is held to signify "bear foot," another name for the bear gens of the Ojibwa.[33]

The Sioux (Dakota)

The Sioux (or, more properly, the Dakota) occupied or claimed a part of northwestern Wisconsin reaching from St. Croix Falls on the St. Croix River southward along the Mississippi to the mouth of Black River near present Trempealeau, and inland for an indefinite distance. This territory was ceded by the Sioux in a treaty signed at Washington on September 29, 1837, in which they gave up all their land east of the Mississippi but did not define the bounds of the tract.[34]

The Sioux and Chippewa were often at war with one another, and each tribe followed the Chippewa River to reach the other.[35] Some of the places named for the Sioux resulted from incidents of that warfare. Sioux River, which joins Lake Superior at Bayfield, recalls a skirmish described in Warren's *History of the Ojibway*. The Sioux lay in wait at the site of Bayfield to ambush the Ojibwa. Two of them crossed to La Pointe on Madeline Island by swimming with a log and attacked a family fishing at night, taking four scalps. Soon thereafter, 150 Sioux came to Chequamegon Point and killed two boys who were hunting ducks. Alarmed by shouting, Ojibwa warriors came to the point and cut off the escape route, killing all but two of the Sioux.[36]

It is safe to presume that not only the Sioux River but also the Little Sioux River and Sioux River Slough in Bayfield County took their names from these or similar incidents. We do not have anecdotes to explain the other uses of the Sioux tribal names: Sioux Creek and the town of Sioux Creek in Barron County, Sioux Portage Creek in Burnett County, and Sioux Coulee in Crawford County. There are Sioux names, personal and otherwise, on the maps which are described elsewhere.

The name Sioux is an abbreviation of the Chippewa-French composite term *Nadowessioux*, also spelled *Nadowessi, Nadowe-is-iw, Naudowasewug*, etc. According to Warren, it meant "like unto adders," also at times rendered as "enemies." The same derogatory label was applied to the Iroquois. The name was unknown to the Sioux until recent times; its use was confined to the French and Chippewa.[37] The tribe's own name for itself, among the Santee or eastern division, was Dakota, and among the Teton or western division, Lakota. The Dakota (Lakota) were divided into several subtribes and were scattered from early times to the present across Wisconsin and Minnesota, and through the Dakotas to Montana. The name Dakota means "united" or "allied,"[38] and in Wisconsin it is confined to a town in Waushara County, where, however, the tribe did not live in recorded times.

The Winnebago

One hundred years after Jacques Cartier sailed up the St. Lawrence to the crags called Hochelaga, and twenty-six years after Samuel Champlain laid out the settlement of Quebec at that place, the first Frenchman set foot on the soil of the future state of Wisconsin.

In 1634 Governor Champlain sent Jean Nicolet to seek out the "People of the Sea" and make peace between them and the Huron. Imagining that he was going to meet the imperial ruler of an Asian people, Nicolet "wore a grand robe of China damask, all strewn with flowers and birds of many colors." He found his sought-for people on the shore of what is today called Green Bay. After their initial fear of the heavenly being who carried thunder (pistols) in both hands, Indians assembled in huge crowds and received him with much ceremony.[39]

The French never called the people of this woodland democracy by their name, *Hochungara* (variously spelled), which has been explained as meaning "big fish people," "people of the parent speech," "fish eaters," and "trout nation." Learning that their Algonquian neighbors called them *Ouinepegouans* (French orthography, now anglicized to

Winnebago), which means "dirty" or "foul smelling," the French called them *Puants*, and at first called Lake Michigan the lake of the Puants and labeled Green Bay on their maps as Bay des Puants.[40]

For three centuries some writers assumed that the common name of these Indians meant that they were unclean, or that the waterways along which they lived were slimy or muddy, or that the shores were strewn with stinking fish.[41] As early as 1648 Father Paul Raguenau tried to set the record straight by explaining that "these people are called Puants not because of any bad odor that is peculiar to them, but because they say they came from the shores of a far distant sea toward the North, the water of which is salt; they are called people of the stinking water."[42] Of Green Bay Father Jacques Marquette wrote in 1673: "They call it as often the Salted bay as the Stinking, which among them is nearly the same thing. It is also the name which they give to the sea." Antoine de la Mothe Cadillac wrote of the "Puans" that "in their persons and habits they are the cleanest men of all the Indians and their women are the least dirty and take great pains to keep their cabins clean and tidy."[43] Alexander Mackenzie wrote (1793) that "stinking lake" was an Indian term (probably Cree) for the sea. Confirming this in his Otchipwe dictionary, Bishop Baraga declared that "the Indians call Lake Winipeg, the great water, the great sea, and use the same expression to speak of the salt-water of the sea."[44] It appears from these remarks that the Winnebago must have originated in the vicinity of either Lake Winnipeg or Hudson Bay. There is no reason to agree with Hennepin's guess that they came from the "South Sea," the Pacific.[45]

The Winnebago were unusual in that they were, except for a few Sioux along the Mississippi and the Oneida immigrants of the nineteenth century, the only group of Wisconsin Indians who did not speak an Algonquian language. Like the Sioux and Iowa, they belonged to the Dakota stock. They are also the only Wisconsin tribe to have reestablished themselves in their old homeland after having been exiled.

From Green Bay the Winnebago moved southward along the Fox River and Lake Winnebago and westward along the Wisconsin River, establishing themselves in southwestern Wisconsin and along the Mississippi as far as La Crosse in the north and south to Rock River in Illinois, where a county bears their name. By treaty in 1832 and 1837 they were induced to surrender all their land in Wisconsin and Illinois and move to northern Iowa. Most of them had to be moved by military force under inhumane conditions. In 1848 they were moved again, to Minnesota, and again to two other locations in that state before being sent to Crow Creek, South Dakota, after the Sioux outbreak of 1862.

Following another treaty in 1865, the peaceful Winnebago were removed, for the last time, to Omaha lands in Thurston County, Nebraska, where many of their descendants remain. However, so many trudged back to Wisconsin that they soon were as numerous there as in Nebraska. Scattering around central Wisconsin, they eked out a living by hunting, fishing, gathering, gardening, selling craftwork, and working for white people. Some took forty-acre homesteads under the Indian Homestead Act of 1875. Eventually small government grants were given to the Wisconsin Winnebago, who were recognized as a tribe in 1963. Their population in 1981 was listed as 1,718, in addition to 1,143 tribal members in Nebraska.

The Winnebago lands—4,116 acres scattered in small tracts over ten counties—now constitute a reservation. The principal concentrations of Wisconsin Winnebago are in five places: near Black River Falls in Jackson County, near Wittenberg in Shawano County, near Wisconsin Rapids in Columbia County, near Tomah in Monroe County, and near La Crosse in La Crosse County. There are also Winnebago who live in the Dells area and participate in the summer powwows at Stand Rock. Recently some Winnebago groups have found a new source of income from bingo games.

The largest single settlement of Winnebago is at Winnebago Mission, seven miles northeast of Black River Falls, with its related community of Sand Pillow, nearby. The population of this settlement is estimated at between two and three hundred. In the 1870s the Winneshiek band, fearing removal to Nebraska, fled from the Mississippi to the pine lands of Jackson County. About 1880 the Reverend Hauser, a missionary of the German Reformed Church (United Church of Christ, founded by Zwingli) established a mission at the present location. Its people have been called the most conservative of all Wisconsin Winnebago in resisting change.[46]

Place names that perpetuate the name of the tribe are Lake Winnebago and the village of Winnebago on the lake, both in Winnebago County; Winnebago Creek in Dodge County; Winnebago Point in Calumet County, on the east side of Lake Winnebago; the town of Fort Winnebago in Columbia County, near Portage; and Winnebago Mission in Jackson County. The many Winnebago individuals commemorated in Wisconsin names are listed in the next chapter.

The Oneida

Oneida County, containing Lake Oneida, and the village and town of Oneida in Outagamie County, derive their names from the Oneida Indians who settled just west of Green Bay in the 1820s and whose descendants still remain there. The Oneida belong to the Iroquois Six Nations of New York. They never lived in Oneida County. The village of Oneida in Outagamie County is the center of the remaining fragments of their reservation, consisting of 2,741 acres in scattered tracts. (At this writing there is a court case pending to determine whether the tribe still has jurisdiction over the 65,000 acres that composed their reservation in 1838.)

During the American Revolution the Oneida and their kinfolk, the Tuscarora, tried to remain neutral while most of the other Iroquois sided with the British. Eventually they were drawn to the American side, but this loyalty helped them little, for they are the only member tribe of the Six Nations which today has no reservation in New York.[47]

Their removal to Wisconsin was brought about by the collaboration of the Reverend Eleazar Williams, a Mohawk and Episcopal clergyman who settled among the Oneida in 1817, and Thomas Ogden, a land speculator. At the urging of Ogden, Williams travelled to Wisconsin with a delegation of Indians and in 1821 engineered a treaty with the Menominee and Winnebago establishing a reservation for New York Indians at the present location near Fox River. Most of the Oneida opposed removal, but the church and the army supported Williams. A large delegation was sent to Green Bay in 1822. In the next two years about 150 Oneida and the same number of Stockbridges (q.v.) came to Wisconsin, the latter settling on the east side of Lake Winnebago.

Migration continued slowly in the next few years. A treaty in 1831 assigned the New York Indians about 500,000 acres. In 1838 this was reduced to 65,000 acres for the Oneida. This area, about twelve miles square, remained their reservation until losses of land accelerated after the Dawes Act of 1887 was applied to them in 1892. Small individual allotments were made, forty-five acres for each person over eighteen years of age, and twenty-six acres for each minor. Although the land was supposed to remain in trust for twenty-five years, it was turned over to the Oneida in fee simple and subject to alienation in 1906. The plots were too small to be economically viable, and unscrupulous whites soon acquired most of the land. Inability to pay taxes or mortgages and the inexperience of the Indians in white business and legal matters led to foreclosures. The policy of sending the young people to distant boarding schools also undermined the cohesiveness of the tribe.

In 1934 the tribe organized a tribal government under the Wheeler-Howard Act. The federal government stopped further allotments and bought 1,200 acres to restore to the Indians. A loan fund was also established. In 1980 the Wisconsin Oneida numbered 3,384 people, of whom well over half lived in the old reservation area. The remainder are in cities such as Green Bay and Milwaukee.[48]

Some of the old culture has been preserved. An annual powwow held at Oneida attracts Indians from other tribes. An industrial park has been established in Green Bay. With bingo profits the tribe has built a luxury motel, a museum, a health center, and a rest home for the aged.

The meaning of Oneida is "standing stone," referring to a large stone at one of the tribe's early villages in New York, for which reason a stone became their national emblem, and the people were called *Oniotaaug*, "people of the place of stone."[49]

The Stockbridge-Munsee

The people of the Stockbridge-Munsee reservation, in Shawano County at the southwest edge of the Menominee reservation, are descendants of immigrant Algonquians from the East. Their total enrollment in 1981 was 948 people, living on 15,000 acres. The Stockbridges are a Mohican remnant named for their former home at Stockbridge, Massachusetts.[50] The Munsee, a Delaware subtribe (also called Muncie, Muncy, etc.), are, in this case, a mixed group earlier called Brotherton, from a Delaware village called Brotherton in Burlington County, New Jersey. That village was sold in 1802, and the inhabitants were merged with another group of Algonquians at the settlement of Brotherton, Oneida County, New York, where they lived for a time under the protection of the Iroquois. Brotherton was composed of Stockbridge Mohican and remnants of several small New England and Long Island tribes, some of them followers of the Mohegan preacher Samson Occum, who settled in 1788 at the New York location.[51] All of them were removed to Wisconsin in the years 1822–33, and along the way they were joined by a band of Munsee previously transplanted to Indiana.

The villages and towns of Stockbridge and Brothertown in Calumet County on the east side of Lake Winnebago commemorate the presence of these eastern Indians there, before the bulk of them moved to Shawano County. Some of their descendants still live in Calumet County.[52]

The Stockbridges were forced out of New York by the same pressures that were placed on the Oneida. Peaceful and educated, they cultivated small farms at their new location. Bishop Jackson Kemper visited them in 1838 and wrote of one family in whose home he spent the night: "The young woman of the house is modest, intelligent, and talks well. She has books, ink, a workstand &c. We had good beds and a good supper which closed with a fine slice of pumpkin pie."[53]

In 1843 the Stockbridges sold half of their land here to the federal government and agreed to move to a reservation west of the Mississippi, although few actually moved. On the unsold half the village of Stockbridge was platted, and here the government unsuccessfully attempted to settle those Indians who wanted to become U.S. citizens. After some discussion, the tribe was reunited, and tribal government was restored. In 1856 the Stockbridges, after negotiating a final treaty with the government, relinquished their land in Calumet County for a cash settlement and a new reservation adjoining the Menominee, where their descendants still live. In the 1870s the pine lands of their reservation were sold under an act of Congress, without notice to the tribe, to a corporation of which a prominent politician was a member, reducing the reservation to half a township (18 square miles). When the timber was gone, the lumbermen moved on, leaving the Indians without resources. In the 1930s, the Bureau of Indian Affairs acquired 14,423 acres of the original reservation and returned it to the Indians.[54]

The Wisconsin Munsee, presently united with the Stockbridge-Brothertons, were part of one of the three main divisions of the Delaware, or Lenni-Lenape, tribe which formerly occupied parts of Pennsylvania and New Jersey. Today most Delawares live in Ontario and Oklahoma; the Wisconsin group is a fragment.

The name Munsee is reputed to signify "wolf," as that was the tribe's totem. Hewitt, however, said the name meant "where stones are gathered together."[55] According to information obtained by Alanson Skinner, the Brothertons (or Brothertowns) arrived at their name in this manner: In 1761 David Fowler, a Montauk Indian from Long Island, New York, visited the Oneida in what is now Madison County, New York. He obtained from them a grant of land on which he invited various Algonquian remnants to settle. As the residents spoke several dialects of the Algonquian languages, they adopted English for communication and called themselves "Brothertowns" to signify their fraternal spirit. However, since the name Brotherton was used by the Munsee fragment in New Jersey, the name may have come from them.[56]

The Iroquois

The Six Nations of Iroquois (Five Nations before 1715) lived in New York State's Mohawk Valley from before the days of the first white settlement until after the American Revolution. That conflict divided the Six Nations and brought severe strain upon them. During the war, General John Sullivan laid waste to several Iroquois villages, and to their crops and orchards, with particular damage to the Cayuga and Seneca tribes.

After the Revolution, numerous Iroquois accepted the British offer of reservations in the Grand River Valley of Upper Canada (Ontario) and on Quinte Bay of Lake Ontario. The largest number who relocated were followers of Joseph Brant, the Mohawk warrior, but some members of the other tribes also migrated. However, none of the Six Nations entirely deserted New York, and all of them are represented there today. Each of them, except the Oneida, still has one or more reservations there. Only the Oneida were induced to migrate in relatively large numbers to other parts of the United States. They were removed to Green Bay, Wisconsin, in the 1830s and their descendants remain there. (See Oneida.)

Although the Iroquois had little direct influence on Wisconsin history, and none resided here before 1820, the names of four Iroquois tribes of the Six Nations are on the Wisconsin map: the Cayuga, the Mohawk, the Oneida, and the Seneca. Only the Onondaga and Tuscarora are unrepresented. In addition, three groups belonging to the Iroquoian language family but not politically part of the Six Nations are represented in Wisconsin place names: the Cherokee, the Huron, and the Mingo.

The Cayuga

The Cayuga once lived on the shores of Cayuga Lake at Ithaca, New York. Today most Cayuga live in Canada, although 300 of them were counted among the Seneca of Cattaraugus in 1972, and a few Cayuga are also listed among the Oklahoma Seneca.

According to Morgan, the Seneca name of Cayuga Lake, *Gwe-ú-gweh*, is translated as "mucky land," but he listed the town there as *Gwä-u-gweh*, "Carrying Place Village," or "place of taking out boats, a portage." Morgan rendered the name of the Cayuga tribe as *Gué-u-gweh-o-nu*, "people of the mucky land." The Cayuga believed that the name referred to a marsh at the foot of Cayuga Lake, near which their settlement was probably established.[57]

In New York the name Cayuga is not only on the lake but also on a county, a state park, a creek, an island, and two towns. It has also been adopted in six other states. In Wisconsin the name was given to a village in Ashland County by Cornell University, of Ithaca, New York, the site of the original Cayuga; the university was a large landowner in the vicinity of Cayuga, Wisconsin.[58]

The Mohawk

The easternmost tribe of the Iroquois confederacy, occupying the region westward from Albany, New York, was the Mohawk. This name by which they are known is from their Algonquian neighbors in Massachusetts or the lower Hudson Valley. Hewitt, a Tuscarora, held that it was "cognate with the Narraganset term *Mohowaùuck*, 'they eat (animate) things,' hence, 'man eaters.'" Cotton Mather in 1699 wrote of the "Maqua's," who were "part of those terrible Cannibals to the Westward."[59] Alternate explanations of this name by Schoolcraft— "wolf country" and "bear country"—have not been accepted. The Mohawks' own name, *Kaniengehaga*, signifies "people of the place of flint."[60]

Today the Mohawks live in scattered locations: St. Regis (Akwesasne) Reservation in Franklin County, New York; on the north side of the St. Lawrence near Cornwall, Ontario; at Caughnawaga near Montreal; on Quinte Bay, Lake Ontario, in Ontario; and on Grand River in Ontario. The Caughnawaga Mohawk were settled in Quebec by the French Jesuits in 1668. The other Canadian Mohawk were resettled from New York to their present locations by the British following the American Revolution.

The Mohawk were never residents of Wisconsin, but their name was attached to Mohawk Valley in Vernon County.

The Seneca

One of the most popular Indian tribal names is Seneca. There are at least sixty-two places named Seneca in twenty-two states, from Vermont to California. Best known of them are Seneca Lake and Seneca Falls, New York.

The Seneca are the westernmost of the Six Nations of New York and are known as "keepers of the western door." Seneca is corrupted from an Algonquian term *assinika*, probably of Mohican or Munsee origin, meaning "stony land" or "place of the stone." The name has the form of the name of a Roman philosopher, but that is the result of corruption by whites. The Seneca tribe's own name is *Nun da-wa-o-na*, "the great hill people." Their oldest village, *Nundao* ("hilly"), was the place where, according to legend, they sprang from the ground.[61]

The Seneca are the most numerous of the Iroquois in the United States. Aside from their people in Canada and Oklahoma, in 1980 there were 5,418 Seneca in New York, most of them living on three reservations totalling 60,000 acres in the western part of the state. In addition, the "Seneca-Cayugas" of Oklahoma numbered 670 people.

Among the well-known Seneca may be numbered Handsome Lake, religious leader (1735–1815); Red Jacket, orator and warrior (1751–1830); Gen. Ely S. Parker, aide to Gen. U. S. Grant in the Civil War (1828–95); and Arthur C. Parker, author (1882–1955).

The Seneca have no connection with Wisconsin, but their name is on a lake in Vilas County, a village in Crawford County, and towns in

Crawford, Green Lake, Shawano, and Wood counties. The name in Crawford County was given at the suggestion of Nicholas Morgan, a settler from Seneca County, New York.[62] It seems reasonable to suppose that the other places received their names in a similar manner.

The Cherokee

Cherokee is one of the most popular tribal names in the United States. Eight states have counties named Cherokee, and fourteen states have other places named for them. Indians sometimes joke about the large number of white Americans who claim to have Cherokee ancestry.

The Cherokee originally inhabited the western parts of North and South Carolina, eastern Tennessee, northwestern Georgia, and northeastern Alabama. They also claimed parts of Virginia and Kentucky. In 1838 most Cherokee, in consequence of a fraudulent treaty signed three years earlier by a minority faction, were removed over the "trail of tears" to northeastern Oklahoma, but a fragment of them, called Eastern Cherokee, still occupies the Qualla Reservation in the Great Smoky Mountains of North Carolina.

The tribe belongs to the Iroquoian language stock but was never a part of the Iroquois confederacy. One of the first to adopt European ways, they were one of that group dubbed "the Five Civilized Tribes." While still in the East, they adopted at New Echota, Georgia, a form of government modeled after that of the United States and also published the first Indian newspaper, the *Cherokee Phoenix*, using an alphabet devised by Sequoyah.

James Adair, a Scottish trader among southern tribes in the 1700s, wrote that "their national name is derived from *Chee-ra*, 'fire,' which is their reputed lower heaven, and hence they call their magi *Cheera-tahge*, 'men possessed of the divine fire.'" Another theory is that the name evolved from a term meaning "cave people" that was applied to them by the Choctaw. Still another writer, John Swanton, supposed that the tribal name came from a Creek term meaning "people of a different speech." No form of Cherokee was used in early times as a national name by the Cherokee themselves. Their own names were *Kithwagi* or *Tsalagi*, terms which are of debated meaning, and *Aniyuh-wiya*, "the real people."[63]

In Wisconsin the Cherokee are memorialized by a village and park in Marathon County, a lake in Dane County, and a park in the city of Madison.

The Huron

On Jacques Cartier's first voyage to Canada in 1534, he recorded some of the vocabulary from the language spoken by the Indians living around the site of the future city of Montreal, from which it has been determined that they were of Iroquoian stock, and probably Huron. Cartier referred to them only as *Sauvages*, "wild men." Samuel de Champlain, who founded Quebec in 1608, called them *Bons Iroquois*, "good Iroquois."[64]

The earliest appearance of the name Huron was in the application of Huronia to the "Huron Country" in the *Jesuit Relations* of 1634–36. By that time they were about the north shore of Georgian Bay.[65]

Father Paul Le Jeune, explaining the name Huron in the *Jesuit Relations* of 1639, declared that some of these Indians wore their hair in ridges, and because of the way their heads appeared to some soldier or sailor, they were called *hures* ("boars"), from which came Huron. In later years the story was repeated by Fathers Francisco Bressani (1653) and Pierre F. X. Charlevoix (1721).[66] It has been accepted by most American writers ever since. J. N. B. Hewitt pointed out that the word *huron* was in use as early as 1358 "as a name . . . signifying approximately an unkempt person, knave, ruffian, lout, wretch."[67] It still appears in French dictionaries.

Nevertheless, the argument for French origin of the tribal name Huron is based on hearsay and guesswork and leaves some questions unanswered. Why would the Hurons alone be named for the scalp lock, which was common to many tribes? Moreover, why would they be branded with a derogatory name when they were friendly allies of the French and were called "good Iroquois"? It seems at least possible that Father Le Jeune's account is only a folk etymological explanation of a gallicized native term.

There the matter rested until 1885, when Russell Errett maintained, in an obscure article, that the name Huron came from *Irri-ronon*, the Iroquois name of the Eries, or "Cat Nation." The French commonly placed an *h* before vowels, writing *Hiroquois* for Iroquois and *Hohio* for

Ohio. So also they appear to have changed *Irri-ronon* to *Hirri-ronon* and then abbreviated it to *Hirron* and Huron. In Errett's view, Huron was essentially the same name as Erie. He believed that both names represented a tribal totem.[68]

There is support for his hypothesis in the fact that the Neutral Nation of Canada, commonly regarded as a Huron subtribe, was called "Cat Nation" by the Iroquois, according to Morgan. In addition, Charlevoix called the Eries "an Indian nation of the Huron language."[69] After being driven from Georgian Bay, some Hurons joined the Erie.

A second challenge to French origin for Huron came from William M. Beauchamp (1907), who called that version a "fanciful story." He pointed out that "the Hurons were not known to the French by this name for some time. It seems to have been used only after visits to their country, and is probably of aboriginal origin." He concluded that Huron was "strongly suggestive of the Huron-Iroquois word ronon, a *nation*."[70]

In the late 1600s one of the Great Lakes, after bearing several temporary names, was called Lake Huron by the French. Hurons driven to Michigan and Ohio by Iroquois warriors became known under their own name, Wendat or Wyandot. Both names, Huron and Wyandot, are now attached to places in several states.

The Hurons were wanderers in Wisconsin between 1670 and 1673 when they were in flight from the Iroquois. They were believed to have stayed for a time on Washington Island, Door County, formerly known, for that reason, as Huron Island. They were also reported at the Potawatomi village of Mehingan and at Chequamegon, on Lake Superior, and along the Lake Superior coast of Michigan. Eventually they settled near Detroit and at Sandusky Bay of Lake Erie.[71]

Long after their departure from Wisconsin, Huron Lake in Waushara County received their name. The Hurons were never reported at that place; it is purely an honorific name.

The Mingo

The Mingo were not a tribe. The name was given by the Delawares to detached groups of Cayuga and Seneca living apart from the main body of their Iroquois brethren. The name apparently became popular as a place name because of its use in James Fenimore Cooper's

Leatherstocking Tales, and so it is discussed herein under names of literary origin. In Wisconsin, Mingo Lake in Burnett County is the only example of this name.

The Algonquin

Algonquin, or Algonkin, is one of the best-known American Indian names. It belongs to the tribe now living in Ontario and Quebec (with a 1980 population of 4,648), but the name was extended, because of language similarities, to the largest family of tribes in North America, the Algonquian, or Algonkian.[72] Champlain's map of 1632 shows the "Algomequins" in the area about Lake Simcoe, Ontario. Marquette spoke of the "allegonquin" language, and Father Gabriel Marest used the spelling Algonquin in 1712.[73] The Algonquin tribe did not live in Wisconsin, but all of the state's indigenous tribes except the Sioux and Winnebago belong to the Algonquian language family.

According to Schoolcraft, the Ojibwa called this tribe *Odishkuagama*, "people of the other or opposite shore," since they lived along the St. Lawrence River opposite the Iroquois who claimed the southern shore. According to Errett, that phrase was mistaken for a name and was applied to all non-Iroquian Indians. William Warren, the Ojibwa, was not consistent. In his *Ojibway Nation* he called the Algonquins *O-dish-quag-um-eeg*, "last water people," but in an article written for Schoolcraft, he claimed that the word meant "broad waters," referring to Lake of the Two Mountains in Canada, their principal home. J. N. B. Hewitt held that the name was from Micmac *algoomaking*, "place of spearing fish."[74] Perhaps we shall never know.

In Wisconsin, Algonquin Park in Brown Deer, Milwaukee County, is the only memorial to this tribe.

The Catawba

There is a story that railroad surveyors working in Price County became inebriated from drinking Catawba grape wine, and so a station was called Catawba.[75] The name has been extended to a civil town.

The tale is undoubtedly just one more of the innumerable myths which spring up to explain strange names. There are at least twenty-one places named Catawba in the United States, and it is probable that several of them (for example, in New Jersey and Ohio) are named for the presence of Catawba grapes. Ultimately, however, the name stems from the Catawba Indian tribe, a group of eastern Siouan speakers who still live in South Carolina. Forty-seven names have been applied to them by Europeans and other Indians. The name Catawba has been attributed to the Cherokee, the Choctaw, and the Catawba themselves.

Few writers have attempted to explain the meaning of this name, but Prof. William A. Read believed it was probably derived from Choctaw *katapa*, "a division," "divided," or "separated."[76] Frank Speck suggested a derivation from native words meaning "people of the river banks."[77]

The Cheyenne

The Cheyenne are known for two historic events. One was the flight back to Montana, in 1878–79, of a group of Cheyenne who had been expatriated to Oklahoma. The story was vividly told in Mari Sandoz's *Cheyenne Autumn*, which was made into a movie.[78] The other event was their alliance with the Sioux and their participation in the battle with Custer at the Little Big Horn River, in Montana, June 25, 1876.

An Algonquian tribe that originally lived in Minnesota, the Cheyenne were pushed into the Plains by the Chippewa at an early date, adopted the horse, and soon were adapted to Plains culture. Modern Cheyenne live on a reservation at Lame Deer, Montana, and on allotted land in Oklahoma.

As in so many other instances, the name by which these people are known is not their own. According to Father Peter Powell, they are *Votostataneo*, "the People." John R. Swanton, however, linked the Cheyenne name to a Dakota term meaning "people of alien speech."[79]

The Cheyenne have not been recorded as residents of Wisconsin, but their tribal name is on Cheyenne Valley, in Vernon County.

3

Personal Names

Their tribes have all been honored in our nomenclature;
some of the greatest chiefs have not; but there are many,
like Tecumseh and Little Turtle, whose valour and high
character would ennoble even a ridiculous name. Their
deeds, too, are our heritage. But for us their tribes will
pass away and leave not even the mounds of the earlier
races. Let us hold fast what we have of their memories in
this state.

> *Maria Ewing Martin,*
> *"Origin of Ohio Place Names" (1905)*

Wisconsin has done a better job than most states in commemorating individual Indians. However, the effort has not always been
free of controversy. For example, "The way to make Oshkosh a metro-
politan city that we all may be extremely proud of is to change its
name!" went an article in the *Northwestern* of Oshkosh, on March 4,
1910. A businessman complained: "I tell you the name Oshkosh is
taken as a huge joke everywhere. . . . They think it is a joke town, a sort
of crossroads rural place, where everything is free and easy and there is
no refinement. Professional stage folk delight in cracking jokes about
Oshkosh—the western town with the funny name. . . . It hurts our social standing and more especially our business relations with the whole
world." And so Oshkosh was torn by debate on the question, "Is our
community's aboriginal name an asset or a hindrance?" It was not the
first time. Historian Reuben Gold Thwaites joined the fray, and told
how, in 1840, the white residents at the mouth of the Fox River on Lake
Winnebago wanted to call the place Athens. The Indians, mixed bloods,
and traders wanted to honor their friend Oshkosh, chief of the Menominee Indians, who was then forty-five years of age. An election was held,
and the name Oshkosh won. "And it was fortunate," Thwaites concluded, "that the election turned out as it did, for the oddity of the name

has been a permanent advertisement for a very bright community. Oshkosh, as hackneyed Athens, would have been lost to fame. Nobody would think of going to 'Athens' to have fun with the boys." Seventy years after its founding, Oshkosh survived a challenge to its name and continued to thrive.[1] Moreover, the trade name "Oshkosh B'Gosh" for overalls manufactured there became as famous as San Francisco's Levis.

Oshkosh is not the only city with an Indian name to become the butt of jokes. Kalamazoo and Keokuk, Medicine Hat and Oskaloosa, Peoria, Wahoo, and Walla Walla have all felt the sting of jokester's barbs, and none are the worse for it. Their unique names have rescued them from a certain obscurity which would have been theirs if they were numbered among the plethora of cities with foreign or conventional names.

Menominee Names

Oshkosh

Chief Oshkosh (1795–1858) was "appointed" chief of the Menominee by Lewis Cass and Thomas L. McKenney, government negotiators at the treaty of Butte des Morts in 1827. By tribal custom, the chief was Josette, but Oshkosh exercised the functions of chief in government relations until his death. In the war of 1812 Oshkosh, like most Wisconsin Indians, had fought for the British, participating in the capture of Mackinac and the attack on Sandusky, Ohio. After the war, Oshkosh became a supporter of the government, even during Indian rebellions such as the Red Bird uprising among the Winnebago (1827) and the Black Hawk War involving the Sauk (1832).

In his position as chief, Oshkosh signed six treaties with the government, one of them through his brother as proxy. His name is variously spelled in these documents. At Butte des Morts, August 22, 1827, it is Oskashe. In the treaty of Green Bay, October 27, 1832, it is "Osh-rosh, the brave (by his brother fully empowered to act)." At Cedar Point, September 3, 1836, his name was written Osh-kosh. In the treaty at Lake Powawhaykonnay, October 18, 1848, wherein all Menominee lands in Wisconsin were ceded, his name appears as Osh, Kosh. The treaty of May 12, 1854, at Falls of Wolf River (Keshena), which cancelled the treaty of 1848, did not, in its original version, have his assent. However, article 6 said that the assent of "Osh-kosh and Keshena" must be se-

Chief Oshkosh, Menominee, 1793–1858. One of the most distinguished of the Menominee chiefs, Oshkosh signed five treaties. His name is preserved as the name of the city of Oshkosh, Winnebago County, where his remains were reburied in 1926. Portrait by Samuel Marsden Brookes, ca. 1852. Photo courtesy of the State Historical Society of Wisconsin WHi(X3)41832.

cured to validate the treaty. Oshkosh was holding out for amendments providing compensation for the land that was given up in return for a reservation on Wolf River. The matter was settled, and he signed on August 22, 1854, his name appearing as Osh-kosh. In his last treaty, at Keshena on February 11, 1856, which assigned two townships of the Wolf River reservation to the Stockbridge-Munsee Indians, his name was again written Osh-kosh.[2]

In the 1848 treaty Oshkosh signed away his tribe's land in Wisconsin, in exchange for a reservation on Crow Wing River, Minnesota. After visiting the Crow Wing site, however, he reversed himself and performed his greatest service to the tribe by leading a campaign to abrogate the treaty. Aided by the Catholic missionary Florimond Bonduel (for whom the town of Bonduel in Shawano County is named) and with the support of the Wisconsin legislature, Oshkosh visited President Millard Fillmore and won his cooperation. At last a new treaty, cancelling the treaty of 1848 and assigning to the Menominee a reservation of 360 square miles along Wolf River, was signed on May 11 and August 22, 1854. Sixty square miles of this was sold to the government two years later as a home for the Stockbridge-Munsee, who had immigrated from the East.

Upon his death in 1858 Oshkosh was buried near Keshena, but on May 25, 1926, he was reburied in Menominee Park in Oshkosh, adjacent to a statue of him which had been erected in 1911. His grandson Reginald Oshkosh spoke at the ceremony.[3] Several writers have interpreted the name Oshkosh as "the brave."[4] However, the evidence appears conclusive that Oshkosh signifies "hoof," "claw," or "nail."[5]

In Wisconsin the name Oshkosh is used for the city and the town in Winnebago County, for Oshkosh Reefs in Lake Winnebago, and for a creek in Menominee County. His name is also on a township in Yellow Medicine County, Minnesota; the county seat town of Garden County, Nebraska; and a railway flag stop in Natchitoches County, Louisiana. A post office in Wells County, North Dakota, bore his name from 1888 to 1894. All these places were named for the Menominee chief, in most cases at the suggestion of former residents of Oshkosh, Wisconsin.

Keshena

About 1829 or 1830 a son was born to Josette, titular chief of the Menominee. Shortly before this, Josette was fasting and in a vision thought he saw a multitude of hawks, the representatives of the thunder phratry, flying swiftly by. From this incident he gave the name *Ke shi' ĕne*, "swift flying," to his son. It was written Keshena.

Keshena succeeded his father as chief, although during his minority Oshkosh acted as chief. Keshena signed a treaty at Stockbridge on February 11, 1856, which gave two townships of land such of the Menominee reservation for settlement by the Stockbridge-Munsee.[6]

Keshena is the name of the principal town of the Menominee reservation, which is the seat of tribal government and includes a school, health services, and tribal court. Keshena is also the name of a lake and a waterfall in Wolf River on the reservation.

Machikanee (Chickeney)

The name of Machikanee Flowage in Oconto County is apparently derived from Menominee Mätshikinĕ' ŭ, "Bad Eagle," a personal name. It appears as Match-a-ken-naew in the treaty of Keshena, February 11, 1856. The name of Chickney or Chickeney Creek on the Menominee reservation is a corruption of this name. Chickeney is given as the name of a band leader who settled at the junction of this creek and Wolf River in the 1850s.[7]

Moshawquit

Moshawquit is the name of a lake in Menominee County. Possible interpretations from Bloomfield's *Lexicon* are *muqsa hkwat*, "the sky is clear," a man's name, and "Bright Sky," a family name. Alanson Skinner listed a Mrs. Mishakwut, "Covered by Clouds," as a resident of the Menominee reservation in June 1919.[8] Agnes Moshoquit, age 77, was named as a Menominee resident on the reservation in 1965.[9] Other possible variations of the name are found in Menominee treaties. In the treaty of Butte des Morts, August 11, 1827, Mishawukewett is listed among the signers. In treaties signed at Washington on February 8 and 17, 1831, the name appears as Mash-ke-wet.[10] This could be the same individual who was called Mosket, a war chief, in 1832.[11]

Neconish

Lake Neconish in Shawano County is named from a Menominee family name, Neka-nes, "Little Leader." Ernest Neconish was one of the Menominee elders who opposed tribal termination in 1958.[12]

Neopit

About 1831 a son was born to Chief Oshkosh and his first wife, Bambani, and was named Neopit, "Four in a Den." He was elected chief of the Menominee in 1875 after his brother Akwinemi was convicted and imprisoned for stabbing a man while under the influence of liquor. Hoffman described Neopit as a full blood, 5 feet 9 inches tall, light brown, with high cheek bones, and resembling a Japanese. Neopit was also said to be a "man of honor and veracity, and universally respected." He was a judge of the tribal court and chief of the Mitawit, or medicine society. Although a "pagan," he allowed his children to be Christianized. He became the father of fourteen children, of whom only two, Reginald and Ernest, were alive in 1892.

Soon after Neopit's death, the Menominee named their largest town Neopit (1980 pop. 1,122). It is the site of the tribally owned lumber mill, established in 1908.[13]

Paiawisit/Pywaosit

Lake Paiawisit in Oconto County and Pywaosit Lake in Menominee County are probably named for the same Menominee individual. It appears that this name is derived from Paye-wehseh, a man's name signifying "Bird Settling Down." Perhaps this is the name listed in the corrupted form Powoisnot as a signer of the treaty of Butte des Morts, August 11, 1827.[14]

Peshtigo

Peshtigo is an important Wisconsin name, yet its origin and meaning are elusive. The city of Peshtigo on the Peshtigo River in Marinette County was the scene of a disastrous forest fire on October 8, 1871. Also in Marinette County are the town of Peshtigo, Peshtigo Harbor, Flowage, Point, and State Wildlife Area (partly in Oconto County), as well as Little Peshtigo River. In Oconto County is Peshtigo Brook, and in Forest County is Pestigo Lake.

My former anthropology professor, the late James S. Slotkin, an adopted Menominee, could not explain this name. Neither could the Menominee Indian Historical Association of Milwaukee. Walter J.

Hoffman listed *Pesh tiko* as the name of the head of one of eleven Menominee bands, the band being named for him. Henry Gannett gave an incorrect explanation, "wild goose river." John R. Swanton wrote that a band of Menominee living on Peshtigo River was called *Pasatiko Wininiwuk*, "Peshtigo River people." *Pesh-tiko*, he said, was "evidently one of the old local groups."[15]

Shawano

About 1721 was born an Indian who came to be called Shawano. His ancestry is cloudy, some claiming that he was the son of a French-Canadian father and an Abnaki mother. However, by 1763 he was chief of the Menominee and was already known to the whites as "Old Chief" or "Old King." In Menominee he was called *Tshekâ' tshakee' man*, or *Cha-kau-cho-ko-man*. The French called him Chawanon, and the English, Shawano, both signifying "Southerner."

On August 17, 1778, Shawano was appointed "Grand Chief of the Menominees" by Canadian governor Frederick Haldimand. In 1821, when he was nearly blind and estimated to be a hundred years old, he died on a visit to Prairie du Chien. According to the scholar of the Menominee, Walter J. Hoffman, "As the name of Old Chief was without doubt applied to him late in life, and the above mentioned certificate (from Haldimand) bears the name of Chawanon (Shá wano), "Southerner," it is probable that he may have been so named earlier in life, and that perhaps the Canadian authorities so designated him . . . because he came from a more southerly tribe."[16]

It was Hoffman's belief that the city and lake named Shawano in Shawano County were named for "an old Indian named Shá wano—'southerner'—[who] formerly dwelt on the shore of the lake."[17] The name is also on a town in Shawano County and a creek in Forest County. It is perhaps this individual, and not the "Old Chief," who is honored by these names. The chief Shawano died in 1821; the later Shawano's name appears as "Shaw-wan-noh, the South," in a treaty signed at Washington on February 8, 1831. The name is spelled the same way, but not translated, in another treaty signed at Washington nine days later, on February 17, 1831. In the Keshena treaty of October 18, 1848, it appears for the last time as Shaw-wan-on.[18] This individual does not appear in Hoffman's genealogical charts.

Tomah

Near Montreal about 1700, Thomas Carron was born of French parents. Carron, who became a trader at Green Bay, married a Menominee woman named Waupesesin (Wild Potato), sister of a prominent Menominee. He became influential in the tribe, and by 1763 he had become speaker for the head chief, known in history as the "Old King" (see Shawano). In 1768 Carron rejected appeals from Pontiac to join the rebellion against the English which occurred in that year. For his loyalty, the British gave him a medal and a certificate naming him a chief. Carron died in 1780 at about the age of eighty.

Carron's second son, born opposite Green Bay about 1752, was named Thomas, a name which the Indians rendered as Tomah or Tomau. His older brother, Konot or Glode, who became acting chief after the death of Old Carron, died in 1804. (The titular chief, also called Old Carron, Old Chief, or Old King, actually continued to hold the title and outlived Tomah.) About 1805 Tomah rejected Tecumseh's appeals to join his Indian confederacy, designed to protect the Indians' land base from further erosion, because he feared the Americans would triumph. In 1813, however, believing that the English had a chance to defeat the Americans, he assembled about a hundred warriors to aid Col. Robert Dickson in the capture of Mackinac and the attack on Sandusky.[19]

Jedidiah Morse reported that "Thomau" died and was buried at Mackinac in 1818 and that over his grave "Mr. Law" (Lawe) erected a monument bearing this inscription:

> Here rests the body of Thomas Carron, Grand chief of the Folles avoine [Menominee] nation, who departed this life July 8th, 1818, aged 56 years, regretted by all who knew him.[20]

If we can accept Hoffman's account of his birth date and the above date for his death, he was sixty-six years old. However, Augustin Grignon claimed that the year of Tomah's death was 1817.[21]

The places named for Tomah are located far from the places where he lived. When a site was chosen for a white settlement in Monroe County in 1855, one of the founders allegedly read that Chief Tomah had once gathered his tribe in this vicinity for a conference (an unverified claim). He suggested the name Tomah for the village, and it was adopted. The name was extended to Lake Tomah, within the settlement, and to the surrounding town.[22]

Watasa/Watosah

Watasa was a Menominee of some importance though not a chief. He is listed as a signer of three treaties and amendments to one treaty, all in a period of eight years.

On October 18, 1848, he signed with an *X* the treaty of the Lake Pow-aw-hay-kon-nay, which gave up all Menominee land claims in Wisconsin in exchange for a reservation at Crow Wing, Minnesota. Therein the clerk wrote his name as Wy-ty-sauh. He also signed the treaty at the Falls of Wolf River (Keshena) on May 11, 1854, which revoked the treaty of 1848, and the amendments regarding financial compensation on August 22, 1854. In both documents the clerk wrote the name as Way-tan-sah. The syllable *tan* may have been a misreading of *tah* in the original. In his last treaty, at Keshena, on February 11, 1856, which assigned two townships of Menominee land to the Stockbridge-Munsee Indians, his name is written Way-taw-say.[23]

There can be little doubt that this is the Indian who is commemorated in the name of Watosah Lake in Menominee County and the names of Watasa Lake and Swamp in Shawano County. If we may connect the name to *wa-tasiw* or *wa-tasam* in Bloomfield's *Lexicon*, it is defined as "he cuts a round piece of him, it; he cuts him, it, in a circle."[24]

Waukau

Waukau is the name of a creek and a village in Rushford Township of Winnebago County and of a lake in Menominee County. Local belief in Winnebago County is that a Menominee family named Waukau lived near the village site until about 1852, at which time they moved north to the reservation on Wolf River. There, Lake Waukau was named by Mitchell Waukau. The name could be related to Menominee *wa·hkow*, "female sturgeon," or *wa·koh*, "fox."[25]

Waukechon

The town of Waukechon in Shawano County was named in 1858 for a Menominee band chief who lived on the Embarrass River near the site of present New London. According to legend, he was killed in 1852 by Mamatosh, an adopted Ojibwa and a medicine man, while on a rice-harvesting expedition down Wolf River. However, his name was signed to two treaties dated later than his supposed murder: Waukechon is listed as the first signer of the treaty at the Falls of Wolf River, May 12, 1854, and the seventh signer of the treaty of Keshena, February 11, 1856. He also signed two earlier treaties, at Cedar Point on September 3, 1836, and Lake Pow-aw-hay-kon-nay on October 18, 1848. In these two documents, his name is spelled Waw-kee-che-un.

One John B. Waukechon, perhaps a son of the chief, served in the Civil War and was wounded at Rome, Georgia. Waukechon is still a family surname among the Menominee. Peter Waukechon was a member of the Menominee Indian Centennial Committee in 1954. There are several opinions on the meaning of this name. One source translates it as "crooked nose"; a similar term, *wa-ketshan*, "hunchback," is listed as a Menominee personal name. The element *wâki*, "crooked," appears in these two forms, but the rest of it is doubtful. Finally, there is a Menominee term, *wahke-cecewan*, which signifies "it flows over something."[26]

Wayka

Wayka Creek and Wayka Rips, or Falls, in Wolf River, bear the name of a leader of the Thunder People who settled in 1852 on the creek named for him, at its junction with Wolf River. The name is also spelled We''ke and We-ka. Wayka is still a family name on the Menominee reservation. Thomas and Anna Wayka were listed as members of the Menominee DRUMS organization in 1951. The meaning of the name is not recorded, but it could be from *wa-kô*, "red fox."[27]

Weyauwega

The name Weyauwega, on a lake, city, and town in Waupaca County, is of obscure origin. Gov. James Doty told Elijah Haines of Waukegan, Illinois, that he gave the post office department the name Wey-au-wa-ya, said by him to be Menominee for "whirling wind." He claimed that the post office substituted -*ga* for -*ya* as the final syllable. According to Doty, this was the name of a Menominee guide in Doty's service in the early days.

Available sources do not confirm Doty's translation of this name. In Bloomfield's *Menominee Lexicon* the nearest approximation of it is *we-*

yawekeh, "old woman." One foolish claim holds that Weyauwega, "pronounced Y-o-wega," is an Indian name meaning "here we rest."[28]

Chippewa Names

Although the Chippewa are by far the most numerous tribe of Indians in Wisconsin and their tribal name is prominent on the map, very few personal names of Chippewa (Ojibwa) Indians have been adopted as place names. The handful that we do have are mainly in French and English.

Billy Boy

One place named for a Chippewa Indian is Billy Boy Dam, on the Couderay River in Sawyer County, upstream from state highway 70. It is named for William Billy Boy, a Chippewa of the Courte Oreilles band, who lived until 1920 in a cabin above the dam site.[29]

Bobidosh Lake

Bobidosh Lake is on the Lac du Flambeau Chippewa Reservation in Vilas County, about 1 1/2 miles east of the site of the old Northwestern railroad depot. Maxine Schmitz, a local historian and lifelong resident of Lac du Flambeau, believes the lake is named for the father of the late tribal leader, Alex Bobidosh. A fullblood like his father, Alex was born in 1890, and at age 75, while president of the Indian Bowl Powwow, he inducted former president Dwight Eisenhower into honorary tribal membership.

The meaning of Bobidosh has not been learned, but it could be a corruption or variation of Obadash, the name of a lake in Iron County (q.v.), which in turn may be a contraction from *obodashkwanishi,* "dragon fly."[30]

Chicog

There is a claim that Chicog Lake and the town of Chicog, as well as Chicog and Little Chicog creeks, in Washburn County are named for a Chippewa Indian. Reportedly he carried the mail on foot from Chandler to Gardner, both of which disappeared over a century ago. Another Indian named Chicog is mentioned in the 1803−4 journal of Michel Curot, a fur trader, but that individual cannot be connected with this area. These places may be named for the skunk, which is the meaning of Chicog in this instance. (See also Chapter 12.)[31]

Mosinee

Mon-so-ne, "Moose Tail," was a chief at Lac Courte Oreilles in the early nineteenth century. The city of Mosinee, in Marathon County, which was settled in 1857, is apparently named for him. According to one account, the postmaster at that place thought the original name, Little Bull Falls, was vulgar, and so a trapper named Connor was asked for an Indian name, whereupon he suggested that "Old Chief Mosinee" be honored, and the name was approved by the citizens.[32]

Nicaboyne

Nicaboyne Lake, Burnett County, has an Ojibwa family name, the source and meaning of which has not been found. St. Croix Chippewa informants could not explain it.

Skinaway/Skanawan

For the explanation of the name of Skinaway Creek in Barron County, I am indebted to Ben Skinaway, vice-chairman of the St. Croix band of Chippewa (1986), who lives at Big Round Lake in neighboring Polk County. He explained that the name Skinaway was from the Ojibway term meaning "young man." In Baraga's dictionary, this word appears in unclipped form as *oshkinawe*.[33]

There is no information to link the name of the stream to a particular individual. It appears likely that the name of Skanawan Creek and Lake in Lincoln County is a mere variation of *oshkinawe* or *Skinaway*.

Potawatomi Names

Big Foot

In the 1820s and early 1830s a Potawatomi village at the west end of Lake Geneva, on the site of present-day Fontana, Walworth County, was headed by Chief Big Foot. In 1827 Shabbona and Sauganash (Billy Caldwell) came from Chicago to this place in order to persuade Big Foot not to join the so-called Red Bird uprising among the Winnebago. The two were temporarily made captive, but Big Foot, though sympathetic to the hostiles, did not join the uprising.[34]

When Mrs. John H. (Juliette) Kinzie and her husband visited this village in 1831, the future Lake Geneva was known under the chief's name: "We descended a long, sloping knoll, and by a sudden turn came full in view of the beautiful sheet of water denominated Gros-pied by the French, *Maunk-suck* by the natives, and by ourselves Big-foot, from the chief whose village overlooked its waters." Mrs. Kinzie's impression of the chief did not match her reaction to the surroundings: "The chief was a large, raw-boned, ugly Indian with a countenance bloated by intemperance, and with a sinister, unpleasant expression. He had a gay-colored handkerchief upon his head, and was otherwise attired in his best, in compliment to the strangers."[35]

In 1836, by terms of the Chicago treaty of 1833, Big Foot's band was compelled to migrate to southwestern Iowa, where they settled on the Nishnabotna River. Ten years later the band was again required, by a new treaty, to move to Kansas. There, at an unknown date, Big Foot died and was buried in the Catholic cemetery at St. Mary's.[36]

Big Foot's name appears in three treaties. In the treaty of Green Bay, August 25, 1828, which set a boundary between the Indians and the lead mines of southwestern Wisconsin, his name is written "Maun-gee-zik, or big foot." In the treaty of Prairie du Chien, July 29, 1829, involving large land cessions, his name is recorded as Maw-geh-set. In the Chicago treaty of September 26, 1833, ceding all Potawatomi lands east of the Mississippi, his name is given as Mang-e-sett.[37]

The chief received his name, according to legend, because of the large tracks left in the snow by his snowshoes as he pursued a deer along the shore of the lake where he lived.[38] In Wisconsin his name continues on Big Foot Beach State Park, which is situated on the southeastern shore of Lake Geneva, adjacent to the city of Lake Geneva. In McHenry County, Illinois, the village of Big Foot is located at the intersection of the state line and U.S. Route 14, only four miles south of Fontana, the site of Big Foot's main village.

Kewaskum

The name of the town and village of Kewaskum in Washington County honors the memory of a Potawatomi band chief who is reported to have lived there about 1850. Reports of him are sketchy. One claim is that Kewaskum died about 1847, the year the town was organized. Paul Radin, in a map of Indian villages on Lake Koshkonong, for various dates, shows "Kewaskum's camp" but does not otherwise identify it. Publius Lawson says it was a temporary hunting camp used from 1847 to 1850 and identifies several other village sites of Kewaskum's band. Kewaskum's followers were homeless wanderers and squatters, since the Potawatomi were legally landless in Wisconsin from 1835 to 1914.

Hoffman (1893) identified Kewäshkum as a Menominee personal name and translated it as "to cause something to turn." Skinner and Smith each listed Kewaskum as a Potawatomi name signifying "turning back on his tracks."[39]

Mishicot

Michicot is the name of a river, a town, and a village in Manitowoc County. It has been called the name of both Chippewa and Ottawa individuals. However, Publius Lawson, whose principal informant was Simon Kahquados of the Potawatomi, identified Mishicot as a Potawatomi whose alternate name was Neatoshing. Mishicot was said to be the father of Joe Sahbe, who had a village at Ellison Bay, Door County. Mishicot also had a daughter named Koshkone, who married Waumegosaka, also called Wampum (1789–1844), a Chippewa of Manitowoc Rapids.

The name Mishicot in its present form cannot be translated, although spurious meanings are in print. *Mishi* means "great," but *cot* is meaningless. The name could be a variant of Menominee Moshawquit (q.v.), which is spelled in several ways.[40]

Shabbodock

John Shabbodock (1870–1950), a Potawatomi Indian, son of Waupaca (q.v.), spent most of his life living in a cabin near Alvin, in Forest County. A former resident of Alvin, Mrs. Lillian Edick, of Sumner, Washington, wrote in 1976 to an inquirer, Mrs. Dolores Miller of Appleton, that she knew John Shabbodock from the time she was sixteen years old. He was a man who loved the land and grew his favorite food, squash, in his garden plot. He searched the woods for ginseng, a lucrative drug plant. He also reportedly sold wild ponies for $10—with the customer obliged to catch them himself.

Another native of Alvin, Beulah Huff, wrote of John Shabbodock's love of music and recalled that he had once made a bow and arrow for her brother in exchange for his playing some tunes on a violin made by Shabbodock's father.

Mrs. Edward Mitchell of Iron River said that Shabbodock was found dead in his cabin in April 1950, at the age of eighty. Shabodock Creek and Lake, in Forest County, were named for him. The meaning of the name is not known. Shabbodock is buried with his father and other family members in the family cemetery four miles south of Marion in Waupaca County.[41]

Waubee/Waupee

Waupee Lake as well as Waupee Creek and Flowage, which join the North Branch of Oconto River in Armstrong Township, Oconto County, probably have the same name origin as Waubee Lake in Lakewood Township of the same county. The first are said to be named for a Potawatomi chief, whose name has been wrongly interpreted as "looking at it." The correct definition is simply "white." *Wabi* and *wapi*, the simpler forms of Waubee and Waupee, are prefixes, almost never standing alone. One Illinois Potawatomi was named Wabimanito, "White Spirit."[42]

Waupee can also be a suffix to a longer name. According to one source, the town of *Nasawaupee* in Door County was named in 1859 for a Menominee Indian who headed a village a few miles to the west.

Waubeka

The village of Waubeka in Ozaukee County is believed to be named for a Potawatomi who about 1850 was chief of a village on the Milwaukee River at the site of present Waubeka. In that year, at age ninety, Waubeka reportedly moved to "Pigeon River," though it is unclear which of Wisconsin's three Pigeon Rivers. Waubeka is said to have been the father of Mequon (q.v.), for whom a town was allegedly named in Ozaukee County. His son-in-law was said to be a son of Solomon Juneau (q.v.), Milwaukee's first mayor. The name Waubeka could be a corruption of *wapikin*, the Potawatomi word for "clay."[43]

Waupaca

The city of Waupaca, in Waupaca Township, is the seat of Waupaca County. From Portage County, the Waupaca River flows through Waupaca to join Wolf River near Weyauwega. These places are named for a Potawatomi Indian who lived in the county.

Waupaca is translated in several ways but probably signifies "white earth." Way-pay-kay is listed as a signer of a treaty at Prairie du Chien, July 29, 1829, but it is not known if he was the same individual as Waupaca.[44]

At Waupaca County Park, four miles south of Marion, Waupaca is buried with other members of his family. A state marker there gives his alternate name as Sam Wapuka, which is not explained. Alanson Skinner translated that name as "looking," and called it a Bald Eagle clan personal name.[45] Waupaca was the father of John Shabbodock (1870–1950), for whom a creek and lake in Forest County are named.

A Sauk Name: Black Hawk

Black Hawk (1767–1838) was a war chief of the Sac or Sauk tribe, which once occupied Wisconsin but removed to Illinois and Missouri in the eighteenth century. Black Hawk was born at the present site of Rock Island, Illinois, in 1767. His rise to fame rests on his effort in 1832 to reoccupy lands in Illinois from which his people had been expelled the year before. In April 1832, he assembled about nine hundred people, including many women and children, at the mouth of the Iowa River opposite New Boston, Illinois, and crossed the Mississippi. Thus began the "war" which ended in Wisconsin four months later.

The Sauk passed their former village site, Saukenuk, without stopping, and moved up the Rock River to join White Cloud, the Winnebago Prophet, at Prophetstown. They were pursued by hastily assembled state militia, who burned Prophetstown on May 10. The probable peaceful intent of the Sauk was transformed into a defensive war when the militia fired on an Indian truce party bearing white flags near Stillman Valley, Illinois, on April 14. Soon after, the militia were routed by a much smaller Indian force. After other engagements at Elizabeth and Kellogg's Grove, Illinois, Black Hawk led his followers into Wisconsin and encamped on Lake Koshkonong and later at Four Lakes (now Madison).

Federal troops under Gen. Henry Atkinson were now pursuing Black Hawk, who led his people north to the Wisconsin River. They were overtaken on July 21 by troops under Col. Henry Dodge and Gen. J. D. Henry at Wisconsin Heights, just south of the site of Sauk City, once the site of a major Sauk town, visited by Carver in 1766. With numbers much depleted and weakened by hunger, Black Hawk here faced a thousand troops while he fought a delaying action to give his people time to cross the Wisconsin River. His prowess on this occasion was praised by Jefferson Davis as "a feat of consummate management and bravery, in the face of an enemy of greatly superior numbers. . . . Had it been performed by white men, it would have been immortalized as one of the most splendid achievements in military history."[46]

With many of his ragged and starving people dropping along the way from exhaustion, Black Hawk hurried over rugged country to the Mississippi, reaching it below the mouth of the Bad Axe River, Vernon County, on August 1. There the troops caught up with them, and they were fired on by cannon from the *Warrior*, a gunboat on the river. Some women with children tried to swim across the river, but many of these were slain by Sioux on the other side. Black Hawk and a few companions escaped to Wisconsin Dells, but after a month he accompanied two Winnebago voluntarily, by his account, to Fort Crawford at Prairie du Chien, where he surrendered to Gen. Joseph M. Street.

He, with two sons, White Cloud, and several others were sent down the river to Jefferson Barracks, Missouri, where Black Hawk was placed in chains and confined for the winter. In the spring he and some others were taken to Washington, where he met the cause of his grief, President Andrew Jackson, and then was confined another month in Fortress Monroe, Virginia. At that place his portrait was painted by George Catlin and Charles Bird King. After being taken on a tour of eastern cities, to impress him with the white man's might, he was returned to Iowa, and lived in a wickiup on the Des Moines River in Van Buren County. There, he dictated his autobiography to Antoine LeClaire, a French-Potawatomi interpreter.[47] He died there on October 3, 1838.

In his autobiography Black Hawk's Sauk name is spelled Ma-ka-tai-me-she-kia-kiak, interpreted as Black Sparrow Hawk. In the only treaty he ever signed, at St. Louis on May 13, 1816, his name is written Mucketamachekaka, or Black Sparrow Hawk.[48]

Although Black Hawk spent only about three months in Wisconsin, he has been memorialized in several place names. These include a village in Sauk County; a lake in Iowa County; islands in the Wisconsin River in Jefferson County and in the Upper Dells, Juneau County; a creek and park in Rock County; a park in Lafayette County; and a ridge in Dane County.

Sioux Names

Wahcoutah

Wahcoutah Island in the Mississippi, Pepin County, is named for a notable Sioux warrior whose name is usually spelled Wacouta, "The Shooter." Other renderings of the name are Wah-koo-ta, Wakooda, Wakouta, and Wakuta. He was a nephew of the notable Red Wing, of Minnesota, and a member of Wabasha's band.[49] The village of Wacouta in Goodhue County, Minnesota is also named for him.

It is reported that Wacouta was the last chief of his band of Dakotas. Although he was unaccustomed to leading his people on the warpath, his braves were free to raid their enemies, normally the Chippewa, whenever they wished. Of him Warren Upham wrote, quoting one Hancock, not otherwise identified:

> Wacouta was very tall, straight and dignified in his demeanor.
> He was also a man of good judgment. His authority was not
> absolute. He rather advised his people than commanded them.
> He encouraged industry and sobriety; was a friend to the mis-
> sionaries, and sent his own children to their schools when he
> was at home himself. . . . This name was borne as a title of
> chieftaincy. With slight differences it was the name of the
> head chief of Issati Sioux about Mille Lacs at the time of the
> captivity of Hennepin and his companions in 1680.[50]

In 1823 Keating mentioned his meeting, at Red Wing's village, with "an old man by the name of Wazekota (Shooter from the pine top)," who, he added, had accompanied Major Long on his previous expedition in 1817.[51] It is apparently Wahcoutah's name, badly corrupted into Warseconta, "who shoots in the Pine tops," that appears after Red Wing's in the treaty of St. Louis, June 1, 1816. In the treaty of Prairie du Chien of July 15, 1830, is the name "Wah-coo-ta, that shoots arrows."[52]

Waumandee

Buffalo County, which is within an area possessed by the Sioux until 1837, has among its place names the second of only two Sioux personal names on the map of Wisconsin. In the county are the village and town of Waumandee, a creek and a lake by that name, as well as Little Waumandee Creek and Waumandee Valley. Sandra Ebert, deputy clerk of Buffalo County, informed me that "the name of Waumandee was suggested by Judge Pierce, at that time a resident of Fountain City. Waumandee is an Indian name, and its English interpretation is by no means certain, but it is supposed to mean 'War Eagle' or 'War Valley.'"[53] My information does not identify the language from which the name came, but that is easily ascertained. Riggs gives *wamdi* and *wanmdi'* as Santee Dakota for "war eagle," and Williamson gives *wanmdi* as "eagle."[54]

Although the origin and meaning of the name are easily traceable, the individual from whom the place names derive is difficult to identify because two prominent Sioux Indians bore this name. One of them, born in Wisconsin or Minnesota between 1780 and 1790, died at the site of Sioux City, Iowa, in 1851. Born a Santee, he was adopted by the Yanktons. He joined his friend Chief Tamaha in backing the American side in the War of 1812, when most Dakotas were pro-British. Later he was a courier for the American Fur Company.

In 1823 William Keating reported meeting "Chief Wamendetanka (War Eagle) generally known as the Black Dog," near the mouth of St. Peters (Minnesota) River. This individual is listed as "Wa-man-de-tun-ka, black dog," among the signers of a treaty at Prairie du Chien on August 19, 1825, although the correct translation is "big war eagle." This chief was apparently not the same person as the other War Eagle, for he signed another treaty at Washington on June 19, 1858, seven years after the death of the other individual. There, his name is listed as "Wa-min-dee-ton-kee, Large War Eagle."[55]

It is possible, however, that War Eagle of the Yanktons is the signer of a treaty at Bellevue, Nebraska, October 15, 1836, wherein his name is spelled Wa-men-de-ah-wa-pe. Though not translated in the treaty, that name is probably composed of the words *wanmdi*, "eagle" (or "war eagle"), and *wa-pi-ya*, "doctor" or "conjurer." This may also be the person listed as "Wa-be-la-wa-con, the medicine war eagle" in a treaty signed June 22, 1825.[56]

The probability is that Waumandee, Wisconsin, is named for the Santee Sioux Indian otherwise known as Black Dog, who signed the treaties of 1825 and 1858, since the Yankton man spent most of his life around Sioux City, Iowa, where he died and was buried in 1851, before Buffalo County, Wisconsin, was organized (1853).[57]

Stockbridge-Munsee Names

Kankapot

At Detroit on February 24, 1837, Henry R. Schoolcraft wrote in his journal:

> Robert Kankapot presents himself with about twenty followers. He is a Stockbridge Indian of Green Bay, Wisconsin, on his way to the East. He is short of funds, and asks for relief. No annuity or other funds are payable, at this office, to this tribe. I deemed his plea, however, a reasonable one, and loaned him personally one hundred dollars. . . . he says he is sixty-four years of age, that he was born in Stockbridge, on the head of the Housatonic River, in Massachusetts.[58]

This individual was a member of a numerous family of Stockbridges (Mohicans from Massachusetts), one or all of whom are commemorated by the name of Kankapot Creek, which runs from northern Calumet County to join the Fox River at Kaukauna in Outagamie County.

The name of one or more members of the Kankapot family appears to be attached to every treaty involving the Stockbridges. In the first, signed at Oneida, New York, on December 2, 1794, are the names of John and Jacob Kankapot. In the treaty of Green Bay, October 27, 1832, is the name of Robert Konkopa, undoubtedly a misspelling of the name of the same person who met Schoolcraft in 1837. A treaty at Stockbridge, Wisconsin, on September 3, 1839, was signed by Robert, Levi, Elisha, Simeon, and Jonas "Konkapot." Each of these five was also listed on a schedule of individuals to be paid for land and improvements, since they were part of a group which had agreed to migrate to Minnesota. On November 24, 1848, another treaty was signed ceding all of the town of Stockbridge on the east side of Lake Winnebago, which was to be divided into lots for Indians wishing to become citizens, while the remainder was to be sold to settlers. Indians not wishing to become citizens would move west of the Mississippi. This treaty was signed by Jacob and Levi Kankapot; Elisha Kankapot was named on a list of valuations for improvements.

The last Stockbridge treaty, February 5, 1856, recognized that the Indians refused to remove to Minnesota and provided them with a reservation of two townships adjacent to the Menominee reservation, where their descendants now live. The treaty was signed by six members of the "Konkopot" family, and in a very unusual turn, two of them were women. The signing Kankapots were Jacob, Elias, Levy (Levi?), Aaron, Louise, and Polly.[59]

Killsnake

John Killsnake was the only Munsee to sign a treaty at Stockbridge on September 3, 1839, ceding to the United States at $1.00 an acre the eastern half of the Stockbridge-Munsee reservation on the east side of Lake Winnebago, a total cession of 23,040 acres. The treaty also provided for payment for the land and improvements of twenty-seven families who agreed to move west of the Mississippi. Killsnake's name is also on a tribal census roll attached to the treaty of November 24, 1848.[60]

His name is on Killsnake River which joins the South Branch of Manitowoc River in Rantoul Township, Calumet County, and on Killsnake State Wildlife Area in Calumet and Manitowoc counties.

Quinney

The village of Quinney in Calumet County takes its name from a member of the Stockbridge (Mohican) tribe of Indians who migrated to Wisconsin in 1833. There are several prominent persons of the Quinney family who figure in the history of these people, but this place is probably named for the celebrated chief Austin E. Quinney, who led the Stockbridge Indians first to Indiana from their temporary New York residence among the Oneida. In 1822 he negotiated a transfer of land

John Waunnacon Quinney, Sr., Stockbridge (Mohican), 1797–1855. He signed the treaty of Stockbridge, November 24, 1848, and made nine trips to Washington on behalf of his tribe. His brother was the chief, Austin E. Quinney, for whom the village in Calumet County is probably named. Painting by A. Hamlin. Photo courtesy of the State Historical Society of Wisconsin WHi(X3)25713.

from the Menominee at Green Bay, land subsequently paid for with money received from New York State for Stockbridge holdings there. The Indians settled on the east side of Lake Winnebago in 1833, but in 1856 a majority of them moved to their present reservation in Shawano County, which is shared with the Brothertons and Munsee, adjacent to that of the Menominee.

Alanson Skinner was informed by Austin Quinney's daughter Harriet that Quinney was a chief of the Wolf Clan and that his native name was Ikuatuam, meaning "on both sides of the river." The name Quinney is said to be from *Quinecan,* "The Dish." George Catlin's portrait of Quinney with his totem, the wolf, in the background is reproduced in Skinner's *Notes on Mahikan Ethnology.*[61]

Quinney's name appears as "Austin Quinny" in the appendix to the Menominee treaty signed at Green Bay, October 27, 1832, along with the name of John W. Quinney. A treaty with the Stockbridges was signed at Stockbridge on November 24, 1848, by "Augustine E. Quinney, sachem," and five other members of the Quinney family.[62] John Waunnacon Quinney, Sr. (1797–1855), apparently a brother of Austin, made nine trips to Washington on behalf of the tribe.[63]

Winnebago Names

Black Wolf

The town of Black Wolf in Winnebago County is named for a Winnebago band chief who in 1828 was living at Black Wolf Point, on the southwest shore of Lake Winnebago near the site of present Van Dyne. At that time Black Wolf's village consisted of ten lodges containing 180 people. According to Augustin Grignon, Black Wolf died before the Winnebago were removed from the state in 1840, but Jipson says he died in 1847. He was the father of Dandy (1793–1879).[64]

We have a description of Black Wolf from Juliette Kinzie, who met him at Fort Winnebago in 1831:

> There was Black Wolf, whose lowering, surly face was well
> described by his name. The fierce expression of his counte-
> nance was greatly heightened by the masses of heavy black
> hair hanging round it, quite contrary to the usual fashion
> among the Winnebagoes. They, for the most part, remove a

portion of their hair, the remainder of which is drawn to the back of the head, clubbed and ornamented with beads, ribbons, cock's feathers, or if they are so entitled, an eagle's feather for every scalp taken from an enemy.[65]

Jipson rendered his name in Winnebago as Shounk-tshunk-saip-kaw and added that he reputedly joined the British in the War of 1812 and took part in the attack on Mackinac. John H. Kinzie's annuity list of November 8, 1832, records Black Wolf as residing at Lake Koshkonong and spells his name as Shoank-tshunk-saip-kaw. His family, consisting of himself, four women, and two children, received $25.81.[66]

His name appears on three treaties. In the Treaty of Butte des Morts, August 11, 1827, it is written as Shoank-tshunksiap; in the Treaty of Green Bay, August 25, 1828, it appears as Shoank-tshunsk-kaw; and in the last, at Prairie du Chien, August 1, 1829, it is listed as Shoank-tsunk-saip-kau. In all three treaties the name is translated "Black Wolf."[67]

Dandy

Dandy Creek and Dandy Creek Flowage in Monroe County are named for a minor Winnebago chief (1793–1870) who was a son of Black Wolf and a nephew of Four Legs, of Lake Winnebago.

Juliette Kinzie, who met Dandy at Fort Winnebago in 1831, explained the peculiar nickname of the chief "to whom with justice was given, by both whites and Indians, the appellation of 'the Dandy'":

When out of mourning his dress was of the most studied and fanciful character. A shirt (when he condescended to wear any) of the brightest colors, ornamented with innumerable rows of silver arm-bands; leggings and moccasins of the most elaborate embroidery in ribbons and porcupine quills; everything that he could devise in the shape of ornament hanging to his club of hair behind; a feather fan in one hand, and in the other a mirror, in which he contemplated himself every five minutes; these, with the variety and brilliance of the colors upon his face, the suitable choice and application of which occupied no small portion of the hours allotted to his toilet, made up the equipment of young Four-Legs [sic]. This devo-

tion to dress and appearance seemed not altogether out of
place in a youthful dandy.[68]

According to Jipson, Dandy was also known as Little Soldier (Mau-nah-
pay-ho-nik). In the 1832 annuity list his residence was given as Barri-
bault (Baraboo) village no. 2. His family then consisted of eight persons,
who received a total of $29.50.[69]

After refusing to go to Iowa with his tribe in 1840, Dandy was captured in 1844 at the head of Baraboo River and fastened to a horse with
ox-chains under the horse's belly. Dandy was still determined to resist
exile and demanded to see Governor Dodge at Mineral Point. Taken to
the governor, he asked to talk in council. There he took a Bible and held
it up, saying: "This good book. You do like say in good book?" When the
governor answered that there was no better book, Dandy spoke again:
"Then, if a man do all it say in this book, what more should he do?" The
governor replied that no more would be required. "Then look at good
book," answered Dandy. "If you find in it that Dandy should go to Turkey River [in Iowa], Dandy will go today; but if not, he will never go to
stay." And he did not go.

He was taken to Prairie du Chien, where it was found that his legs
were so blistered by the chain that he could not walk for three weeks.
According to Jipson, he was turned over to the soldiers, and a corporal
carried him on his back to a buggy. When he was left unguarded, presumed unable to walk, he jumped from the buggy and escaped to the
woods. He lived the rest of his life along the Wisconsin River, dying in
1870 at the age of seventy-seven at Petenwell Bluff, near Necedah, 255
feet above the river. August Derleth called him "a symbol of the uncon-
querable spirit of the Indians who loved their land, the red men like
Yellow Thunder, Red Bird, and Black Hawk."[70]

Decorah

In 1729 a French officer, Sabrevoir de Carrie (or Joseph de
Caris, according to Kellogg), won the favor of Hopokoekaw (q.v.), a Win-
nebago maiden and chief styled "Glory of the Morning" who lived on
Doty Island, where the Fox River flows north out of Lake Winnebago.
From their union sprang a notable line of chiefs and persons prominent
in tribal and state history.[71] "At the present time," wrote Paul Radin in

Spoon Decorah, ca. 1805–1889. A member of the noted Decorah family, of French-Winnebago ancestry, son of "Old Gray-Headed Decorah" and younger brother of Little Decorah. Three other tribesmen, at different times, were named Spoon Decorah. Several topographic features in Trempealeau County and the village of Dekorra in Columbia County are named for members of the Decorah family, but writers disagree on which places are named for which individual. Cabinet view by E. R. Curtis, Madison. Photo courtesy of the State Historical Society of Wisconsin WHi(X3)12668.

1921, "there is no clan as numerous as the descendants of that family."[72] The father of the line, de Carrie, was killed in battle at Quebec in 1759, but his descendants have spread the family name—in the forms Decorah, Decorra, Decoria, and Dekorra—over the map of five states.[73]

The oldest son of Hopokoekaw and de Carrie was Choukeka De Kaury, or Spoon Decorah (1730–1816), who signed the treaty of St. Louis on June 3, 1816, and died the same year at Portage. (Because at least three other Decorahs were called "Spoon," this name has caused some confusion, and at least one writer has mistaken it for the Winnebago meaning of Decorah.)[74] The second son, Buzzard Decorah, was the father of Big Canoe, or One-eyed, Decorah (1772–1864) and Waukon Decorah (ca. 1775–1868). Big Canoe, like all the Decorahs and most Indians of his region and generation, fought for the British in the War of 1812.

Most Winnebago were neutral in the Black Hawk War of 1832, and according to Gen. Joseph M. Street, it was Big Canoe (along with a man identified as Chaetar) who delivered the Sauk chief Black Hawk to him at Fort Crawford, August 27, 1832. (Black Hawk, however, said he came voluntarily.)[75]

According to Charles Hexom, Decorah Peak, Decorah Cave, and Decorah Prairie in Trempealeau County are named for Big Canoe, but Thomas Hughes claimed that these places are named for Old Decorah, son of Spoon Decorah. Old Decorah (ca. 1747–1836) was the father of Little Decorah (1797–1887) for whom the township of Decoria in Blue Earth County, Minnesota, was named.[76]

Waukon Decorah, the brother of Big Canoe, is perhaps the most notable of the family. He signed five treaties between 1828 and 1846, in which he is listed under his Winnebago name Wau-kon-haw-kaw (variously spelled), translated in the treaties as "Snakeskin." His portrait was painted by James O. Lewis, and he lived to see his given name, shortened to Waukon, attached to the seat of Allamakee County, Iowa, and his family name, Decorah, to the seat of Winneshiek County in that state.[77] Other geographic names originating with this family include that of the vanished village of Decora, in Montcalm County, Michigan, and Decorra, a current village name in Henderson County, Illinois.

In Wisconsin, besides the features mentioned in Trempealeau County, this illustrious name is used for the village of Dekorra, in Columbia County, so spelled by action of the county board, and for Decorah Beach on Lake Winnebago, Winnebago County. The cemetery at Winnebago Mission, Jackson County, is called Decorah Cemetery, and the family name may be seen on gravestones in that place.[78]

Funmaker

Funmaker Flowage is a tributary of Black River in eastern Jackson County. It is a dammed-up drainage ditch, part of a conservation area. It is named for George Funmaker, Sr., a Winnebago who is buried in Decorah Cemetery near Winnebago Mission. The grave marker gives the years of his life as 1860–1947.

According to Frances Perry of Black River Falls, Funmaker was a member of the Bear Clan, whose homestead was in this part of the central plain. His Bear Clan name, she wrote, is badly translated: "Actually, it refers to the antics of a bear cub; [it] probably means 'Laughing-at-his-antics,' probably Old Funmaker's vision-quest name." Funmaker is still a family name among the Winnebago.[79]

Little Thunder

Little Thunder Flowage in Jackson County is named for a Winnebago Indian who is sometimes called Good Thunder (ca. 1795–1863). In 1832 he headed a village at Fond du Lac and in that year participated in the Black Hawk War on the side of the whites. In John H. Kinzie's annuity list of November 8, 1832, his name is recorded as Wau-kaun-tshah-nik-ka, "Small Thunder," of Nau-Paw-Saw, or Locust Tree Village. His family then consisted of four men, six women, and four children, who received the sum of $51.63.[80]

In 1840 Little Thunder was removed with his people to Turkey River in northeastern Iowa. In 1848 they were moved again to Long Prairie, Minnesota, and still again in 1855 to Blue Earth County. Their final removal, after a short time in South Dakota, was to the present reservation in Thurston County, Nebraska, in 1865, after which the chief died.

During the Sioux rebellion of 1862, Little Thunder remained steadfast to the whites. After his final removal, grateful Minnesota settlers placed his name on a village established in 1871 on the vacated site of his village in Blue Earth County.

Thomas Hughes gave the Winnebago form of his name as Wakunt-chapink and said he signed treaties in 1832, 1837, and other years. After examining all twelve treaties to which the Winnebago were a party, I do not find the above name or any name which is translated as Good

Thunder. However, the name Wa-kun-cha-nik-kah, "Little Thunder," is attached to a treaty signed at Washington, November 1, 1837. Another treaty, signed at Washington on February 27, 1835, lists as a signer Waw-kon-chau-hoo-no-kaw, "Little Thunder."[81]

Mazomanie

Mazomanie, the name of a Dane County village near Madison, is a corruption from Mau-ze-mon-e-ka, "Iron Walker," the name of a Winnebago Indian, son of Whirling Thunder, who had a village at the site of Watertown in the early 1830s.[82]

His name is written as Mau-zay-mau-nee-kaw, "Iron Walker," on John H. Kinzie's annuity list of November 8, 1832. At that time, his family or band consisted of two men, seven women, and twenty children, who received a total annuity of $73.75.[83]

In October 1836, Iron Walker was charged with the murder of Pierre Paquette, a well-known trader at Fort Winnebago. According to one report, a rival trader named Daugherty convinced the Indian that Paquette was cheating in his role as distributor of government goods to the Indians.[84] Mazomanie, as he was known, was first convicted, then acquitted in a second trial. After that, he apparently remained in seclusion for the rest of his days.

According to Frederic Cassidy, the village of Mazomanie was named in 1855 at the suggestion of Edward Brodhead of New York, one of the founders. Cassidy believes that the choice of the name may have been influenced by anticipation of the coming of the railroad, which occurred in 1856. Mazomanie's name is related to the Winnebago term *maaz-na-coe-nah*, "railroad." Today the name is also attached to a state wildlife area.[85]

There was also a Sioux chief named Mazomanie, but he lived in Minnesota. His name appears as Mazo-manie, "Iron That Walks," in a treaty signed July 13, 1830, at Prairie du Chien, and Maz-zo-ma-nee, "Walking Iron," in the Treaty of Washington, June 19, 1858.[86]

Mitchell Red Cloud

Mitchell Red Cloud, Jr., born in Jackson County, Wisconsin, on July 2, 1925, was only sixteen when the United States entered World War II. As soon as he was eligible, he joined the Marines and served with Carlson's Raiders in the Pacific.

In December 1945, at the age of twenty, Red Cloud published, in the

Wisconsin Archaeologist, an account from Winnebago tradition of the surrender of the Sauk chief Black Hawk in 1832, in which he supported Black Hawk's claim that the surrender was voluntary.[87] He was also an informant to Nancy Lurie in her master's thesis, "Trends of Change in Patterns of Child Care and Rearing among the Wisconsin Winnebago."[88]

War came again in Korea only five years after the end of World War II. This time Mitchell Red Cloud joined the army and became a corporal. On November 5, 1950, at the age of twenty-five, he was killed by Chinese troops while manning a machine gun to protect fellow soldiers. Posthumously, the congressional Medal of Honor was presented to his mother, Nellie Red Cloud, by Gen. Omar C. Bradley.

In 1957 the city of La Crosse dedicated Red Cloud Park in his memory. On September 2, 1957, Labor Day, Red Cloud Highway Memorial Park at the powwow grounds in the village of Winnebago Mission, Jackson County, was likewise named in his honor. State route 54 is Red Cloud Highway.

Mitchell Red Cloud is buried in Decorah Cemetery at Winnebago Mission, where a monument was dedicated to his memory on May 30, 1967. A post of the Veterans of Foreign Wars in Friendship, Wisconsin, was also named for him.[89]

Waushara (Big Fox)

A lake and a county in Wisconsin are named for a local Winnebago chief called Fox or Big Fox. His name appears as Wau-shay-ray-kay-kaw on John Kinzie's annuity list at Fort Winnebago, November 8, 1832.[90] He headed a village located on present Fox Lake in Dodge County. Its Winnebago name was Day-wau-sha-ra (*day* meaning "lake," and *waushara*, "fox"). Cram's map of 1839 showed this village as Waushara, an abbreviation of its Winnebago name. Today, as a white village, it is called Fox Lake. In 1851 the name Waushara was transferred to a new county formed two tiers to the north.[91]

Winneshiek

Several topographic features in Wisconsin and neighboring states are called Winneshiek. This was the name borne by several generations of prominent Winnebago chiefs during the last two hundred years, and they were sometimes confused with one another.

The first Winneshiek, also called Mawa-ra-ga, is believed to have

Winnebago Indians: John Black Hawk (*left*), unidentified (*center*), and Winneshiek III (*right*). Winneshiek III died near Black River Falls in 1887 or 1888, according to conflicting accounts. The Winneshiek genealogy is complicated because of similar names of various individuals. Several geographic features in Wisconsin are named for members of this family. Copy from print lent by Alan R. Sawyer, 1957. Photo courtesy of the National Anthropological Archives, Smithsonian Institution.

been born about 1777 on Doty Island, at the north end of Lake Winnebago. One of his wives was reputed to be a sister of Wabokieshiek (White Cloud), the Winnebago prophet who aided Black Hawk and the Sauks in 1832. The elder Winneshiek headed a village of two or three hundred people at the site of Freeport, Illinois, in 1827, but by 1829 the band had removed to La Crosse, Wisconsin.

Winneshiek had two notable sons. The first, called in Winnebago Waukonchawkoohaw, "Coming Thunder," but generally known as Young Winneshiek, was born at Portage in 1812. Young Winneshiek, at age fifteen, was active in the Red Bird "uprising" of 1827, during which he was captured by Col. Henry Dodge and held hostage for two weeks at Galena, Illinois.

During the treaty conference at Prairie du Chien in July 1829, government negotiator Caleb Atwater reported: "It became my duty, in order to effect the views of the United States, to gain over to our interest, Winnesheek, the principal Chief of the Prairie Le Cros. . . . As the readiest way to effect my object, I sent for his son, gave him many presents."[92]

Upon the outbreak of the Black Hawk War in 1832, the younger Winneshiek and his brother Short Wing aided their uncle, White Cloud, in behalf of the Sauk. Both were captured at the Bad Axe River on August 2, 1832, and held captive for several months at Jefferson Barracks, Missouri.

The elder Winneshiek died near Hokah, Minnesota, in 1835, and the band leadership passed to his son, Coming Thunder. By treaties signed in 1832 and 1837, the Winnebago were forced to surrender all their lands in Illinois and Wisconsin, and in 1840 they were moved by military force to northern Iowa. By 1845, the younger Winneshiek apparently was trusted sufficiently by the U.S. government to be "appointed" as "head chief." In 1859, after two more removals, the Winnebago were living in Blue Earth County, Minnesota, when Winneshiek aroused the ire of the government by refusing to cede any more land and questioning the Indian agent's accounts. He was therefore "deposed" for "insubordination," but the Indians continued to regard him as their chief. After the Sioux rebellion of 1862 the Winnebago were compelled to remove to Crow Creek, South Dakota, and three years later, to Thurston County, Nebraska. From there, Winneshiek attempted to return to Wisconsin, as many of his people already had done. Descending the Missouri River by canoe in 1872, he fell ill and died on the Iowa reservation in Doniphan County, Kansas.

The third Winneshiek, also called "the Younger" in some accounts, has been described as a younger brother of the second Winneshiek, and in others he is called a son. He is reported to have died near Black River Falls in 1887. He was survived by his brothers, No-gin-kah, or Little Winneshiek, and John Winneshiek.

The name Wee-no-shee-kaw in the Treaty of Green Bay, August 28, 1828, is that of the first Winneshiek, for his son was then only sixteen years old. A treaty signed at Washington on February 27, 1855, lists as a signer "Wau-kon-chaw-koo-haw, The Coming Thunder, or Win-no-shik," representing the Winnebago, English, and Sauk names, in that order, of the eldest son of the senior Winneshiek.[93]

The name Winneshiek is Algonquian, perhaps from the Sauk, and has been given several unsavory translations: "A dirty person," "stinking," "muddy," and "bearded." Through misunderstanding, similar definitions have been given for Winnebago (q.v.). John Blackhawk, a grandson of Winneshiek II, maintained that the name was composed of *Winne* (short for "Winnebago") and *shiek*, "leader."[94]

Wisconsin places named for Winneshiek are probably named for Winneshiek II (1812–72). These include Winneshiek Bluff, Winneshiek Bottoms, Winneshiek's Landing, and Mount Winneshiek in Trempealeau County; Lake Winneshiek in Crawford County; Winneshiek Bluff and Slough in Crawford and Vernon counties; and Winneshiek Wildlife Refuge in Crawford, Grant, and Vernon Counties. There are also places named Winneshiek in Illinois, Iowa, and Minnesota.[95]

Yellow Thunder

Wau-kaun-zee-kaw, Yellow Thunder (1774–1874), was a Winnebago chief who figured prominently in the history of southern Wisconsin. He is commemorated by Yellow Thunder Park, near his last homestead in Sauk County.

Yellow Thunder's village was located from 1828 to 1832 at Yellow Banks on the Fox River near Berlin, in Green Lake County.[96] On John Kinzie's annuity list of 1832 he is named Wau-kaun-tshah-zee-kaw, Yellow Thunder. His family consisted of two men, three women, and four children, who received a payment of $33.19.[97]

In 1828, with several Indians, including his wife, a daughter of White

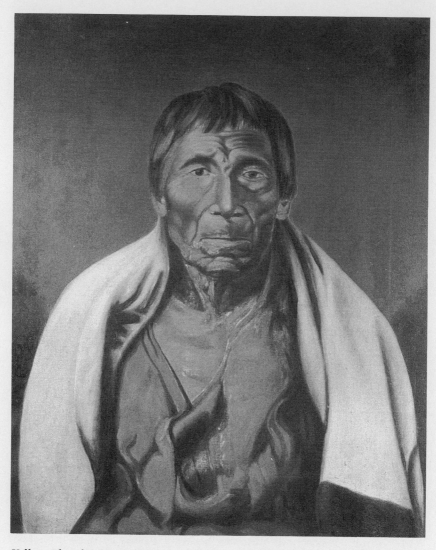

Yellow Thunder, Winnebago, 1774–1874. He had a village from 1828 to 1832 at Yellow Banks of the Fox River near Berlin, Green Lake County. He was forcibly deported to Iowa in 1840, but returned on foot. He bought 40 acres in Delton Township, Sauk County, and died there in 1874. Yellow Thunder Park, near his last home, perpetuates his name. Painting by G. D. Coaten. Photo courtesy of the State Historical Society of Wisconsin WHi(X28)1197.

Crow, later known as Washington Woman, he visited New York and Washington, where the group had a meeting with president-elect Andrew Jackson.[98]

He signed the Treaty of Prairie du Chien, August 1, 1829, wherein his name appears as "Waun-kaun-tshaw-zee-kau, yellow thunder." That treaty assigned boundaries for the various tribes. In another treaty, signed at Washington on November 1, 1837, the Winnebago gave up all their land east of the Mississippi and agreed to move to Iowa within eight months. In the list of signers appears "Wa-kun-cha-koo-rah, Yellow Thunder."[99]

Apparently Yellow Thunder did not understand the treaty. When he learned that the treaty compelled him to go west of the Mississippi, he declared he would not go. However, he was tricked into compliance. In 1840, together with Black Wolf (q.v.), he was invited to Fort Winnebago ostensibly to hold a council and receive provisions. When the gates were shut behind them, they were seized and conveyed beyond the Mississippi. According to August Derleth,

> The method of taking Yellow Thunder for his removal was in itself disgraceful . . . no sooner had he come than he and those others who had accompanied him "were put in the guard house with ball and chain, which hurt the feelings of the Indians very much, as they had done no harm," said John T. de la Ronde, of the American Fur Company. Yellow Thunder wept at this disgrace, but he had all the same a keen understanding of the whites. He had no intention of being parted from his land, and before long he led a small part of the Winnebago back to the upper Baraboo valley on foot.[100]

According to Norton Jipson, Yellow Thunder presented himself to the land office at Mineral Point and asked if Indians could enter land. On receiving an affirmative answer, he bought forty acres on the west bank of the Wisconsin River in Delton Township, Sauk County. Reportedly he built two log huts and cultivated five acres in corn, beans, and potatoes. During his feast, large numbers of Indians (up to 1,500 according to Jipson's inflated estimate) usually gathered in his vicinity. In 1840 he was said to have had a summer village sixteen miles upriver from Portage. Jipson says he sold his land just before his death in 1874. It was said that when he paid his taxes he placed in his pouch a kernel of corn for every dollar paid, and when he sold out, he demanded a dollar for every kernel.[101]

When Yellow Thunder died at the supposed age of one hundred, he was given a Catholic burial near his homestead and near the grave of Washington Woman and other family members.[102] The Sauk County Conservation Committee has erected a monument and plaque to Yellow Thunder at his grave site.

A Seminole Name: Osceola

It may seen strange that the name of a Florida Indian should be given to places or features in five Wisconsin counties. However, more places in the United States are named for this Indian than for any other. He was widely regarded as a hero for his resistance to the exile of the Seminole people from their homeland. His reputation was enhanced by Capt. Mayne Reid's popular novel *Osceola the Seminole*, published in New York in 1858.

Osceola (ca. 1803–38) was not a chief, and his life was short, but his mark on history is enduring. He joined Chief Micanopy in refusing to sign the Treaty of Payne's Landing, April 23, 1835, which provided for removal of the Seminole Indians to Oklahoma. When Gen. Wiley Thompson called a parley to induce consent from the holdouts, tradition has it that Osceola drove his knife through the treaty and declared that he would never sign it. The general seized Osceola and placed him in irons. Osceola feigned a change of heart to secure his release, then began guerrilla resistance from the swamps. When 110 soldiers under Maj. Francis Dade marched to capture him, all but three of the pursuers were killed in a battle near the site of Bushnell, Florida, on December 28, 1835. Osceola was wounded soon afterward in a skirmish on the Withlacoochee River but escaped. Gen. T. S. Jesup called a pretended peace parley, to which Osceola came in good faith under a flag of truce. With several followers, he was seized and imprisoned at Fort Moultrie, South Carolina, where he died within three months, on January 30, 1938. Shortly before his death, his portrait was painted by George Catlin.

The name Osceola is from Creek *Assi-yahola*, "Black Drink Singer." Medicine men of the highest importance were called *yaholi*. The Creeks and other southern Indians brewed a black drink from the leaves of yaupon (also called cassine), a caffeine-rich shrub of the holly family (*Ilex vomitoria* or *Ilex cassine*), which was much used in councils and festivals.

Osceola's name has been adopted for places in twenty states. In Wisconsin it is on no less than eight places: a bluff in Grant County; islands in the St. Croix River, Polk County; lakes in Polk and Vilas counties; a town in Fond du Lac County; and another town, as well as a village and creek, in Polk County.[103]

An Abnaki Name: Samoset

After the Pilgrims landed at Plymouth Rock in December 1620, the winter passed before they met their first Indian. Indeed, the Indians were "skulking about," wrote William Bradford, "but when any approached near them, they would rune away." He continued:

> But about the 16. of *March* a certaine Indian came bouldly amongst them, and spoke to them in broken English, which they could well understand, but marvelled at it. At length they understood by discourse with him, that he was not of these parts, but belonged to the eastrene parts, wher some English-ships came to Phish, with whom he was acquainted, & could name sundrie of them by their names, amongst whom he had got his language. He became profitable to them in acquainting them with many things. . . . His name is Samaset.[104]

Samoset told them of Squanto, who had been taken as a slave and lived for a time in England, and of the sachem Massasoit, both of whom he introduced to them in a few days. With Massasoit they made a peace which lasted as long as he lived, more than fifty years.

Samoset was an Abnaki Indian, sagamore (Abnaki, "chief") of Pemaquid, at the site of present Bristol, Maine, and had been living in the Cape Cod area about eight months. It is believed that he was brought there from Maine by Captain Dermer. Not long after meeting the Pilgrims, Samoset returned to Maine, and in ensuing years deeded two large tracts of land in Maine to English settlers. His second and last cession took place in 1653. It is believed that he died soon thereafter. It is supposed that his name, from Osamoset, signified "He Walks over Much."[105]

In all of New England there are no places named for Samoset. A town in Manatee County, Florida, and an Illinois Central Gulf freight stop in Alabama are apparently his only monuments outside Wisconsin. His name in this state is on Samoset Lake in Drummond Township, Bayfield County.

Samoset is also the name of a council of the Boy Scouts of America with headquarters at Wausau. It is situated in the old Milwaukee railroad station which became famous as the logo of a leading insurance company.

4

Women's Names

Only five Indian women are known to be commemorated in place names of Wisconsin. Two of them are known by French names, and one, who never lived in the state, is known by an Iroquois name. Three of them are remembered mainly because of their white husbands or their distinguished descendants or both.

This does not necessarily indicate that the Wisconsin Indians held women in low esteen. In most tribes, descent was traced through the female line, and women were the absolute masters of their lodges and children. But most Indian personal names on the map were put there by white people. It was they who leaned toward perpetuating the names of chiefs and warriors, who were usually men.

Hopokoekaw

On September 25, 1766, Jonathan Carver, ascending the Fox River southward from Green Bay, arrived at what was later called Doty Island at the top of Lake Winnebago, where the twin cities of Menasha and Neenah are now located. Carver reported: "Here the queen who presided over this [Winnebago] tribe instead of a sachem, received me with great civility, and entertained me in a very distinguished manner, during the four days I continued with her."[1] Carver gave no name for the "queen," but we know her as Ho-po-koe-kaw, mistranslated as "Glory of the Morning," a Winnebago woman who married the French officer Sabrevoir de Carrie and started the distinguished Decorah family (q.v.). De Carrie was killed in battle against the British in Quebec, September 13, 1759, but his name, in the form Decorra, Decorah, Dekorra, etc., is still prominent among the Winnebago. Radin declared that "there is no family as numerous as the descendants of that family." However, he downgraded the rank assigned to Hopoekaw (to which form the name is usually shortened) by Carver. According to Radin,

73

"Her position and that of her children . . . was, however, due to the fact that she married a Frenchman named Decora. She was not the chieftainess of the tribe nor were any of her children, strictly speaking, chiefs of the tribe."[2]

Details about the life of Hopoekaw are sketchy. She was fictionalized in William Ellery Leonard's poetic drama, *Glory of the Morning*.[3] She is commemorated in Wisconsin by the name of Hopokoekau Beach in Fond du Lac County. According to Frances Perry, the name should be Hamp-ho-goo-wiṅga, "day where comes woman," referring to the false dawn that lights up the sky before sunrise, then disappears.[4]

Madeline

Madeline Island, largest of the Apostle Island group in Ashland County, Lake Superior, is situated three miles offshore from the town of Bayfield. The village of La Pointe at its western end was an important Ojibwa town and trading center from early times. The island is named for Madeleine Cadotte, wife of fur trader Michel Cadotte (1764–1836). Her Indian name was Equaysayway, "Travelling Woman." She was a daughter of Chief White Crane and grandmother of Chippewa historian William W. Warren. Madeleine was baptized under her French name by the priest at the Sault Ste. Marie at the time of her marriage to Cadotte.[5] The spelling of the island name has been anglicized.

Marinette

The city and county of Marinette are named for a woman of mixed parentage, Marinette Farnsworth (1791–1863). Her mother was a Menominee, a daughter of Wabashish (the Marten), and her father was Bartholomew Chevalier, of French descent. Her given name was reportedly from a combination of Marie Antoinette, the name of the French queen at the time of her birth.

We know little about Marinette, described as "a blooming young woman, bright and intelligent," before her marriage at Mackinaw at an unknown date to a Canadian named John B. Jacobs. The couple had several children, of whom two were living in 1876, when we have our first account of her. For unknown reasons, Jacobs abandoned Marinette at Mackinac. Afterward, William Farnsworth, who had settled at Menominee River in 1822, was attracted to her, took her for his wife, and brought her and her children to Menominee River, where the city of Marinette now stands. Of the children born to them, George Farnsworth was recorded as a resident of Green Bay in 1876. The senior Farnsworth, who reportedly deserted Marinette in 1832, was lost in Lake Michigan when the steamer *Lady Elgin* sank in a collision off Evanston, Illinois, in 1860. According to E. S. Ingalls, Marinette died in 1863, at the age of 72, "highly honored by all the residents about the river. She . . . had been looked to as a mother by nearly all early settlers and Indians, for she had always been ready to assist the needy and comfort the distressed. The first orchard of apple trees was set out by her and is still bearing."[6]

Marinuka

Marinuka Lake, near Galesville, Trempealeau County, is named for a Winnebago woman (1802–84) described as a daughter of Winneshiek and a granddaughter of Decorah (although which of the several persons of these names is meant, we are not informed). It is reported, erroneously, that Marinuka was a "princess"; that she was the last of a celebrated family, which is also untrue; and that she was buried at midnight with pagan rites, her head pointing north, which cannot be verified.[7] According to Frances Perry, Marinuka's head should have faced west toward the spirit world, the setting sun.[8]

Tekakwitha

In 1656 a girl who became known as the "Lily of the Mohawks" and was the first North American Indian candidate for sainthood in the Roman Catholic Church was born in a Mohawk village at the site of Auriesville, New York. No one knows her earliest name, but around her tenth year she was called Tekakwitha (*Te-ka-kweeta*, "One Who Puts Things in Order" or "She Hesitates"). The child of Kahenta, an Algonquin captive who was a Catholic, and a Mohawk chief named Kenheronkwa, she was orphaned at four years of age by smallpox. The child survived the disease but incurred facial scars that later painters omitted from her portraits.

Reared by her pagan uncle Onsegonga and his wives, she aroused the anger of her foster father by rejecting a prospective husband he chose for her and by refusing to work on the Sabbath. When a treaty permitted French Catholic missionaries to live in the Iroquois settlements, Teka-kwitha adopted the religion of her mother and was baptized at age twenty, on Easter Sunday, 1676. The Jesuit priest Jacques de Lamber-ville, who inducted her into the church, gave her the Christian name Catherine, rendered in Mohawk as Kateri.

Harassed by unconverted tribesmen, from whom her uncle failed to protect her, Kateri managed with the help of Father de Lamberville and a Christian Oneida named Hot Ashes to escape in 1676 to the Christian Mohawk settlement at La Prairie, near Montreal, Quebec. Among the birches beside the St. Lawrence River she erected a cross and made the spot her personal retreat for prayer and penance.

Kateri joined the Confraternity of the Holy Family, took a vow of chastity, and wore a blue blanket in honor of her adopted patron, the Virgin Mary. She fasted excessively and inflicted personal torment upon herself in the tradition of medieval ascetics. Weakened by self-neglect and perhaps by her earlier bout with smallpox, she died on Wednesday of Holy Week, April 17, 1680, at age twenty-four.[9]

The Mohawk village of Caughnawaga ("at the rapids"), which has stood at its present site since 1717, within sight of the towers of Montreal, is the last resting place of Kateri Tekakwitha. Her remains were placed at the Mission of Saint Francis Xavier after being removed from Côte Ste. Catherine, named for her patron saint, site of the old vil-lage six miles downriver. *Kateri*, a quarterly magazine promoting the memory and the sainthood candidacy of the "Lily of the Mohawks" is published at Caughnawaga.

Ten biographies of Kateri Tekakwitha in six languages have been published. She has also been the heroine of a play, was pictured on a Canadian postage stamp, and is portrayed in several paintings and nu-merous statues in the United States and Canada.[10] Because of several cures and remarkable events attributed to her intercession, two of which were mentioned by Charlevoix as early as 1743, Catholic author-ities in Baltimore first proposed her name for beatification in 1883. In 1942 the title Venerable Kateri Tekakwitha, the Servant of God, was be-stowed upon her. On April 15, 1980. Pope John Paul II granted her the title "Blessed," which was formally bestowed at the Vatican on June 22.

The geographic names honoring Kateri Tekakwitha are located far from the places where she lived. In 1952 two Catholic priests—Fathers Robert Hogan of Marinette, Wisconsin, and Claude LeClair, of Manitowoc, Wisconsin—purchased for a summer retreat two hundred acres of land surrounding Mud Lake, in Langlade County, Wisconsin. They changed the name of the lake to Tekakwitha, and it so appears on maps today. Along with a summer retreat home, the two priests erected near the lakeshore a statue of Kateri Tekakwitha, a chapel, and guest cottages.[11] Another statue of Kateri Tekakwitha stands outside St. Anthony's Catholic Church on the Chippewa reservation at Lac du Flambeau, Wisconsin.

On the Sisseton Sioux reservation in South Dakota, a mission, hospital, and orphanage were named for Kateri Tekakwitha. Father John J. Pohlen, a founder of these institutions, proposed in 1939 that the name Tekakwitha be given to a postal substation at Sisseton. Tekakwitha, South Dakota, was added to the list of post offices, but it closed in 1978.[12]

5

French-Indian Personal Names

French names which occur all through our early state
papers as Indian agents or other government employees
in the then recently acquired west are almost invariably
those of French mixed-bloods already resident in the
region.

Louise S. Houghton,
Our Debt to the Red Man *(1918)*

No Europeans enjoyed a more harmonious relationship with the native Americans than the French. Their voyageurs and *coureurs des bois*, and some of their officers, married Indian women on a scale matched only in Spanish America, and from these unions arose a numerous progeny of mixed bloods known in Canada as *métis*, a term equivalent to *mestizo* in Spanish America.[1]

The French empire in America, thinly populated though it was, once included the entire drainage basin of the Great Lakes and the Mississippi with all their tributary waters. It ran north to Hudson Bay, southward to the mouth of the greatest river on the continent, and west to the Rocky Mountains. Although France lost its North American empire in 1763, writes Dr. Patricia Ourada, "echoes of her reign ring through every roll call of the Menominee Indians."[2] The same can be said of nearly every tribe with which the French established contact. Of the Ojibwa, William Warren wrote in his tribal history: "The Ojibways learned to love the French people, for the Frenchmen, possessing a character of great plasticity, easily assimilated themselves to the customs and mode of life of their red brethren. . . . no nation of whites have ever succeeded so well in gaining the love and confidence of the red men, as the Franks."[3]

Many of the mixed-blood Indians retained French names and became

78

chiefs, interpreters, and people of influence. Among the Winnebago, Paul Radin wrote, "a person with French blood has always been the chief; only they could accomplish anything among the whites."[4] Their names, in turn, became attached to our maps as place names, furnishing a lasting record of their influence.[5]

Cadotte

One of the French-Ojibwa families whose members were important in Wisconsin history, and left the names of some of its members on the map, was called Cadotte.

The Cadottes were descendants of one Monsieur Cadeau who came to the Ojibwa country in 1671, in the entourage of the French envoy Sieur de St. Lusson. His son John (or Jean) Baptiste Cadotte (as the name was then and subsequently spelled) became a trader among the Ojibwa and was engaged for a time with Alexander Henry, who in his *Travels and Adventures* mentions Cadotte frequently. John was married by a Catholic priest to an Ojibwa woman of the Awause clan and settled at Sault Ste. Marie. She bore him two sons, John (Jean) Baptiste Cadotte, Jr., and Michael (or Michel) Cadotte, who also became traders with the Indians. In 1796 the younger Jean guided the explorer David Thompson in his search for the source of the Mississippi River.

Both young Cadottes were well educated for their time and were influential in the Lake Superior region. Both married Ojibwa women, Michel's wife being the daughter of White Crane, hereditary chief at La Pointe, on present-day Madeline Island. Michel Cadotte, had two sons, Jean Baptiste and Michel, who were captured or enticed by the British during the War of 1812 to come to Drummond Island in Lake Huron, where they were given the option of going into confinement for the duration or acting as interpreters and using their influence to sway the Ojibwa. They chose the latter, participated in all the principal Canadian battles, and were present at Tecumseh's death at the Thames, October 5, 1813. Jean Baptiste was severely wounded and became a British pensioner. Michel lost his arm and went back to La Pointe, where he was living in 1852. His father had died there in 1836, at age seventy-two.

Mary, a daughter of the elder Michel Cadotte, married Lyman Warren, a fur trader, in 1821. Mrs. Warren was three-quarters Indian and could speak no English. This couple were the parents of Ojibwa historian William W. Warren, who was born at La Pointe in 1825 and died at St. Paul, Minnesota, on June 1, 1853. He left a partially complete history of the Ojibwa, which was published by the Minnesota Historical Society and from which much of this information was obtained. About 1838, after ending his tie with the American Fur Company, Lyman Warren moved to the Chippewa River in Wisconsin, where he had been appointed farmer, blacksmith, and subagent to the Ojibwa. He located his post a few miles above Chippewa Falls, and his wife died there on July 21, 1842.

Jean Baptiste Cadotte, Jr., established a trading post on Yellow River in present Chippewa County, at a place then called Cadotte Falls. When a village was platted there in 1878, it was called Cadott. Also named for him are two Cadotte lakes, one in Burnett County and the other in Chippewa and Rusk counties.[6]

Du Bay

Louis Dubé, a Frenchman from Montreal according to some accounts, came to Green Bay around 1800 and took as a wife a daughter of Pewatenot, a Menominee chief. They became the parents of Jean Baptiste Dubé, who is better known as Du Bay and frequently signed his name that way. The date of his birth has been given variously as 1802, 1806, 1807, or 1808, and 1810. Other facts about him are equally hazy. One account gives Detroit as his birthplace. Du Bay contributed to confusion about his lineage by claiming at one time to be a "Chippewa half-breed," and on another occasion he wrote to Indian Commissioner T. R. Crawford that he was a "half Breed Menominee."[7]

His marriages are also obscure. It is said that his first wife was a Chippewa, but the dates of duration of that marriage are unknown. His son Louis, born about 1831, was the only one of his children listed as a Chippewa half-blood in 1838, although at that time he purportedly had two children by another woman.

He next married, at an unknown time, Madeleine, a daughter of Menominee chief Oshkosh. According to the census of 1850, he was forty-two years old in that year and Madeleine was thirty. Six of his children were listed, aged from one to nineteen years. According to Du Bay's biographer, Merton E. Krug, "Du Bay exerted a great deal of influence among the Menominee Indians as a half-breed of that tribe, as he had among the Chippewas the decade earlier as a Chippewa half-breed."[8]

While still in his teens, Du Bay reportedly became a trader for the American Fur Company at Saginaw and Kalamazoo, Michigan, and was an interpreter for Gov. Lewis Cass. It is said that in 1831 he moved to Sault Ste. Marie and started his own fur business. The precise date he returned to Wisconsin is not known, but it is believed that he inherited his father's fur business on Wolf River, in Menominee country. During the Black Hawk War of 1832 he was appointed a lieutenant colonel by territorial governor Cass but did not actively serve in the conflict. He was an interpreter for the government in a treaty with the Chippewa at St. Peter's (now St. Paul), Minnesota, on July 29, 1837, and there signed his name Jean Baptiste Dubay. In the Menominee treaty of October 18, 1848, he signed as a witness, John B. Dube.[9]

Du Bay was active in many enterprises, but fur trading ranked first until about 1850. Before that date, he traded at Du Bay Prairie, on the lower Wisconsin River near present Boscobel and established himself at Du Bay Point, formerly *Nay-osh-ing* ("place of the point"), near present-day Knowlton on the Wisconsin, prior to 1835. He also worked for the American Fur Company as manager of their post among the Chippewa at Lac du Flambeau. In 1840 he acquired Joseph Rolette's post among the Winnebago at Fort Winnebago, near Portage, and continued activity there as well as elsewhere until 1857.

He also carried out a profitable lumbering operation along the Wisconsin at Du Bay Point. In 1852 he established a stage line between Fort Winnebago and Stevens Point. He was an organizer of the Wisconsin River Navigation Company, which aimed to dam the river for navigation purposes. Finally, he was postmaster at Eau Pleine, in Portage County.

Du Bay's active career was ended on August 13, 1857. On that date he was involved in an altercation with William S. Reynolds, a white man who had begun construction of a house on land claimed by Du Bay. Du Bay killed Reynolds with a shotgun. The sheriff barely saved Du Bay from a lynch mob. After two trials at Madison, both of which resulted in a hung jury, Du Bay was set free. He retired to Du Bay Point, where he remained until his death on January 11, 1887.

Du Bay Point is now under the water of Lake Du Bay, an artificial lake in the Wisconsin River created by the construction of Du Bay dam just below the junction of the Little Eau Pleine in Portage County, thirteen miles above Stevens Point. Just below the dam is Du Bay County Park. These places all commemorate an important but shadowy figure in Wisconsin's history.

Grignon

The Grignon family, according to Louise Houghton, is "permanently identified with the pioneer history of Wisconsin." The first of that name to be associated with Wisconsin was Pierre Grignon, a French voyageur of the Lake Superior region and an independent trader of Green Bay before 1763. His first wife was a full-blooded Menominee, and his second wife, Louise Domitilde, was the métisse daughter of Charles Langlade (q.v.). Pierre fathered nine children; among his sons were Amable, Augustin, Charles, and Louis, all of whom were prominent in the Green Bay–Fox River area. Amable was a trader for the Northwest Fur Company about 1820. Charles established a business at Fort Winnebago and is recorded as an interpreter at the Menominee treaty of Washington, February 17, 1831.[10]

Pierre and Louis were farmers at Green Bay. Louis married a Chippewa woman who spoke no English. He had a distinguished career. In the War of 1812 he held a British commission. In 1829 he chaired the first public meeting in Green Bay, which petitioned Congress for a road to Chicago and improvements in the Fox and Wisconsin rivers. Best known of the Grignons, perhaps, was Augustin, who established a farm and store at present Kaukauna on the Fox River. He held a British captain's commission in 1814 and took part in the capture of Fort McKay at Prairie du Chien. Late in life he wrote (or dictated) his memoirs, "Seventy-Two Years' Recollections of Wisconsin," which were published by the State Historical Society.[11]

Place names commemorating the Grignons are Grignon Lake in Menominee and Oconto counties, and Grignon Park in Outagamie County.

Augustin Grignon, French-Menominee, 1780–1860. He was a member of a distinguished métis family, and was a farmer and storekeeper at Kaukauna, Outagamie County. A lake in Menominee-Oconto Counties and a park in Outagamie County commemorate the Grignons. From a dagguereotype. Photo courtesy of the State Historical Society of Wisconsin WHi(X3)24630.

La Motte

La Motte Lake near Keshena on the Menominee reservation bears the name of a well-known nineteenth-century Menominee. His name is signed (as La Motte) to three treaties, at Lake Pow-aw-hay-kon-nay, October 18, 1848; Falls of Wolf River, May 12, 1854; and Keshena, February 11, 1856.[12]

Langlade

One French Canadian is sometimes called "the father of Wisconsin." He was Charles Michel de Langlade (1729–1800), for whom Langlade County and the village of Langlade in that county are named. Born at Mackinac to a French father, Augustin M. de Langlade, and an Ottawa mother named Domitilde, Charles was educated by Jesuit priests at Mackinac and studied briefly at Montreal. In 1754, at age twenty-five, he was married at Mackinac to Charlotte Bourassa, an Ottawa Indian.

Langlade engaged in the fur trade at Sault Ste. Marie and in 1756 formed a partnership with the Chevalier Repentigny, French commander at that place. After the French defeat by the English, Langlade moved his business to Green Bay.

Not surprisingly, Langlade aided the French in their battle for North America. He is said to have planned the ambush that resulted in the defeat of the British general Braddock on Pennsylvania's Monongahela River in 1755. With his Indian contingent he joined the French commander Montcalm at Fort George, New York, in 1757, and was active in the defense of Quebec in 1759–60. After the French surrendered, he did not join Pontiac's revolt against the English but warned western garrisons of the intention of his tribesmen. At this time he moved to Green Bay, where he spent the rest of his life except when away on military campaigns.

Most of the French settlers remained indifferent to the outcome of the Revolutionary War, but Langlade, along with most of the Indians, supported Great Britain. He was with Burgoyne's army in the invasion of New York, but because of friction with the British commander, he deserted with his Indian followers before the critical battle of Saratoga (October 8, 1777). Despite this incident, the British in 1780 appointed him Indian agent and later superintendent, with a lifetime annuity of $800. Langlade died at Green Bay in 1800, four years after the final British evacuation of the Northwest.[13]

Perrote

Perote Lake on the Menominee reservation and Perrote, a former Soo line railroad station, were named for Sabatis Perrote, a judge of the Menominee Indian court in the early twentieth century.[14]

Poupart

Poupart Lake, on the Lac du Flambeau Indian Reservation, Vilas County, has the name of a well-known Chippewa family of that community. Among recent members of the family are the late Josephine Poupart and her three brothers, Ben, Paul, and William, all of whom worked as guides.

Poupart is a French word for a large edible crab.[15]

Saint Germaine

In the late seventeenth century a French soldier named Jean François St. Germaine deserted the French army and married an Ojibwa woman. In the neighborhood of Vilas County, several of his descendants were fur traders and interpreters. In 1747 Antoine St. Germaine was a fur trader in this area. Leon St. Germaine was a Chippewa interpreter in the War of 1812 and was employed by the American Fur Company at Lac du Flambeau. Another member of the family worked for the Northwest Company. St. Germain or Germaine is still a family name among the Ojibwa of northern Wisconsin.

In Vilas County the family name, minus the final *e*, was given to the village and town of St. Germain, Big and Little St. Germain Lakes, and their drainage streams flowing into the nearby Wisconsin River, St. Germain and Little St. Germain rivers. There is also a Germain Lake in adjacent Gogebic County, Michigan.

In the village of St. Germain is a statue of "Chief St. Germain," a romantic invention of the Chamber of Commerce, shown in Plains Indian costume.[16]

6

Literary and Legendary Names

> The new Americans had sought to keep something of
> the poetry when they retained many of the Indian place-
> names, beautiful in sound and suggestion. The names of
> Indian villages were often kept, even when the original
> inhabitants had been ruthlessly expelled.
>
> *Constance Rourke*, The Roots of American Culture
> and Other Essays *(1942)*

The last century was a curious time. It was the century in which America's first people made their last stand against foreign conquest and also the century in which they aroused the most romantic and sympathetic interest among white writers and their readers. Novelists, playwrights, essayists, and poets, in the course of their productions, used a number of Indian and pseudo-Indian names. By that route, many of these names found their way onto the map of an expanding country looking for names for its new settlements.

Names from James Fenimore Cooper

One of the most influential writers of the nineteenth century was James Fenimore Cooper (1789–1851) of New York. Most of his writings were set in the then still remembered late colonial period, and they aroused much interest. Although Cooper may not be highly regarded today, his books are still fondly remembered by many Americans of earlier generations and remain in print today. *The Last of the Mohicans*, *The Deerslayer*, and the series of *Leatherstocking Tales*, among his large output, are not forgotten. One of the names taken from Cooper is Iowa's nickname, Hawkeye, which is attached to several inconspicuous place names in that state. It was from the Delaware appellation for a white scout in *Last of the Mohicans*.[1]

Mingo

Cooper is perhaps the man mainly responsible for the popularity of Mingo as a place name. It was made widely known in the *Leatherstocking Tales*, particularly in *The Pathfinder* (1840), as a name bestowed by the Delaware on the Iroquois. Although applied to alleged villains by Cooper and other writers, such as the poet Henry Whiting,[2] the name was attractive enough to get on the map in at least twenty-three places in eleven states, including Mingo Lake in Burnett County, Wisconsin.

Mingo is not an artificial name. Lewis H. Morgan held that "the Delawares call the Senecas Mingwa-o, hence I think the historical word Mingoes, a word for the Iroquois." James Mooney called *mengwe* an Algonquian word meaning "stealthy, treacherous." Dunlap and Weslager called it a borrowed Iroquois word meaning "males" or "men." A. S. Anthony, coauthor of a Delaware (Lenape) dictionary, went further and defined it as a Delaware word meaning "glans penis." It may be that some Indians, like some whites, used this anatomical term as an epithet.[3]

The name Mingo was used historically as a label for detached bands of Iroquois, mainly Cayuga and Seneca, living in Pennsylvania and Ohio. The name in these states may be a record of their former residence there. Elsewhere it may be either a transfer name or evidence of the influence of Cooper and perhaps other writers, such as Whiting.

Horicon

For Wisconsin, the most important name from Cooper's writing is Horicon. It is the name of a city in Dodge County and of a nearby marsh that contains both Horicon National Wildlife Refuge and Horicon State Wildlife Area. Every fall large flocks of migrating wild geese spend some time at these places and attract crowds of bird watchers.

Horicon was the name Cooper applied to Lake George in upper New York State. In 1839 a group of settlers from that vicinity came to the Wisconsin place then called Hubbard's Rapids. At a meeting held in the home of one of them, William Larrabee, the settlers voted to rename the place Horicon.[4]

Cooper explained, in his introduction to *The Last of the Mohicans* (1826), his reasons for the use of Horicon:

Looking over an ancient map, it was ascertained that a tribe
of Indians called "Les Horicons" by the French, existed in the
neighborhood of this beautiful sheet of water [Lake George].
As every word uttered by Natty Bumpo was not to be received
as rigid truth, we took the liberty of putting the "Horicon"
into his mouth as the substitute for "Lake George." The name
has appeared to find favor, and, all things considered, it may
possibly be quite as well to let it stand, instead of going back
to the House of Hanover for the appellation of our finest sheet
of water.[5]

According to Hodge, Horicon was marked on a map of 1671 as a
people living on the headwaters of the Hudson River, west of Lake
Champlain. Beauchamp (1907) said that *Horikans* was shown on an
early map as the name of an Indian people living west of Lake George.[6]
Cooper did not invent the name but transferred it. Later it was transferred again to a town and small lake in Warren County, New York. The
town does not appear on current maps, but the lake name remains. It
was adopted from there for Horicon Lake, Ocean County, New Jersey;
for Lake Horicon in Otsego County, Michigan; and for the Wisconsin
places.

On the meaning of the name, opinions clash. E. M. Ruttenber suggested that Horicon might be a corruption of Mohican ("Wolf"), the
name of a tribe living about Lake George. John G. Shea thought that
Horicon was a misprint for a variant spelling of Iroquois. Cooper himself believed that Horicon meant "Tail of the Lake," because it was a tail
to Lake Champlain.[7]

Names from Longfellow's *Hiawatha*

No writer has inspired the adoption of more Indian names
on the American map than Henry Wadsworth Longfellow, who published *Song of Hiawatha* in 1855. Romantic interest in the Indian, fired
in an earlier generation by Cooper, was still current, and Longfellow's
epic poem was immediately successful. The Indian names and tales
which form the Hiawatha story were borrowed mainly from Henry R.
Schoolcraft, who had served for twenty years (1821–41) as Indian agent
at Sault Ste. Marie and Mackinac, Michigan. Longfellow's Siouan names
were taken from tales of the Sioux written by Mary Eastman, who ob-

served those Indians while her husband, Capt. Seth Eastman, was stationed at Fort Snelling, Minnesota.[8]

The name of the poem's hero, Hiawatha, is on a spring in Janesville, Rock County; on a park on the shore of Rice Lake, Barron County; on a lake in Vilas County; and on Hiawatha Heights near Menomonee Falls, Waukesha County. The name is also found in at least ten other states.

Hiawatha is the name of an Iroquois folk hero whose actual existence is debated. His name was substituted for that of the Ojibwa deity Manabozho in a composite legend of the Ojibwa of Lake Superior. Before Longfellow's poem, the name Hiawatha was known to only a few scholars and was spelled in various ways. Lewis H. Morgan, for example, spelled it Ha-ya-went-ha. The historic Hiawatha (ca. 1570), it is maintained, was a Mohawk sachem, a spokesman and collaborator of Dekanawida, an Onondaga reformer, orator, and peacemaker who united five warring Indian nations into the League of the Ho-de-no-sau-nee, the Longhouse People, or Iroquois. According to Morgan, Hiawatha was elevated, after his death, to a place in the Iroquois pantheon. Morgan translated his name as "the man who combs," from the tradition that Hiawatha combed snakes from the head of an Onondaga Hero. J. N. B. Hewitt, the Tuscarora ethnologist, held that the name means "he makes rivers." To Schoolcraft, the name signified "a person of very great wisdom."[9]

Nokomis

Following in importance only Hiawatha and his Dakota wife, Minnehaha, in Longfellow's poem, is his grandmother, Nokomis, who gave birth, after a tryst with the spirit Mudjekeewis, to Wenonah, who was to become Hiawatha's mother. Since Wenonah died in childbirth, it was Nokomis, "daughter of the moonlight," who reared Hiawatha "by the shores of Gitche Gumme" (Lake Superior).

Nokomis is authentic Ojibwa for "grandmother."[10] In Wisconsin the name is on a town in Oneida County; Lake Nokomis, astride the line of Lincoln and Oneida counties; North Nokomis Lake in Oneida County; and Lake Nokomis in Bayfield County.

Apukwa

Apukwa Lake in Vilas County (on some maps mistakenly written as Apeekwa, a word which does not appear in any Ojibwa dictionary) has an Ojibwa name signifying "bulrush," or more properly, reeds or cattails. During Hiawatha's fight with Mudjekeewis, his father, the latter, in defending himself,

> Seized the bulrush, the Apukwa
> Dragged it with its roots and fibres
> From the margin of the meadow
> From its ooze, the giant bulrush....[11]

Mishe Mokwa

Mishe Mokwa, the Great Bear, is mentioned in *Hiawatha* as a monster which was the "terror of the nation." The poem tells how the animal was killed by Mudjekeewis:

> Then he swung aloft his war-club
> Shouted loud and long his war-cry,
> Smote the mighty Mishe Mokwa
> In the middle of the forehead,
> Right between the eyes he smote him.[12]

There can be little doubt that the village of Misha Mokwa in Buffalo County received its name from *Hiawatha*, although inquiries indicate that local residents are unaware of the source or meaning of the name.

Onaway

Onaway Island in Sunset Lake, Waupaca County, is a name from *Hiawatha*, but it is not easily explained. At Hiawatha's wedding feast Chibiabos sang:

> "Onaway! Awake beloved!
> Thou the wild flower of the forest!
> Thou the wild-bird of the prairie!"[13]

From this passage it has been assumed that Onaway means "awaken," and it is so explained in the glossary appended to some editions of the poem. In Baraga's *Otchipwe Language,* however, the term for "I awake" is *nin goshkos.*[14] The context of Chibiabos's song in *Hiawatha* suggests that his words are addressed to an imaginary sweetheart named Onaway. It is a love song.

Onaway has been adopted as the name of a village and state park in

Presque Isle County, Michigan, and a town in Idaho. Variants of it appear to be Onawa, an Iowa town and a lake in Maine; Onoway, a town in Alberta; and Onway, a lake in New Hampshire. None of the variants can be found in standard Ojibwa sources, and the name may be artificial.

Osseo

Osseo, a town in Trempealeau County, bears the name of a legendary Ojibwa figure whose story was first published in Schoolcraft's *Algic Researches* (1839). The name is also in *Hiawatha*, where Osseo is called "Son of the Evening Star." His story is told by Iagoo at Hiawatha's wedding feast:

> And he said in haste: "Behold it!
> See the sacred star of Evening!
> You shall hear a tale of wonder
> Hear the story of Osseo,
> Son of the Evening Star, Osseo!"[15]

Osseo post office, established in 1865, undoubtedly took its name from *Hiawatha*, since Schoolcraft's legends in *Algic Researches* never enjoyed a wide circulation. The name Osseo was also given to places in Michigan, Minnesota, and Ontario.[16]

The name has the earmarks of manufacture by Schoolcraft, who was a notable fabricator of names, from Ojibwa *oôsima*, "father." By his account he also manufactured the name of Iosco, Michigan, by merging *os*, from the word for "father," with other fragmented syllables. It is my opinion that the name Osseo is a meaningless pseudo-Indian invention.[17] H. W. Kuhm attempted to connect it to Menominee terms for "bear" or "stony place," but Schoolcraft was not familiar with that language, and no place having this name is in Menominee territory.[18]

Pukwana

In the opening lines of *Hiawatha*, Gitche Manitou, the Great Spirit, is about to call all the tribes to the Pipestone Quarry for a peace conference. As a signal to them, he lit a peace pipe, and

> All the tribes beheld the signal
> Saw the distant smoke ascending
> The Pukwana of the Peace-Pipe.[19]

In Wisconsin, the Ojibwa word for "smoke" as given in *Hiawatha* is attached to Pukwana Beach on Lake Winnebago in Fond du Lac County. The only other Pukwana in the United States is a small village in Brule County, South Dakota. My inquiry at that place in 1976 revealed that the origin of the name was not known to the resident I questioned, but his pronunciation was *Puck-wánna*.

Wabasso

Wabasso Lake in Vilas County probably derived its name from the white rabbit in the Hiawatha story. There, Shawondasee proclaims:

> "Ah! my brother from the North-land,
> From the kingdom of Wabasso,
> From the land of the White Rabbit!"

The name is close to Baraga's term *wâbos*, "rabbit."[20]

Wabeno

Wabeno, "dawn man," is a word common to the Menominee, Ojibwa, and Potawatomi. According to Walter J. Hoffman, it was applied to "a certain class of mystery men who profess prophecy, prescribe medicinal preparations, and, more particularly, make and dispose of love powders and hunting medicines."[21]

In the Midewiwin, or medicine society, of all three tribes, the Wabenos were second in rank to the priests. In the Hiawatha story, Iagoo presents the Wabeno as an evil magician:

> "In the lodge that glimmers yonder,
> In the little star that twinkles
> Through the vapors, on the left hand,
> Lives the envious Evil Spirit,
> The Wabeno, the magician."[22]

The village and town of Wabeno in Forest County could have obtained their names directly from the Potawatomi who lived in that vicinity or from Longfellow's poem.

Waubeek

Hiawatha was listening one day to the boasts of his spirit father:

Then he said, "Oh Mudjekeewis
Is there nothing that can harm you?
Nothing that you are afraid of?"
And the mighty Mudjekeewis,
Grand and gracious in his boasting,
Answered saying, "There is nothing,
Nothing but the black rock yonder,
Nothing but the fatal Wawbeek!"[23]

Upon hearing this, Hiawatha broke the rock into fragments, which he threw at Mudjekeewis, blaming him for the death of Wenonah, Hiawatha's mother.

Despite a minor spelling difference, it is likely that Waubeek Mound and the town of Waubeek in Pepin County took their name from the Hiawatha story. The same can be said for Waubeek, Iowa; Wawbeek, Alabama; and Wabeek Lake in Michigan.

The glossary to one edition of *Hiawatha* defines *wau-beek* as "a rock." Baraga's dictionary has *ajibik* as the word for "rock."[24] Other Indian names signifying "rock" are, or have been, on the Wisconsin map, but their spelling is quite different from that in *Hiawatha*.

Other Literary and Legendary Names

Maiden Rock

In the summer of 1823, as Major Stephen Long's expedition was ascending a wide place in the Mississippi called Lake Pepin, their guide pointed to a bluff which rose 450 feet on the Wisconsin side of the river. It was then called, as it is now, Maiden Rock. William Keating, historian of the expedition, recorded the guide's narration of the Dakota legend about the place and included a picture of the bluff in his published account.

According to the story, there lived at the Dakota village of Keoxa—a few miles downriver where Winona, Minnesota, now stands, an Indian maiden called Winona ("first-born daughter"). Her parents had promised her in marriage to a distinguished hunter and warrior. However, Winona loved a hunter of lesser renown and rejected the proposed spouse. When her parents insisted upon the undesired union, Winona chose what appeared to her to be the only solution. While her band was encamped at Lake Pepin, she climbed the bluff and threw herself to her death on the rocks below.[25]

A quarter-century later the same story was told, with some variations, by Mary Eastman (and by others before and since).[26] Mrs. Eastman was inclined to brand the story a myth, but she pointed out that the Dakotas defended its authenticity. Whatever the truth may be, the story resembles several others of dubious credibility. According to Keating, the story was told to Major Long in 1817 by Wazecota, an alleged witness to the event.

The name Maiden Rock is today attached to a town and a village below the rock, in Pierce County, Wisconsin. The name of the legendary maiden was given in 1853 to the settlement of Winona, Minnesota, now a city and county seat, and the following year to the township and county. A slough through which the Mississippi once flowed is called Lake Winona. The Winona for whom these places were named has been called the cousin of the last Dakota chief, named Wabasha; others say she was a daughter of Red Wing, also a notable chief. Generally, however, the name is attributed to the legendary Winona, who, according to Mrs. Eastman's informants, lived a century earlier.[27]

In Wisconsin, the name Maiden Rock is attached not only to the legendary spot in Pierce County, but also to geological features in Iowa, Jackson and Pepin counties. The name Winona (or Wenona, Wenonah, etc.) is also given to several places in other states, but most of these places appear to be named for Wenonah, the mother of Hiawatha in Longfellow's poem. Whatever the spelling, no place in Wisconsin is named for a historic or legendary Winona.

Monona

The name of Lake Monona at Madison, which gives its name to a town on the lake's southern shore, has long been a puzzle. Before 1849 it was called Third Lake in the chain called Four Lakes, the others being named, in this period, Kegonsa, Waubesa, and Mendota (q.v.). In 1849 the name Monona was given to Third Lake by Frank Hudson of Madison. Prof. Frederic Cassidy believes the name was borrowed from the township of Monona, in Clayton County, Iowa.[28] The village of Monona, in the township of the same name in Clayton County, was reportedly named in 1847 for an Indian girl who, hearing that her white lover had been killed by Indians, jumped from a bluff into the Mississippi

River. According to one account, those "who named the town discovered the girl's name was Winona, but the name remained unchanged." Iowa also has a western county called Monona, named in 1851.[29]

The lover's leap story is a common one and is immediately suspect. The fact that the name Monona appeared in identical form in three widely separated places within four years suggests that the name is not a mistaken application of the name of the renowned Winona, but has its own origin. It does not appear in Indian vocabularies of the region, Algonquian or Siouan. It is probable that the name is an artificial one from some forgotten literary work. The most likely source is a play called *Oolaita; or, The Indian Heroine,* by Lewis Deffebach, published at Philadelphia in 1821.[30] The scene is set among the Sioux of Minnesota at Lake Pepin of the Mississippi, which is near the site of Winona's village. In the play, Monona is a crafty and treacherous old man who seeks a forced marriage with the gentle maiden Oolaita, who loves Tallula, a younger man. To avoid the unwanted union, she threw herself into Lake Pepin. The plot resembles the Winona legend and several others that are quite unrelated to actual Indian customs. This play, however, precedes the first known publication of the Winona story, by Keating in 1823.[31] In 1828, J. C. Beltrami told a story similar to Deffebach's but gave the heroine's name as Oholaitha.[32] This story or variants of it apparently were widely current at the time. Since villains are seldom honored in place names, the name Monona was probably chosen for its pleasing sound. There are several spurious explanations of Monona, which are best relegated to the footnotes.[33]

Onalaska

The city, town, and lake called Onalaska, all in La Crosse County, owe their name to a Scottish poet who was never in the United States and who was, incidentally, also responsible for the spread of the name Wyoming (q.v.). Thomas Campbell (1777–1844) in 1799 published his first long poem, the popular *Pleasures of Hope*. In one passage of this poem, Hope, the "angel of Life," accompanies the pilot whose bark is "careening o'er unfathomed fields" as far as "Oonalaska's shore."[34] The name Oonalaska was already in existence as that of an island in the eastern Aleutians off Alaska. The U.S. post office eventually established there was originally called Ounalaska, but its name was changed to Unalaska in 1898. As Onalaska, the name came to be attached to towns or cities in Arkansas, Texas, Washington, and Wisconsin. Owing to the popularity of Campbell's poem, the name was adopted in Wisconsin, reputedly at the suggestion of tavern owner William C. Rowe, and spread from there because a resident of Wisconsin founded the Carlisle Lumber Company, which in extending its operations to other states also transferred the name.[35]

Onalaska and Unalaska are but two of the variant spellings this name has had. It is apparently the residue of a longer name, the meaning of which is in controversy. Some hold that it is Aleut for "this great land"; others trace it to an Aleut term meaning "dwelling together harmoniously."[36]

Viroqua

The name of the city and town of Viroqua in Vernon County has long been a mystery. The name was given in 1854 by the county board, but no one knows why. Gannett (1905) said the name was from a version of the title, Duke of Veragua, given to Columbus and his descendants. Other stories tie the name to an Indian actress, an Indian princess, a chief's daughter, and an Indian girl in an unidentified novel.[37]

I suspect that the name is from a novel entitled *Viroqua; or, The Flower of the Ottawas, a Tale of the West* (1848), written by Emma Carra (probably a pseudonym). The story is of a romance between an English officer and Viroqua, the beautiful daughter of Wampanoag (*sic*), the chief of the Ottawa tribe. Pontiac's siege of Detroit (1763), the scene of the story, and other events interrupt their romance, but the pair is at last united in marriage when peace arrives.[38] The author chose the name of the New England tribe that met the Pilgrims and gave it to the Ottawa chief. The novel is apparently based on the debatable account, mentioned by historians Francis Parkman and Howard Peckham, of a love affair between Maj. Henry Gladwin, British commander at Detroit in 1763, and an Indian girl named Catherine. According to the story, Catherine warned Gladwin of Pontiac's intended attack.[39] The siege of Detroit also figures in another novel that gave rise to place names, John Richardson's *Wacousta* (see below).

The name Viroqua is probably a manufactured name, although it has a resemblance to Viracocha, the name of both a Peruvian deity and the eighth Inca, who died in 1440.[40] The terminal syllable *-qua* is commonly attached to Algonquian women's names, but the rest of the name, *Viro-*, is undefinable. The author of Viroqua made little effort to use credible names for her characters and perhaps lacked a broad knowledge of Indian history.

Waucousta/Wacousta

Both fictional and historical accounts of the French and Indian War and of Pontiac's rebellion, which followed it, have contributed place names in states of the old Northwest.

In 1832 Maj. John Richardson (1796–1852) of the British army published a novel of Pontiac's rebellion (1763) entitled *Wacousta; or, The Prophesy*.[41] In the novel, Wacousta is the Indian name of Reginald Morton, a fictional white "renegade" who advised Pontiac during the uprising. His role has been outlined by literary critic Louise Barnett: "This renegade, rather than the Indian leader Pontiac, is the intransigent spirit behind the frontier war of 1763. Endowed with the typical attributes of the stereotype, Wacousta out-Indians the Indians: he performs marvelous physical and military feats, devotes himself wholly to revenge, and is unsurpassingly bloodthirsty and unmerciful to captives."[42] Wacousta's villainous character seems to be inspired by stories of another white ally of the Indians from another time, Simon Girty.

Wacousta's role as an enemy of his own people did not prevent his name from being adopted for places in three states. In Wisconsin this name, in the variant spelling Waucousta, is the name of a village in Fond du Lac County, dating from the 1840s. In 1839 the name Wacousta was given to a post office and village in Clinton County, Michigan. Wacousta is also a township name in Humboldt County, Iowa.

Wacousta is not an Algonquian name, but it may have been suggested to Richardson by the name Wacouta (q.v.), "The Shooter"; a Sioux Indian of Minnesota. Wacouta was a contemporary of Richardson.[43]

Wyoming

In the early 1700s, a Delaware Indian village stood along the Susquehanna River at the site of the present-day city of Wilkes-Barre, Pennsylvania. The Delawares called the settlement and the surrounding valley *M'chewomink*, "upon the great plains." Whites simplified the name in various ways, including Chiwaumuc, Waiomink, Wajomink, Wiawomic, and finally, Wyoming. So was born a famous name, which was later to be given to some twenty places. In Wisconsin it became the name of towns in Iowa and Waupaca counties and of a valley in Iowa County.

The name was not famous until a battle and a poem made it so. The battle occurred during the Revolutionary War, on July 3, 1778, when white settlers were attacked by a force of 1,100 men, consisting of 400 British soldiers and Tories, and 700 Iroquois Indians, all commanded by Maj. John Butler. The attackers killed enough settlers to secure the name Wyoming massacre for this event.[44] Thirty-one years after, in 1809, the Scottish poet Thomas Campbell published in London his book *Gertrude of Wyoming: A Pennsylvania Tale*, which memorialized the massacre in a pro-American way. The first lines picture a desolated community just after the blow fell:

> On Susquehannas's side, fair Wyoming
> Although the wild-flower on thy ruin'd wall
> And roofless homes a sad remembrance bring
> Of what the gentle people did befall,
> Yet thou wert the loveliest land of all.[45]

The heroine was fictional, but incidents of the tragedy were not. Campbell's work became popular, and soon the name Wyoming became popular, being adopted as a place name from Rhode Island and Ontario to the far West, where in 1869 it was given to a state. All places named Wyoming, except for two creeks in Alaska, were named before the state was, and commemorate the now nearly forgotten valley in Pennsylvania and its bloody massacre. Campbell was also responsible for another Wisconsin name, Onalaska (q.v.).

Sand Pillow: An Authentic Winnebago Tale

Near the Winnebago village of Winnebago Mission in Jackson County is an Indian community of new housing. A sign announces that this place is called Sand Pillow, a name which at once arouses interest. This community is not shown on maps, nor is it listed in the USGS printout of Wisconsin place names, but it assuredly exists, and behind its name lies a quaint tale. I am grateful to Frances R. Perry of Black River Falls for the following account of it.

The old men tell a story that long ago the men of the Black River band and of the Tomah band camped together. The

Tomah men brought tents and all the comforts. The Black River men brought each a blanket. When it came time to bed down, the Tomah men put up their tents and made themselves comfortable. Each man of the Black River band scooped a hollow, piled up the sand at the head, laid down his blanket, rolled up in it and went to sleep.

Later it came back to the Black River band that the Tomah (Blue Wing) band had laughed at them. "They are so poor that they use sand for pillows," they said.

Now to laugh at a Winnebago when he is serious is an insult and it is never forgotten. But lately when the new housing unit was finished there was a contest to decide the name for it as it was separate from the Mission. Melinda Walker Greengrass remembered the story and knew that to give the humiliating name to a respected place would cancel the insult. (Winnebagoes will wait years until these things right themselves). So Melinda entered the name in the contest. It won and she received the $25.00 prize.

This account is a combination of notes from Melinda herself and from Bernard Eagle.[46]

7

The Spirit World

One night long ago a Menominee Indian dreamed that
Manabush, grandson of Ko-Ko-Mas-Say-Sa-Waw (the
earth) and part founder of the Mitawin or Medicine
Society, invited him to visit the god. With seven of his
friends the Indian called on Manabush, who granted their
request to make them successful hunters. One of the
band, however, angered the god by asking for eternal life.
Manabush, seizing the warrior by the shoulders, thrust
him into the ground and said, "You shall be a stone, thus
you will be everlasting." The Menominee say that at
night kindly spirits come to lay offerings of tobacco at
the rock, and that if one looks closely he can see their
white veils among the trees. The legend is that when the
rock finally crumbles away, the race will be extinct.

Text of roadside sign at Spirit Rock,
Menominee Indian Reservation,
Keshena, Wisconsin

There are numerous places in Wisconsin named Spirit (Manitou), and
there is probably an interesting story behind most of them. Unfortunately, the stories have seldom been recorded and are now forgotten.
The names continue, however, as a testimonial to the cosmic beliefs of
a people who saw all of nature's creations as living things.

Most common are the Spirit Lakes, in Bayfield, Burnett, Douglas,
Menominee, Oneida, Price-Taylor, and Vilas counties. North Spirit
Lake straddles the line of Price and Taylor counties. Price County also
has a Spirit Rock. Out of Spirit Lake in Price County flows Spirit River,
to join the Wisconsin River just below Tomahawk in Lincoln County.
The last few miles of the river's course, widened by a dam, is called
Spirit River Flowage.

Manitou

Manito or *Manitou* is the term for "a spirit" in Ojibwa, Ottawa, and Potawatomi.[1] Father Claude Allouez, speaking of the Ottawa in 1666–67, wrote: "The savages of the region recognize no sovereign master of Heaven and Earth, but believe there are many spirits—some of whom are beneficent, as the Sun, the Moon, the Lake, Rivers, and Woods; others malevolent, as the adder, the dragon, cold, and storms. And in general, whatever seems to them either helpful or hurtful they call a Manitou, and pay it the worship and veneration which we render only to the true God."[2]

The name Manitou is on the Wisconsin map in various forms and combinations. Manitou Island is in the Apostle Islands in Lake Superior, Ashland County. Two of Schoolcraft's companions remarked on June 21, 1832, that this island, which they called Spirit Island, was venerated or feared by the Indians, who never camped on it.[3] Big and Little Manitou falls are in Black River, Pattison State Park, Douglas County. These falls are a mile apart, and the first of them, descending 165 feet, is the highest waterfall in Wisconsin. According to Indian belief, several spirits lived in Big Manitou Falls. One could hear their voices or war songs above the roar of the Falls of the "Great Spirit." It was believed that the spirit Manabozho (Neinibozho, Winneboujou, etc.) rested at Little Manitou Falls when on hunting expeditions.[4]

Manitou Rock is in Winnebago County. Manitou Lake is in Eureka Township, Polk County. The name of Monito Lake in Langlade County is only a spelling variation of Manitou.

Manitowish River flows from Vilas County into Flambeau Flowage in Iron County. The village of Manitowish in Iron County is named for it. In Vilas county, Manitowish is the name of a lake; a village, and a town there are called Manitowish Waters. Father Baraga listed Manitowish as Ojibwa for "small animal (a marten, a weasel, etc.)." The name may be related to *Manito-waise-se,* Tanner's name for "spirit beast," reportedly named by the Ojibwa for "evil spirits in the waters here."[5]

Manitowoc, according to Grignon, is a Menominee name meaning "the home or place of the spirits." Hoffman thought it meant "much game," and Hathaway misunderstood it to mean "devil's den."[6] Grignon's explanation is much the preferred one. The name is used for the city and county of Manitowoc; the Manitowoc River, which flows from Calumet County into Lake Michigan at Manitowoc; Manitowoc Rapids in that river; Little Manitowoc River, a tributary of the Manitowoc; and the town of Manitowoc and Manitowoc Rapids, as well as Manitowoc Harbor at the city of Manitowoc.

Miniwakan/Wakanda

Miniwakan Lake in Langlade County has a Dakota (Sioux) name meaning "spirit water."[7] The same name is found in areas of present or former Sioux occupation in Iowa and North Dakota, but the name in Wisconsin is in Algonquian territory. It is, therefore, a name given by whites for reasons of euphony or whimsy.

In the same class is Wakanda Park in the city of Menomonie, Dunn County. The name is often interpreted as "Great Spirit" in Dakota and related languages. Stephen R. Riggs translated it "to reckon holy or sacred, to worship."[8]

Devils

Devils Lake in Sauk County is the white man's interpretation of the Winnebago name *Day-wa-kun-chunk*, "Sacred Lake." The story is told that "many years ago a Winnebago was engaged in a fast and prayer for blessing on the bank of this lake, crying aloud to the Supreme Being for twenty days. He saw an animal resembling a cat rise to the surface. The animal told him he would live a long happy life and his predictions came true."[9]

This is one of thirty-three Wisconsin names containing the word *devil* listed by the U.S. Geological Survey. The word has been applied to places by whites because of a misunderstanding of the names given to them by the Indians. There is, in fact, in native cosmogony, no single evil spirit comparable to the Devil of the Christians. There are many spirits of all shades from good to bad, called Manito by the Algonquians and Wakan by the Siouans. As Ruth Landes has explained it, "In the world-view provided by Ojibwa religion and magic, there is neither stick nor stone that is not animate and charged with potential hostility to man."[10] The Algonquians indicate the malevolent or beneficent nature of a spirit by a prefix before Manitou and its variants; the Siouans use a suffix for the same purpose after the name Wakan.

Europeans simplified these words so that we have innumerable names on the map resulting from their translations. Whites commonly thought of Indians as "devil worshippers" because of their propitiation of evil spirits, and so Indian words meaning "spirit" or "sacred" or "mysterious" were simply put down as "devil."

The "Devil" names in Wisconsin, besides the one mentioned and the state park around it, include Devil creeks in Ashland, Lincoln, Rusk, and Sawyer counties; Devils Creek State Wildlife Management Area, Rusk County; Devils lakes in Bayfield, Burnett, Fond du Lac,[11] Forest, Marinette, Sawyer, Vilas and Washburn counties; Devils Elbow, a bend in Adams County and another in Waupaca County; Devils Gate, a valley in Pepin and Pierce counties; Devils Cauldron (a bay), Devils Island, and Devils Shoal in Ashland County; Devils Island in Dodge County; Devils Chair (a summit) in Sauk County; Devils Corner, a locale in Pepin County; Devils Marsh in Polk County; Devils Monument (pillar) in Monroe County; Devils Head and Devils Nose (cliff) in Brown and Manitowoc counties; and Devils Washbowl (basin) in Sauk County. Some of these places (as in Fond du Lac County) may have been named by whites for their own devil; it is not possible now to sort them out. But it is documented that some were named by interpretation of Indian names.

Medicine

To American Indians, the term *medicine* referred not only to curative agents, but to anything mysterious or powerful. There was a spiritual component in medicine, and its highest practitioners were both priests and doctors.[12]

The word is found in numerous place names throughout the United States, mostly in English, but in every instance where the origin of such a name has been traced, it has been found to be of Indian origin. Usually there is something considered grand or mysterious about the place to which such a name is attached. Sometimes it was the site of a remarkable happening.

In Wisconsin, Medicine Lake in Three Lakes Township, Oneida County, and Medicine Brook, a tributary of Peshtigo River in Stephenson Township, Marinette County, are examples of this group of names.

Windigo

Windigos were a race of giant cannibals who were believed by the Ojibwa and Ottawa Indians to inhabit an island in Hudson Bay and were universally feared. The Swampy Cree who lived in that region also lived in fear of the Windigos.[13] William Keating told of a band of Ojibwa northwest of Lake Superior who resorted to cannibalism during a famine in 1811. From that incident, Windigo Lake in that part of Ontario received its name.[14]

Numerous tales of the Windigos were told by northern Indians, one of which was recorded by Schoolcraft in *Algic Researches* (1839).[15] The Windigos are also mentioned in Longfellow's *Song of Hiawatha*, wherein Mudjekeewis tells Hiawatha:

"Cleanse the earth from all that harms it,
Clear the fishing-grounds and rivers,
Slay all monsters and magicians,
All the giants, the Wendigoes,
All the serpents, the Kenabeeks,
As I slew the Mishe-Mokwa."[16]

Windigo is on place names in Ontario, Michigan, and Wisconsin. In the Badger State the name was given to Windigo Lake in Bass Lake Township, Sawyer County, west of Lac Courte Oreilles Indian Reservation.

Winneboujou

The name of the village of Winneboujou in Douglas County is simply one of several ways of spelling the name of the spirit, culture hero, and miracle worker of the Great Lakes tribes who was adopted by Longfellow as the leading figure in his Indian epic under the name Hiawatha. The name appears in numerous writings in a variety of spellings—Manabozho, Manabush, Winne-bozho, and many others. Although he was what we could call a deity, he was not worshipped.[17]

8

Material Culture

In things relating to common life the language of the
Indians is remarkably rich. They, in many cases, have
several names for one and the same thing under different
circumstances. They have ten different names for a bear,
according to its age or sex. Similarly they have a number
of names for a deer. They have one word for fishing with
a rod, another for fishing with a net, another for fishing
with a spear or harpoon. Such words do not in the least
resemble one another.

David Zeisberger (1721–1808),
"A History of the Indians"

Names relating to Indian cultural activities usually appear on the
map in English translation, and most of them were put there by
whites. However, they are descriptive of the Indian presence, and since
my focus is on the function of names as a cultural record, they are
treated here.

Gardens

In the summer of 1831, Henry R. Schoolcraft and his party
arrived by canoe at the Ojibwa village of Pukwaewa on the Namekagon
River. The inhabitants were off on a summer hunt, but their gardens
were left in good order: "We found eight large permanent bark lodges,
with fields of corn, potatoes, pumpkins, and beans, in fine condition. . . . The corn fields were partially or lightly fenced. The corn was
in tassel. The pumpkins partly grown, the beans fit for boiling. The
whole appearance of thrift and industry was pleasing."[1]

All Wisconsin tribes, to some degree, depended upon crops for a
living. Their gardens or fields gave rise to some place names. Elsewhere,
I mention Lac Vieux Desert as one of these (see Chapter 17). Several

other names are in English, but all refer to native agricultural activity. These include Garden Lake in Bayfield County, Planting Ground Lake in Oneida County, and Plantation Lakes in Iron and Oconto counties.

Powwow

Powwow is a word from the eastern Algonquians, but it spread across the country, among both Indians and whites, at an early date. General Trobriand, at Fort Berthold, North Dakota, wrote on September 22, 1867: "I was informed that the three chiefs, accompanied by the principal personages of their tribes, would call on me presently to have a pow-wow; that is to say, a conference to discuss their affairs; what we should call in English a solemn talk."[2]

Perhaps the earliest appearance of this word in print was by Roger Williams (1643), who defined the Narraganset word *powwaw* as "a Priest."[3] The sense of the word, over time used as both a verb and a noun, has included medicine man, conjuring over a patient, a dance, a feast, and a council or conference. In the last sense it has been used much by whites. Among Indians at present it chiefly refers to a social gathering featuring dances and ceremonies.[4] Several Wisconsin tribes hold summer powwows, which attract other Indians as well as whites from afar.

Powwow has become a name for a lake in Gogebic County, Michigan, and a river and pond in Rockingham County, New Hampshire. In Wisconsin we have Pow Wow Campground in Trempealeau County. Although spelled here as two words, it is usually written as one word.

Sugar-Making Places

It was Menaboju who discovered that the maple-tree could produce sugar. He went one day into the forest, made an incision into a maple-tree, found the exuding sap to be sweet, made sugar of it, and since that period the Indians have imitated him.
> *Ojibwa legend quoted by Johann Georg Kohl,*
> Kitchi-Gami *(1860)*

The town of Sugar Creek in Walworth County obtains its name from a stream which originates there, the name of which is a translation from its Potawatomi name, *Sisibakwat sepee*. It is reported that in the spring of 1836 a Potawatomi band made a thousand pounds of maple sugar at Sugar Creek in the town of Lafayette. According to local history, "From some immemorial time the numerous sugar-maple trees along the valley of the creek had been tapped."[5] Other Sugar Creeks are in Crawford and Door counties.

The white people adopted from the Indians the practice of making maple syrup and sugar,[6] and this activity by both races has had a colorful influence on the place names of the states where maple syrup and sugar production has been or is still being practiced. In Wisconsin twenty-nine place names relate to sugar, meaning maple sugar.

A grove of sugar maple trees is commonly called Sugar Bush, which gave rise to the names of the villages of Sugar Bush in Brown and Outagamie counties, Sugar Bush Hill in Forest County, Upper, Lower, Middle, and Little Sugarbush lakes on the Lac du Flambeau Indian Reservation in Vilas County, and Sugarbush creeks in Ashland and Vilas counties. There are Sugar Bush lakes in Outagamie and Washburn counties, and Sugarbush (one word) lakes in Ashland, Polk, and Washburn counties.

Temporary sugar-making camps were established in the sugarbush in late winter or early spring, which are recalled by the creek, lake, town, and village named Sugar Camp in Oneida County, and Sugar Camp Hill in Douglas County. In Vernon County is the village of Sugar Grove and a feature called Sugar Grove Ridge. Sugar Grove Valley is in Sauk County, Sugar Lake is in Rusk County, and Sugar Island in Dodge County. Lastly, there is Sugar River in Dane County. One lake, in Wood County, carries the Ojibwa name for a maple forest, *Manakiki*.[7]

Trade

In view of the one-time importance of the Indian trade in Wisconsin history,[8] it is remarkable that few names on the map refer to it. The personal names of traders are often preserved as place names, but the activity itself is less commonly noted. However, we do have Big Trade Lake, Little Trade Lake, and the village and town of Trade Lake in Burnett County. Out of Big Trade Lake flows Trade River, which falls into the St. Croix in Polk County. On the river in Burnett County is the village of Trade River. One other Wisconsin place name referring to trade is Traders Bayou in Waupaca County.

The Indian origin of these names is indicated by J. N. Nicollet, who recorded the Ojibwa name of Trade River as *Attanwa Sibi* in his journal and Attanwa or Attanwan River on his maps.[9] Baraga's words for "trade" in the commercial sense are *atâwewin* and *atandiwin*.[10] From the verb *atâwe*, "trade," came the name of the Ottawa tribe of Indians.

Implements, Ornament, Raiment

Dish or Bowl

Two Wisconsin names refer to a dish or bowl. Mishonagan Creek and Swamp on Lac du Flambeau Reservation, Vilas County, have an Ojibwa name which apparently means "big dish or bowl."[11] The reference is probably to the bowl-shaped appearance of the swamp.

The **Ontonagon** River rises in Vilas County and joins Lake Superior at Ontonagon, Michigan. The name appears to be composed of Ojibwa *onâgan*, "dish or bowl," and the prefix *ont-*, from Ojibwa *ond*, which Baraga says "in compositions, alludes to the reason or *origin* of (something); to the *place* from which, or out of which, some object comes or is obtained."[12] If this assumption is correct the name broadly means "where dishes are obtained." This could refer to some kind of clay or wood used in making dishes or bowls, which was obtained in this locality.

There are alternative views. One says the word for "bowl" in this name relates to the shape of the river's mouth. William T. Boutwell wrote in his journal for June 19, 1832, that the name was for a chief called On-a-gon, "Bowl." Verwyst in this instance rejects Baraga's definition "my dish," for the explanation of one Antoine Gaudin: "place where game is shot by guess." There is also an apocryphal story that an Indian woman lost a dish in the river and shouted *"Nindonagan!"* ("There goes my dish!").[13]

Nepadoggen Creek

Nepadoggen Creek is a stream which flows a mile and a half into Beaver Brook in Clayton Township of Polk County. It has an Ojibwa name which was explained by Archie Mosey, a local St. Croix Ojibwa, to Frank Werner of Spooner as "an Indian name for scrapings from hides of wild animals used for medicinal purposes (no particular animal)."[14] In Baraga's *Otchipwe Language* the word most nearly approximating this name is *nabidoigan,* "a needle to take up with something on a string or thread."[15]

Moccasin

Of names of articles of clothing used by Indians, only one has become a Wisconsin place name: moccasin. This aboriginal name for a shoe originated with eastern Algonquians, from whom it was adopted into English. From the word *mawhcasun* of the Virginia Algonquians, or *mokkussin* of the New England Naticks, to the *makisin* of the Ojibwa is but a short step.[16]

Places named Moccasin are likely to be topographic features so named because of a fanciful resemblance to a moccasin. In Wisconsin we find Moccasin Bend in the Wisconsin River, in Dewey Township of Portage County; Moccasin Creek, near Nekoosa, in Wood and Portage counties; and four lakes named Moccasin—Moccasin Lake in Elcho Township, Langlade County; Moccasin and Little Moccasin lakes in Three Lakes Township, Oneida County; and Moccasin Lake in Land O' Lakes Township, Vilas County.

Paint and Vermillion

Almost any stream named "Paint" is so named because Indians obtained from such places clay used in making paint for the adornment of their persons and possessions. Wisconsin has but one Paint Creek, located in Chippewa County.

The most popular paint among Indians was the brilliant orange variety called by the whites vermilion or vermillion. It was made from a mixture of the appropriate kind of clay with bear's grease. Vermilion as a place name, either in English or aboriginal form, is not as common in Wisconsin as in certain neighboring states, such as Minnesota. Baraga's Ojibwa name for "Vermillion Lake" (not identified as to location) was *Onamani-Sagaigan.*[17]

In this state, the name Vermillion (spelled here with a double *l*) is present only in its English form (from French *vermillon*). It is found on Upper and Lower Vermillion lakes and Vermillion River, in Barron County. Vermillion River flows from Lower Vermillion Lake to join Yellow River near Barron.

Pipes and Pipestone

Ceremonial pipes were important items in American Indian diplomacy. As noted in my discussion of Calumet, possession and display of such a pipe was a guarantee of safe conduct among hostiles, and the smoking of it was always preliminary to councils and negotiations. According to Jonathan Carver (1766), when Indian peace emissaries gathered,

> They bear before them the Pipe of Peace, which I need not inform my readers is of the same nature as a Flag of Truce among Europeans, and is treated with the greatest respect and veneration, even by the most barbarous nations. I never heard of an instance wherein the bearers of this sacred badge of friendship were ever treated disrespectfully, or its rights violated. . . . It is used as an introduction to all treaties, and great ceremony attends the use of it on these occasions.[18]

Of Indian cultural items, the pipe ranks with the tomahawk as an item frequently noted in place names. In Wisconsin it appears on the map in French, English, and perhaps two Indian languages. **Lake Poygan** in Winnebago and Waushara counties is one of the native place names signifying "pipe." This lake is traversed by the Fox River from west to east, and receives the Wolf River from the north. Father Verwyst was convinced by an Ojibwa informant that this name was from *opwagan*, the Ojibwa name for "pipe," and that it might have reference to the shore of the lake and one its connecting rivers.[19] However, it could be of Menominee origin. On T. J. Cram's map of 1839 the Wolf River is called *Pauwaygun*, which is very probably his version of the Menominee name, since Wolf River flows from Menominee territory. The Menominee word for "pipe," *ohpuakan*, is almost identical to the Ojibwa,[20] as is the Potawatomi *o-paw-gan*.[21] Albert Jenks (1901) thought that this name came from a Menominee term given by him as *Po-wa-hé-canne*, said to signify "threshing wild rice," but this appears to be but a wild guess.[22]

The name Poygan is also used for a town in Winnebago County and a marsh in Waushara County. In Land O' Lakes Township, Vilas County, the name of Boygan Lake is only a spelling variation of Poygan.

On Pine River, a tributary of Lake Poygan from the west, is the village of Poy Sippi, in Waushara County. In this name, *Poy* is clearly a fragment from Poygan. Of this name, Philip Poulette, secretary-treasurer of the Waushara County Historical Society, Wautoma, writes: "I believe it was an Indian name contraction of Poygan Sippi, meaning Pipe River. The Pine River goes into Lake Poygan and I suspect the river made the stem of the pipe and the lake the bowl."[23] Huron H. Smith said the name resulted from the shape of the river at the village site.[24] There is no basis for Father Verwyst's belief that *Poy Sippi* was from *Bwan-sibi*, "Sioux River," for the Sioux were never in this region.[25]

Another "pipe" name in Wisconsin in **Sheboygan,** given to a city, a county, a river, and several other features. Its origin is the same as that of Cheboygan, Michigan. Father Verwyst thought that this name was from Ojibwa *jibaigan,* "any perforated object, as a pipe stem." B. F. H. Witherell identified She-boy-gan as meaning "a hollow bone."[26]

To this writer it appears that the *Che* (*She*) in Cheboygan (or Sheboygan) is a contraction from Ojibwa *kitchi,* "great," joined to *boy-gan* (from *opwagan*), "pipe."[27] The reason for the name may be the fancied resemblance of some curve in the Sheboygan River to a pipe. However, there are some apocryphal stories about the name. One relates: "A squaw gave birth to her 12th son. The proud father made the rounds of the tepees [*sic*] to spread the glad tidings. At the first, when questioned concerning the sex of the new aborigine, he replied: 'She boy again.'"[28] The use of the Dakota word *tepee* is but one sign that this story is not from the Ojibwa. Another wild story, from Joshua Hathaway (1854), held that Cheboygan was from Chippewa *Shawb-wa-way-gun,* which expressed a tradition "that *a great noise,* coming under ground from the region of Lake Superior, was heard at this river."[29]

Sheboygan was applied first to the river, and from that came a cluster of names: the city and county of Sheboygan; a waterfall, a marsh, and a town in the county; the city and town of Sheboygan Falls; Sheboygan Bay and Lake; Sheboygan Marsh State Wildlife Area; Sheboygan Point; and Sheboygan Reef.

In English, we have a village called Pipe and a Pipe Creek in Fond du Lac County, and in Pierce County Pipe Lake as well as North Pipe Lake. Pipe Lake in Johnston Township of Polk County was so named, according to Frank Werner of the Polk County Historical Society in Spooner, because the shape of the lake resembles that of a pipe.[30]

Calumet County and Calumetville, Fond du Lac County, in former

Stockbridge Indian territory, have their names from the old French term for "pipe," which became so clearly identified with the Indian pipe (perhaps from its use as a baking soda trademark) that it was been mistaken for an Indian word. (See Chapter 17.) Calumetville is located only two miles north of the village of Pipe, a name given in translation from Calumet.

Pipestone

Indian pipe bowls were usually made of a red stone called pipestone by the whites and known scientifically as catlinite, for George Catlin, the painter of Indians who visited and illustrated the famous pipestone quarry in Minnesota, which is featured in Longfellow's *Hiawatha* and is now a national monument. Places where pipestone was abundant were important enough to be regarded as neutral ground, and several place names in Great Lakes states resulted from the presence of the esteemed substance.[31] In Wisconsin, Pipestone Creek and Falls in Sawyer County are named for it.

Snowshoes

Snowshoes are an American Indian invention without which winter travel in northern forests would have been impossible. Baraga's *Otchipwe Language* lists eight terms for snowshoes, their appurtenances, and uses.[32] None of the Indian terms appear on the Wisconsin map, but we are reminded of the one-time importance of this native contrivance by the presence of Snowshoe Lake in Ashland County and again in Polk County. Both appear to have been named for their shape.

Tomahawk

Andrew White, an early missionary to Indians in Maryland, wrote that "they also use in warres, a short club of a cubit long, which they call a Tomahawk."[33] This is the instrument listed as "Tamahake, a hatchett," in Strachey's Virginia Indian vocabulary. The term was applied to both clubs and cutting tools and was quickly adopted into English.[34] Tomahawk became a familiar place name, even in places where the word was unknown to local Indians.

Tomahawk is a common place name in Wisconsin, although the word has no close resemblance to any Wisconsin Indian term. It is commonly applied to lakes because of some perceived similarity in shape, but probably also, in some cases, merely to have a "savage-sounding" name.

A cluster of Tomahawk names in Lincoln County stems from Lake Tomahawk, which is generally believed to have been named for its shape. In the late seventeenth century, it is said, a band of about two hundred Ojibwa had a village here. According to a promotional book published in 1912 by the Tomahawk Club in the town of Tomahawk, the Indians originated the name, and the lumbermen later adopted it.[35] However, the name in this form cannot be from any Wisconsin Indian language. From Tomahawk Lake in Lincoln County came the names of Tomahawk River, which flows into it, and of the city and town of Tomahawk.

In adjacent Oneida County are Tomahawk and Little Tomahawk lakes. The village of Lake Tomahawk is on the shore of the larger lake and gives its name to the town. The lake is said to be named for its shape,[36] but one would have to greatly stretch one's imagination to see such a shape in this lake. Two other Tomahawk Lakes are in Barnes Township, Bayfield County, and Casey Township, Washburn County.

Fishing and Trapping

Indian activity connected with fishing and trapping has given rise to a number of place names. Nearly always these names have been translated into English, and occasionally into French, but their existence is nevertheless a measure of native influence on geographical names, and so deserves mention here.

Bear Trap

Beartrap Creek, between Ashland and Odanah in Ashland County, has a name translated from Ojibwa *Makodassonagani sibi*, according to Father Verwyst.[37] In addition, there is a Bear Trap Lake in Polk County, another lake called Beartrap in Washburn County, and Beartrap Falls in the West Branch of the Wolf River, Menominee County. There are many more translated names than we know about in Wisconsin.

Fence: A Deer Trap

The name of the village of Fence in Florence County originates from the early Indians' method of killing deer. In the fall of the

year a large brush fence was built and a picket fence placed directly behind it. Deer were driven toward the fence and, upon jumping over the
brush, landed on the sharp pickets.[38]

Torch

Members of several Wisconsin Indian tribes fished by
night with the aid of torches, usually made from pine knots. With this
illumination, fish were speared, not only in inland lakes but also in
Lake Michigan.[39]

There is no question but that this practice caused the French to give
the name **Lac du Flambeau** (Torch Lake) to the lake in Vilas County, a
name today also borne by the Ojibwa village and reservation centered
there. There also can be little doubt that fishing by torchlight is the
source of the name of Flambeau (or Turtle Flambeau) Flowage in Iron
County, out of which flows the Flambeau River, which joins the Chippewa in Rusk County. From the river came the names for the town of
Flambeau in Rusk County and Flambeau Ridge in Chippewa County.
Indian torchlight fishing is also the reason for the names of Torch Lake
in Vilas County and of Torch River in Ashland and Sawyer counties.
There are also rivers and lakes named Torch in the upper and lower pen-
insulas of Michigan.

Wannigan

The Abnaki had a word for "a trap," *waniigan*, which was
adopted into the language of loggers, campers, and sheepherders. The
word also resembles Cree *wanihigan* or *wunehi'kun*, "trap." Normally
written as *wanigan*, the word was heard in old-time logging camps from
Maine to the Pacific. The meaning varied. It was sometimes a place for
storing clothing, shoes, tobacco, and other supplies. At other times it
was a houseboat or raft used for carrying food and tools during logging
drives along rivers. It could also be a camp commissary and office car in
railroad work camps housing gandy dancers (track workers).[40] It was a
sheepherder's name for the supply wagon, which was also a solitary
camp. It was also a box or chest sometimes called *yannigan* bag, containing food and gear. The term *wanigan*, in the last-named sense, has
been used among backpack campers.

Another variant of this term is *wangan*. In Piscataquis County,

Maine, the name for Wangan River has been interpreted from the Abnaki as "the bend." If that interpretation is correct, the similarity to *wanigan* must be coincidental. In Ojibwa, *wanikan* is "a hole in the ground" (sometimes these were caches, sometimes game traps), and *winigan* is "marrow bone."[41] *Wanigan* appears to be an extreme example of how much the meaning of a native word can vary in white usage.

As a place name, Wanigan (or its variants) is found in several states. In Wisconsin the Wannigan Rapids are on the Chippewa River in Sawyer County. In Hayward a restaurant is called Wanigan, and *Wannigan* is the name of a houseboat used in a logging show at that place. "Wannigan Days" is a celebration, including a parade, which is held every July at St. Croix Falls, Polk County. Elsewhere, there is a Wanagan Creek in Gogebic County, Michigan, and a Wannagan Creek on the north boundary of Theodore Roosevelt Memorial Park in Billings County, North Dakota. Winigan is a village in Sullivan County, Missouri.

Weirs and Fish Traps

From Father Claude Allouez we have an early description (1670) of an Indian fish weir in Fox River:

> From one bank of the river to the other they make a barricade by driving down large stakes in two brasses of water, so that there is a kind of bridge over the stream for the fishermen, who, with the help of a small weir, easily catch the sturgeon and every other kind of fish, which this dam stops, although the water does not cease to flow between the stakes. They call this contrivance Mitihikan, and it serves them during spring and part of the summer.[42]

Mitihikan as used by Allouez is equivalent to Father Baraga's Ojibwa term *mitchikan*, which is defined as "fence."[43] Some of the various "Fence" place names in Wisconsin are apparently derived from the contrivance described by Allouez. Verwyst explicitly includes among them Fence Lake, which lies within the Lac du Flambeau Indian Reservation in Vilas County.[44] It is reasonable to suppose that Fence Lake in Wausaukee Township, Marinette County, derived its name from the same source.

From the devices described by Allouez we can be reasonably sure also that these place names originated: Fishtrap Creek in Ashland and Sawyer counties, Fishtrap lakes in Sawyer and Vilas counties, and Fishtrap Rapids in the St. Croix River, Burnett County, which were mentioned, but not named, in Nicollet's journal, August 7, 1837.[45]

Lodges and Villages

Tepee

Whites looking for "Indian" names to give to places often pick names which do not belong in the areas where they are applied. One of these is Tepee, the name of a lake in Cumberland Township of Vilas County. This word, sometimes spelled *teepee* or *tipi*, is from the Dakota, or Sioux, language and simply means "a dwelling."[46] Whites adopted it as a name for any Indian lodge, regardless of type, and of tribe or location, and so it appears also as a place name not only in Wisconsin, but in Iron County, Michigan, and elsewhere.

Wigwam

Wigwam, an Algonquian term for "a dwelling," found in similar form from the Atlantic to the Mississippi and beyond, was adopted into English at an early date. Unlike the portable tepee of the Plains Indians, a wigwam was a more permanent structure, made of a framework of poles covered with bark or with rush mats, according to season.

William Penn, borrowing from the Delawares, used the term *wigwam* in 1683.[47] White Americans saw fit to give the name Wigwam to the building in Chicago where Abraham Lincoln was nominated for president in 1860. The word has been written as *wigiwam* in Ojibwa, *wigwam* in Potawatomi, and *wig-wom* in Ottawa.[48]

Wigwam is a place name in several states. In Wisconsin we have Wigwam Slough in La Crosse and Vernon counties.

Villages

Native names for "village" or "settlement" appear on the Wisconsin map in three languages. The name of Odanah, the principal settlement on the Bad River Reservation of the Ojibwa in Ashland

County, is from the Ojibwa word for "village." Father Baraga spelled this word *odêna*,[49] and in that form it is the name of a place on the Algoma Central Railway just north of Sault Ste. Marie, Ontario. The spelling as found at Bad River is matched by Odanah, Manitoba. In Madison, Wisconsin, are Odana Park, Odana Road, and Odana Hills Golf Course.

Menekaunee, a post office at Marinette, has the Menominee name for "settlement," "city," "village," or "town." The sites at the mouth of Menominee River now occupied by the cities of Marinette, Wisconsin, and Menominee, Michigan, were once Menominee village sites, and the place where legend says the people originated. To them, therefore, the river was known as *Minikani Se'peu*, "village or town river."[50]

Taycheedah was the name of two Winnebago villages shown on Cram's map of 1839. The first place, from which the name has vanished, was at the foot of Lake Koshkonong. The second was at the foot of Lake Winnebago just east of present Fond du Lac. Here the name survives on a village, a creek, and a town. The name has been translated by Smith as "camp by a lake."[51] Norton Jipson interpreted the name as "lake dwellers," from *Day-cheera*, Winnebago name for the site of Fond du Lac, composed of *Day* ("lake") and *chee* ("dwellers") plus *"ra* or *da* as a final syllable," which Jipson called a definite article.[52]

Potch-Chee-Nunk does not appear on maps, but it is recognized by official highway signs on U.S. 45 three miles north of Wittenberg in Shawano County. It consists of a log cabin housing a Winnebago family and an Indian cooperative gift shop selling craft work of Wisconsin tribes. I was told by a Winnebago woman at the shop on June 25, 1977, that the name of this place means "house or village in the woods." In seeking the elements of this name in Jipson's Winnebago vocabulary, I found the following: *paij-ra*, "woods, forest"; *che-ra*, "house"; and *chee-nuk-ra*, "village."[53] The first and third terms make as good a match to this name as one can normally find.

Prehistoric Sites

Wisconsin contains numerous visible sites of prehistoric Indian occupation or activity, including quarries, cemeteries, manmade mounds, and garden sites. Some of these places have been given names, and a few have been preserved as state or local parks. Their names, though given by another race of people, deserve notice as another mark of aboriginal influence.

The oldest archaeological site in Wisconsin—as old as 10,000–12,000 years—is Silver Mound Park, one and a half miles west of Alma Center, in Jackson County. The mound is a natural elevation containing quarries where Indians mined quartzite for stone tools. Whites mistakenly thought silver had been mined here.

The 52-acre Copper Culture Mounds State Park in Oconto contains two hundred burials belonging to a culture dating back to 3000 B.C. It is named from the use of copper by these people in the manufacture of weapons and implements. This metal was apparently brought from the Lake Superior region.

The Woodland Culture, which emerged about the beginning of the Christian era, produced the mound builders, who left their earthworks in innumerable places in Wisconsin. The commonest type of Indian mound in Wisconsin is the effigy mound, made in the shape of animals, birds, or reptiles. Among them are also found linear and conical mounds. Most of these mounds were used as burial sites and have yielded numerous artifacts. The height of effigy mounds is seldom more than three feet, though one attains six feet. The longest effigy mound, a panther figure in Marquette County, is 575 feet long.

Lizard Mound State Park near West Bend, Washington County, is a 31-acre site containing thirty-one mounds, mostly effigies of panthers and birds, but containing one lizard effigy, for which the park is named. There are also linear and conical mounds at this site.

Sheboygan Indian Mound Park is a 14-acre park in the city of Sheboygan, which contains five deer and two panther effigies.

Kingsley Bend Indian Mounds, four miles east of Wisconsin Dells, contains effigy mounds dated 700–1000 B.C.

The town of Moundville in Marquette County is named for its numerous prehistoric Indian mounds.

The late-arriving Middle Mississippi Culture, which reached Wisconsin about A.D. 1200, established the notable village in Jefferson County to which the discoverers attached the Mexican name *Aztalan* (q.v.). This site is now a state park, notable for its two temple mounds, or truncated pyramids, similar in shape to, but smaller than, those at

Cahokia, Illinois, and at sites along the lower Mississippi and in Mexico.

Numerous mound sites scattered about Wisconsin, at Devils Lake, Lake Koshkonong, places in Grant County, and elsewhere, including sites on private lands, remain unnamed.[54]

9

Ethnicity, Gender, Rank, Occupation, and Age

When Columbus first landed upon the shores of this continent, in his attempt to discover a western passage to the Indies, he imagined that he had accomplished the object of his expedition, and that the island of San Salvador was one of those islands of the Chinese sea, lying near the extremity of India, which had been described by the navigators.

Acting upon this hypothesis, and also perhaps from the similarity of features and physical conformation, he gave the Islanders the name of Indians, which appellation was universally adopted, and extended to the aboriginals of the New World, as well as of Asia.

From decision of Supreme Court of California in The People v. Hall *(4 Cal. 399), October 1, 1854, holding that persons of Oriental origin were included in the statute barring Indians from testifying against white persons. Quoted from Robert F. Heizer and Alan F. Almquist,* The Other Californians.

Indian as a Name

Because Christopher Columbus thought he was in the East Indian islands in 1492, he called the inhabitants Indians. The name became indelibly fastened to them, and no satisfactory substitute has been found. The most popular current alternative name, Native American, is a designation that any person born in America can claim, and Amerind is a clumsy hybrid used only by academics. We are stuck with a name for the aboriginal Americans which belongs also to the population of a huge Asian nation.

One fact which makes "Indian" hard to shed is that it is graven permanently on our map, on an endless variety of topographic features and political units. How could we dispose of the state of Indiana, and its capital, Indianapolis? Would Florida sacrifice the name of Indian River, which has become identified with quality citrus fruit? What would become of ten places named Indianola, and thousands of other place names which contain the word Indian? Such toponymic surgery is hard to imagine.

Despite the accidental transfer of the erroneous name Indian to the New World, its appearance on the map adds a unique and colorful quality. Americans seeking a romantic tie to the past have been inclined to link the name Indian, as well as Indian names, to things having no connection with the Indians, and to use names that are, moreover, misplaced or inappropriate. Consider the suburbs and real estate developments with names such as Indian Ridge, where there is no ridge and no record of aboriginal occupancy; or Navajo Hills, where we have no hills and no Navajo; or Squaw Valley in California, where that Algonquian word is out of place.

The misnaming habit goes back a thousand years to the time when Eric the Red gave the name Greenland to the largest chunk of ice outside of Antarctica. In this respect, our naming customs differ from those of Indians whose rule was that every place name must be appropriate to the locality.

Perhaps the only harm that can come from this is that unwary persons might draw false conclusions from these names. If any persons assume that names *always* have some relation to local history, topography, or folklore, they may be misled. They may discover that viewing Indian names and other names as cultural artifacts may at times be as misleading in its way as are Piltdown Man, the Cardiff Giant, and the Kensington stone in theirs.

Of course, not all places called "Indian" are inappropriately named. For instance, the village of Indian Ford in Rock County does indeed occupy the spot where Indians forded the Rock River.[1] It is also probable that many of our Indian Creeks and Indian Lakes were once Indian camp or village sites, although specific information is often lacking. Also, many geological features, with names such as Indian Head, are named for their fancied resemblance to Indian profiles.

The *Alphabetical Finding List of Wisconsin Geographic Names*, issued by the U.S. Geological Survey, lists forty-nine places having the word "Indian" in their names, and one with "Injun" (Big Injun Lake, Menominee County). Prof. Frederic Cassidy lists eight "Indian" place names in Dane County alone, some of which are on the USGS list; four of them are no longer in use. Some place names on these lists (e.g., names of cemeteries) do not meet the definition of "place name" adopted for this book, but the frequency of their occurrence is of interest.

Indian Head Flowage, Polk County, takes the name given to the region of northwestern Wisconsin bordered by the St. Croix River, which forms part of the Minnesota boundary. The river course as seen on the map forms an outline which could be likened to an Indian profile. Also named for its shape is Indian Head Rock at Fountain City, Trempealeau County.[2]

Indian Creeks rank first numerically among features named for the Indian. There are at least thirteen Indian Creeks in Wisconsin, in addition to Indian Chain Creek (Oneida County) and Indian Grave Creek (Jackson County). The origin of the last name may be self-explanatory. However, we have no hard data on any of them, except for Cassidy's remark that Indian Creek, an old name for a tributary of Lake Mendota in Dane County, was so named because it was frequented by the Winnebago.[3] In fact, all of the places named "Indian" that Cassidy lists were formerly associated with activities of the Winnebago.

The tiny crossroads settlement of Indian Creek in Polk County is named for its location on Indian Creek. This stream flows into Clam River in Burnett County, near the Big Bend Lake portion of the St. Croix Indian Reservation.

Wisconsin has nine Indian Lakes, as well as an Indian Camp Lake (Forest County) and an Indian School Lake (Sawyer County). The last two names are self-explanatory. Indian Camp Lake is in an area of present Potawatomi occupation; Indian School Lake is near the Lac Courte Oreilles Chippewa Reservation.

Six places are called Indian Point, and one (in Winnebago County) is named Old Indian Point. The USGS lists two Indian Cemeteries, plus one Indian Hill Cemetery, but they must have overlooked a few. Cassidy lists two places in Dane County called Indian Springs (although only one use of the name is current) and Forest County has another Indian Springs.

The other examples of features called Indian each occur but once. They are Indian Castle, a summit in Iowa County; Indian Church in Juneau County; Indian Heights and Indian Hill in Dane County; Indian Hollow in Crawford County; Indian Lookout Tower and Indian Mound Campground (so called from the presence of Indian burial mounds) in Oneida County; Indian Ridge in Monroe County, and Indian River in Forest County. Indian Shores is a settlement in Winnebago County, and Indian Slu (or Slough) is in Buffalo County.

The adoption and persistence of these names is a measure of the romantic interest in Indians in previous generations, as well as its continuation in later times. The settlers, while crowding the Indians out of the land, seemed intent on commemorating the expelled occupants.

Half Breed

The term "half breed," used in the last century, always bore a negative and pejorative tone, and thankfully, it is no longer used. However, there is an example of it on the map of Wisconsin, at Halfbreed Rapids in the Wisconsin River, Oneida County.

Yankee

Rev. John Heckewelder wrote in 1818 that New England Indians were unable to pronounce the word *English*, which emerged in their speech as *Yengees*. He further explained:

> This name they now exclusively applied to the people of New England, who, indeed, appeared to have adopted it and were, as they still are, generally through the country called *Yankees*, which is evidently the same name with a trifling alteration. They say they know the *Yengees*, and can distinguish them by their dress and personal appearance, and that they were considered to be less cruel than the Virginians or *long knives*.[4]

The French visitor the Marquis de Chastellux (1782) independently confirmed Heckewelder's view of the origin of the term Yankee: "This is a name given derisively, or merely jestingly, to the inhabitants of the far eastern states [New England]. It is thought to come from a tribe of

Indians whose lands were occupied by the first settlers, and who lived between Connecticut and the state of Massachusetts."[5]

Yankwi is also the name for Englishmen in the Delaware traditional history, the *Walum Olum.*[6] There are others, however, who claim Dutch origin for the name Yankee, and some who argue that its origin is unknown.[7] "Yankee" was at first confined to New England. Later, it was used by southerners to denominate northerners, and finally, by World War I, it became a synonym for American.

Yankee is a place name in several states, including Wisconsin. There is a Yankee Hollow in Grant County and another overlapping Green and Lafayette counties. Yankee Lake is shared by Marinette and Oconto counties and Yankee Joe Creek is in Sawyer County.

Lenawee

Lenawee Creek and Lake in Bayfield County have a name meaning "man," in the sense of "human being," from either the Delaware or Shawnee language in slightly corrupt form. It is here identical to the name of a county in southern Michigan.[8]

The Shawnee word for man has been written as *illeni, ilani,* and *linneau;* the Delaware word is recorded as *leenew* and *lenno.* It is not hard to see how the name Illinois (originally *ilini,* plural *iliniwek*) arose from this word as used in Illinois. Lenawee in Wisconsin is a white introduction. No Wisconsin tribal language possesses the *l* sound.[9]

The Ojibwa equivalent of Lenawee is *Anishinabe.*[10] Strangely, it does not appear as a place name in Wisconsin. In western Ontario, however, is Anishinabi Lake, and in the city of Kenora, Ontario, is Anicinabe Park.

Squaw

Wisconsin has thirty-two places named Squaw, but the word is not from any language of Wisconsin Indians. At first the word "squaw" for a woman was confined to the Algonquian languages and dialects of southeastern New England, especially the Narraganset and Natick. The word was used in the present form by Roger Williams in 1643. It diverges from that form in other languages, even in the immediate neighborhood. Trumbull's *Natick Dictionary* (1903), based on John Eliot's *Indian Bible* (1663), lists *squa, squaas, squas,* and *squa'us,* all as singular for woman, and adds that the term was "rarely used by Eliot except in compound words." The term for a married woman was quite different: *mittamuus.*[11]

Away from New England the term for woman became *ochqueu* in Delaware, *kwê* in Potawatomi, *ikwê* in Ojibwe, and *ikwäwa* in Fox.[12] But only *squaw*, as Roger Williams spelled the Narraganset word, was adopted into English and became a place name as far away as Alaska. Deploring such transfers, Edward Everett Hale wrote: "It is much to be regretted that a careless habit of thought takes it for granted that an Indian word of one locality is a good Indian word of another, and that names may be transferred from North to South or from South to North at the free will of an innkeeper or a poet. Such transfers of words, which in the beginning amount almost to falsehood, cause more confusion and more as time goes by."[13] The spread of this term is a measure of the influence of New England on American culture. The distribution of it is also an illustration of migration and settlement patterns and an indication of the limits of New England influence.

It should be noted that "squaw" has come to be seen as a derogatory epithet and has normally had such connotations when used by whites in the past and in the present. When used in a place name, Squaw usually recalls some incident involving an Indian woman (or women), although the incident is seldom recorded and apparently was soon forgotten.

Wisconsin has Squaw Creeks in Ashland, Forest, Jackson, Langlade, Lincoln, Lincoln-Price, Marathon-Wood, Marinette, Menominee, Monroe, Price, Price-Oneida, Sawyer, and Vilas counties. There is also a Squaw Lake Creek in Sawyer County. Squaw Lakes are in Langlade, Lincoln, Marinette, Oconto, Outagamie, St. Croix, Sawyer and Vilas-Oneida counties. Oconto County also has a Little Squaw Lake, and Vilas County has a White Squaw Lake. There are Squaw Bays in Bayfield, Dane, and Sawyer counties, a Squaw Island in Door County, Squaw Mound and Squaw Flowage in Jackson County, and Squaw Point in Bayfield County. The particular reason for the application of these names has not been found. Only in a remote way are they an example of native influence.

Ogema

The Ojibwa term for chief is *ogima.* From it came the names of the village and town of Ogema and Ogema Millpond, all in

Price County.[14] Lake Ogemaga in Oneida County is perhaps a name corrupted from Ojibwa *ogimakwe*, "queen," or literally, "woman chief."[15] These two names are apparently not given in honor of any particular individuals.

Warrior

The Indian warrior is honored by the name of Warrior Lake in the Lac du Flambeau Indian Reservation in Vilas County, but no particular reason for this designation has been discovered.

Papoose

Papoose is another of those eastern Algonquian words which was adopted into English and has become so familiar that it is often presumed to be a term known to all Indians. The word was used by the Narraganset and was recorded as *papoos*, "A childe," by Roger Williams in 1643.[16] Similar terms were used in other New England languages, but the Algonquian words for child in the upper Great Lakes region are different. In Ojibwa, it is *abinodji*, from which is named a waterfall in Presque Isle River, Gogebic County, Michigan.[17]

Papoose, introduced by whites, is commonly used in Wisconsin. There are Papoose Creeks in Jackson, Lincoln, and Vilas counties. Marinette and Oconto counties each have a Papoose Lake; Vilas County has Papoose and Little Papoose lakes. No particular reason seems to exist for these names other than whimsy.

10

Trails and Portages

The whole country was a thick forest, through which our
only road was a foot-path, or such as, in America, is
exclusively termed an *Indian path.*

Alexander Henry (1764)

Trails

Wisconsin in early days was crisscrossed by a web of Indian trails linking all parts of the future state, and reaching into surrounding areas. Some of these trails were later followed by the white
man's roads and railroads because they took into account the topography in such a way as to provide the easiest and safest passage. The military road from Green Bay to Prairie du Chien is an example of such an
adaptation.[1]

Indians as a rule gave no names to their trails, but generic words for a
trail appear on the map. **Mikana,** a village in Barron County, has the
Ojibwa name for "road." The name **Mecan** (*mikan*) is a variation of this
term. It is preserved in the name of a town in Marquette County, a river
tributary to the Fox in Waushara, Marquette, and Green Lake counties,
the Mecan-Princeton Canal in Green Lake County, as well as in Mecan
Springs and Mecan Lake in Waushara County.[2]

Kikaigon, according to Father Baraga, was the Chippewa name for a
"mark to guide travellers, or to point out dangerous places on the
road."[3] That is the probable origin of the name of **Kakagon** River and
Kakagon Slough in Ashland County.

Some trails established by white people have been given Indian
names for romantic reasons. One of these is the **Wazeka** Trail in Jackson
County, which follows state route 54 from Black River Falls to and beyond the Winnebago settlements northeast of town. *Wazeka* (or
Wazika) is the Winnebago word for pine, or white pine.[4]

Tuscobia Trail is a 74-mile-long hiking and horseback trail which follows an abandoned railroad right-of-way from Rice Lake to Park Falls. Its name, taken from that of a village in Barron County, is of obscure origin but is not from a local language. One claim holds that "in Indian terminology, 'Tuscobia' means 'a very level place'."[5] This view probably originates in cryptic statements made by Schoolcraft concernng the name Tuscola, in Michigan.[6] The language origin is not given in either case. From surface appearances, Tuscobia could be a corruption of the name of Tuscumbia, Alabama. This is said to be the name of a Cherokee chief, but it is from the Choctaw language—*tàshka* (*tuska*), "warrior," plus *àbi* or *ambi*, "killer." It has also been speculated that the name is from Choctaw terms meaning "warrior rainmaker."[7] If it seems strange to have a southern name in northern Wisconsin, consider Alabama Lake in Polk County.

Portages

In Indian and frontier days in the Great Lakes region, travel was frequently done by canoe. By following interconnected lakes and rivers, travellers could cover thousands of miles with only a few interruptions where it was necessary to cross overland carrying canoes and baggage from one lake or waterway to another, or across projecting spits of land, or around rapids and waterfalls. The English called these breaks "carrying places." The French called them *portages*. The Ojibwa Indians called them *onigam;* while the Winnebago name for a portage was *wa-wa-na,* literally, "to put (canoe) on shoulder."[8]

A remarkable system of canoe routes and portage trails was laid out by the Indians. Years later whites dug canals along Indian portage routes, and built roads and railroads beside them. In early days the portage routes were considered to be important strategic points and were frequently mentioned in treaties. In the Treaty of Greenville (1795), Anthony Wayne reserved several enclaves of land at portage sites, where cities often arose.

The most important of these sites in Wisconsin is now occupied by the city of Portage, in Columbia County. It was the only land break in a water trail from Niagara to New Orleans. Here the Fox River flows within two miles of the Wisconsin. The Fox River is connected to Lake Michigan by way of Green Bay and Lakes Winnebago, Butte des Morts,

Poygan, and Puckaway. The Wisconsin leads to the Mississippi just below Prairie du Chien. The Fox-Wisconsin waterway was first described
by Father Jacques Marquette in his account of his journey to the lower
Mississippi in 1673.[9] It was a major avenue of travel for more than 150
years thereafter. At this portage in 1828 the U.S. Army built Fort Winnebago to guard the portage route. In 1831 the Winnebago agency house
was built here and still stands as a historic attraction. The digging of a
canal across the portage route began in 1838, but many failures and interruptions occurred before it was finished in 1851. For a half century
small steamboats plied the canal; after 1910, pleasure boats were the
main users. In 1951, after one hundred years of use, the canal was closed
by the U.S. Army Corps of Engineers.[10] The old Portage trail today is followed by **Wauona** Trail, a footpath having a name adapted from the
Winnebago word for "portage."[11]

Although the city of Portage is the main memorial of the canoe travelling days, there are other portage names which recall long-forgotten
portage routes. Portage County is named for the Plover portage, eight
miles long, which connected the Wisconsin River near present-day Stevens Point with the Wolf River at what is now Waupaca, via the Plover
and Waupaca Rivers.[12] Portage Point and Portage Park in Door County
are on Lake Michigan at the eastern end of the Sturgeon Bay Ship Canal,
which connects with Green Bay. Formerly, the canal route was a portage
path. Marquette used it on his return from his trip down the Mississippi
in 1673 and again on his last trip to Illinois in the fall of 1674. In Vilas
County, canoe travellers could portage from Big Portage Lake to Little
Portage Lake, and then follow Portage Creek to the Wisconsin River.

The portage names are a mark of aboriginal influence on the land, but
their own names for portages are scarce on the map. As indicated,
Wauona is one of the few Indian portage names still preserved. The
Ojibwa word for "portage," *onigam* or *onigum*, survives in Michigan,
Minnesota, and Canada.

11

Descriptive Names

So much geography there is in their names. The Indian
navigator naturally distinguishes by a name those parts
of a stream where he has encountered quick water and
forks, and again, the lakes and smooth water where he
can rest his weary arms, since those are the most interesting and more arable parts to him.

Henry David Thoreau, The Maine Woods *(1864)*

Colors

Black River

J. N. Nicollet, on his map of 1843, showed the Black River
at La Crosse with the Winnebago name "Sappah or Black River" as he
understood it.[1] Frances Perry wrote that the river was called *Nee saip* or
Nio-sep by those Indians. Black River Falls in Jackson County was
called *Ni ho kha wa ne ey ja*, "where the black water goes over the
rocks."[2] The river received its name because of the dark color given to
the water by the tannin resulting from decaying vegetation.

Miscauno Creek

Miscauno Creek is a tributary of the Menominee River in
Beecher Township of Marinette County. A widening of the creek halfway from its source is called Miscauno Pond. At its mouth a large island
is called Miscauno. These places are in former Menominee territory, but
their names are approximate to the Ojibwa and Ottawa term for "red,"
given in its inanimate form by Andrew J. Blackbird as *miskwa*.[3] Baraga's
term is the same, but he also lists *miskonigade* for "it is red, painted
red." Miscauno could be the residue of that term.[4]

Waubee/Waupee

Waubee Lake and Waupee Creek and Lake in Oconto
County have the same name; the spelling variation has no significance.

This is a prefix meaning "white" which, in some Algonquian languages, is attached to the names of white objects, such as, in Ojibwa, swan (*wabisi*), white duck (*wabini nishib*), and white feather (*wabigwan*).[5] However, Waubee and Waupee in Wisconsin may be from a personal name.

Whitewater

Whitewater, in Walworth County, is a name translated from an Algonquian language (*wabi'skĭŭ nipe'ŭ*). Gov. James Duane Doty was quoted as saying that it was the Menominee name, meaning "white water." Solomon Juneau is reported to have said: "The river Whitewater is called by the united tribes of Chippewa, Ottawa and Pottawattamies, Wau-be-gan-nau-po-cat, meaning *rily, whitish water*, caused by white soft clay, in some parts of it."[6]

Yellow Lake and River

Yellow Lake in Burnett County has its name from Ojibwa *Ossawa gami*. The lake name was also transferred to the river flowing from it to the St. Croix, and to the village of Yellow Lake. On Nicollet's map of 1836–37, he gave the native name of Yellow River as *Wassawa Gomig* (actually, "Yellow Lake"). On his 1843 map he showed "Wassawa or Yellow L. & R."[7]

Necedah

Another Yellow River joins Castle Rock Flowage, an artificial lake in the Wisconsin River in Juneau County. Its name is from Yellow Lake, the Winnebago name of which is preserved in the name of Necedah on a bluff, lake, village, town, and wildlife refuge in Juneau County. The name Necedah is formed from the Winnebago words *Ne-* ("water"), plus *ce* or *zee* ("yellow"), and *day-ra* ("lake").[8]

Location and Direction

Names referring to location, character, or direction of a place are an interesting and little-known class of Indian names. Whether a place was far or near, high or low, to the right or left; whether a lake was long or short, shallow or deep; whether a river was crooked or straight; whether land was marshy, sandy, wooded, grassy, or rocky—all were matters which affected the ease of travel from one place to another.

Eska Lake in Taylor County has a name from Ojibwa *ishkwa*, "end, last in a row." It is the third in a row that begins with Lake Eleven and Richter Lake in Grover Township. This name closely resembles that of Esquagama Lake in Aitkin County, Minnesota, which is also the "last lake" in a row of three.[9]

Nemadji River flows from Carlton County, Minnesota, into Douglas County, Wisconsin, and enters Lake Superior at the city of Superior. When one enters the harbor from Lake Superior, between Wisconsin and Minnesota Points, Nemadji River is to the left, and St. Louis River is about five miles to the right. Because of its position in relation to St. Louis River, Nemadji River received its name, meaning "left hand," from the Ojibwa Indians. J. N. Nicollet on his map of 1843 recorded the river name in French, "Riv. a gauche."[10]

Okauchee Lake in Waukesha County has its name from Ojibwa *okitchi*, meaning "the right side of something."[11] The name was apparently given because the lake is to the right of Lac La Belle, if one looks north. Skinner's derivation from Potawatomi *okatci*, "something small," is neither precise nor fitting, since the lake is one of the largest in the area, covering more than 1,100 acres.[12] From Okauchee Lake the name Okauchee was given to a village.

Packwaukee is the name of an island in the Fox river and of a village and town in Marquette County. The name appears to be a combination formed from Ojibwa *bâgwa*, "shallow," plus *aki*, "land," or in Potawatomi, *Päkwa'we*, "it is shallow." However, Father Verwyst held it to be from Ojibwa *bagwaki*, "forest opening."[13]

The names of **Pacwawong Lake** and Pacwawong Spring in Sawyer County are apparently derived from Ojibwa *bâgwa*, "shallow," + *ong*, "place." The name of **Pocquayahwan** Lake in Douglas County is probably explained in this passage from the journal of J. N. Nicollet, August 9, 1837: "The geographic language of the Chippewa is richer than ours. Places where there are islands covered with bushes and trees dividing up the savanna and places where a river resembles a lake are called by them packwayanwan." *Pakway*, in Nicollet's account, is probably from Ojibwa *bagwa*, "shallow," and *anwan* signifies "it is."[14]

Pensaukee is the descriptive name of several features in Oconto and Shawano counties. The name probably originated on the Pensaukee River, which flows from Shawano County to join Green Bay at the village of Pensaukee in Oconto County. In the view of Father Verwyst, the name was from Ojibwa *pindsagi*, "inside the mouth of a river." [15] From the river and village the name was extended to the town of Pensaukee, Pensaukee Shoal, and Pensaukee State Hunting Grounds in Oconto County. Pensaukee Lake in Shawano County is the source of the North Branch of Pensaukee River, which joins the main stream in Oconto County.

Shapes

Lake names used by Indians commonly describe their shape. Father Baraga described *bakegama* as the "separation of a lake, where a lake is divided in two branches by a projecting point."[16] On the map, this name is usually **Pokegama** (the interchangeability of *b* and *p* is of no significance), and in this form is on numerous places in northern Wisconsin. Pokegama and Little Pokegama Rivers join St. Louis River at Superior in Douglas County. The larger river, approaching its outlet, widens into Pokegama Bay. In the city of Superior is Pokegama Park. Lakes named Pokegama are in Barron, Burnett, Sawyer, Vilas, and Washburn counties. Barron County has Pokegama Creek, which empties into Mud Lake, which in turn is connected to Pokegama Lake in Chetek Township.

Another name descriptive of shape which was used by the Ojibwa in Wisconsin and Minnesota is *Sissabagama*, sometimes spelled *Shishebagama* or *Shishebogama*. It is defined as a "lake with arms running in all directions" or "every-which-way lake."[17] On the line of Oneida and Vilas counties is **Shishebogama** Lake, having a shape which makes its name fitting. In Sawyer County are Sissabagama and Little Sissabagama lakes. The larger lake is connected to Sand Lake by Sissabagama Creek.

Kenong Go Mong Lake in Racine County, according to a report by Racine County surveyor John Nelson, is believed to be named for an Indian who died on the lake at the age of 107. Another individual believed that the name was "Indian for sunfish." There is no record of the aged Indian, and this name does not mean "sunfish" in any local language.

Very likely this is a Potawatomi name, meaning "at the long lake." The name resembles Kenogami, the name of two lakes in the Timiskaming district of Ontario, which signifies "long lake," and Kenogaming, a lake in the Sudbury district, the name of which, signifies "at the long lake" in Ojibwa. A lake in Minnesota, source of the Crow Wing River, was mentioned by Schoolcraft in 1832 under the Ojibwa name "Kaginogumaug or Long Water." Another possibility is that the name derives from Kenago-gaming, "at the eel (long fish) lake."[18]

Other Descriptive Names

The village and town of **Aniwa** and Lake Aniwa are in Shawano County. In Ojibwa, according to Verwyst, "*aniwa* refers, as a prefix, to superiority, e.g., *aniwagabawi*, he is taller than the rest, *aniwakkiso aw mitig*, that tree is taller than the rest."[19] Father Baraga's dictionary lists *Aniwia* (*nind*), "I precede him, I surpass him, beat him." The location of the name Aniwa, however, suggests Menominee origin. In that language the word *ani·w* indicates "more, farther, beyond, too far." Thus it also indicates superiority, as the Ojibwa term does.[20]

The name of **Kawaguesaga** Lake in Oneida County is perhaps related to *Kau-wau-ka-mig Sah-kie-gan*, as written by John Tanner for a lake in Canada, and defined by him, from Ojibwa, as "Clear water lake." The name of Kawagami Lake, in Ontario, is defined as "Clear Lake" by J. B. Tyrrell. *Saga* is a clipped form of *sagiegan* (*Sah-kie-gun*, etc.), Ojibwa for "inland lake"; -*gami* is the term for a larger lake.[21] Another translation for the Wisconsin lake name, "Lake of many bays," has no support in Ojibwa language sources.[22]

The name of Wisconsin's largest city, **Milwaukee,** is not difficult to explain, yet there are a number of conflicting claims made concerning it. The letter *l* in Milwaukee may be a survival from the seventeenth-century Miami form of the name, since the *l* sound is absent from other Wisconsin native languages. Two forms of the name appear in a treaty with the Menominee signed at Washington on February 8, 1831. It refers to the "Milwaukee or Manawauky River." The latter name, though spelled in slightly variant ways in old documents, means "good land" in Ojibwa, Potawatomi, and Menominee. Father Baraga explained it from "*mino*, good, and *aki*, or *akki*, earth, land, the fine land." The same interpretation is given by the scholar of Potawatomi, Prof. Charles Hockett.[23]

B. F. H. Witherell said the Menominee name was *Me-ne-aw'kee*, "rich or beautiful land," but Augustin Grignon associated it with *man-wau*, "an aromatic root."[24] Among the unlikely explanations of this beautiful name are "great council place," "a promontory," "a suckhole," and "fire water."[25] Places with identical or similar meanings besides those mentioned below are Minaki, in Manitoba, and Lake Maniwaki, Minnesota.

In Wisconsin the name Milwaukee is also given to the Milwaukee River, Milwaukee County, and the suburbs of West Milwaukee and South Milwaukee. Elsewhere, places named for Milwaukee include a village in Lackawanna County, Pennsylvania; a town in Northampton County, North Carolina; a creek in St. Clair County, Michigan; Milwaukee Lake in Marquette County, Michigan; Milwaukee Lake in Lake County, South Dakota, named by settlers from Milwaukee, Wisconsin; and the town of Milwaukie, Clackamas County, Oregon, named in 1847.[26]

Minong might be another variation of an Ojibwa name for "good place," but it has also been interpreted as "blueberry place," and is treated here with other floral names in Chapter 13. Minong is the name of a village and town in Washburn County, and in the seventeenth century it was applied to Isle Royale in Lake Superior.

Minonk Lake in Vilas County has the same name as a village in Woodford County, Illinois. The same name appears on Thevenot's map of 1681 as that of a village or region near the Arkansas River. Since the name appears to be Algonquian, it is out of place there.

Minonk is closely related to Minong, Minooka, and Milwaukee, so far as its meaning is concerned. The most likely definition is from Ojibwa, "a good place."[27]

Minooka Parkway Estates and Minooka Park Beach in Waukesha County have a name which is not native to Wisconsin. Minooka is a village name in Grundy County, Illinois, but it probably originated from a village named Minooka near Scranton in Lackawanna County, Pennsylvania. One writer interpreted the name as Delaware, composed of *mino*, "good," and *aki*, "land." Another interprets the name as meaning "good land" but adds "it does not belong in the region."[28]

In the Brinton-Anthony Lenape dictionary, "fine land" or "good land" is *Wulamike*, and "earth" or "ground" is *haki*.[29] The name is more closely matched by the Ottawa *Me-no au-ky*, "good land,"[30] but an Ottawa name would be out of place in Pennsylvania. Minooka is an Algonquian name and quite clearly means "good land," but its place of origin remains in doubt.

The name of **Nadjack** Lake in Marinette County is perhaps a variation of the name of Nagak Lake is Oceana County, Michigan. That in turn could be a contraction from Ojibwa *nagikiwad*, "it is nothing, it is worth nothing."[31] This, however, is only a guess, as no confirming data are available.

Nagawicka Lake in Delafield Township, Waukesha County, has its name from Ojibwa *negawicka*, "there is sand." Others simply interpret it as "sandy."[32]

Lake **Napowan** in Waushara County apparently is named from the Ojibwa term *nibiwan*, meaning "it is wet, damp." Perhaps swampy surroundings inspired the name.[33] The name also approximates *nibâwin*, "sleeping, sleep," but this seems to be an unlikely name for a lake.

Negani Lake in Iron County has its name from Ojibwa *Nigani*, meaning "foremost, in the lead." The identical meaning is given to the name of the city of Negaunee, Michigan.[34]

The village and town of **Neshkoro** in Marquette County have their name from the Winnebago words meaning "salt river." *Nee-skoo* (or *nee-skoe*) signifies "salt"; the terminal *ro* is an abbreviation and alteration of *nee-shanak-ra*, "river."[35]

Neshota River flows out of Brown County into Manitowoc County, where it is also called West Twin River. At the city of Two Rivers, it meets its sister stream, East Twin River, just before the united river enters Lake Michigan. The site of the city of Two Rivers was called Neshota, or Nashotah, by all the Indian tribes of the region. Also derived from the river name are the names of Neshota County Park in Brown County, Neshotah Park in Manitowoc County, the village of **Shoto** on West Twin River, and Shoto Lake in Manitowoc County. Although the name is variously spelled by different authors, all agree that it signifies "twin." It has been given as *Nijode* in Ojibwa, *Nisho-ta* and *Nĭchôtê* in Potawatomi, and *nisiwan* ("two") in Menominee.[36] In Waukesha County this name appears again, on Upper and Lower Nashotah Lakes and the adjacent village of Nashotah.

In 1823, Major Stephen H. Long's party stopped at a "small stream, designated by the name of Pektannons, a diminutive of Pektannon, a neighboring stream. . . ." It was probably the east branch of what is now called the **Pecatonica** River. The two streams flow out of Lafayette County, join in Green County, and eventually the united stream enters the Rock River at Rockton, Illinois. According to Keating's account, the meaning of this stream name "in the Sauk language is *muddy*, and it is remarkable that the same name has been applied to the Missouri by the Sauks."[37] In view of the designation of the Missouri as Pekitanoui, etc., by Hennepin, Marquette, and Marest, which was translated as "muddy water" by the latter, it is reasonable to suppose that Pecatonica is a variation of that name. S. A. Mitchell's map of 1836 shows "Pektanon or Muddy R."[38]

Big and Little **Quinnesec** Falls on the Menominee River between Marinette County, Wisconsin, and Dickinson County, Michigan, are said to receive their names, allegedly referring to smoke or fog, from the spray caused by the falls. Father Gagnieur considered this name, in Ojibwa, a "contraction of Rakwannesec, a place of smoke or fog," and others have accepted that view.[39]

However, there is no *r* sound in Ojibwa or the other Algonquian languages of Wisconsin. In Ojibwa, *pakwene* or *pashkine* means "there is smoke"; *awân* means "it is foggy." These forms cannot be reconciled with the *q* in Quinnesec. The letter *q* does not appear at all in Baraga's dictionary, the letter *k* being substituted.[40] It appears more likely that *Quinnes* comes from *Kiwanis*, "noise," to which is added *ec*, for *aki*, "place, ground," or *aka*, "where." A credible translation of Quinnesec would be "where it is noisy."[41]

Kiwanis Park in Waupaca County is named for the well-known civic organization, the name of which, in Ojibwa, means "noise" or "noisy."

The name of **Sasacat** Creek and Lake in Langlade County is apparently taken from Ojibwa *sasaga* (plural *sesagag*), which is defined by Baraga as "it is full of brushwood (a place in the woods)."[42]

Some time before 1839, a place on the Wisconsin River in Marathon County was called Big Bull Falls for a cataract in the river. One W. D. McIndoe proposed the adoption of the Ojibwa name **Wausau** for the settlement which grew up there.[43] Bishop Baraga, who spelled the word *wâssa,* defined it as "far, afar off, a great way off, distant."[44]

The Menominee name for this place is identical to the Ojibwa. Hoffman reported the Menominee story about it: ". . . an Ojibwa was at one time walking by a hunter's cabin in the direction of the place where this town has since been built, and as the hunter asked the Indian where he was going, he replied, 'wâ'sâ, wâ'sâ,—far, far,' meaning to a great distance."[45]

More probably the place was named for the far-off view from nearby Rib Mountain (elevation 1,940 feet) or simply for its pleasing sound. There was an Ojibwa chief named Wassau who signed a treaty at Saginaw, Michigan, September 19, 1820, but there is no evidence that this place was named for him.[46]

The name Wausau is also on the town and on Lake Wausau, a wide place in the Wisconsin River at Wausau. Wausau in Washington County, Florida, was named by a settler from Wisconsin.[47]

Wausaukee River, lake, village, and town, in addition to Little Wausaukee Creek, in Marinette County apparently have their name from *wassa-aki,* which means "far-away land" in Ojibwa and Potawatomi.[48]

The name of Lake **Winneconne** and the village and town of Winneconne in Winnebago County is of disputed meaning. Bloomfield relates the name to human skulls.[49] Skinner matched this name with *winikani,* his spelling of the Menominee word for "skull." He added that the place was "named because of the large number of bleached human skulls and bones said by the Menomini to have been scattered about on the field of a battle, perhaps one of the battles between the Sauk and French."[50]

Father Verwyst interpreted the name as signifying "a dirty place," from Ojibwa *winikaning,* and related it to the flats around Winneconne.[51] M. J. Smith of Omro, Wisconsin, provided the following information:

> Miss Daisy E. Rogers, now deceased, had this to say about the naming and meaning of Winneconne in the foreword to her "Winneconne," the history published in 1949, 100 years after it was first laid out as "Winnekona":
> "This is Winnekaning, Ojibwa for the land of dirty water; Winnekaning for Wauna ko-big, chief of the Menomini: land

of skull and bones: feasting place, from ween (marrow) and kaning (Deer bones)."

Miss Rogers noted later that in the late 1870's a Milwaukee daily used the spelling "Winneconne." Just when it was changed to the present spelling she did not note.[52]

12

Names from Fauna

Some of the savages derive their origin from a bear,
others from a moose, and others similarly from other
kinds of animals. . . . You will hear them say that their
villages each bear the name of the animal which has
given its people their being—as that of the crane, or the
bear, or of other animals.

> Nicholas Perrot, "Memoirs on the Manners,
> Customs and Religions of the Savages of North
> America" (1721)

Mammals

Before white demand for beaver skins changed the hunting practices of Indians of the Great Lakes region, wrote Charlevoix,
"the bear held the first rank with them."[1] One measure of the bear's importance is the abundance of places named for it.

The village of **Mukwonago** in Waukesha County is on the site of a
former Potawatomi village of this name. It has been suggested that the
name is from Ojibwa *makwanagoing*, "bear lair, or place where the bear
lies."[2] *Maw-kwa* or *maw-quaw* is Potawatomi for "bear." It is the same
in Ojibwa, though it is spelled *makwâ* by Baraga.[3] From the name of the
village of Mukwonago came the identical name of the adjacent lake,
river, park, and town. Another Mukwonago Lake is in Sawyer County.

Mukwa, "bear," is the name of a town and a state wildlife area in
Waupaca County.

Moquah is merely a spelling variation of this Ojibwa word. In Bayfield County is a village named Moquah, and in the nearby Chequamegon National Forest are Moquah Natural Area and Moquah Bar-
rens Wildlife Area. **Moquash** Lake in Ashland County may have its
name from Ojibwa *makowiass*, "bear meat."[4]

J. N. Nicollet, in his journal of August 9, 1837, mentioned "Sleeping

Bear River, also called Nibigomawin."[5] Today this stream, in Douglas County, is called **Nebagamon** Creek. The same name has been extended to Lake Nebagamon and to the village of Lake Nebagamon, also in Douglas County. Father Verwyst called this name a corruption of *nibe-gomowin*, signifying "watching for game at night in a boat."[6] Comparing these names with terms in Baraga's *Otchipwe Language*, we find *nibâwin*, "sleeping, sleep," and *nabek*, "male bear." Some combination and telescoping of these terms apparently produced Nebagamon.[7]

Piscasaw Creek rises in Walworth County and flows south to join the Kishwaukee River in Boone County, Illinois. On mid-nineteenth-century maps the name of this stream was *Pisgasaw*, *Piskasaw*, and *Pishkashaw*, among other variations.

The name appears to be badly corrupted from its original form, and we can only guess that it evolved from aboriginal names for "buffalo." The Indians in Illinois named the Fox River of the Illinois for that animal, and the word was recorded by Marquette as *pisikiou*, by DeLiette as *Pestequoy*, by Charlevoix as *Pisticoui*, by Keating as *Pishtako*, and by John Long as *Peshekey*. On Cram's map of 1839, this river is labelled Pashtic or Fox River. A survivor of these old names may be seen in the name of Pistakee Lake, a wide place in Fox River in Lake and McHenry counties, Illinois. A Potawatomi chief who signed treaties in 1832 and 1833 was named Pesheka, "Buffalo." It is conceivable that someone confused the creek with Fox River under its old name, and wrote the name in its present twisted form. Other guesses are possible, but data are lacking.[8]

In the fur-trapping days, no animal was more eagerly sought than the beaver. As long as European demand for beaver hats continued alongside the Indian desire to trade for the white man's goods, the pressure on the beaver continued. As the animal became scarce, Indians fought each other for the hunting and trapping grounds and were more caught up in an alien economy.

The former importance of the beaver is indicated by the presence of the animal's image on the logo of the Hudson's Bay Company and on some Canadian coins, and by its name on the map. Lewis H. Morgan, the nineteenth-century ethnologist, devoted a book to this animal.[9]

The number of places named for the beaver may not seem large in view of its former importance, but the names are found wherever the animal was abundant. **Ahmeek** Lake in Bayfield County, Amik Lake in Price and Vilas counties, and Amik Island in Douglas County all have the Ojibwa name for "beaver" in variant spellings.[10]

The name of **Amicoy** or Amacoy Lake (local spelling) in Rusk County is perhaps related to *amikwaj*, "hole of a beaver," *amikwons*, "young beaver," or *amikogan*, "beaver's bone."[11]

A cluster of names in and about Waukesha County apparently have their names from the Ojibwa or Potawatomi name for "beaver dam"— *okonimawag*. This includes the city and town of **Oconomowoc**, Oconomowoc Lake and a village of the same name, as well as Upper Oconomowoc Lake. Moreover we have Oconomowoc River in Waukesha and Jefferson counties and Little Oconomowoc River in Waukesha and Washington counties. Father Verwyst, who offered the above version of the origin of Oconomowoc, believed that there were several beaver dams in that neighborhood.[12]

One of Wisconsin's most picturesque names is **Beaver Dam**, given to a city and a town in Dodge County, situated on Beaver Dam Lake, which is fed by Beaver Dam River and Beaver Creek. Indian origin of these names is indicated by Cram's map of 1839, which shows what is now Beaver Dam River as Ahmic River. Verwyst (1916) has *Okwanim*, "beaver dam," for this place.[13]

Carcajou, an unincorporated locality in Jefferson County, is named for the wolverine, an animal no longer found in Wisconsin. According to Chamberlain, carcajou is a corruption of the French form of the Cree word *kitwâ'kas*. Both the animal and places named for it are better known in Canada. Schoolcraft reported that "the Chippewa Indians called the wolverine 'Gween-guh-auga,' which means underground drummer. This animal is a great digger or burrower." Bishop Baraga's Ojibwa name for the wolverine was *swingwaage*.[14]

Chickaree is an uncommon place name. Its only occurrences found by this writer are on lakes in Colorado and in Vilas County, Wisconsin. It is called an "imitative" name for the red squirrel by Mathews, who does not indicate its origin.[15] "Chickaree" was used but not explained by Henry David Thoreau.[16] Friederici identified *chickaree* as an Algonquian word but did not name the specific language.[17] It is not found in the vocabularies of Wisconsin Indians.

The Ojibwa word for "squirrel" is *atchitamo*, which is composed of *atchit,* "head first," and *-amo,* "mouth," from its habit of descending trees head first.[18] In the *Hiawatha* glossary, *Adjidaumo* is defined as "red squirrel." The spelling difference is insignificant. Longfellow has Hiawatha speak to the squirrel: "Boys shall call you Adjidaumo / Tail-in-the-air the boys shall call you!"[19] The Ojibwa name for "squirrel" is slightly abbreviated in **Chittamo,** the name of a Soo Line railway station in Washburn County.

Related to the foregoing is "chipmunk," for the little ground squirrel, of which several species are found. Chamberlain wrote of it:

> There can be no doubt of the Indian origin of this name of the striped ground squirrel (*Sciurus striatum*), of which many variants, *chipmonk, chipmunk,* etc., occur. It is derived from *atchitamo,* the word for "squirrel" in Ojibwa and some closely related dialects. . . . Long, in his vocabulary published in 1791, gives the Chippeway (Ojibwa) word for squirrel as *chetamon,* and by the middle of the present century [nineteenth], the word was current in the English of Canada in the form *chit-munk,* which clinches the etymology.[20]

Chipmunk in Wisconsin is on the map in Chipmunk Coulee and South Chipmunk Coulee in Vernon County, North Chipmunk Coulee in Vernon and La Crosse counties, Chipmunk Ridge in Vernon County, Chipmunk Rapids in Pine River, Florence County, and Chipmunk Rapids in the North Branch of Pike River, Marinette County.

Lake **Koshkonong** is a wide place in Rock River in Rock and Jefferson counties. It has a tributary creek with the same name, and east of it is the town of Koshkonong in Jefferson County. No less than half a dozen explanations of the meaning of this name are recorded. Perhaps the earliest is by Lewis Beck, who in 1823 mentioned a Winnebago village on Rock River as "Coscoenage (or republic)." That name is not in Winnebago vocabularies and, if at all genuine, must be Algonquian. There is no word for "republic" in any language of that region. Juliette Kinzie, wife of John H. Kinzie, the Winnebago agent at Fort Winnebago, saw this lake in 1831 and wrote that its name meant "the lake we live on." In Black Hawk's autobiography, recorded by the French-Potawatomi Antoine LeClaire, this place is called *Goosh-we-hawn,* with no explanation.[21]

A unique and unlikely explanation of this name was reported by Isaac T. Smith in his journal of 1835–36:

> Thiebeau, the old French trader, an early French trader at Beloit, told me that the name Koshkonong was of Winnebago derivation, and means "the place where we shave" as when he and another trader first came into the country, they left their razors at the lake, and would travel around among the Indians trading for furs; but when they wanted to shave, they returned to their headquarters at the lake. The Pottawattamies had a village on the east side, and their named signified "the lake we live on."[22]

Cram's map of 1839 shows this lake as Koskonong and spells the name of the creek the same way. Father Verwyst in 1892 thought the name was from Ojibwa *gwaskwaning*, "jumping," but there is nothing in the character of the lake to fit such a meaning.[23]

The most recent effort to explain this name is that of Prof. Frederic Cassidy, a notable language scholar, who concluded that it is a contraction from one of the Algonquian languages of the region, probably of the Ojibwa term *kackäwanung*, signifying "where there is a heavy fog" or "where it is closed by fog."[24] However, terms for "fog" in the local languages don't match well with Koshkonong: Ojibwa *awân* or Potawatomi *winisiwan*.[25] Moreover, this lake is no more prone to fogginess than hundreds of others in Wisconsin, yet no other has such a name.

Dr. Cassidy correctly warns against etymologizing words "as if they might change their forms at any time without making much difference in the meaning."[26] Unfortunately, Indian names on the map are often corrupted and do not match well with vocabulary or dictionary entries of any local Indian language, whereupon the author is forced to seek the nearest agreement that can be found and also search records and maps for clues as to the meaning as understood by early observers. Dr. Cassidy's terms, as indicated, do not correspond well with the linguistic sources, and other data are scarce or contradictory.

There is a word in Potawatomi and Ojibwa which corresponds more closely to this name than any other. It is *kokosh* or *cocosh*, signifying "hog."[27] The terminal *ong* is merely a suffix denoting "place." If we accept this as the origin of the lake name, we have to presume that it once had an initial *ko*, which was transposed to the middle of the word, and that the name would have originally meant "hog place." This explanation, "hog place," was in fact given in an anonymous documentary source listed but rejected by Dr. Cassidy. The pioneers were not bound by the rules that etymologists must obey. It seems that this explanation does less violence to the structure of the word than any other, and we know that such transpositions of syllables are commonly made.

Words for "hog" are found in Indian place names in other states, and some Indians adopted the animals from whites. In 1781 General Proctor, travelling along the Allegheny River in western Pennsylvania, wrote that "we arrived this morning at an old Indian settlement called Hog's town." That place, abandoned twenty years earlier, was called Goshgoshing, "place of hogs," by the Delawares. Several villages of Delaware and Seneca Indians near the site of present Newcastle, Pennsylvania, were known collectively as "The Kuskuskies." This name was written as Goschgoshing or Goshgoschunk by the German speaking Moravian missionaries and likewise signified "place of hogs."[28]

These names have not survived in original form, but variants are preserved. One is Kokosing River, Knox County, Ohio, in former Seneca territory. It is a close cognate of the Ojibwa and Menominee term for "hog," *kokosh*, and its usual rendering in Potawatomi, *cocoosh*. Cocoosh Prairie in Branch County, Michigan, has a name which is pure Potawatomi for "hog." Hog Creek and Hog Creek Lake in adjacent St. Joseph County may have some connection with it.[29]

But why would Indians name a place for the white man's hog? Some Indians adopted the hog, but there is no evidence that this was done in Wisconsin. Some Indians, for example, the Cherokee, applied to the hog the term they already had for the opossum. But this did not happen in Wisconsin. One possible clue to the use of this name in this place is the presence of numerous effigy mounds about Lake Koshkonong, some of which represented unidentified animals, which may have been likened to hogs.

The moose is no longer found in Wisconsin, but places named for it in the state are a measure of its former range. The name **Moose** occurs on the map of six Canadian provinces and sixteen American states, including some in which the animal has never been seen in the historic period except in captivity. A few of these names may be the result of confusing this animal with the elk. Alexander Henry exhibited this tendency, also mentioned by Carver, when he wrote: "The Indians . . . killed two elks, otherwise called *moose-deer.*"[30]

"The Moose," wrote Jonathan Carver in 1768, "has feet and legs like a camel, its upper lip much larger than the under, and the nostrils of it are so wide that a man might thrust his hand into them a considerable way. . . . Most authors confound it with the elk, deer, or carrabou, but it is a species totally different."[31]

This largest member of the deer family received its name from the New England Algonquians, "a name given to the animal," wrote Trumbull, "from his habit of stripping the lower branches and bark from trees when feeding; *moss-u,* 'he trims' or 'cuts smooth,' 'he shaves'."[32] The Ojibwa word for "moose," *mons,* is not seen in Wisconsin,[33] although the Ojibwa had a moose phratry and used the animal's name in personal names.[34]

The name Moose is most often seen in the names of lakes and rivers, probably because the animal is frequently seen wading in water as it browses on aquatic plants. The name was attached to some features because of their fancied resemblance in shape to the moose or its antlers, and in others because a moose was shot at those places.

With one exception, moose place names in Wisconsin are in the northern part of the state. Only one of these names, Moose Junction in Douglas County, refers to a populated place. There are Moose Lakes in Bayfield, Douglas, Iron, Langlade, Marinette, Sawyer, and Waukesha counties. Bull Moose Lake is in Rusk County, and Iron County has Little Moose Lake. Moose Park is in Sheboygan County, and Moose Springs is in Langlade County. There are two Moose Rivers, one in Sawyer and Ashland counties, the other in Douglas County. Sawyer County has Little Moose River. Iron County has Moose Creek, Moose Ear Creek is in Barron and Rusk counties, and Moose Ear Lake is in Barron County.

Indian names for "rabbit" were given to several Wisconsin places. There is very little difference in the form of this name among the Ojibwa, Potawatomi, and Menominee tribes. **Wapoose** Lake and Little Wapoose Lake in Forest County probably received their names from the Menominee. *Wapus* Ridge on the Menominee reservation is the same

Dan Waupoose, Menominee chief, 1943. The names of Wapoose Lake and Little
Wapoose Lake in Forest County and Wapus Ridge on the Menominee Reservation are
spelling variations of waupoose, meaning "rabbit." It is not clear whether these places
are named for the animal, or for members of the Waupoose family. Photo by the U.S.
Navy, Algiers, Louisiana, 1943. Courtesy of the National Archives.

name in variant spelling. There was once a Menominee chief bearing
this name, but it is uncertain whether any place was named for him.[35]

The Ojibwa word for "rabbit" is given as *wâbos* by Bishop Baraga.[36] A
town in Ontario has the name in this form. **Waboo** Creek in Ashland
County could be named from a slight corruption of this Ojibwa word. So
also is Wabasso, the name of the white rabbit in the *Hiawatha* story. In
that form it is the name of a lake in Flambeau Township, Vilas County.

Perhaps no wild animal is as widely distributed in North America as
the raccoon, which occurs in southern Canada and in every state of the
continental United States, excluding Alaska. Like many animals of

North America, this nocturnal roamer was first described in Virginia, where John Smith wrote: "There is a beaste they call *Aroughcun,* much like a badger, but useth to live on trees as squirrels doe." In William Strachey's Powhatan vocabulary the animal was variously called *racone, arrathcune,* and *Arathkone,* "a beast like a fox." The meaning of the name is "hand scratcher."[37]

Most raccoon place names are along water courses, which may be because of the animal's preference for foraging on the banks of streams and lakes. Places named raccoon, or coon in its abbreviated from, are numerous in Wisconsin, but only a few places bear the animal's name in the languages of Wisconsin tribes. These are **Ashippun** Lake in Waukesha County, the village and town of Ashippun in Dodge County, Old Ashippun in Dodge County, and the Ashippun River in Waukesha and Jefferson counties. This name could be from either Potawatomi *ä'shpûn* or Menominee *ä'sepan.*[38]

In Wisconsin the name is found in its conventional spelling only on **Raccoon** Creek in Rock County. However, at least twenty-three map features are called Coon. These include Coon Bluff in Sauk County; Coon Branch in Lafayette County; Coon Creeks in Dunn, Dunn–Eau Claire, and La Crosse counties; Coon Fork Creek and Lake, as well as Coon Fork Park in Eau Claire County; Coon Gut Creek in Eau Claire County; two Coon lakes in Menominee County, besides others in Oneida, Polk, and Rusk counties; Coon Prairie in Vernon County; Coon Rock (a locality) in Iowa County; Coon Rock (a pillar) in Juneau County; Coon Rock Cave in Iowa County; Coon Slough in Vernon County; and Coon Valley, a feature in Grant County and a village in Vernon County.

The skunk, wrote Jonathan Carver, when in danger would eject from behind a stream of water having an odor so powerful "that the air is tainted with it for half a mile in circumference." For that reason, he explained, the French called the animal *Enfant du Diable,* "Child of the Devil," or *Bête Puant,* "Stinking Beast." The English sometimes called it a polecat, after an Old World animal of a different character, but the native word "skunk" soon prevailed. John Josselyn wrote *squnck,* probably from the Massachuset language or dialect, although some have supposed it to be an early evolution from Abnaki *seganku.* The radical is said to signify "urinator."[39]

The Ojibwa called the beast *she-gagh* or *jikâg*, the Cree *sikak*, the Menominee *shikak*, and the Foxes *cecacqua*. Some of these forms have influenced place names.[40] By both Indians and whites the word "skunk" was attached to things with repulsive odors; for example, whites gave the name skunk cabbage to *Symplocarpus foetidus*, and Indians gave their name for skunk to wild garlic (*Allium canadense* L.).[41] This fact has caused disputes about the origin of such place names as Chicago.

Generally, **Skunk** is not a popular place name; but Wisconsin is an exception. Perhaps because of the fact that the animal is numerous here. At least fifteen place names include Skunk. There are Skunk Creeks in Langlade-Lincoln, Oneida, Rusk (two), and Wood counties. Skunk Lakes are in Forest, Oneida, Portage, Washburn, and Waupaca counties. Racine County has Skunk Grove, and Skunk Hollows are found in Green Lake, Pepin, Trempealeau, and Vernon counties.

The Ojibwa term for "skunk" is seen in **Chicog,** the name of a lake, town, and two creeks (Chicog and Little Chicog) in Washburn County. Chicag or Chicog was the name of an obscure Ojibwa chief,[42] but there is no proof that these places were named for him. It is uncertain whether Chicago Creek in Bayfield County is named for wild garlic or onions, for the skunk, or for the city of Chicago, Illinois. The village of Little Chicago, in Marathon County, is undoubtedly named for the windy city which drew its name, according to Joutel's account of 1687, from wild garlic growing there.[43] Several Wisconsin places are apparently named for the city of Chicago. (See Chapter 13, "Names from Flora.")

At present there is no populated place in Wisconsin that bears an Indian name for the wolf, which once roamed the state. However, the **Wolf** River, which begins in Forest County and joins Lake Poygan in Outagamie County, has its name in translation from the Menominee name. Skinner wrote it as *Muhwä' o Sepe'u*, "Wolf River"; Hoffman rendered it as *Maqwäi' o oshi' piomĕ*, "wolf, his river."[44] The Wolf River is the major waterway running through the Menominee reservation.

Another place name is connected to the wolf. The name of the village and town of **Wonewoc,** in Juneau County, is explained by Verwyst as a derivation from Ojibwa *wonowag*, pronounced *wo-no-waug*, signifying "they howl, e.g., wolves." Baraga has *wonawin, wawonomin*, "howling," as the last entry in his *Otchipwe Language*. The *Hiawatha* vocabulary lists *Wahono'win* as "a cry of lamentation." However, in Ojibwa "wolf" is *maingan*.[45]

Birds

Unlike other animal names, very few aboriginal bird names have been adopted into English. However, a number of native names of birds survive as place names.

Ondaig Island in St. Louis River, Douglas County, probably has its name from the Ojibwa word for "crow," given as *andek* by Baraga and *ondaig* by Haines.[46]

Lake **Wingra,** smallest of the Four Lakes at Madison, Dane County, apparently has its name from the Winnebago word for "duck." Charles Brown stated that the name was in use in 1837 and appeared on maps as Lake Weengra in 1844 and 1848.[47] Professor Cassidy found that the name was already on maps in 1839, on one as Weengra Lake and on another as Wingra. Cassidy's Winnebago word for it is *wiçra*. In Jipson's Winnebago vocabulary, the word for "duck" is given as *winx*. Cassidy says the lake was once a great resort for ducks.[48]

It seems certain that **Kenu** Lake in Vilas County has its name from a variant spelling of Ojibwa *kiniw*, which Baraga explained as "War-eagle; a kind of eagle that remains almost every day very high in the air. The Indian warriors wear his feathers as an ornament on their heads. These feathers are rare, and not easy to be obtained."[49]

An ordinary eagle is called *megisi* in Ojibwa. **Eagle** River, which joins the Wisconsin River at the city of Eagle River, seat of Vilas County, was called Migisiwisibi by the Ojibwa.[50]

The name of **Nekuk** Island in St. Louis River, Douglas County, from its surface appearance, could be considered as a variation of *nikag*, the Ojibwa plural for "wild geese." An alternative, from *nigi*, "Otter," is possible, but the former is a closer match.[51]

Puchyan River and Lake in Green Lake County probably derive their names from Winnebago *pai-ja*[n], "heron." A local belief is that the name means "little woods," but that interpretation is not supported by Winnebago vocabulary sources.[52]

Bena Lake in Vilas County draws its name from the Ojibwa word for "partridge," *biné*. Sometimes this name is spelled *pena*.[53]

The white pelican is found in Wisconsin, and the Ojibwa name for it is on several places, though variously spelled. **Chetac** Lake in Sawyer County, once the site of a Chippewa village which was visited by Schoolcraft in 1831, is one of them. Chetek is the name of a lake, river, city, and town in Barron County. It, too, is understood to be from the Ojibwa word for "pelican." This is the lake mentioned by Ojibwa historian William Warren as *Sha-da* ("pelican") *sagiegan* ("lake").[54]

Places named **Meeme** or Mimi are usually named for the wild pigeon or dove, from Ojibwa *omimi*. (The name could also be connected with *méme*, "woodpecker," although no one has done so.) Examples in Wisconsin are the Meeme River and the town of Meeme in Manitowoc County where the Meeme River joins the Pigeon River. Named from its tributary, the Pigeon River joins Lake Michigan on the north edge of Sheboygan. The name of Mimi Lake in Bayfield County is a mere spelling variation of Meeme.[55]

Almost all writers agree that the name **Kewaunee** means "prairie chicken," given with only slight differences in Ojibwa, Ottawa, and Potawatomi.[56] It is the name of a county on the Door peninsula and of a city, river, and town in that county. Kewaune, Kee-waw-nay, and Kee-waw-nee are variant spellings of the name of a Potawatomi chief who signed treaties on October 16, 1826, October 26, 1832, and April 22, 1836, but it is not ascertained whether these places were named for him.[57]

Father Verwyst's assertion that this name is from *Kakiweonon*, "I cross a point of land by boat," has little support. He confused Kewaunee with Sturgeon Bay to the north.[58]

Lake **Waubesa** in Dane County has the Ojibwa name for "swan," although the tribe did not live there and did not name the lake. According to Professor Cassidy, the name was chosen in 1854 by Lyman W. Draper, director of the State Historical Society of Wisconsin. Draper found *wabisi* given as the word for "swan" in an Ojibwa dictionary and changed the spelling to Waubesa. The name was apparently given to what was formerly called Second Lake because of the story that a large swan had been killed at that place.[59]

A variant spelling of this name, **Waubeesee,** has been given to a village and lake in Racine County, perhaps from the Potawatomi language, but the details are not available.

Fish and Fishing Activity

Fishing was an important activity among Wisconsin Indians, and still is in some places. Most Indian villages were located along lakes or streams not only because most travelling was done by water, but also for the availability of fish. Consequently, a number of Wisconsin water features are named for fish or for fishing activity.

In Ojibwa, the most prevalent of Wisconsin native languages, *keego* or *gigo* is the generic name for "fish."[60] **Keego** Lake in Vilas County is "Fish" Lake. The name of **Kekegama** Lake in Washburn County appears to be a corruption from *keego*, "fish," joined to *gama*, "lake."[61]

The diminutive of *keego* (or *kego*) is *kegonsa*, "little fish." Lake **Kegonsa** in Dane County was given its name in 1854 by Lyman C. Draper of the State Historical Society of Wisconsin. Today Kegonsa is also the name of a village and of the state park which adjoins the lake.[62]

Ashegon Lake in Sawyer County is named for the bass. Baraga spells this name Ashigan.[63]

Minnemac Lake (sometimes written Minemac) in Sawyer County has the Ojibwa name for "catfish." An Ojibwa who signed a treaty at Fort Industry (Toledo), Ohio, on July 4, 1805, is listed as "Monimack, or Catfish." Hodge lists "Manumaig (*Myänamäk*, catfish)" as a Chippewa gens. This name appears in various places and in several Algonquian dialects as Marameg, Maramech, Muramik, Merrimac, Winemage, Winnemac, etc. In some places, it is assigned to species other than the catfish.[64]

Yahara River in Dane and Rock counties is believed by some to receive its name from the Winnebago word for "catfish," and some people call it Catfish River, which was its name before Yahara was officially adopted in 1855. "However," says Professor Cassidy, "it is either a bad translation or the actual Winnebago word (*How-wix-ra*) has been greatly distorted in being 'simplified' for readers of English."[65] In Jipson's Winnebago-English vocabulary the word is *howix*. Frances Perry of Black River Falls says that her Winnebago friends agree with Cassidy's evaluation and she writes the word for "catfish" as Jipson did.[66]

No one can be sure today how Yahara came to be, as it cannot in this form be matched with anything we know. However, since the river was known to the early inhabitants as Catfish River, it seems likely that they learned the name from the Indians.

Cisco is a contraction of Siskawit, Siskiwit, or Siskowit (etc.), the name given to several species of fish found in the Great Lakes and their tributary waters. Among them, authors have included whitefish, lake trout, lake herring (*Coregonus artedi*), lake mooneye (*Coregonus hoyi*), and a salmon (*Salvelinus namaycush* var. *siscowet; namaycush* is a corruption of the Ojibwa name for trout). *Siscowet* (etc.) is said to be a French-Canadian contraction of the Ojibwa term *pemitewiskawet,* "that which has oily flesh." [67]

J. N. Nicollet first noted a stream named for these fish when he recorded "Shishkaweka Sibi (Fish River)" in his journal of August 11, 1837. [68] That stream is now called the **Siskiwit** River. It joins Lake Superior in Bayfield County. The name has also been given to a bay and lake in that vicinity, and to Little Sikiwit Lake, all in Bell Township. In Drummond Township of Bayfield County is Cisco Lake.

The name **Muskellunge,** sometimes in variant spelling, is more commonly used in Wisconsin place names than the name of any other fish. The name is apparently of Ojibwa or Cree origin. Alexander Henry, while at Lake Nipissing, Canada, wrote, "Among the pike, is to be included the species called, by the Indians, *masquinonge.*" [69] Bishop Baraga wrote of it: "*Maskinonge* (Otchip.), the ugly fish (Jackfish) from *mâsk,* disfigured, ugly, and *kinonge,* fish, or, it may be a kind of Jackfish who has a peculiar hump on his back." [70] Except for the uncommon sturgeon, the "muskie" is the largest freshwater fish of the Great Lakes region. Catching one is the dream of many anglers, and the hope of landing one is the lure of many resorts. This may account for the popularity of the name on water features, for the fish is not so abundant as to explain it otherwise.

Only in Quebec is this name spelled as Baraga has it. That province has a village, county, lake, and river named Maskinonge. By inserting *ll* into the word, in place of *n,* we have strayed from the correct Indian form.

There are Muskellunge Lakes in Ashland, Bayfield, Lincoln, Oneida, and Vilas counties; Oneida also has a Muscallonge Lake. Vilas County has Big Muskellunge Lake. Muskellunge Creeks are in Ashland, Grant, Lincoln, Oneida, and Vilas counties.

The common contraction, **Muskie,** is widely used in lake and stream names. There are Muskie Lakes in Iron and Oneida counties. Muskie Springs Lake is in Bayfield County. Little Muskie Lakes are in Iron, Oneida, and Vilas counties. In variant spelling, Musky, we have Musky Bay in Oneida County and two bays of that name in Sawyer County.

Pike River, a not very important stream, empties into Lake Michigan at the city of **Kenosha.** The city takes its name from the Potawatomi name for "pike." In the early 1830s, the locality was known to Indian traders as Kenosha. The first post office, established there in 1826, was named Pike. When settlers met the next year to choose a permanent name for the settlement, they chose Southport, because it was the most southerly port on Lake Michigan in Wisconsin. However, when the place was chartered as a city in 1850, the former name of Kenosha was restored. The name was also given to the county.[71]

At least two other Wisconsin names may represent a native name for "pike." One of them, though debatable, is **Oconto.** Swanton listed a Menominee village, *Oka'to wini-niwûk,* "pike place people," at the mouth of the Oconto River in Oconto County. Bloomfield's *Menominee Lexicon* lists *Okâ·w* for "pike" and *oka·qtow* as the "place name 'Oconto.'" Hoffman lists *okâ'wa* as Menominee for "pike," but derives the place name from *Okan'to,* "boat paddle."[72] Oconto is also the name of the county and town in which the city of Oconto is located, as well as the name of a creek, river, and bay. Oconto Falls is a city on the Oconto River, some twenty miles west of Oconto.

The city of **Kaukauna** is on the Fox River in Outagamie County, east of Appleton. Here the rapids of the Fox River required canoe travellers to portage. The place was first mentioned by Father Claude Allouez in 1670: "On the eighteenth we passed the portage called by the natives *Kakaling,* our sailors dragging the canoes among rapids, while I walked on the river-bank."[73] Today the rapids are eliminated by locks.

Father Allouez misunderstood the name, since the sound of *l* is absent from all Wisconsin Indian languages. Father Verwyst believed the place was originally called *Okakaning,* meaning, in Ojibwa, "pike fishing ground." Hoffman agreed on the essential meaning of the name from which Kaukauna evolved, but derived it from Menominee *ogâq'kanĕ,* "the place of pike." He said that the Indians formerly fished there for pike, "*Okâ'wa.*"[74]

Namekagon River flows from Namekagon Lake in Bayfield County, crosses Sawyer and Washburn counties, and joins the St. Croix River in Burnett County. According to Verwyst, the name means "place of sturgeons." (Cf. with Baraga's name for sturgeon, *namé*, and *Nahma*, the sturgeon in *Hiawatha*.)[75] In Bayfield County, Namekagon is also the name of a village, a town, and a recreation area.

According to Nicollet, *Namekawegon* was the Ojibwa name for a "sturgeon dam" in the St. Croix River at present Gordon, in Douglas County. It was a natural obstruction in the water.[76]

The city of Sturgeon Bay in Door County has its name in translation from the Menominee name *Noma'wiqkito* (or *wikitu*). It is on the site of a former Menominee village, the inhabitants of which were called Sturgeon Bay people.[77]

The sucker, a bottom feeder of northern lakes, regarded as a junkfish, was called *name'bin* by the Ojibwa. At times the name was also applied to the carp, a fish introduced from Europe.[78] Upper and Lower **Nemahbin** lakes in Waukesha County probably have their name from the Potawatomi, a tribe closely allied to the Ojibwa. In Schoolcraft County, Michigan, Namebinag Creek has the Ojibwa plural form of this name.[79]

Wapogasset is the name of a lake nearly three miles long lying in both Lincoln and Garfield townships of Polk County. Locally it is believed to carry the Chippewa Indian name for "sucker." The name is probably derived from *wapagessi*, which Baraga gave as the name of a "kind of large carp."[80] These two kinds of fish, as noted above, were not always distinguished from one another. According to Frank Werner of the Polk County Historical Society, early white settlers called this lake Sucker Lake. The name did not favor the easy sale of lots on the lake shore, and so the name was changed back to Wapogasset, which it remains today. The name is also attached to a tributary branch or brook.[81]

Namegosh Lake in Bayfield County has the Ojibwa name for "trout" in almost pure form. (As *namaycosh* this name appears as the specific part of the scientific name of a species of siscowet, q.v.) Baraga spells it *name'goss*. The first part of the name, *name'*, is a generic word found in the name of other fish species, including sturgeon and sucker.[82]

In Douglas County, near the city of Superior, the **Amnicon** River dashes madly over granite rocks, forming spectacular Amnicon Falls in the present Amnicon State Park, then plunges into Lake Superior at Amnicon Bay. The river has a tributary called Little Amnicon. Amnicon is also the name of the town which includes the falls. Several writers agree that this name is from the Ojibwa word *aminikon*, "spawning ground," and that it was given because fish from Lake Superior ascended this stream in order to spawn.[83]

Clam River, a tributary of the St. Croix in Burnett County, has its name in translation from the Ojibwa. J. N. Nicollet recorded it on his map of 1843 at Kayeskikan or Shell River.[84]

Reptiles

Lake Kenabee in Polk County has a name which is very probably a mistaken rendition of *Kenabec*, Ojibwa for "snake." The name may have been suggested by that of Kanabec County, Minnesota, which is named for the Ojibwa name of the Snake River, which rises there and runs to the St. Croix River. Baraga, who generally renders *k* sounds with a *g*, spelled this word *ginêbig*. Schoolcraft wrote of *Gitchy Kenabec* "or Great Serpent, of their mythological and allegorical fictions." Alexander Henry narrated: "From prayers, the Indians now proceeded to sacrifices, both alike offered to the god-rattlesnake, or manitokinibic."[85]

Chewelah Lake in Vilas County has a name which does not belong to any language of this region. The probability is that it was transferred from Washington State by some white traveller. In Stevens County, Washington, are a town, creek, and peak named Chewelah. The Indian tribe of that region was the Spokane, of the Salishan linguistic stock. According to Rev. Myron Eells, *Cha-we-lah* was their name for a small striped snake and "was applied to that place [Chewelah Creek] either because the snake abounded there or because of the serpentine appearance of the stream." There was also an Indian legend that an old chief saw a snake reaching from mountain to mountain, and so the place was named for the serpent.[86]

Mekanac Point is a cape on Pelican Lake in Oneida County. Its name is obviously a mere variation of Mackinac. It is the Ojibwa name for "turtle," which is listed by Baraga as *Makinâk* or *mikkinâk*.[87] The name in various forms is found in several states, including the famous island and strait in Michigan, as well as places in Illinois and Minnesota.

Insects

In an account of the survey of the Wisconsin and Upper Michigan boundary by Capt. T. J. Cram, a Michigan author wrote: "At times swamps would have to be traversed as well as almost impenetrable windfalls and thickets; lakes, rivers and marshes often had to be crossed, and if in mid-summer, clouds of mosquitoes, black flies and gnats (the Indians 'no-seeums') were ever present day and night to make one's existence almost intolerable."[88]

In the same time period, Henry David Thoreau's Indian guide in *The Maine Woods* called these tiny, nearly invisible insects "no-see-ems." Thoreau gave this account of the insect at Telos Lake: "Here first I was molested by the little midge called No-see-em (Simuliam nocivum, the latter word is not the Latin for no-see-em), especially over the sand at the water's edges, for it is a kind of sand-fly. You would not observe them but for their light-colored wings. They are said to get under your clothes, and produce a feverish heat, which I suppose was what I felt last night."[89]

Western Indians applied this pidgin name to buffalo gnats and it was also adopted into the language of logging camps.[90] *No-see-em* (or *no-see-um*) is not a word that appears in any Indian vocabulary or dictionary, because it is an improvisation, by Indians, from English. It does not belong to a single tribe, but its origin is an example of the adaptability of language. "No-see-um" is an invented word which apparently was adopted from the Indians by frontier whites. That entitles it to consideration here.

In Wisconsin, **No-se-um,** variously spelled, appears four times as a place name. On the Menominee Indian Reservation are Noseum Creek and Noseum Lake. In Vilas County there is a Nosseeum Lake, sometimes called Nosseum, in Phelps Township and another in Winchester Township.

Obadash Lake in Iron County is a name apparently abbreviated from Ojibwa *Obodash-Kwanishi*, "dragon-fly, mosquito eater."[91] It seems highly probable that the name of **Bobidosh** Lake (q.v.) in Vilas County is a corruption from Obadash or Obodash, although that lake is named for an individual Indian.

The melodic name of **Wauwatosa,** possessed by a city in Milwaukee County, is of disputed origin. One view is that it is named for Wau-wau-to-sa, "Great Walker," a Sauk chief who signed a treaty at Washington on October 21, 1837.[92] The name is plainly mistranslated by the clerk. Moreover, since the Sauk then lived in Iowa, and had never lived at the site of Wauwatosa, one wonders why a Sauk name would be chosen for that place, which was established in 1841. Another erroneous explanation holds that *wawato'sä* is Potawatomi for "what he works for, what he earns."[93]

Father Verwyst is doubtless correct in holding that the name of Wauwatosa is a corruption from *wawatessi*, Ojibwa for "firefly."[94] The name compares well with three other examples: *Wahwah-taysee*, the firefly in *Hiawatha; wawatessi*, "glow-worm," in Baraga's *Otchipwe Language;* and *waw-wa-tais-sa*, "lightning bug," in Tanner's captivity narrative. Moreover, the same name in slight variation, Wawatosa, is on an island in Lake Minnetonka, Hennepin County, Minnesota. It is maintained that this name, originally spelled *Wawatasso*, came from the *Hiawatha* poem, and means "little firefly."[95] The Wisconsin name is older than Longfellow's poem, but the meaning is probably the same. Near Sayner, in Vilas County is Wah Wah Tay See resort, which spells its name as in *Hiawatha*.

13

Names from Flora

The dominant character of the vegetation of a region is always an important factor in shaping the culture of that region. . . . The prevalence of certain plants often gave origin to place names.
Melvin R. Gilmore, Uses of Plants by the Indians of the Missouri River Region *(1919)*

Indians were heavily dependent upon the plant world for their subsistence. Trees furnished material for their lodges, canoes, snowshoes, dishes, cordage, and fuel. Wild plants were widely used for food, medicine, dyes, and other purposes. One plant, wild rice, was of major importance to the northern tribes and one tribe was named for it. Rushes, or stems of the common cattail, were woven into mats and used as lodge coverings. In addition, and somewhat surprisingly, cultivated plants were grown as far north as Lake Superior. Among these were not only those plants which were domesticated by Indians, including corn, beans, pumpkins, and squash, but others introduced by white men, especially potatoes.[1] One might expect that native names of plants would be prominently displayed in place names, and so they are.

Trees

The city and town of **Antigo** in Langlade County are reputedly named from the Ojibwa name of the Spring River which runs through the city. From there the name has been transferred to an island in Pelican Lake, Oneida County. Antigo is clipped from a longer name which has been written *Neequie antigo seepi, Nequi-antigo-seebah,* and *nikwi-antigo-sibi.* It has been translated as "balsam evergreen river," and "water running under evergreens." The word *antigo* alone is said to signify "evergreen." The third word, *seebi, seebah,* or *sibi,* signifies river. Baraga does not list evergreen; his terms for balsam are *pap-*

shkigiw and *nominigan.* In my view the origin and meaning of *antigo* are unsolved.[2]

Red Cedar River flows south from Red Cedar Lake in Barron county to join the Chippewa River in Dunn County. The present name is a translation of its Ojibwa name as recorded by J. N. Nicollet in 1841 when he mentioned "Mishwagokag, or Red Cedar River, which falls into the Chippeway river."[3]

The name of the hickory tree, of which the most common species is the shagbark hickory (*Carya ovata*), is adapted from a term used by the Renape (Powhatan) Indians of Virginia. According to John Smith, the name *pawcohiccora* was applied by them to a milky substance created by beating and drying the hickory nuts and mixing the powdery product with water. A. F. Chamberlain wrote: "From the cluster words *pawcohiccora*, etc., transferred by the whites from the food to the tree, has been derived *hickory.* The latter form was in use by 1682."[4]

This important hardwood is found mainly in southern Wisconsin. Its name has been given to thirteen places: **Hickory** Corners in Oconto County; Hickory Flat in Iowa County; Hickory Grove, a village and town in Grant County, and a village in Manitowoc County; Hickory Hill in Monroe and Dane counties; Hickory Hills in Calumet County; Hickory Point in Dodge and Polk counties; Hickory Ridge in Sauk and Vernon counties; and Hickory Ridge Trail in Chippewa County.

Maples were important to northern Indians as the source of sap for the manufacture of maple syrup and sugar, which was done in the month of March. Whites learned the process from the Indians,[5] and the one-time prevalence of the industry is indicated by the presence in northern Wisconsin of names such as Sugar Bush, Sugar Camp, and Eau Pleine, the French name for "maple tree." The aboriginal names for "maple" are not commonly preserved, but **Manakiki** Lake in Wood County has the Ojibwa name for "maple forest."[6] (See Chapter 8.)

Minocqua Lake and the town and village of Minocqua, all in Oneida County, appear to be named from the Ojibwa term *minakwa*, "a number of trees standing together."[7]

The white pine (*Pinus strobus*) was a mighty pillar of Wisconsin's economy in the last half of the nineteenth century. The pines that remain add much to the attractiveness of the northern woods. These trees were not of major importance to the Indians, although the sap was used in medicine and the knots for torches. Wisconsin's map, however, contains names for "pine" in at least two of the Indian languages.

On **Pine** Lake in Waukesha County is the village of **Chenequa,** which appears to have the lake's name in Ojibwa. The aboriginal name may have been given by Increase Lapham, early mapmaker and historian, who wrote in 1844: "The Indian name is Chenequa or Pine, given in consequence of a few pine trees having been found on a small neck of land or island in this lake."[8]

Near Pine Lake is Chenequa Springs. Pine Lake, together with nearby Beaver and North lakes, are called Chenequa Lakes. Another Chenequa Lake is far to the north in Bayfield County. This name, in Ojibwa, has been corrupted from its original form. Baraga's word for "pine" is *jingwak*, pronounced *shingwak*. In Vilas County, **Jingwak** Lake has the name in Baraga's orthography. The Potawatomi equivalent is *chikwak*.[9]

The other pine names in Wisconsin are from the Winnebago and refer specifically to the white pine. Lake **Wazeecha** lies in Wood County. In Crawford County in southwest Wisconsin are the village and town of Wauzeka, as well as Wauzeka Cave and Wauzeka Ridge. In Jackson County, which contains Wisconsin's largest Winnebago community, is Wazeka Trail. These names conform closely to Radin's Winnebago term for "pine," *wazika* (also given by him as *wazi;* the *ka* could represent *ska,* "white").[10] Frances Perry, scholar of the language, says Wazeka means "White pine," *ka* being a masculine referent in a personal name. Jipson's Winnebago vocabulary has *wa-zee* ("pine") and *ska* ("white").

Another variation of the Winnebago name for "pine" or "white pine" is **Waucedah,** the name of a former village in Adams County. It continues as the name of a village in Dickinson County, Michigan. It is reported to signify "large pine." In Winnebago the correct form for that would be *wa-zee-xa-tay.*[11] Possibly the name could mean "pine place" (which would be *wa-zee-a-ja* in Winnebago), as does the Minnesota town name of Wasioja, of Sioux origin.[12]

The tamarack or American larch (*Larix americana*) is a coniferous tree which grows in boggy places and is common in northern Wisconsin. Also referred to by Bartlett as Hackmatack, the name, he wrote, was "generally thought to be derived from some of the Algonkian dialects of Canada or the New England States," possibly from *ackmatuk* or *ackmestuk,* "wood for bows and arrows."[13]

Because of its eastern origin, all tamarack names in Wisconsin were placed by whites. There are at least twenty-seven of them, mostly in the northern part of the state. Only one settled place is called **Tamarack,** a village in Trempealeau County. There are nine Tamarack Lakes, three Tamarack Creeks, three Little Tamarack Creeks, two Tamarack Swamps, a Tamarack River and Upper Tamarack River (both in Douglas County), a Tamarack Valley, Tamarack Coulee, a Tamarack Creek Wildlife Area, and Little Tamarack Flowage.

Berries

The town of **Meenon** and Meenon County Park in Burnett County are named from the Ojibwa plural word *minan,* usually applied to blueberries (*Vaccinium* spp.). These are common in the north woods, ripening in early August, and are prized by both bears and humans.

Minong is the name of a lake, village, and town in Washburn County, and is generally held to signify "blueberry place" (*Min* = "whortleberry," i.e., blueberry, plus *ong,* "place"). It has also been interpreted, especially in the ancient name of Isle Royale in Lake Superior, as "good high place." Minong, Wisconsin, is not especially high. It is level, but it is blueberry country.[14]

The name of the town of **Nekimi** in Winnebago County is, like many puzzling names, a probable fragment of a longer name. Verwyst called it an Ojibwa word for "wild gooseberry," but Baraga's word for that fruit is *jabomin,* which Tanner wrote as *Sha-bo-min* (see Chebomnicon, below).[15] Clearly this name is something else. It may have been clipped from the Ojibwa or Menominee name for "high blueberry bush." Tanner gave the name of this shrub as *Ne-kim-me-nah-ga-wunje.* The terminal *ga-wunje,* attached to the names of numerous plants, is thus explained by Tanner: "The word ga-wunje, added to the name of any fruit or berry, indicates the wood or bush."[16]

Henry R. Schoolcraft, ascending the Wisconsin River on August 26, 1825, met several canoes of Menominee, and (he wrote): "They presented me a couple of dishes of a species of berry, which they called *Neekimen-een,* or Brant-berry. It is a black, tasteless berry a little larger than the whortleberry."[17]

J. N. Nicollet in his journal of August 11, 1837, recorded the name of "Mashkigi Minikani Sibi or Cranberry River." It flows into Lake Superior in Bayfield County, and is today called **Cranberry** River, in translation from its Ojibwa name.[18]

Pembine, the name of a village and town in Marinette County, has a variant spelling of the name of Pembina, a widely known settlement on the Red River of Minnesota–North Dakota in fur trading days. The present town, Pembina, North Dakota, is situated at the mouth of Pembina River about three miles south of the Canadian border.

According to Baraga the name is a reduction from Cree *nipimina,* "watery berries," i.e., high bush cranberries (*Viburnum trilobum,* or other species of *Viburnum*). Nicollet linked it with Ojibwa *anibimin,* but apparently confused it with the *assimina* or pawpaw tree of Missouri and Illinois. Keating (1823) traced the name to Ojibwa *anepeminan,* which is only a variation of Nicollet's term.[19]

The last-named term might have been garbled into **Pemebonwon,** the name of a river which joins the Menominee in Marinette County. The stream, incidentally, flows through the town of Pembine. An apocryphal story is told about it, according to which a man from Green Bay, having heard that the stream was good for fishing, asked a French Canadian where he could find good trout fishing. The Frenchman, pointing toward the river, replied "La Pemene c'est bon won," meaning, "The Pemene, it is a good one."[20] Pemene (q.v.) was a name which is reported to have been applied to the river at times, although it properly belongs to a waterfall in Menominee River.

Chebomnicon Bay on the south shore of Madeline Island of Lake Superior, Ashland County, has a name which is said to mean "gooseberry place." Dwight Kelton wrote it *"Shabominikan* Bay, *Zhabo'minikan."* It has also been rendered in English as "gooseberry patch." *Shabomin* is Ojibwa for "gooseberry"; *-ikan* signifies "there are."[21]

Raspberry River, a tributary of Lake Superior in Bayfield County, was called "Miskwi Minikan or Raspberry River" in Nicollet's journal of 1837, and "Miskwimin or Raspberry River" on his map of 1843. *Miskwimin* in Ojibwa signifies "red berry."[22] Raspberry Bay takes its name from the river.

Tanner's Ojibwa word for "raspberry" was *miskwamin.* The last half of this word, *wamin,* was apparently chopped off to create the name of **Wamin** Lake in Langlade County. Wamin alone has no meaning, since the *wa* belongs to *miskwa,* "red."[23]

The town of **Metomen** in Fond du Lac County probably takes its name from Menominee *mita men*, "heartberry," i.e., strawberry. An alternative explanation, "grain of corn," does not fit any local vocabulary.[24]

Other Floral Names

The name of **Onimish** Lake in Forest County does not precisely match any term in the language of either the Ojibwa or Potawatomi of that area. The nearest approximation of it is Ojibwa *ominik*, "bud, browse, sprout." The *sh* might represent the diminutive form.[25]

The smoking mixture used by Great Lakes Indians was called *kinnickinick* (variously spelled). It was a mixture of tobacco, sumac leaves, and the inner bark of red willow or a species of dogwood, though the contents varied in different places. The word signifies "it is mixed," and may be derived from Ojibwa *kinikinige*, "he mixes," from the root *kinika*, "mixed."[26]

Frontier literature has frequent references to *kinnickinick*, and it has produced place names in several states. At Fort Winnebago where her husband was Indian agent in 1830, Juliette Kinzie wrote: "I watched the falling of the ashes from their long pipes, and the other inconveniences of the use of tobacco, or kin-ni-kin-nick, with absolute dismay."[27]

In Wisconsin the **Kinnickinnic** (so spelled) River flows to Lake Michigan at Milwaukee, and along its banks winds Kinnickinnic Parkway. Another Kinnickinnic River joins the St. Croix in Pierce County. From this river are named a state park near its mouth, a sand bar, and a state fishery area. Also named for the river is the town of Kinnickinnic, St. Croix County, through which the river flows.

Aside from corn, the only important grain eaten by North American Indians was wild rice, *Zizania aquatica* or *Zizania miliacea*. It was not cultivated, but rather was harvested in canoes along the waterways and lakes where it grew. Its main distribution was, and is, in the northern parts of states bordering the Great Lakes and in Canada. Because this region was inhabited almost entirely by Algonquian-speaking tribes, their name for "wild rice" has flourished as a place name. It is *menomin* or *manomin*, compounded of *meno*, "good," and *min*, a generic term for berries, fruits, and grains. The frequency of its occurrence, though limited geographically, is greater than that of any other name for an indigenous American food plant.

As discussed in Chapter 2, an Indian tribe living about Green Bay and its tributaries and connecting waters was called Menominee because of the importance of wild rice in its food supply. It was of equal importance, however, to the Ojibwa, Ottawa, Potawatomi, and Winnebago tribes. Jonathan Carver (1766) called wild rice "the most valuable of all the spontaneous productions of that country."[28]

It is not always easy to determine which places called **Menominee** (and its variant spellings) are named for the tribe and which for the plant. It seems likely that such places in areas once inhabited, or still inhabited, by the Menominee Indians are named for them. This includes the Menominee River, which joins Green Bay at Marinette, and the Menomonee River which joins Lake Michigan at Milwaukee, together with the places named from it near Milwaukee. Likewise, the Menominee River, a small stream in Grant County of southwestern Wisconsin, which is outside former Menominee territory and also outside the rice-growing region, seems to bear the name of the tribe because of their travels in that region, where they once had a battle with the Sauk. Of course Menominee County, which is coterminous with the present Menominee reservation, bears the tribal name.

However, the city and town of Menomonie, in Dunn County, are located far from the area of Menominee occupation and are doubtless named for the grain. So also is Menominie Lake, located in the city of Menominie, as well as Munnomin Lake in Iron County and Manomin Lake in Waupaca County. According to one writer, **Shioc** River in Outagamie and Shawano counties, and the village of Shiocton in Outagamie County, derive their name from the Menominee designation *Mäno'-mänê Sa'iak*, "Wild rice along the banks."[29] (For another opinion, see Chapter 11.)

It is probable that many of the forty-one place names in Wisconsin which contain the word "rice" (mostly creeks and lakes), were named in translation from Indian names. For example, Rice Lake in Barron County, according to Ojibwa historian William Warren, was "always known to the Ojibways by the name of Mush-ko-dah-mun-o-min-ekan, meaning Prairie Rice Lake, and to the French as Lac La Folle."[30]

Joseph N. Nicollet, travelling north on the St. Croix River on August 3, 1837, thirty-eight miles from the Mississippi, reached the junction at the "Wabizipinican River emerging from the [East] bank. Wabizipin is a kind of fruit produced by a very prolific aquatic plant on the Mississippi. This fruit is very useful to the Indians who eat it and call it swan potato."[31]

It was, however, not a fruit but a tuberous root, probably from one of *Sagittaria* species, or arrowhead plant. The French, as shown elsewhere (p. 192) called this and other wild tubers *pomme de terre*, "apple of the earth," and today the Wisconsin stream is called Apple River.

Another Algonquian word for a kind of wild potato is *wapato*. It probably originated with the Cree or Ojibwa and was carried to the far northwest by hunters or trappers of the Hudson's Bay Company. There it was adopted into the Chinook jargon, and so it happened that Lewis and Clark in 1805 gave the name Wappatoo to an island at the junction of the Willamette and Columbia Rivers.[32] In Wisconsin the name **Wapato** is on Upper and Lower Wapato Lakes and Little Wapato Lake, all in Oconto County. In this instance, the name may originate in Menominee *wa-patow*, "mushroom."[33] Also in Oconto County is White Potato Lake, a name translated from its former Menominee name *Wapasipaniuk*.[34]

It is probable that many of the **Potato** place names in Wisconsin are translations of old Indian names, although it is difficult to separate them from others that have always been called "Potato." There are Potato Creeks in Marathon, Rusk, and Washburn counties (the name in Rusk County being given also to a flowage and state wildlife management area). There is also a Potato Hill in Juneau County, together with Potato Lakes in Rusk and Washburn counties, Potatoe (so spelled) Lake in Barron County, Potato Rapids in Marinette County, Potato River in Ashland and Iron counties, and Potato River Falls in Iron County.

Some of these places are probably named for domesticated potatoes introduced by whites and early adopted by the Indians, which remain an important crop in Wisconsin. However, the word *potato*, like the tuber itself, is of aboriginal origin. The name is from the Taino language of Haiti, and entered Spanish as *patata* or *batata*. Originally it was applied to the sweet potato, a member of the morning glory family, but it was transferred to the Andean tuber of the nightshade family, now called potato.[35]

Some other names for "potato" from languages indigenous to Wisconsin are on the map, or have been in the recent past. Potato Lake in Rusk County was formerly Opinikaning Lake. Its name was formed of *opinikan* (Ojibwa, "potato") and the terminal *ing* ("place"). Of the same origin is Penokee, the name of a range of hills and of a former village in Ashland County. It is a corruption of Ojibwa *opinikan*.[36]

When Juliette Kinzie in 1830 was en route with her husband and party to Fort Winnebago via the Fox River, she wrote: "We reached Lake Puckaway late in the evening of our second day from Butte des Morts. . . . This lake has its name from the long flags or rushes which are found in its waters in great abundance, of which the squaws manufacture the coarse netting used in covering their wigwams."[37] The lake mentioned by Mrs. Kinzie is part of the Fox River in Green Lake County, and still retains its old name, probably of Ojibwa or Potawatomi origin. On August 26, 1825, Schoolcraft camped on this lake and called it **Puckwa**.[38]

The Menominee word for these "rushes" (cattails, *Typha latifolia*, in this instance) is *nepiaskon*.[39] On Cram's map of 1839 is the name **Neepeeuskun** Lake, which is today in southwestern Winnebago County. Its name is translated into Rush Lake, which has been attached also to a nearby village. However, the old Menominee name, spelled *Nepeuskun*, is preserved in that of the town which surrounds the lake.

On August 11, 1837, Joseph Nicollet recorded in his journal the name of a tributary of Lake Superior in present Bayfield County as "*Pakwaika Sibi* (Rush River)." In his map of 1843 he changed the spelling to Apakwa. Today it is simply Rush River.[40]

Nicollet's map spelling, Apakwa, is nearly identical to *Apukwa*, the Ojibwa name for "bulrush" in *Hiawatha*. Another variation, **Apeekwa**, is the name of a lake in Flambeau Township, Vilas County.[41]

The U.S. Geological Survey lists in Wisconsin five Rush Creeks, six Rush Lakes, one Rushes Lake, and one Rushes River. Some of these may be translations from old Indian names, but the data are not available.

Cram's map of 1839 shows **Scuppernong** Creek as a tributary of Bark River east of Fort Atkinson, Jefferson County. The location is in present-day Palmyra Township. On today's maps it is called a "river" in Jefferson County, but a "creek" in southwestern Waukesha County, where it originates. Scuppernong is one of the oldest introduced Indian names in Wisconsin.

In the southeastern United States, scuppernong is known as an indigenous variety of light green grape (*Vita muscadina* or *rotundifolia*). The present name comes from Scuppernong Lake and River in Washington and Tyrell counties, North Carolina, where this grape was first noticed in the eighteenth century. The name of the lake and stream came from the Indian designation for the swamp land in that vicinity, *askup' onong*. The language is not specified in the sources, but the region, adjacent to Albemarle Sound, was occupied by Algonquian speakers.[42]

Squash was domesticated by Indians in ancient times and its name is shortened from its Narraganset appellation. "*Askútasquash*, their Vine aples," wrote Roger Williams in 1643, "which the *English* from them call *Squashes* about the bignesse of Apples of severall colours, a sweet light wholesome refreshing."[43]

Squash, or pumpkins (*Cucurbita*), together with beans and corn, formed the "three sisters" cultivated by all North American Indians in regions where growing conditions permitted. Carver wrote:

> They have also several species of MELON or PUMPKIN, which by
> some are called Squashes, and which serve many nations
> partly as a substitute for bread. Of these there is the round, the
> cross-neck, the small flat, and the oblong squash. The smaller
> parts being boiled, are eaten during the summer as vegetables;
> and are all of a pleasing flavour. The cross-neck, which greatly
> excells all the others, are usually hung up for a winter's store,
> and in this manner might be preserved for severall months.[44]

In the southwest and in Latin America, squash became an art motif. In several states it gave rise to place names. Wisconsin has two **Squash** Lakes, one each in Vilas and Oneida counties. They may have been named for their shape.

Wabigon is the Ojibwa word for "flower, bloom, blossom." Specifically, it has also been applied to the water lily and the trailing arbutus. **Wabigon** is the name of a lake in Bayfield County. In variant spelling the name is on Wabikon Lake, Forest County, where it may have come from the local Potawatomi, and on Wahbegon Island in St. Louis River, Douglas County.[45]

Winooski is the name of a swamp and of a former village in Sheboygan County. They were named by early settlers for a town and river of the same name in Chittenden County, Vermont. James and Lucinda Stone from Vermont settled on the site of Winooski in 1846 and were soon joined by others. The village of Winooski was named on January 27, 1853.[46] The name in Vermont is from the Abnaki word for "onion," and in fact, the Winooski River of Vermont was called Onion River in 1837 by Capt. Frederick Marryat, an English traveller. The Wisconsin stream on which Winooski once stood is also called Onion River. It is a tributary of the Sheboygan.[47]

Chicago: Onion or Skunk?

Chicago is sometimes identified with onion or garlic, and sometimes with skunk, as the aboriginal words for each are similar in central Algonquian languages. Wisconsin names associated with the skunk are mentioned under faunal names.

Several places in Wisconsin are apparently named for the city of Chicago, Illinois. Included among them are Chicago Bay, Sawyer County; Chicago Corners, Outagamie County; Chicago Junction, Washburn County; Chicago Point, Oneida County; Chicago Point, Waushara County; and Little Chicago, Marathon County.

The plant origin of Chicago's name was recorded by Henri Joutel, a survivor of LaSalle's Texas expedition, who reached the site of the future metropolis on September 25, 1687: "We continued walking until Thursday the 25th, when we arrived at a place which is named Chicagou, which, according to what we could learn, has taken this name from the quantity of garlic which grows in this district, in the woods."[48]

The name is from the Illinois *chicacwa,* and identical in Miami, but equivalents are found in other Algonquian languages. Albert Gatschet (1904) linked the name of Chicago in the Peoria dialect "to the existence of a species of *leek,* from a radix *shikzhik,* to smell."[49] (See also "*Chicog*" and "*Skunk.*")

14

Water Names

The names of rivers, of lakes and of diverse places in
Otchipwe or Cree, are still in use to attest, in future
times, the existence of these languages and reclaim their
rights to first possession. Obliged to disappear before the
white man, the haughty savage will compel the invader
to preserve these first denominations, at the risk,
however, of seeing them disfigured.

Bishop Frederic R. Baraga (1797–1868),
A Dictionary of the Otchipwe Language

Wisconsin is abundantly supplied with lakes and streams, especially in the northern part of the state. The more than three
thousand lakes that dot the landscape are a legacy of the glaciers which
receded ten thousand years ago and today are a tourist attraction.

Native names of water features have proven to be more resistant to
change than most others. Of course, the majority of them now have
non-Indian names, often in monotonous repetition. For instance, Wisconsin has seventy-three Mud Lakes, forty-two Round Lakes, and
thirty-two Silver Lakes. Indian lake names are not often duplicated, and
so they offer not only relief from monotonous repetition but also a colorful and fitting dash of originality to the map.

Most Indian lake and stream names in this book are treated under
other headings. Here I consider only a few which include generic terms
for "lake," "stream," and "water."

Bayou

Bayou is a topographic term common in some southern
states, especially along the lower Mississippi and the Gulf of Mexico.
However, it is also found in Michigan and Wisconsin, doubtless as a leg-

acy from the French, although it is not originally their word. An early mention of *bayou* is in the writings of J. C. Beltrami: "Below Red River [of Louisiana] the Mississippi may be said to be tributary [to?] itself, for all the issues found along its banks, and which are called *Bayoux*, are properly speaking, only Vents or passes which it has formed for itself, to carry off its waters, in periods of overflow, into the sea."[1]

The term *bayou* is French in orthography, and from the Louisiana French it entered into English, but its ultimate derivation is Choctaw. It has not been adopted into conventional French. Several of the standard references derive it from Choctaw *bayuk*, variously written *bayouc*, *bayouk*, and *bayouque* by early writers. It is defined as a backwater, minor river, marshy inlet or outlet of a lake or river, branch of a delta, a small sluggish stream, or dead branch of a stream. In practice *bayou* is applied, in the lower Mississippi Valley, to all of these features.[2]

Byington's *Dictionary of the Choctaw Language* does not list *bayuk*; it has *bok* for "a brook, a creek; a natural stream of water less than a river; a river, as *Bok humma*, Red river." But *bok* is listed in no fewer than seventeen combinations, many of which could have been corrupted into *bayuk* or *bayou*. One of them, not necessarily the true source, is *bok ushi*, "lit., the son of a river, a rivulet; a brook, a branch . . . a rill."[3]

In Wisconsin, six bayou names are listed, five of them in Waupaca County. The largest of these features, Traders Bayou in Mukwa Township of Waupaca County, is an Oxbow lake created by a change in the course of Wolf River. The others are named Jenny, Lowell, Miller, and Toms. In Winnebago County, Hogers Bayou, just west of the city of Omro, is a backwater of Fox River.

Lake Michigan

Lake Michigan forms all of the eastern boundary of Wisconsin. Named for it are Michigan Bay in Namekagon Lake, Bayfield County; Michigan Creek, Forest County; and Michigan Island, one of the Apostle Islands in Lake Superior, Ashland County.

Michigan and its variants mean "great lake" in the languages of the Algonquian tribes of this region. It was a generic term applied to any large lake, and apparently to Lakes Superior and Huron, as well as to Lake Michigan. Some examples from the literature include:

Gitche-gitche-gum-me (Ojibwa): "big, big lake." Tanner, *Narrative of Captivity*, 399.

Kitchi-gami (Ojibwa): Lake Superior. Baraga, *Otchipwe Language* 2: 194.

Kitchigamink (Algonquin): "great lake." Lahontan, *New Voyages* 2: 739.

Metchigami8i (Metchigamioui) (Illinois): "grand lac" (great lake). Le Boulanger, "French-Illinois Dictionary," 108, 160.

Mischigoning (Miami): "at the great lake" (applied to Lake Michigan). Hennepin, *New Discovery* 1: 62.

There is no ground for claiming that Lake Michigan was named for the Michigamea, an affiliated Illinois tribe which did not live near it. Neither is there evidence supporting belief that it was named for fish weirs or for a variety of fish, or that it means "stinking water" or "a bone with hair."[4]

Tichigan Lake and the village named for it in Waterford Township, Racine County, have a name which appears to be related to Michigan. It is apparently a shortened version of *tchi-i-gi-tchi-gami*, Potawatomi for "the great inland lake," according to Simon Pokagon, or *tchigi-kitchi-gama*, Ojibwa for "along the great lake, on the sea," as given by Baraga. This may be compared with Tichegami, the name of a lake in Quebec, taken from Montagnais *tshishe kamu*, "it is a large water."[5]

Mississippi River

The Mississippi forms the western boundary of Wisconsin from the point where it receives the St. Croix at Prescott in Pierce County, southward to the Illinois line. Its name is doubtless from the Ojibwa language,[6] although it is identical or similar in other Algonquian languages of the region. Because the river was in the French domain for so many years, and the earliest settlements were made on the upper river rather than the lower, it received its present name from the northern tribes, although the river's name became attached to a southern state in the Muskhogean language area.

The pious Father Marquette wrote in 1673 that he "safely entered Mississippi on the 17th of June, with a Joy that I cannot express." Nonetheless, he soon tried to rename it Rivière Conception; other French-men tried to affix to it the names of the French statesmen Buade and Colbert. The Spanish called it Río del Espíritu Santo, "River of the Holy Spirit," but only the native name was used after the middle 1700s.

Popular lore holds that Mississippi means "father of waters." In 1777 the botanist William Bartram, visiting Louisiana, called the Mississippi "the great sire of rivers."[7] At least nine other foolish explanations of this name are in print, none of which has the slightest foundation in fact.

Thevenot's map of 1681 correctly called the river "Mitchisipi ou grand Rivière." In January 1699 the Jesuit priest Julien Binneteau wrote from Illinois, "I have recently been with the Tamarois, to visit a band of them on the bank of one of the largest rivers in the world which, for this reason, we call the Missisipi or 'the great river.'" Concurring, Father Hennepin, a chaplain with La Salle, declared that the river of the Illinois "falls into that of Meschasipi; that is, in the Language of the *Illinois*, the Great *River*."[8] Identical or similar statements were made by Fathers Vivier, Le Boulanger, Charlevoix, and others, each of which is borne out by reference to native vocabularies.[9]

Nebish/Nippersink

When examined, many Indian names of water features are mundane. Some simply signify "water;" and others describe character-istics of the lake or stream; some are named for flora and fauna, and others commemorate events.

Nebish Lake in Vilas County has an Ojibwa name which signifies nothing more profound than "water."[10] An island south of Sault Ste. Marie, Michigan, in St. Mary's channel, has essentially the same name, Nee-bish. There is also a Nebish Lake in Beltrami County, Minnesota.

Closely related to these is the name of Nippersink Creek in Wal-worth County. Basically it is the same as Nipissing, the name of a lake in Ontario. Its characteristic element is *nipisse* (or *nippisse*), a dimin-utive of *nippi* or *nippe* ("water"), signifying "small water, a pool or pond," to which is added *ink*, meaning "at" or "place" in Ojibwa and Potawatomi.[11] The Canadian lake is large, although small in comparison to Georgian Bay, which is connected to it by the French River.

Neenah

At the northwest corner of Lake Winnebago, where the Fox River exits northward to Green Bay, is the city of Neenah. It is partly on the mainland and shares half of Doty Island with its neighboring city, Menasha. The name Neenah is from the Winnebago word for "water."[12] It seems to be an appropriate name for a place nearly surrounded by water. The name is also given, at this place, to a town as well as to Neenah Channel and Point.

Elsewhere is Neenah Creek, which emerges from Adams County, passes through Neenah Lake at Oxford, in Marquette County, and empties into Fox River in Fort Winnebago Township, Columbia County.

Nekoosa

Nekoosa is a paper mill city on the Wisconsin River in Wood County. It is said to have been named in 1893 for the Nekoosa Paper Company.[13] The name is clearly Winnebago but has been variously interpreted. Several writers translate it as "running water."[14] A Winnebago Indian named Nekousaa, "the main channel," signed a treaty at St. Louis on June 3, 1816.[15] The Winnebago name for the Mississippi is given by Jipson as *Neekoosa-ho-xa-tay-ra*, "water large."[16] Nekoosa is perhaps the residue of a once longer name. A variant spelling of this name is on Nikusa Island in the Dells of the Wisconsin River.

Neosho

Neosho, a village in Dodge County, has a Siouan name which may be of Winnebago or possibly Osage origin. Huron H. Smith called *neosho* (or *niozho*) a Winnebago word for "small water hole."[17] Such a word is not listed, however, in Jipson's Winnebago manuscripts.

It is possible that the name is of Osage origin and is from Kansas or Missouri. Neosho is the name of a river that rises in Morris County, Kansas, and flows into Grand Lake of the Cherokees at Miami, Oklahoma. In Kansas it gives its name to the towns of Neosho Falls and Neosho Rapids, to Neosho Lake, and to Neosho County. In Missouri is the town of Neosho, seat of Newton County. Neosho in that region is from the Osage word *ni-o-shó-de*, "the water is smoky with mud." Related terms are *ní-o-sho-dse*, an Osage and Omaha word meaning "smoky, muddy, turbid and roily water," and *Ni-sho-dse*, the Osage name for the Missouri River. From one of the last two terms came Neodesha, the name of a town in Wilson County, Kansas.[18]

Rock River/Sinissippi

The Rock River flows south from the Horicon Marsh in Dodge County, and just below the town of Horicon it widens into island-studded Sinissippi Lake. The river continues in a generally southwesterly direction, giving its name to Rock County, and eventually discharges into the Mississippi just below the city of Rock Island, Illinois.

The name Sinissippi is from *Assini-sippi*, meaning Rock River in the language of the Sauk and Foxes, whose last major settlements east of the Mississippi River were near the mouth of the Rock River. The river was also "Rock River" to the early Illinois Indians, the Potawatomi, and the Winnebago. The river took its name either from Rock Island in the Mississippi above its mouth, or from the rocky bottom in its lower course. As early as 1718 the river was shown on De Lisle's map as "Assenisipi ou R. a la Roche." Charlevoix called the river "Assenesipi, or river of the rock; because its mouth is directly opposite to a mountain [sic] placed on the river itself, where travellers affirm rock-chrystal is to be found."[19]

The early appearance of the name suggests that it came from the Illinois, but it was continued by the Sauk who settled on the river after 1750, and who, in the words of Maj. Morrell Marston (1820), described the point of land formed by the junction of the Rock and Mississippi rivers as *Sen-i-se-po Ke-be-sau-kee* or Rock River Peninsula.[20]

According to Keating (1823), the "Sinsepe" was called *Weroshanagra* ("Rock River") by the Winnebago.[21] Thomas Jefferson proposed in 1784 that a portion of the territory "through which the Assenisipi or Rock River runs, shall be called Assensipia."[22]

The name Sinissippi is of special interest for three reasons. It indicates that several tribes could have the same name, in their respective languages, for a particular feature. Second, it shows that Indian names are not necessarily temporary, but instead can last for centuries. Finally, we see that a river can have the same name throughout its length, and not necessarily several. These views have been subject to unwarranted challenge.[23]

Sinnipee Creek

Sinnipee Creek in Grant County has a name composed of Sauk *assini*, "rock," plus *nipi* or *nipee*, "water." The rocky character of the country through which it flows makes the name especially appropriate. The name has also been given to a cemetery and school in that locality.[24]

15

Topography

One new fact, which we realized as we heard our Indians
discuss the trip, was that not only every stream but every
prominent hill, strange tree, large rock, unusual land
formation, and body of timber had its individual name.
Therefore, when Wajapa returned from the trip and
named to Iron Eye the details of our route, that old chief
sat down and made a perfect map of the country we had
traversed with our route marked on it by all those natural
features he knew well by sight and hearsay.

Thomas H. Tibbles, *Buckskin and Blanket Days*
(1969)

Chequamegon

On Lake Superior's shore in Bayfield and Ashland counties, Chequamegon Bay is shielded from the lake by a sliver of land
called Chequamegon Point and by Long Island, which was cut off the
peninsula by the waves in historic times. "Point Chegomegon," wrote
Carver (1765), "might as properly be termed a peninsula, as it is nearly
separated from the continent . . . by a narrow bay."[1] About 1665,
Ojibwa, Ottawa, and Huron Indians fleeing from the Iroquois settled
around this bay and on adjacent Madeline Island. Not long afterward Father Claude Allouez started a mission station at Chequamegon. The
settlement here was called *La Pointe* by the French. A village of that
name on Madeline Island (formerly Isle De Tour) was long an important
fur trading center, and it is also the birthplace of Ojibwa historian
William Warren. About 1765 Alexander Henry wrote that "Chegouemi-
gon might at this period be regarded as the metropolis of the Chipe-
ways." Nearby the Ojibwa still occupy Red Cliff Reservation above Bayfield, and Bad River Reservation east of Ashland.[2]

There are several explanations of the meaning of Chequamegon, which is an Ojibwa name. According to Father Verwyst, it is a "corruption of *chagaouamigoung,* the French method of spelling *jagawamikong* (pr. *shaw gau-wau-me-kong*), which means a long narrow strip of land running into a body of water, such as a lake or bay." W. J. Hoffman spelled this name *Shagawamikongk* and defined it as "Long sand bar beneath the surface." E. D. Neill, in a note to Warren's *Ojibway Nation,* related it to *jâbonigan,* "a needle."[3]

Gogebic Range

A range of hills stretching across northwestern Iron County, from the Ashland County line to Hurley on the Michigan boundary, is called Gogebic Range. The average elevation of this range, which is paralleled by the Soo Line railroad, is about 1600 feet. It was initially notable for its iron ore deposits. The name was first attached to Gogebic Lake, in adjacent Gogebic County, Michigan, from which it was adopted in 1853 by the Gogebic Mining Company, and next transferred to two now vanished post offices in Michigan. Among conflicting theories of the name's origin, the most credible seems to be that it comes from either the Ojibwa word *âjibic,* meaning "rock," or *ogidâbic,* "on the rock."[4]

Menasha/Maunesha

The city and town of Menasha in Winnebago County are said to receive their name from *Minä'si,* the Menominee word for "island." That is fitting, for the city shares with Neenah the occupancy of Doty Island at the north end of Lake Winnebago, where the Fox River exits northward.[5]

This name closely approximates that of Maunesha River, which rises in Dane County and joins Crawfish River in Dodge County. There are, however, two reasons for doubting their sameness. One is that Maunesha River is in former Winnebago territory; the other is, as Professor Cassidy has noted, that Cram's map of 1839 and other early documents recorded it as Nauneesha. Cassidy believes the later name is a corruption of the earlier one, but the reverse might instead be true.[6]

The name Nauneesha cannot be matched closely with any Winnebago words except *man-us-ka*, "sweet grass," and *me-nee-sha*, "year," which is an unlikely name for a stream.[7]

The present name is a fairly close match with *Mina'she*, the Potawatomi word for "island," and could have been applied to the stream by someone familiar with that language.[8]

Minnesuing

The name of Minnesuing Lake and Creek in Douglas County is probably only a variation of the name of Munising, Michigan, which is Ojibwa for "island place." *Minnis* (here made into *Minnes*) signifies "island"; the *u* is a superfluous intrusion; *-ing* is a prepositional suffix. The name was probably given because there is a small island at the north end of the lake,[9] and the stream was named for the lake.

Muscoda

Muscoda is the name of a village in Grant County and of an island in the Wisconsin River in Iowa County. This name clearly approximates the word for "prairie" (or "meadow") in several Algonquian languages. In Ojibwa it is *mashkodê*.[10]

Variations of this name in other states are Mascoutah, Illinois; Muscatine, Iowa; Muskoda, Minnesota; and Muscotah, Kansas. In *Hiawatha* is "Muskoday, the meadow." The Muscoda post office was named Muscody in 1843. Supposedly it was named for English Meadow, which in turn had been named for two Englishmen killed there by the French in 1763.[11]

Muskeg

In this report of 1841 on the hydrographic basin of the upper Mississippi, Joseph Nicollet wrote that ". . . there is what the Chippeways call a *mashkeg*, and the Sioux *wiwi*, or swamp, or elastic prairie, which is the head-spring of a small river that empties into the river of the rock, one of the tributaries of the Sioux river."[12]

Boggy, marshy lands were called *mashkig, maskeg, maskig, maskik, muskak,* or *muskeek* by the Cree, Ojibwa, and other Algonquian tribes, from the Great Lakes to Hudson Bay and westward as far as these tribes extended.[13] The name has been adopted into English as *muskeg*, and it is a common place name in the Great Lakes region and Canada. The Cree living in the wilderness of the Hudson Bay drainage region were called Muskego by the Ojibwa and Swampy Cree by the whites.[14]

In Wisconsin this name appears on Muskeg Lake, near Phelps, in Vilas County, as well as on Muskeg Creek, a tributary of Iron River, and the village of Muskeg, both in Bayfield County. Bad River, a tributary of Lake Superior in Ashland County, is the present name of a stream known to the Ojibwa as *Maskesipi, Maskigo, Mushkeesebe,* or *Mashki-sibi.*[15] The swampy character of its lower course was the cause of the name.

In Racine and Waukesha counties this name appears as Muskego, probably abbreviated from the Potawatomi *mashkig-ong,* "swampy place." Essentially it is the same name as Muskegon, Michigan, which was called Maskigo in a treaty with the Ottawa on March 26, 1836.[16] Muskego is the name of a creek in Racine County. In Waukesha County are Big and Little Muskego Lake, as well as Muskego Creek, Marsh, Canal, and the city and town of Muskego.

Okee

Okee is a village on the south side of the Wisconsin River in Columbia County, opposite Merrimac. The name is an Algonquian word for "earth, land, country or soil," given in various related languages, dialects, or orthographies as *akhew* (Menominee), *aki* or *akki* (Ojibwa), *ku* (Potawatomi), and *aukee* (Ottawa).[17]

Pewaukee

Pewaukee is the name of a river, lake, village, and town in Waukesha County. It is apparently the residue of a longer name. Father Verwyst thought it was a corruption from Ojibwa *nibiwaki,* "swampy" (literally, "water land"). B. F. H. Witherell, however, said that the correct name was *Pee-wau-nau-kee,* Menominee for "the flinty place."[18]

Sinsinawa

This is the name of a creek, a mound, and a village in Grant County. The mound, a natural hill which was the site of a skirmish in the Black Hawk War, is the site of St. Clara Convent. The name of this place has been spelled Sinsinahwah, Sinsinawa, Sinsinewa, Sinsiniwa, Sinssinniwa, and Susseneway.[19]

The first part of the name could be corrupted from *aseniki*, Sauk-Fox for "stony," or from *assini*, "stone"; the last part could represent *nawi*, Sauk-Fox for "middle."[20] Such an interpretation does not answer how *ki* was converted to *si*, but the other explanations of this name which are in print present greater problems. These propose the word *jinawe*, not identified as to language, which one writer inteprets as "home of the young eagle," and another as "rattlesnake." *Jinawe* is an Ojibwa word for "rattlesnake" in Baraga's dictionary, but it seems a poor match for Sinsinawa.[21]

Suamico

Suamico is the name of several places in Brown and Oconto counties, on the west shore of Green Bay. In Brown County are Big and Little Suamico lakes, as well as Suamico River, town, and village. To the north, in Oconto County, a town and village are named Little Suamico.

Swanton said that Menominee Indians living on the sand dunes at Big Suamico on Green Bay were called *Mätc sua' mäko Tusi'nini*[u] or "Great Sand Bar People." Alanson Skinner, who gave the same definition, said Big Suamico was an ancient Menominee village site at the mouth of the river and along the bay shore. He called the site famous in Menominee folklore, mythology, and history.[22]

An alternate view from Father Verwyst is that Suamico is a corruption from *ossawamigoing*, "place of the yellow beaver." However, Verwyst was not familiar with this locality or with the Menominee language.[23]

Totogatic

From Totogatic Lake in Cable Township, in southwestern Bayfield County, the Totogatic River winds its tortuous way through corners of Sawyer, Washburn, Douglas, and Burnett counties before finally discharging into the Namekagon, an affluent of the St. Croix River.

Father Verwyst linked this name with Ojibwa *totogan*, "bog," and defined it as "boggy river." Baraga's definition of *totogan*, "trembling ground," is compatible with that view.[24] Henry R. Schoolcraft, who reached this stream by canoe on July 31, 1831, gave a curious account of the name: "The name is indicative of its origin. Totosh is the female breast. This term is rendered geographical by exchanging *sh* for *gun*. It describes a peculiar kind of soft or dancing bog."[25]

Nicollet's 1843 map showed this river as the *Totokitig*, and near its junction with the Namekagon indicated "Women's Portage." This may give some support to Schoolcraft's association of the name.

The name is also on Totogatic Lake State Wildlife Management Area in Bayfield County, Totogatic River State Wildlife Management Area in Sawyer County, Totogatic Flowage in Sawyer and Washburn counties, and Totogatic Park in Washburn County.

The name of Wequiock for a bay of Green Bay, and for a small village and church in Brown County is related to Ojibwa *wikweia*, "there is a bay," with the termination "ock" (from *aki*), signifying "land." *We-quiock* is "bay land."[26]

16

Commemorative Names

As with other human endeavors in which the form
survives long after the substance is lost, so the name
alone often remains.
      George F. Shirk, Oklahoma Place Names (*1974*)

The designation "commemorative name" could be applied to all of
the personal and tribal names listed in this book. Many of the
names of features which have been translated into English or French are
also commemorative. Listed here are names recalling historic or legendary events which have not been treated earlier. Most of these seem to
have been placed by white people, and most relate to warfare. Indians
gave commemorative names (though not honorific ones), but few of
these have survived. The following names are linked with the Indian
history of Wisconsin and thus are another measure of aboriginal influence on the map.

Battle Hollow, Battle Island, and Battle Slough, in Wheatland Township, Vernon County, mark places associated with the misnamed battle
of the Bad Axe, the last incident of the Black Hawk War. (The Bad Axe
River is really about five miles north of the site of the fighting.) At
Battle Hollow, two miles south of the present village of Victory, on August 1, 1832, fleeing Sauk Indians led by Black Hawk were attacked as
they attempted to cross to the west side of the Mississippi by troops
under Gen. Henry Atkinson, U.S. Army, Gen. W. D. Henry, Illinois militia, and Col. Henry Dodge, Wisconsin militia.

The steamboat *Warrior* also fired on the Indians, although Black
Hawk was trying to surrender. Other Sauks who reached the Iowa side
of the river, mostly women and children, were killed by Wabasha's
Sioux Indians; still others who had rafted down the Wisconsin as the
main body travelled overland, were fired on by artillery at the mouth of
the Wisconsin, miles to the south. It is estimated that only 150 Indians

survived the so-called Black Hawk War, out of more than 900 who crossed from Iowa into Illinois at the Yellow Banks in early April.

A number of places in Wisconsin are named for commanders in the Black Hawk War. Dodge County, Dodgeville, and Fort Atkinson are among them. Black Hawk is also commemorated by the names of several places.[1] (See pp. 50–53.)

Bloody Lake is the local name for an oxbow lake formed by the Pecatonica River in Lafayette County, about a mile north of Woodford. Here a skirmish of the Black Hawk War occurred on June 16, 1832, when twenty-one Wisconsin volunteers led by Col. Henry Dodge overtook seventeen Indians, said to be Kickapoo allies of Black Hawk. In the fight, three volunteers were killed and one was seriously wounded. All of the Indians were killed. "Thus was our land made safe for settlement," reads a marker placed here in 1927 by the Rhoda Hinsdale Chapter of the DAR of Shullsburg and the town of Wiota. When the author visited this spot on April 17, 1960, the marker stood in a tangle of brush on a farm rented by a Swiss immigrant named Schulthess. It has since been removed to a more accessible location in nearby Black Hawk County Park, on the Pecatonica River.[2]

According to archaeological evidence, the site of **Council Grounds** State Park along the Wisconsin River near Merrill in Lincoln County, was occupied about A.D. 600 by sedentary Indians of the Woodland culture. When the French arrived in the area three hundred years ago, the Chippewa were living along the river, including this site, supporting themselves by wild rice gathering, horticulture, and hunting. According to tradition, Indian councils involving the Chippewa and neighboring tribes were held here.

The land containing the present park was ceded by the Indians in 1837. It remained in the public domain until 1880, when it was purchased by a business man who sold it to a lumber company. In 1924 the city of Merrill bought 425 acres of the land for a city park, but gave it to the state fourteen years later for one dollar. The state named it Council Grounds State Park and opened it to camping, picnicking, hiking, fishing, and swimming.[3]

There is a Council Bay in La Crosse County, as well as Council Creek and Council Spring in Monroe County. No specific information has been found relating to these places.

Deathdoor Bluff, a feature at the tip of Door County peninsula, has a name which is the English translation of Porte des Morts (q.v.), a name given by the French, after an earlier Indian name, to the water passage into Green Bay between Washington Island and the mainland. The name commemorates a legendary disaster which overtook a flotilla of canoes laden with Winnebago (or Noquet, by another account) warriors en route to attack the Potawatomi. The invaders were drowned when a storm overturned the canoes and dashed them against the rocks. Door County also received its name from this alleged event.[4] (See also Chapter 17.)

Retreat, a village on Highway N, Vernon County, is located on the trail followed by Black Hawk's band of Sauk in their retreat to the Mississippi River, where the final battle of the Black Hawk War took place on August 1–2, 1832.[5]

The name of **Soldiers** Grove, a village in Crawford County, was changed from Pine Grove in 1873 in order to eliminate a duplication. The present name commemorates the encampment here, in late July 1832, of a band of soldiers pursuing Black Hawk's fleeing Sauk Indians.[6]

The village of **Victory,** situated on the Mississippi River in Vernon County, about three miles below the mouth of the Bad Axe River and two miles above Battle Hollow, is named for the "victory" of white troops over Sauk Indians led by Black Hawk near this place on August 2, 1832. Since the Indians were greatly outnumbered, in a weakened and starving condition, trying to surrender, and most of the victims were women and children, several observers felt that the incident reflected little credit on the troops.[7]

17

French-Indian Place Names

> In general, I note everywhere that the names given to
> places in these regions by the French or the Americans
> (the latter transplanting them from the French) are of
> Indian origin and no more than a mere translation of
> these native names into both modern languages.
> Therefore, it is of great interest to the history of
> geography to preserve the relationship of these names
> [to] retain their etymology and recall their origin.
>   The Journals of Joseph N. Nicollet *(1837)*

Next to the Indian names, the French names, both personal and to-pographic, are the oldest names on the Wisconsin map. Frequently investigation reveals that many French place names are simply translations of Indian names. To show the full measure of native influence on the state's map, these names must be included in this account.

To determine the ultimate origin of French names, it is necessary to examine the journals, letters, and reports of those early explorers, missionaries, and other visitors who were literate and comprehensive in their writings. The work here is historical, not linguistic.

The sources do not always tell us what we want to know, because details that interest us were not always seen by early writers as worthy of notice. On that account the ultimate source of some names remains unknown or in doubt. However, enough information has been recorded so that we can greatly expand the history of Wisconsin as told in its names.

Butte des Morts. At Oshkosh in Winnebago County is Lake Butte des Morts, through which the waters of the Fox and Wolf rivers, united just to the west, are carried into Lake Winnebago. A village on the north-western shore of the lake has the name Butte des Morts, French for "hill of the dead." There are conflicting stories about the origin of this name.

Some chroniclers, such as Peter Pond (1773–75), simply described it as a burying place;[1] others held that battles occurred there between the French and the Fox Indians, or between Indian tribes. The account of Juliette Kinzie (1831) relates that "The Butte des Morts, or Hillock of the Dead, was the scene long since of a most sanguinary battle between the French and the Mis-qua-kees, or Foxes. So great was the carnage of the engagement, that the memory of it has been perpetuated by the gloomy appellation given to the mound where the dead were buried."[2]

A stone marker near the Butte des Morts post office gives the "Indian" name of this place as *Mas-pa-qua-te-no.* That is not a close match to any Menominee terms, but the name could be related to the Ojibwa *Mishi Pikwadina,* "Great Hilly (place)."

Courte Oreilles. The Courte Oreilles ("Short Ears") band of Ojibwa, who live about the five-thousand-acre Lac Courte Oreilles in Sawyer County, inherited their name from a band of Ottawa who once lived on the shore of the lake. When explorers Radisson and Grosseilliers came to this place in 1659, they found Ottawa Indians, whom they called "Short Ears" because they had cut the rims off their ears. The Ojibwa called the sheet of water at that place *Odahwah sahgaegan,* "Ottawa Lake," because of the tradition that, around 1750, a party of their hunters found on its shores the frozen body of an Ottawa. It later became and still remains the home of the Ojibwa of Lac Courte Oreilles Reservation, who numbered 1,811 persons in 1981. The name has also been given to Little Courte Oreilles Lake and to Courte Oreilles River, which drains the lake. English-speaking settlers spelling the name according to their own phonetics turned it into *Couderay,* the name of a river and village in Sawyer County, and Coudray, a lake in Barron County.[3]

Des Moines. In Burnett County is Des Moines Lake. It is clearly not a local name, but a transfer from Iowa, through which runs the Des Moines River that gives its name to the state capital.

The first white men to see the river were apparently Father Jacques Marquette, Louis Joliet, and their party, but they did not record the name. They did, however, record the name of an Indian tribe of the Illinois which lived on its banks, the Moingouena.

The preponderant evidence is that the river was named for the tribe. On his map of 1684, Jean-Baptiste Franquelin (who was never in America) showed a "R. des Maingoana" in the wrong place, Illinois, but a vil-

A portion of a map of New France by Jacques Bellin, Royal French Marine engineer, ca. 1745. Four tribal regions are shown in capital letters: Pays des Renards (Country of the Foxes), Otchagras (Winnebagoes), Les Sakis (Sacs or Sauks), and Pays des Mascoutens (Prairie People, sometimes miscalled gens de Feu).

lage of Maingona in the right place, west of the Mississippi. In 1688 he corrected his earlier error. The English mapmaker Senex in 1718 placed "Moingona R." where the Des Moines now is. De Lisle in 1718 showed "la Moingona R." in the same place. Charlevoix in 1721 wrote of "La Riviere des Moins ou Moingona."

Throughout the eighteenth and early nineteenth centuries the river continued to be known by this tribal name, although the tribe itself vanished from the records by 1810. Only in the nineteenth century did several foolish explanations of this name appear: "Demon" River, River of Monks, River of Mines, River of Means, "the Lesser," "the Middle," and "river of the Mounds." A widely held view, originating with J. N. Nicollet, is that the name Moingona or Moingwena "is a corruption of the Algonkin word Mikonong, signifying at the road."[4]

It is hard to imagine how the consonant *k* could replace the vowels in the original name. Moreover, there is no documentary evidence to support Nicollet's view, although it has been adopted by several later writers.

In the Miami language the word *mong'wa* means "loon."[5] The loon is listed as a Miami gens by Lewis H. Morgan, who also found a loon gens among the Ojibwa, Potawatomi, and Shawnee.[6] De Gannes and other early writers asserted that there was no significant difference between the Illinois language and that of the Miami.[7] No term closer to Moingwena or Moingona has been found than the Miami term for "loon." It seems probable that the name of this Illinois tribe was taken from their totemic bird or a totem of one of their subdivisions. A relic of this old name is the name of the village of Moingona in Boone County, Iowa.

Des Plaines/Eau Pleine. The Des Plaines River rises in northern Kenosha County and flows generally southward into Illinois, joining the Kankakee in Grundy County to form the Illinois River. Early canoe travellers portaged from the South Branch of the Chicago River into the Des Plaines in order to reach the Illinois and the Mississippi. The first white men known to have crossed the portage were Marquette and Joliet's northbound party in 1673 and La Salle's band of explorers in 1682. In 1848 the streams were connected by a canal.

Local people believe that the name of the Des Plaines River means "River of the Plains." In its present, corrupted form it can be read that way, but the early forms of the name, as traced by Hermon Dunlap Smith, clearly indicate that something else was intended. The river was earlier called Eau Pleine, ("full of water"), French-Canadian name for the maple tree, so named for its sap.[8] Maple trees are still abundant along the river. The name is aptly commemorative since Indians made syrup and sugar from the maple and taught that art to Europeans. According to William Keating (1824), the Potawatomi name of the stream was *Sheshikmaoshike sepe* ("river of the trees which flow").[9] The French form of this name, through the years, was written as Au Plaines, Aux Plaines, Deplaine, O'Plaine, Plane, Plein, and in many more ways. In Gurnee, Illinois, one of those corruptions survives in the name of O'Plane Street. In Marathon County, Wisconsin, the old, correct name is preserved in the name of Big and Little Eau Pleine Rivers, which are tributaries of the Wisconsin, and Eau Pleine Reservoir.[10] According to Hiram Calkins (1849) the Chippewa name of the Eau Pleine, was (in somewhat garbled form) *She-sheg-e-ma-we-she can Se-be,* "Soft Maple River."[11]

Eau Claire. The city and county of Eau Claire are named for the Eau Claire River which joins the Chippewa at Eau Claire. In 1843 J. N. Nicollet called it the Wayokomig River on his map, and Clear Water River in his journal. In 1859 Hiram Calkins gave the river name in garbled Ojibwa as "Wahyaw con-ut-ta-qua-yaw Se-be—Clear Water River, now known as Eau Claire." These renditions may be compared with Baraga's " *Wâkami* or -*magad.* The water is clean, clear."[12]

There is another Eau Claire River which joins the Wisconsin in Marathon County, and still another which flows out of the connected chain of Eau Claire Lakes (Upper, Middle, and Lower) in Bayfield County into the St. Croix River in Douglas County.

Fond du Lac. The city of Fond du Lac occupies the south end of the shore of Lake Winnebago, and according to Alanson Skinner, the Menominee called the site *wanika miu,* "End of the Lake," which the French translated into Fond du Lac.[13] A similar translation, from Ojibwa, led to the name Fond du Lac for the western end of Lake Superior, the present site of the cities of Duluth, Minnesota, and Superior, Wisconsin. The Ojibwa term *waiekwagâm,* in Baraga's dictionary, signifies "at the end of the lake."[14]

For Fond du Lac, Wisconsin, the surrounding town and county, as well as the Fond du Lac River, were named.[15]

La Crosse. Zebulon Pike, who visited the site of the present city of La Crosse on September 12, 1805, noted the origin of the name: "Passed . . . a prairie called Le Crosse, from a game of ball played frequently on it by the Sioux Indians."[16] While ascending the Mississippi with Major Stephen Long's expedition on June 27, 1823, William Keating wrote:

> The party reached Prairie la Crosse in time to encamp there; this has been incorrectly called the Cross (*crux*)[17] prairie. The name of this spot is derived from a game much in favour among the Indians; it is played with a ball, and is probably not very unlike some of the games of the white man. This prairie being very level and fine, is admirably well calculated for this purpose, and was formerly much frequented by the Indians.[18]

The French name La Crosse for this game is believed to result from comparison of the ball bat used in it to a bishop's crozier or staff. The Ojibwa name of the game was *baggatiway*. Brief descriptions of it are given by Alexander Henry and William W. Warren, and it is described at length by Stuart Culin.[19]

The name was given to the site of La Crosse, Wisconsin, by white men. The Winnebago, in whose former territory it is situated, called it *He-nook-was-ra*, "Woman's breasts" (Jipson) or *Enookwasaneenah*, "River of the woman's breasts" (La Crosse River), according to Spoon Decorah. The reference was to a pair of sloping bluffs near the mouth of the La Crosse River.[20]

The game of la crosse was played by all tribes in the Great Lakes region, and beyond. Outside Wisconsin, the name has been given to places in seven states and Canada. From Prairie La Crosse, Wisconsin, were named the city and county of La Crosse, La Crosse Ridge, the La Crosse River, and the Little La Crosse River.

Lac du Flambeau. The custom of spearing fish at night by torchlight was widely practiced by northern Indians, and it has given rise to a number of place names in the region. For this practice the Ojibwa Indians called one lake in Vilas County *Wauswagaming*, "at the lake of torches." The French translated it into Lac du Flambeau, shown on government maps as Flambeau Lake. The village of Lac du Flambeau located there is the seat of the Lac du Flambeau Indian Reservation, established by treaty in 1854, which had an enrollment of 1,485 persons in 1981.

This name has also been attached to the surrounding town, to the Flambeau River, which runs from Flambeau Flowage in Iron County to Chippewa River in Rusk County, and to the village of Flambeau in Rusk County.[21] (See also Torch Lake, Torch River).

Lac Vieux Desert. Ojibwa Indians once planted garden crops on the shore of a large lake which lies astride the border of Gogebic County, Michigan, and Vilas County, Wisconsin. They called their settlement *Ketekitiganing*, "the garden place," or "place of fields." The French, finding the "old deserted fields" of the Indians, mapped the lake in 1718 and gave it the name it still retains, Lac Vieux Desert. A small band of Ojibwa Indians still occupies a tract on the north shore of the lake. Out of the lake on its south shore flows the Wisconsin River.[22]

Pomme de terre, "earth apple," was the French name for Indian "potatoes." Anglos often translated this simply as "apple." The name was applied to several tuberous plants eaten by Indians, including wild turnip (*Psoralea esculenta*), Jerusalem artichoke (*Helianthus tuberosus*), arrowhead (*Sagittaria latifolia*), and wild sweet potato (*Convolvulus pandurata*).

J. N. Nicollet, descending the Mississippi, wrote in his journal, September 16, 1836: "Along the sandy left bank we find an abundant growth of a climbing plant that is attached to small trees. Its root is a tubercle the size of an ordinary apricot that Indians eat and call *pomme de terre* [ground nut or Indian potato]."[23] The French name is on Pomme de Terre Slough, Buffalo County. (See also Potato.)

Porte des Morts. At the tip of the peninsula which separates Lake Michigan from Green Bay is a strait about five miles wide. Beyond it lies Washington Island, accessible by ferry from Gills Rock, where farmers descended from Icelandic immigrants continue to raise potatoes. There is a legend that the Winnebago (or the Noquets, in another version) sent a flotilla of canoes through this passage to attack the Potawatomi. A storm arose which overturned the canoes and dashed them against the rocky shore. There were no survivors. The Indians gave the watery graveyard a commemorative name, which has not survived, but the French translated it as Porte des Morts, "Door of the Dead." The name has been retained for the strait. When the adjoining peninsula, with its offshore islands, was organized into a county in 1851, it was called Door County. (See also p. 185, Deathdoor Bluff).[24]

Of this place poet Jens Jacobsen has written:
Porte des Morts the Frenchmen called it,
And the English called it Door;
But the Indians thus had named it
In the ages long before.[25]

Prairie du Chien, situated on the Mississippi in Crawford County, about three miles north of the Wisconsin River, is the second oldest settlement in Wisconsin (after Green Bay). Jonathan Carver, who visited the Indian village at that place in 1766, said it was "called by the French la Prairie les Chiens, which signifies the Dog Plains."[26]

William Keating, who came to this place on June 19, 1823, wrote: "The Prairie has retained its old French appellation, derived from an Indian who formerly resided there, and was called the Dog." He assumed that there was formerly a "family of the Dog Indians," which had become extinct.[27] However, both Louise Kellogg and R. G. Thwaites asserted that the Indian village at that place belonged to the Foxes, and that it was named for Chien (Dog), a Fox chief.[28]

Nicholas Perrot established a fur trading post at Prairie du Chien in 1685, but the first white settlers arrived about 1775. The town remained largely French until well into the nineteenth century.

Prairie du Sac. Since the middle of the eighteenth century, this place in Sauk County has been called Sauk Prairie in English, and for it are named the twin villages of Prairie du Sac and Sauk City. The visit of Jonathan Carver to the large Sauk village at this place in 1766 has already been mentioned (see Sauk). Sac is the usual French spelling of this tribal name.[29]

Racine. The city and county of Racine have their name from the French appellation of the Root River, which joins Lake Michigan at Racine. The French name, in turn, is a translation of an Indian name of uncertain origin, but perhaps from Potawatomi, where it signifies "root." Publius Lawson gave the Potawatomi name of the river as *Che pe kat aw sebe.* Gailland's Potawatomi word for "root" was *otchê' buk-in.*[30]

Our first description of the Root River is from the French missionary M. Jean François Buisson de St. Cosme, who paddled south from Milwaukee, reaching this stream on October 11, 1698. Starting in the morning, he wrote: "at an early hour we reached Kipikaoui, about eight

leagues farther." The site is identified by Louise Kellogg as that of pres-
ent Racine. Having been informed by the Indians that they could reach
Illinois by an easier route than the Chicago portage, by ascending the
Root River and then portaging to the "Pesiou" (the present-day Fox
River of the Illinois), his party tried that route. However, finding the
water too low, they returned to Lake Michigan and followed its shore to
Chicago.[31]

Trempealeau. When Jonathan Carver was on the Mississippi in 1766,
he noted that "About fifty miles below this lake (Pepin) is a mountain
remarkably situated; for it stands by itself exactly in the middle of
the River, and looks as if it had slidden from the adjacent shore into the
stream. . . . Both the Indians and the French call it the Mountain in the
River."[32] In the next century William Keating, historian of Long's expedition, wrote that on June 28, 1823,

> the party reached the spot which has been described, by all
> travellers, as a great natural curiosity, though in fact, it
> presents nothing extraordinary. It is termed by the voyagers,
> the *Montagne qui trempe dans l'eau*. This, which we under-
> stand to be but the Indian name for it, means "the mountain
> that soaks in the water." It is a rocky island corresponding
> with the adjoining bluffs and separated from the left bank of
> the river by a narrow sluice.[33]

The words *trempe l'eau* were run together with an *a* inserted to form
Trempealeau, the name of the village which stands today at that place
and also the name of the surrounding county. Five miles up river from
the town is Trempealeau River, which flows into the Mississippi. It was
called Bluff Island River on Keating's map and Mountain Island River by
J. N. Nicollet.

18

State Names

> He was named Susquehanna, he was named Mississippi;
> Every River and State in the Indian Tongue,
> Every park, every town that is still to be sung. . . .
> *Vachel Lindsay, "Doctor Mohawk,"*
> Collected Poems *(1952)*

Twenty-seven American states have native American names, although some of them are so distorted or obscure that their origin and meaning is debated. Eleven Indian names of other states are on the map of Wisconsin. As with other transfer names, their presence is in part a reflection of the nostalgia felt by settlers for their old homes. Others, however, especially western or southern names, are present for other reasons. These reasons are rooted in various historical events which influenced people in widely scattered places. These names are another thread in the fabric of names which illustrates American cultural experience.

Alabama Lake, in Polk County, is named for the state which was admitted to the union in 1819. The lake was so called because the early settlers on the southwest shore in 1890 came from Alabama. The state is named for a tribe of the Muskogee or Creek confederacy whose residence was once in central Alabama in the vicinity of present-day Montgomery. In 1854 some of these Indians, after a sojourn in Louisiana, were given a reservation together with the related Coushatta or Koasati tribe, in Polk County, Texas, where most of their descendants still live. Others are in Louisiana and Oklahoma.

The synonymy for Alabama in Hodge's *Handbook of American Indians* contains thirty-three variations, but those most commonly seen in the literature are *Alibamo* and *Alibamu*. Hodge interpreted the name as "thicket clearers." Elsewhere it has been defined as "weed gatherers" or "vegetable gatherers," meaning, in broad terms, "those who clear the

land for agricultural purposes." Dr. William A. Read called Alabama a
Choctaw name; Swanton suggested *albina* (Choctaw, "to camp") as a
possible source of the name. Byington's Choctaw dictionary gives
Halbamo as the Choctaw name for the Alabama tribe, but provides no
definition. The name is not listed in Loughridge's Muskokee dictionary.
Alabama is obviously much corrupted from its original form and perhaps
is beyond definition. That was the conclusion of John P. Harrington.[1]

The village of **Alaska,** and East and West Alaska lakes are found in
Kewaunee County. The Alaska, Wisconsin, post office was established
in 1867, the year that the territory called Alaska was purchased from
Russia. The lakes were named for the village.[2]

Alaska is from an Aleut name apparently first applied by the Russians to the Alaska peninsula. Three persons have been credited with
proposing this name for the region formerly called Russian America:
Secretary of State William Seward, Senator Charles Sumner, and General H. W. Halleck. Indeed, all three of them had proposed the name, independently of one another.

The name Alaska has been spelled Alashka, Alayeska, Alyeska, etc.,
and defined as "great country" or "great land." Prof. J. Ellis Ransom
(1940) said that the original Aleut form was *Ala'xsxq*, "the object toward which the action of the sea was directed." Alaska was admitted to
the union as the fiftieth state in 1958. Its name has been given to at least
six places in the lower forty-eight states.[3]

The village of **Arkansaw** in Pepin County draws its name from
Arkansaw Creek, a tributary of the Chippewa River, on which it is situated. The stream has a tributary, the Little Arkansaw. Named in 1852 by
William Holbrook, the creek bears the name of the state of Arkansas as
it is pronounced, which is found on the map in this way only in Wisconsin. The state is ultimately named for its principal indigenous Indian
tribe, better known as Quapaw, whom Marquette called Arkansea when
he met them in 1673. Akansea (also written Akamsea, etc.) is thought
to be a corruption of Siouan words meaning "south wind people." The
same meaning has been given for Kansas. Muriel Wright believed the
two terms were related. Baird's history of the Quapaw, however, calls
this an Algonquian word, obtained from the Illinois whom Marquette
met on his journey down river. The name was attached to at least two
Quapaw villages, then to the great river which rises in the Colorado

Rockies and joins the Mississippi in Arkansas. From the river the territory and then the state were named.[4]

Iowa as a legal name for a piece of land was first used on October 9, 1829, when the legislature of Michigan Territory, then having jurisdiction over the land which became Wisconsin, decreed that the name of Iowa County be given to the region south of the Wisconsin River, between the Mississippi and Lake Michigan. Lieut. Albert Lea first applied the name of Iowa informally in 1835 to a district in the land which was to become the state of Iowa. In the next year that region, then inhabited almost entirely by Indians, was made a part of Wisconsin Territory. Lea wrote that he chose the name "from the extent and beauty of the Iowa River which runs centrally through the District."[5] Since Iowa Territory was not created until 1838, and the state was organized in 1845, Iowa County in Wisconsin possessed the name before Iowa Territory.

The Iowa River, to which the name was informally attached in earlier times, was named for the Iowa (or Ioway) tribe of Indians who lived in its valley. The name has been spelled in diverse ways, but the first to use it in its present form was Thomas Hutchins, whose map of 1778 shows "Riviere Iowa" for the present Iowa River, and "Iowa Town" situated on the Illinois side of the Mississippi.[6] The tribe's own name, *Pahoja* or *Pahuja,* has been translated as "gray snow" by Dr. Edwin James (1819) and "dusty nose or face" by Rev. William Hamilton (1885). It seems unlikely that Iowa is derived from these names or from the word *iowa* defined in Riggs's *Dakota-English Dictionary* as "something to write with, a pen or pencil."

At least a dozen unacceptable explanations of the name Iowa are in print. Riggs gave the Dakota (Sioux) name for the Iowa tribe as *Ayúhba,* "sleepy ones." It is possible, perhaps probable, that the tribal name as we know it evolved from that.[7]

The Iowa, who are closely related to the Winnebago, gave up their lands in Iowa in a series of treaties ending in 1838. Some of their descendants occupy a small reservation on the Kansas-Nebraska border, and others live in Oklahoma.

Kansasville, a village in Racine County, is named for the state of Kansas. In earlier years this place was successively called Brighton and Dover, for places in England. It acquired its present name in the 1850s owing to the agitation over the Kansas-Nebraska Act (1854), which compromised the slavery issue. This is but one of many instances of political influence on place names.

The state was named for the Kansas Indians, a tribe of the Siouan language family. The name has been spelled in numerous ways, but popularly the Indians of this tribe were called Kaws, and Kaw became and remains the colloquial name of the Kansas River.

The authoritative view is that *Kansa* (English plural, Kansas) means "south wind people." The tribal name was generally pronounced *Kansa* or *Kasa*, given the sound of *au* or *aw*, hence *Kaw*. Other views of the meaning of Kansas include "smoky" and "swift."[8]

There is a **Kentuck** Lake in Forest and Vilas counties, a Kentuck Creek in Vilas County, and a **Kentucky** Creek in Lafayette County. The erroneous definition of Kentucky, "dark and bloody ground," originated in a misunderstanding of a statement made by Cherokee chief Dragging Canoe to agents of the Richard Henderson Company in March 1775. They had met at Watauga, Tennessee, to negotiate a land purchase. A Virginia commissioner, William Campbell, appointed to examine the purchase, met at Washington Court House, Virginia, with Samuel Wilson, who had been present at the "treaty" conference. Wilson's remarks were reported as follows: "that when the sd: Henderson & Co. proposed purchasing the lands below the Kentucky, the Dragging Canoe told them it was the bloody Ground, and would be dark, and difficult to settle it."[9] Later this remark gave rise to "Dark and Bloody" or "Bloody" as descriptions of Kentucky. One of these terms was used by Thomas Filson, Andre Michaux, and Charles F. Hoffman to describe the land called Kentucky. However, none said that the descriptive terms emanated from the word "Kentucky."

The best evidence is that Kentucky is Wyandot Iroquoian for "plain" or "meadowland." It is notable that the Mohawk-Iroquoian name for La Prairie, Quebec, is *Kentake*. Harrington is doubtless correct in concluding that Kentucky is "the Wyandot-Iroquois word for plain."[10]

The village of **Minnesota** Junction in Dodge County was located on a railroad that was expected to reach and cross Minnesota Territory. It is located on both the Milwaukee (Chicago, Milwaukee, St. Paul, and Pacific) and Northwestern railways, which cross one another at that place. Minnesota Channel in Douglas County is a place in the St. Louis River that separates Superior, Wisconsin, from Duluth, Minnesota.

The state of Minnesota is named for the Minnesota River, which joins the Mississippi at Mendota, outside St. Paul. The river was called St. Peters from exploratory days until changed by Congress on June 19, 1852, in response to a request by the territorial legislature, which had already adopted the name for the territory in 1849. The name Minnesota was originally given to the river by the Dakota Indians, and it was recorded as *Waddapawmenesotor* by Carver in 1767. In Santee dialect *watpa* means river and *mi'-ni-so-ta* means "whitish water." The name was given to the river for its cloudy appearance from the silt it carried. Romantics misconstrued this name and incorrectly rendered it as "sky blue water" and "sky tinted water."[11]

Missouri Creek in Dunn and Pepin counties and Little Missouri Creek in Dunn and Pierce counties are named for either the state of Missouri or the Missouri River. The name comes from the Illinois-Algonquian name given to the Siouan-speaking Missouri tribe, which occupied the banks of the great river a short distance upstream from its mouth at the time of Marquette's trip down the Mississippi in 1673. He called these Indians *8emess8rit* (8 = *ou*) on his map; the river was called by the Algonquian name Pekitanoui (in French orthography), which signifies "muddy." (See Pecatonica.)

It was long assumed, erroneously, that Missouri was an Algonquian term meaning "big muddy." However, on October 27, 1897, an editorial by Col. W. F. Switzler, editor of the Boonville, Missouri, *Democrat*, asserted that Missouri signified "wooden canoe people." His view was based on an article of unknown date and authorship (perhaps W. W. Tooker) which appeared in the *Brooklyn Eagle* of New York.

This view is easily confirmed as correct, except that the word "wooden" is superfluous. *Missouri* (variously spelled) is the name for any boat, including skin-covered ones, in the language of the Illinois. The French word *canot*, "boat," is rendered as *misso8ri* in Le Boulanger's "French-Illinois Dictionary" (1718); canoe is translated as *missuli*, and *emasuliaki* is "boatmen, canoemen" in the Peoria lexicon of Albert Gatschet (1904). The name of the Missouri River in Peoria was *emäs'-ulia sipiwi*, "river of boatmen." Thomas Forsyth, agent to the Sauk and Foxes in 1827, reported that the Illinois called the Missouri people *Miss-sou-li-au*, "Canoe-men," because they travelled in canoes. The differences between the orthography of Gatschet and Forsyth from that of

Le Boulanger is due to the fact that the latter's dictionary was in the Kaskaskia dialect, in which *r* was substituted for *l*.

The nineteenth-century articles on Missouri are forgotten, and standard works continue to speak of the "big muddy." However, John R. Swanton in 1952 interpreted Missouri as "(people having) dugout canoes," and John Harrington (1955) interpreted it as "canoe havers."[12]

Nebraska Hollow in Richland County may have been named because of agitation over the Kansas-Nebraska Act of 1854 (see Kansasville). The state took its name from that applied to the Platte River by the Iowa, Omaha, and Oto Indians. The native name meant, as the French name does, "flat water," "shallow water," or "broad water." The missionary William Hamilton held that Nebraska was from the French *platte* (as then spelled), meaning "broad," a translation of native names signifying the same thing. Ne-brath-kae or Ne-prath-kae in Ioway and Ne-brath-kae in Omaha, or as some speak it, Ne-bras-ka." Other writers agree. Dr. Edwin James, physician with Long's expedition to the Rocky Mountains (1819), offered *Ne-bres-kuh* as the Omaha word for "flat water" and *Ne-bras-ka*, Oto for the same thing.[13]

The village and town of **Oregon** as well as Oregon Branch are all in Dane County. The village was named in 1847 for the town, which was named for the Oregon Territory, and the branch, a tributary of Badfish Creek, was named for the town.[14] Oregon Territory was much in the public mind in the 1840s, when it comprised all the land now included in the present states of Oregon, Washington, and Idaho, plus parts of Montana and, by U.S. claim, part of British Columbia. The controversy with Great Britain over its possession gave rise to the slogan "54-40 or fight" during the 1844 presidential campaign. Oregon has been given as a name to thirty-five places in seventeen states, not including some that have disappeared. Most were given during the 1840s.

The name Oregon was first applied to the Columbia River in 1765, although the river's mouth was not "discovered" until 1792, by Capt. Robert Gray, who named it for his trading ship. The river was already well known to Indians, trappers, and explorers as far east as the Great Lakes.

On August 16, 1765, Robert Rogers petitioned the king and his ministers for support for an expedition to find "the river called by the Indians Ouragon." Jonathan Carver, on information supposedly obtained from Sioux, Assiniboine, and Cree Indians (1765), called "the Oregon or River of the West" one of the four principal rivers of North America.[15] He was not explicit as to the source of the name, but there is reason to believe it came from the Cree or Ojibwa.

In the early nineteenth century Oregon was at times used as an alternate name for the Columbia River. President Thomas Jefferson (1803) called it "Oregon or Columbia." In 1817 William Cullen Bryant's poem "Thanatopsis" contained the lines "or lose thyself in the continuous woods / where rolls the Oregon and hears no sound." John Wyeth (1832) wrote of the "Oregon river whence the territory takes its name."[16]

The name Oregon was officially applied to the region drained by that river in the Anglo-American agreement of 1818 providing for the joint occupation of the territory north of the 42d parallel, west of the Rocky Mountains, and in the treaty of June 18, 1846, which finally fixed the 49th parallel as the boundary between Canada and the United States from the continental divide to the Pacific. Oregon became a state in 1858.

The controversy over the meaning of this name is too involved to review fully here. The name is evidently of native origin, as Rogers asserted, but it is not from the language of tribes living in the Oregon region. In 1921 T. C. Elliott set forth several guesses as to the origin of the name. One of them was that Oregon came from *ouragon*, the French adaptation of the Caribbean native word for "hurricane." He held that "river of storms" might be the meaning of Oregon.[17]

This view cannot be reconciled with the testimony of Rogers that the name came from the "Indians," although he did not give the language origin. Other guesses came into print in the next two decades, but the one set forth in 1944 by George R. Stewart found its way into present reference books. He held that the name was taken by mistake from the name *Ouaricon/sint* applied to the Wisconsin River on a map published in the 1703 edition of Baron de la Hontan's *New Voyages*.[18]

However, Robert Rogers, who first used the name Ouragon in 1765, was well aware that there was no connection between those two rivers. Rogers was acquainted with Carver, who had travelled on the Wisconsin, which he showed as Ouisconsin on his map. Carver also showed an unnamed lake in the west of present Minnesota out of which flowed a stream labelled "heads of Origan." Rogers, moreover, in a second petition dated February 11, 1772, referred to both the "Ouisconsens" and the "Ouragon." He also outlined his proposed route for reaching the

"Ouragon." He would begin at the Falls of St. Anthony (present Minneapolis), follow the St. Pierre (Minnesota) river to its source, and then portage to a tributary of the Missouri. He would follow the Missouri to its beginning, and then portage across the divide "into the great River Ourigon."[19]

From Elliott's article in 1921 to Stewart's in 1944, diverse views on Oregon were given by several authors, but none of them noted Bishop Baraga's place name list in his *Otchipwe Language* (1878), in which he listed "*Orâgan,* or *Oyagan.* (Cree) plate, vase; (Otchip.), *onâgan.*" Moreover Watkins' *Cree Dictionary* (1938) defines *oyakun* as a "pan, a dish, a basin, a bowl, a cup."[20] As indicated elsewhere, the Chippewa form of the word *onâgan* is the probable source of the name of the Ontonagon River in Wisconsin and Michigan.

The first article which, in my view, gives unequivocally the correct origin of Oregon was published in 1959 by Vernon F. Snow. In this well-documented contribution, Snow called "Ouragon an Indian noun referring to a vessel or dish of birchbark," which entered the French vocabulary during the fur-trading era.[21] That is abundantly confirmed. La Potherie's account of Perrot (1665–70) used *ouragon* as a word for "dish." Lahontan used *oulagon* as the Algonquin word for "cup," this tribe having no *r* sound.[22] *Ouragon* was given as the Lake Superior Chippewa word for "a bark dish" in the Raudot memoir (1710).[23] There are numerous instances of "ouragon" used in this sense in the *Jesuit Relations,* some of which are cited in Snow's 1959 article. Father François de Crepieul (1697), a missionary among the Montagnais, complained that a missionary "eats from an *ouragon* (dish) that is very seldom cleaned or washed."[24]

In an article replying to Snow, Malcolm Clark (1960) argued that the Montagnais (of Quebec) was the only tribe which used the word *ouragon* (and its variants).[25] We know, however, that something similar to it was used by all Algonquian-speaking tribes of the Great Lakes region and by some beyond it.

The question now arises, since the domain of the Cree and other Algonquian tribes never extended to the west of the continental divide, how did the word become attached to a river in the far Northwest? And why was it given to a river? We know that some Algonquian words had reached the far Northwest before white settlement began, and they could only have been introduced by Indian or white trappers working for the fur-trading companies. Among these words is *wapato*, referring to the tuberous *Sagittaria* or arrowhead plant, which Lewis and Clark found in use on the Columbia. They applied the name (as Wappatoo) to an island at the mouth of the Willamette River.[26] The Chinook jargon spoken in the region included this word and also the Cree word *mitass*, "leggings," said by Gibbs to have been imported by the Canadian French; *siskiyou*, "bobtailed horse," also from the Cree; and *tatoosh*, Ojibwa for "female breasts."[27] The last two became geographical names. It is true that Oregon is not listed in Chinook jargon vocabularies, but the presence in them of the other words of Algonquian origin suggests that Oregon was introduced in the same way that they were.

We can only speculate that the name could have been given to the great river for the same reason that the French gave the name Platte to the river called Nebraska by the resident Indians. The stream was flat, spread out like a dish, and so is the Columbia along parts of its course. So they called it *ouragon*, or "dish" river. Or, alternatively, some bowl-like formation in its valley could also have caused the name to be given to it, since *ouragon* applied to several types of utensils. The origin of Oregon, in general terms, seems clear. The manner of its adoption is not, but that is not a vital defect.

The town of **Texas** is in Marathon County. The name of the lone star state has been given to at least forty places in twenty states. Most of them were named during the patriotic fervor of the Texas War of Independence (1836) and the Mexican War (1846–48). Some were named for individuals from Texas who had "Tex" or "Texas" as nicknames.

Texas received its name from a term meaning "friends" or "allies" which was used as a greeting by the Hasinai, a Caddoan-speaking tribe of the lower Rio Grande region. The Spanish often spelled it *Tejas* and erroneously applied it to the region, to the tribes, and to groups of tribes. An account of the origin of the term was given in a letter written by Father Damian Massanet in 1689:

> As soon as the Indians became aware of our presence, they made for the wood, leaving to us the rancheria, together with the laden dogs, which they had not been able to drive fast enough when they fled. The Indian who served as our guide himself entered the wood, and called to the others, declaring that we were friends, and that they should have no fear. Some

of them—and among them was their captain—came out and embraced us, saying: "Theches! techas!" which means "Friends! friends!"[28]

Some writers, without supporting evidence, have tried to connect the name Texas with Spanish *tejer*, "to weave," owing to the grass huts of the natives, or *tejas*, "cobwebs."[29]

19

Transfer Names

> Passionate love for their homes and sentimental attach-
> ment to familiar names by which they had known their
> streams and mountains, geographical locations and gather-
> ing places, strongly characterized these people. In re-
> membrance of those loved spots they brought old names
> to bestow on features of the western country; and thus
> the nomenclature of the ancestral domain became that
> of their home in the West. This robbed the new country
> of some of its strangeness, created a sense of friendship,
> unity, and permanence which strengthened them in the
> tremendous task of rebuilding their homes and farms,
> governments and schools.
>
> *Clark Foreman*, A History of Oklahoma (1942)

These remarks describe the attachment to familiar places shown by the Five Civilized Tribes who were removed from southern states to Oklahoma during the 1830s. The result of that sentiment was the transfer of names from the old habitations to the new. The same sentiment was shown by white immigrants from the East, who brought names westward along with their material possessions. Places named in nostalgic remembrance of the homes from which settlers came reveal the many places of origin from which Wisconsin was peopled in its early days. Another reason for the name transfers was the effect of historic events. The war with Mexico, the push toward Oregon, the California Gold Rush, the Civil War, and the purchase of Alaska had an influence on place names in Wisconsin and elsewhere. Another influence, already examined, is literary. Places mentioned in poetry and fiction, often based on actual events, caused names to be established in Wisconsin. Those borrowed names which are ultimately of American Indian origin are reviewed here.

The name of **Allequash** Creek, Lake, and Spring in Vilas County is not from the resident Ojibwa Indians, for the *l* sound is not in their language. It seems likely that these features were named by whites for the Allegash River of Maine, a principal branch of the St. John. It is mentioned at length by Thoreau in *The Maine Woods*, which describes his canoe travels on this and other rivers of Maine. Citing his Penobscot guide, Polis, Thoreau translated Allegash as "hemlock bark." William Willis, an Algonquin scholar, also citing a Penobscot Indian, said "The Indians gave the name, meaning 'Bark camp,' to Allegash Lake from the fact of their keeping a hunting camp there."[1]

Another scholar, Lucius Hubbard, substantially agreed on this interpretation, calling the name of the lake and river a probable contraction of *Allegaskwigam'ook*, "bark cabin lake."[2]

Since Wisconsin was a part of Canada during the British regime in the Northwest, it is perhaps fitting that our neighboring country should have its name on at least one Wisconsin feature: **Canada** Ridge in Buffalo County.

The name Canada was originally the local Indian name for a town, which was applied by the French to a territory around the site of the present city of Quebec. Heckewelder was no doubt correct in his assumption that ". . . it is highly probable that the Frenchman who first asked the Indians in Canada the name of their country, pointing to the spot and to the objects which surrounded him, received for answer *Kanada*, (town or village), and . . . believed it to be the name of the whole region, and reported it to his countrymen, who consequently gave to their newly acquired dominion the name of *Canada*."[3]

Jacques Cartier visited Stadacona (Quebec) and Hochelaga (Montreal) on his second voyage to America in 1535–36. He spoke of Donnaconna, the chief of Stadacona, as the "King of Canada," which reached from the Isle of Orleans, just below Stadacona, upriver perhaps a dozen miles beyond present Quebec. Cartier wrote of the "Kingdoms of Hochelaga and Canada, of us called New France," and said that "the Canadians with eight or nine villages alongst the river be subject unto them." Upriver from the mouth of Saguenay, he declared, "followeth the Province of Canada, wherein are many people dwelling in boroughs and villages. There are also in the circuit and territories of Canada, along and within said river, many other Ilands, some great and some small."

In the vocabulary of Iroquoian words, probably Huron, recorded by him, the word *canada* was defined as "a Towne."[4] So, once again, as in the case of Mexico, and the continents of Asia and Africa, we find a very local name extended to embrace a much larger region.

In Kewaunee County is a cluster of places having the name **Casco.** It is on a village, a creek, a millpond, and a locale called Casco Junction. The origin of the name is either Casco Bay at Portland, Maine, or the village of Casco, on Pleasant Lake, Cumberland County, Maine. It is reported that the first settler at Casco, Wisconsin, in 1855, was Edward Decker from Casco, Maine.[5]

This name, according to Fannie Eckstorm, is "thought by some to be from the Abnaki word for "heron," although that view was rejected by two leading scholars. She said, with reservations, that this name might be a clipped form of *aucocisco,* the name attached to the shore of Back Bay, Portland, by John Smith in 1614. She believed that the first half of the word was from *wakw,* which is Micmac and Malecite for "head of a bay." The latter half, *-cisco,* she continued, was from Micmac *sisgog* or *seskow,* as recorded by different authors. This term means "mud," and so "head of the bay, mud," or "muddy bay" might be the true meaning. She concluded, "No name could better fit this when the ebbtide has drained it."[6]

At least four names from California were introduced to Wisconsin by adventurers returning from the California gold fields to which a stampede began in 1849. **Coloma,** an unincorporated community in Waushara County, is named for a settlement in Eldorado County, California, which developed around Sutter's mill after the discovery of gold in January 1848. The name came from *Ko-lo'-ma,* the name of a village of Maidu Indians which once stood in that locality. In 1848 its name was recorded as Culloma. The meaning has not been determined.[7]

Escanaba Lake in Vilas County is apparently named for the city of Escanaba, Michigan, which lies at the mouth of Escanaba River in Delta County of that state. The generally accepted translation of this name, as given on a state historical marker at the north end of the city, is "flat rock." Escanaba is not a very close match to words signifying "flat rock" in Baraga's *Otchipwe Language,* which has *nabaga* for "flat" and *ajibic* for "rock."[8]

A map by Bela Hubbard (1840) does show, in Upper Michigan, "Osqua na be konk sepe (Flat rock R.)" emptying into Lake Superior in present Alger County. Prof. Bernard Peters, however, believes this name really means "Slippery Rock River." On today's maps it is called Rock River.[9]

From surface appearances it is possible to surmise that Escanaba is adopted from Ojibwa *Eshkam nibiwa,* "more and more, increasing."[10] One of Father Chrysostom Verwyst's several explanations is that Indians called the site of the Michigan city *Misconabe,* meaning "red man."[11] This, however, does not conform to Indian naming customs. A convincing conclusion as to the significance of this name cannot now be given.

The New York influence is shown by a cluster of places called **Genesee** in Waukesha County. There we find the three Genesee Lakes (Lower, Middle, and Upper), the village and town of Genesee, and the village of Genesee Depot. The village of Genesee was named by Benjamin Jenkins for his former home in Genesee County, New York. When residents of Genesee refused permission for a railroad to pass through their settlement, the railroad bypassed them and in 1852 the village of Genesee Depot was established a mile to the northwest.[12]

Genesee County, New York, was named for the Genesee River, which joins Lake Ontario at Rochester, or for its valley. The name of the river has been spelled in several ways, and appears as Geneseo on a city in Livingston County, New York. The definition of Genesee by Lewis H. Morgan as a Seneca name is commonly accepted: "It is worthy of remark that the root of the word Genesee was the name of the valley and not of the river, the latter deriving its name from the former. *Gen-nis'-he-yo* signifies "the beautiful valley," a name most fittingly bestowed."[13]

Lackawanna Lake in Oconto County was named either from the city of Lackawanna, New York, a suburb of Buffalo, or for the Lackawanna River, a tributary of the Susquehanna in Luzerne County, Pennsylvania. The name is a corruption of the Delaware Indian *Lechau-hanne,* "the forked stream."[14]

Mendota, the largest of the Four Lakes at Madison, Dane County, has a Dakota name borrowed from Minnesota. There it is the name of a town at the junction of the Minnesota and Mississippi rivers, which is also the site of Old Fort Snelling. Of this name, Stephen R. Riggs wrote: *"mdo-te, n. the mouth* or *junction of one river with another* (a name commonly applied to the country about Ft. Snelling, or mouth of the St. Peters [now Minnesota R.]; also the name appropriated to the establishment of the Fur Company at the junction of the rivers, written Mendota); *the outlet of a lake."*

Undoubtedly the name Mendota became well known from the publication in 1848 of Mary Eastman's *Dahcotah, or Life and Legends of the Sioux.* It was in the same year, according to Prof. Frederic Cassidy, that the name Mendota was given to Fourth Lake at Madison by Frank Hudson of that city, "for its euphony and its association with Indian legends."[15]

The village of **Merrimac** on the Wisconsin River in Sauk County was first called Matt's Ferry and then Colomar about the middle of the last century. One J. G. Train is credited with having the name changed to Merrimack, after a county and river in New Hampshire. The final *k* was later dropped. The town of Merrimac was named for the village. At the outset of World War II, an ordnance plant was constructed here.

The Merrimack River flows south from New Hampshire into Massachusetts, thence east into the sea at Newburyport. Its name has been spelled as now since Cotton Mather recorded it this way in 1699. In Massachusetts, however, the place names derived from it are spelled without the *k:* Merrimac and Merrimacport in Essex County.

The name Merrimac in this form was the name of a Confederate warship in the Civil War. It was adopted by villages in West Virginia and Illinois and for a canyon in Nevada. Several similar names derived from local Algonquian languages are also on the map: Maramec, Oklahoma; Meramec River in Missouri; and Minemac Lake in Wisconsin (q.v.). Franquelin's map of 1688 showed an Indian village named Maramec in Illinois. The Kalamazoo River in Michigan, during the French occupation, was called Meramec. Probably related to these also is Winnemac, a Potawatomi personal name. Outside of New England, these names are usually translated as "catfish," and sometimes as "sturgeon."[16] It is probable that all of them are related to the New England names.

The name in New England, from its location, is probably from the Pennacook, an Algonquian tribe. Some writers have interpreted it to mean "deep place" or "place of noises."[17] These explanations are a poor match with available vocabularies of the region. A more likely analysis would be that the name evolved from *monac,* "abundance," plus *lamek,* old Algonquian for "fish" or "sturgeon." This view relates the name also to the name of Alemeck Bay, New Brunswick, and *amal meekw,* Malecite for "mackerel."

We have seen how Meramec and its variants become Minemac and Winnemac in Algonquian languages lacking the *r* sound. The reverse change, from *n* or *l* to *r,* is also seen.[18]

Neshonoc Creek and Lake in La Crosse County have a name apparently borrowed from Pennsylvania. In the Quaker state Neshannock is the name of a stream, village, and township in Mercer County, and of a waterfall in Lawrence County.

Neshannock Creek in Pennsylvania enters the Beaver River in Lawrence County. G. P. Donehoo called its name a corruption from the Delaware name Neshaminy. John G. Heckewelder, early missionary to the Delawares, used the form Nishannok, interpreted as "both streams" or "two adjoining streams." Some Delawares from the region about Neshaminy Creek in the western part of the state settled along Beaver River near Kuskuski. Donehoo considered it a coincidence that the stream should be given the same name as the historic stream on the Delaware. Among the first white settlers in the western region of the state were some Scotch-Irish Presbyterians, who brought the name of the historic Neshaminy Church with them. Neshaminy Creek, which joins the Delaware in Bucks County, reportedly took its name from *Nischam-hanne,* "two streams," signifying a stream formed by the junction of two branches.[19]

The village of **Niagara** in Marinette County was so named because the Quinnesec Falls in the Menominee River were compared to Niagara Falls, New York. The name of the village was extended to the town. Little Niagara Creek in Eau Claire County appears on maps as early as 1888. Locally it is believed that the name was given because of a small waterfall near the junction of the creek with the Chippewa River.[20] Niagara Escarpment in Door County is named for the Niagara limestone which underlies much of the Midwest and here reaches the surface.

The Iroquois Indians, in whose territory the famous Niagara cataract was located, did not apply that name to the falls but, according to some, to the Niagara River, or, according to others, to the neck of land which the portage road followed between Lakes Erie and Ontario.[21] In Seneca and other Iroquois dialects or languages, Niagara and its variants are usually defined as "the neck," although an alternative meaning, "bisected bottom land," has also been suggested.[22]

The Mohawk form was given as *O-ni-ag-a-ra* by Lieut. Gov. Cadwallader Golden in 1741. Ethnologist Lewis H. Morgan (1851) said that a Seneca village at the mouth of the Niagara River was called *Neahga* in their dialect and *Oneagara* in Mohawk. He connected the name to their term for "neck," a supposition which appears to be sustained by Chafe's Seneca dictionary.[23]

The village of **Norwalk** in Monroe County has a disguised Indian name. The name for this place was chosen by S. McGarry, original owner of the town site, because of his former residence near Norwalk, Ohio, which in turn was named for Norwalk, Connecticut.[24] This name evolved from an old Mohegan word adopted by whites in 1650. According to a Connecticut historian, it was once supposed "to commemorate a purchase from the natives of territory measured by one day's *Northwalk* from the [Long Island] Sound but the orthography used in the early appearances of the name does not favor this explanation, and common sense rejects it; it is almost certainly Indian, modified by English lips."[25]

According to J. Hammond Trumbull, nineteenth-century Algonquian scholar, this name occurs in colonial records as Norwaake, Norwauke, Norwaack, and Norwake. He maintained that "the fact that modern spelling of the name was not generally adopted for ten years after the purchase and settlement of the town is sufficient reason for rejecting the traditional derivation. . . . The name seems to be the equivalent of Nayaug, Noyack, Nyack, etc., 'a point of land.'"[26]

Oneonta Lake in Goodman Township, Marinette County, is named from the city of Oneonta in Otsego County, New York. The name is from the Oneida or possibly the Mohawk term meaning "stony place." Schoolcraft's vocabularies give *onehya* as the word for stone in Mohawk, and *onia* as the same in Oneida and Onondaga.[27]

The village of **Ontario** in Vernon County was named in 1837 at the suggestion of O. H. Millard, a settler from Ontario County, New York.[28] The New York county was named for Lake Ontario, on which it is situated. Ontario has become an attractive name in the United States. Eight states have one or more places named Ontario, some for the lake, some for the Canadian province, and some for other places called Ontario.

The name is Iroquoian, but there is a difference of opinion about the meaning, with formidable scholars having varying beliefs. Louis Hennepin, seventeenth-century explorer-priest, reported that the name meant "beautiful lake."[29] The same meaning was given by Lewis H. Morgan to the Mohawk form of the name, *Skanodario.*[30] Prof. J. A. Rayburn, Canadian place name scholar, identified the name with *Kanyatariiya*, which he linked with the Mohawk name for "Handsome Lake."[31] W. M. Beauchamp held that Ontario "was not only the name of a great lake, but in its full form is also the title of the principal Seneca chief (Handsome Lake), and was borne by the prophet of the New Religion."[32]

The identity of the lake name and that of the noted religious leader is coincidental, neither being connected to the other. Still another view was given by Horatio Hale in his *Iroquois Book of Rites:* "Ontario is derived from Huron *yontare*, or *ontare*, lake (Iroquois *oniatare*), with this termination (*-io*, "great"). It was not by any means the most beautiful of the lakes they knew, but in the early times, when the Hurons dwelt on the north and east of it and the Iroquois to the south, it was to both of them emphatically 'the great lake.'"[33]

Oswego Lake in Vilas County is named for the city of Oswego in Oswego County, New York. Oswego was an ancient trading post in the Iroquois country. Its name was the Oneida and Onondaga designation of Lake Ontario. Beauchamp called Oswego one form of a well-known name meaning "flowing out," or more exactly, "small water flowing into that which is large." Morgan listed four dialectical variations of this name, and also translated it as "flowing out." Oswego is situated on Lake Ontario at the mouth of Oswego River.[34]

The village and town of **Otsego** in Columbia County were settled by people from Otsego County, New York, who apparently named it for their former home.[35] Otsego, a name of Iroquois origin, is related to *Otsaga*, given by Morgan as the Mohawk name for Cooperstown, New York. He called its signification lost, but others translated it as "place of the rock."[36]

Rockaway Beach, in Calumet and Winnebago counties, is a settled area with an Anglo-sounding name that actually belongs, in different form, to an Indian tribe of Long Island, New York. Their territory reached across the island from north to south, and included land now within the boroughs of Queens and Brooklyn, and between the land of the Canarsies on the west and the Matinecocks and Merricks on the east.

Rockaway is a corruption of the aboriginal name first recorded by the Dutch as *Rechouwhacky* and *Rochqua Akie,* which was turned into Rockaway as early as 1656. "Sandy land" is the meaning of this disguised Indian name. Rockaway became a popular place name in New York and elsewhere. It is on nine places on Long Island as well as places in six states from New Jersey to California.[37]

Saginaw Lake in Webb Lake Township, Burnett County, has a name borrowed from Michigan. The name there was originally on Saginaw Bay of Lake Huron, from which it was extended to the river that empties into the bay, and to the city and county of Saginaw. Saginaw is a borrowed name in eight states.

The meaning of Saginaw is in dispute. Perhaps the most widely held view is that Saginaw River and Bay are named for the Sauk Indians, who are reported to have occupied that area before whites arrived. The Ottawa Indian writer Andrew J. Blackbird asserted (1887) that "Saginaw is derived from the name [of the] O-saw-gees, who formerly lived there."[38] The other chief claim is that Saginaw means "outlet of a river." Some hold that the Sauk were named *Saukie-uck,* "people of the outlet," because of their residence on the bay, instead of that place being named for them. This view was first given by Cadillac (1718) who wrote that "the Sauk tribe is so called because Sauky means mouth of the river."[39]

However, the correct name of the Sauk is *Osaukie-uck,* "yellow earth people," according to their own traditions. The Indian agent to the Sauk in 1827, Thomas Forsyth, wrote that "the original and present name of the Sauk Indians proceeds from the compound word, Sakie, alias, A-saw-wee-kee literally Yellow Earth." The older spelling of the tribal name is suggested by the names of Ozaukee County, Wisconsin, and Osakis Lake, Minnesota.[40]

Father Verwyst (1892) called Saginaw a "corruption of Osaginang (place where the Sacs used to live)," but later (1916) he changed his view, saying that the name came from Ojibwa *saging* or *saginang,* "at the mouth of a river."[41] It is significant that none of the variant spellings of Saginaw include the initial sound of *a* or *o*, although that was indisputably a part of the Sauk tribal name. Even if the Sauk lived about Saginaw Bay, as tradition holds, the similarity between the tribal name and the place name is probably coincidental. Saginaw Bay, according to J. H. Trumbull, was named "from the mouth of the river which flows through it to the lake."[42]

Sandusky, in Washington Township, Sauk County, is listed by the U.S. Geological Survey as a "populated place." Rural folk of my generation would call it "a wide place in the road." Its presence, however, is a sign of settlement from Ohio. The place was named for Sandusky, Ohio, by William Dano and Joshua Holmes.[43]

Sandusky is a Wyandot Indian name which seems to have been a generic term widely used by the Indians of northwestern Ohio. Two Wyandot villages, Lower and Upper Sandusky, formerly existed at the sites of the present towns bearing those names. On Sandusky Bay, an arm of Lake Erie, the English in 1749 established a trading post called Fort Sandoski, which was burned by the Indians in 1763.

The present city of Sandusky, Ohio, did not receive its name until the 1820s, although "Lac Sandouske" was shown on Popple's map of 1733. With one exception, explanations of this name invariably connect it with water. The other claim erroneously links the name with an alleged Polish trader named Sadowsky who left Poland in 1756 and made his way to Ohio, where he was killed by Indians. However, the appearance of this name in Ohio precedes the date of the alleged settlement by Sadowsky.

Interpretations of this name, from Wyandot, include "water," "cool water," "pure water," and "large bodies or pools of water." Sandusky is the name of populated places in eight states, each of them named for the Ohio city.[44]

The town of **Saratoga** in Wood County has a Mohawk Indian name from New York which has been adopted in fourteen states. The name is on several places in the Empire State. The original Saratoga (now Schuylerville) was the place where Americans captured Gen. John Burgoyne's army on October 17, 1777. In honor of the event, Saratoga County, Saratoga Lake, and the city of Saratoga Springs, New York, were named later. The fame of the historic Saratoga was later eclipsed by the reputation of the resort at Saratoga Springs, and most of the Saratogas in other states are named for it.

Several interpretations of this name have been made, but the most convincing one was given by E. M. Ruttenber and Daniel Brinton, who held that the name arose from Mohawk words for "beaver place." Moreover, they wrote, the Mohicans called the place by a name having the same meaning in their language.[45]

Lake **Tahoe** lies in the high Sierras on both sides of the California-Nevada border just west of Carson City, Nevada. Mark Twain camped there in the 1860s and admired the spectacular scenery. Gold seekers crossed the Sierras through Donner Pass just to the north, and so the name of the lake became known.

Tahoe is from the language of the Washoe Indians, who still live in Nevada near Carson City. The name has been defined by Kroeber as the generic name for "lake," and by Carlson as a Washoe word meaning "big lake or water."[46]

Wisconsin has three lakes named for this now popular tourist attraction, in Iron, Lincoln, and Racine counties.

The name of **Telulah** Springs at Appleton, Outagamie County, is probably from Tallula in Louisiana and Mississippi. It could have been brought north by Civil War veterans, as it was in Illinois. *Talula* is Choctaw for "bell." The name was given, for unknown reasons, to Cherokee settlements in Georgia and North Carolina, where it survives today in both states, on a creek in North Carolina and two villages in Georgia. However, it is not a Cherokee word.[47]

Tioga is a tiny settlement in Hendren Township, Clark County. Its name is that of a river which flows from Pennsylvania to join the Chemung River at Corning, New York. Tioga is also the name of counties and villages in each of those states. The name was originally applied to an Indian village composed mainly of Delawares at the confluence of the Chemung and Susquehanna rivers, at the site of present Athens, Pennsylvania.

Lewis H. Morgan derived Tioga from *Tä-ya-o'-ga*, in the Cayuga dialect of Iroquois, signifying "at the forks," and referring to the convergence of several trails at that place. Heckewelder believed, however, that it meant "a gate, a place of entrance" (from *Tiao'ga*) because a trail at that point led from Delaware lands into Iroquois territory. Morgan's view, "at the forks," is accepted by George P. Donehoo, by William Beauchamp, and by Mooney and Dunn.[48] Tioga is a borrowed name in nine states.

Tippecanoe Lake in Vilas County and Tippecanoe Park in the city of Milwaukee have names borrowed from Indiana's Tippecanoe River. It is famous for a battle which took place on November 7, 1811, at the junction of that river with the Wabash. A village of Shawnee, Potawatomi and other Indians established there by Tecumseh was approached by about nine hundred militia led by William Henry Harrison, apparently intent on dispossessing the inhabitants. In Tecumseh's absence, his brother Tenskwatawa, the Prophet, on the evening of November 6 sought a parley to be held the next day.

The Indians, expecting no resolution to their situation, decided to strike first, and before dawn on November 7, they attacked the soldiers' camp. However, sentries gave the alarm, the Indians were dispersed, and the village was destroyed. The prestige won in this incident helped propel "Tippecanoe" Harrison into the presidency in 1840.

The name given to the river by the Miami, in whose territory it was located, was *ke-tap-kwon*, the name of the buffalo fish, which was formerly abundant in the river and its tributaries. According to J. P. Dunn, Tippecanoe is a corruption of *Ke-tap-e-kon-nong* (i.e., *ketapekon* town or place), which was the name of the Indian town at the mouth of the river. The last part of the name was twisted into "canoe," which is not a North American Indian word.[49]

Towanda Lake in Vilas County has a Delaware Indian name from Pennsylvania. There Towanda is the name of a creek which joins the Susquehanna River below the town of Towanda, the seat of Bradford County. According to the missionary John Heckewelder, this place was known to the Delawares as *Tawundeunk*, "where we bury the dead," because the Nanticoke buried their dead there.[50] This view fits very well with the Delaware term *tauwundin*, "burial place," in Brinton and Anthony's Lenape dictionary.[51]

Other views are less convincing: (1) that it is a contraction from *tanawunda*, "swift water, or rapids"; or (2) that it is corrupted from the name of a Susquehannock village located there.[52] The somber meaning of Towanda has not prevented it from being adopted as a place name in Illinois and Kansas, as well as on this Wisconsin lake.

Walla Walla Creek, which runs into Partridge Lake in Waupaca County, has its name from the far Northwest. It is one example of what is called reduplication, or repetition of sounds in a name. Pago Pago, Samoa, is another example. Walla Walla is the name of a small river which runs out of northeastern Oregon and joins the Columbia at Wallula, in the state of Washington. Wallula is simply a variant form of Walla Walla, which is also the name of a town and county in this region of southeastern Washington.

This name is originally that of a small Indian tribe, closely related to the Cayuse and Nez Perce, which is now on the Umatilla reservation in Oregon. According to Swanton, Walla Walla means "little river." Explanations by other writers include "small, rapid river," "running water," and "rapid stream."[53]

Where **Wyalusing** Creek joins the Susquehanna River in Bradford County, Pennsylvania, is a village with the same euphonious name, a contraction from *Machiwihilusing.* Two miles below it once stood a Munsee-Delaware village of the same name, which is said to mean "place of the old man," from an ancient warrior who lived there. The Moravian Brethren missionaries called this place Friedenshütten, "tents of peace," but the native name, as presently modified has prevailed.[54]

The state of Indiana gave this name to a creek and Wisconsin borrowed it for a village, town, and state park which occupies the high bluffs at the mouth of the Wisconsin River, in Grant County. The original name-giver was Robert Glenn, an early settler from Wyalusing, Pennsylvania, who thought that this place resembled his former home town.[55]

Yolo, a one-time flag stop on the Northwestern railway in Clark County, had a name which now survives only on a cemetery. It is named from the town and county of Yolo, in California. The name was taken from that of a Wintun Indian village, but it has not been defined.[56] This is one of several Wisconsin names resulting from the California Gold Rush.

The village of **Yuba** in Richland County has its name from that of a Maidu Indian village which formerly existed at the site of present Yuba

City, in Yuba County, California. The Yuba River, which passed by that place, was named by Johann Sutter, who had settled in the vicinity a few years earlier.[57]

Like Alaska, in Kewaunee County, the name of **Yukon** Creek in Oneida County was probably inspired by the Alaska purchase of 1867, or perhaps by the 1898 gold rush. The Yukon River heads in tributary waters of Lake Bennett, in Canada's Yukon Territory, and flows through Alaska to the Bering Sea. Its Athapascan Indian name was first obtained by Hudson's Bay Company fur traders, who explored the upper river and established Fort Yukon in 1847. The Russians explored the lower river in the 1830s, and established a post at Nulato in 1841. The lower Yukon and its delta was then and is now occupied by Eskimos (Inuit), who called the river *Kuikpak*, meaning "Big River." The Athapascans of the interior called it *Yukonna*, "Great River."[58]

The Alaska-Yukon gold rush of 1898 caused the adoption in four Wisconsin places of the name of a small tributary of the Yukon River in Yukon Territory, Canada, where an important gold strike was made. The stream was called Klondike, a name adopted for villages in Kenosha and Oconto counties, and a lake in Vilas County. In Grant County, the variant spelling of Klondyke was given to a park. The word is corrupted from an Athapascan native term of uncertain meaning. It has been interpreted as "deer," "deer river," and "hammer water," from the native custom of pounding sticks into shallow streams to support salmon nets.[59]

20

Names from South of the Border

Almost invariably the original Indian names of Mexican
towns are descriptive designations. To the uninitiated,
many of these names may appear "unpronounceable" at
first glance, due to the fact that as written they represent
an attempt to convert, phonetically, the sounds of Indian
words into Spanish as it was written four centuries ago.
Even the resourceful Spaniards were balked by the tongue-
twisting complexities of a few Indian place names, but
being always a practical people they simply corrupted the
pronunciation of the Indian names in the interests of
expediency, just as West Coast Americans have corrupted
the pronunciation of the Spanish-Mexican place names
in California in a way that often would be unrecognizable
to Spanish-speaking people.
        "Mexican Place Names," Amigos *1 (August 1942)*

The United States map is strewn with aboriginal names which originated in Mexico, the other Central American countries, the Caribbean region and South America. The reasons for this are: (1) many of
these names in the Southwest were given when that region was part of
Mexico; (2) numerous aboriginal words from the Latin American region
were adopted into French, Spanish, and English, and are scarcely recognized as borrowed words. Prominent in this category are names of flora
and fauna, but also such words as *canoe, hurricane, pampa,* and *savanna;* (3) the Mexican War (1846–48) caused an abundance of Mexican
place names to be adopted, particularly the names of places where
battles took place; (4) sympathy for liberation struggles, especially that
of the Cubans in the nineteenth century, caused many places to be
named Cuba and Havana; (5) important literary-historical works, such

as William Prescott's (1786–1859) *Conquest of Mexico* and *Conquest of Peru* popularized names from those countries; and (6) in addition to the ordinary attraction of exotic names, there was the association of some of these names with mineral wealth.

The Caribbean

Despite its identification with North American Indians, the **canoe** has not taken its name from any of their languages. It is from the Arawakan language stock of the West Indies. It is said that Columbus borrowed the word from the Haitian *kanoa* or *canoa* and carried it to Spain, from whence it found its way into French and English on the North American continent.[1] In Wisconsin this very American word is in **Lost Canoe** Lake in Vilas County.

Cuba was once a popular North American place name, and nearly all of the places named for the largest of the Antilles received their names before the Spanish-American War of 1898. The reason was American sympathy for the Cuban independence struggles of the nineteenth century, which were likened to our own war for independence.

The name of the island is generally connected with *Cubanacan*, an Arawak term meaning "center or middle." It was the name of a now-extinct tribe which occupied the island at the time of Spanish discovery, and it is still the name of a mountain chain in central Cuba.

Cuba City, a village in Grant County, is the second Wisconsin place to carry this name. According to legend, it was named Yuba about 1870, but was soon changed to Cuba, and later Cuba City. A place called Cuba City was listed in Kewaunee County in 1880, but it has long since disappeared.[2]

In our earlier history, the term **hurricane** was applied not only to violent storms, but also to their effects, such as fallen trees and stormswept ground or any recently devastated area.[3]

Hurricane is an adaptation of the Spanish *huracán*, which in turn was adopted from the Carib Indian *huracan*, according to William A. Read. Bartlett, likewise, over a century ago, traced the origin of the word to the West Indian natives, who applied it to violent storms.[4] Daniel Brinton found that the Indians of the Central American mainland had adopted the word as a name for a deity:

In the legends of the Quiches [a Mayan tribe of Guatemala] the mysterious creative power is HURAKAN, a name of no significance in their language, one which some have thought they brought from the Antilles, which finds its meaning in the ancient language of Haiti, and which, under the forms of *hurricane, ouragon, orkan,* was adopted into European marine languages as the native name of the terrible tornado [*sic*] of the Caribbean sea.[5]

Skeat, like Barton, believed that the word was Haitian, in which case it must be from Taino, an Arawak language, and not the Carib, as presumed by some others.[6] In Wisconsin the name **Hurricane** is on an island in the Mississippi and a village in Grant County.

Mexico

In 1836 Judge N. F. Hyer discovered the remains of an ancient Indian village along the Crawfish River in Jefferson County. The twenty-one-acre site was once stockaded and contained the ruins of mounds which later archaeologists classified as Middle Mississippian. Judge Hyer imagined that this northernmost mound-builder site was the legendery **Aztalan** (usually spelled Aztlan), which Aztec tradition named as the original home of those people before they began their migration to south central Mexico. The name and tradition had been mentioned by Alexander von Humboldt.

Consequently, Judge Hyer named this place Aztalan. In 1950 the state acquired the site and named it Aztalan State Park. Aztalan is also the name of the nearby village and the surrounding town.[7]

The *Encyclopaedia Britannica* says that *Aztlan* means "Aztec place" in Nahuatl; another source links the name with the Nahuatl words *atl,* "water," and *an,* "near." (The same meaning has been assigned to Anahuac.) The name Aztec has been explained at least five ways.[8]

Aztlan is the name given by militant Chicanos to the southwestern part of the United States which was taken from Mexico in 1848.[9] In 1864 some delegates to the new Arizona territorial legislature wanted to create a town as territorial capital, to be called Azatlan (variant spelling), but nothing came of it.[10]

Chapultepec is listed by the U.S. Geological Survey as a locality in Trempealeau County. Originally it was the name of a 200-foot-high ele-

vation near Mexico City which was captured by General Winfield
Scott's troops on September 13, 1847. It is one of many Mexican place
names adopted in the United States as a consequence of the war with
Mexico. This name comes from the Aztecs and is said to signify "grass-
hopper hill."[11]

Mexico Creek in Forest County is another name that was adopted as
a result of the Mexican War. *Mexico, Mexihco,* or *Metzxihco (Meh'-hee-
co)* was originally the Nahuatl (Aztec) name for the territory in which
their capital, Tenochtitlan, now Mexico City, was located. It was "the
place of Mexihtli, the eponymous god . . . of the Aztec tribe, born during the years of wandering." He was the war and sun god, the chief god
and protector of the city, otherwise called Huitzipochtli. *Mexico* in its
original form is said to signify "in the navel of the moon" or "in the
center of the moon."[12]

South America

An unverified story is told of the origin of the name **Chili**
for a village in Clark County. A railroad crew arrived there one January
day in the 1870s. Their task was to erect a depot sign with the name
Cedarhurst. Since the weather was exceedingly cold, one man remarked
that it was the chilliest place he had ever been, so the name was
changed to Chili.

Chili is a name of Aztec origin applied to the hot peppers of the
American tropics (*Capsicum frutescens* or *Capsicum annuum*). It is
probable, however, that this place was named for the Republic of Chile,
which during the nineteenth century was often called Chili. Chile, of
course, is not named for the pepper plants, but its name origin is obscure. It is suggested that it comes from an ancient Auracanian tribal
name which survives in the name of the island of Chiloe, or that it is
from an Aymara word meaning "cold."[13]

Most places in the United States which are called **Lima** are so
named from the capital of Peru. (Often it is pronounced *Lime'-ah*, instead of the more correct *Leem'-ah*). The name of this Quechua (Inca)
Indian city was corrupted by the Spanish from the Indian name *Rima*
or *Rimac* when the Spanish named this city their colonial capital in
1535. Rimac was a god whose temple "was repaired to by countless

members from all parts of the realm," according to Prescott. The name
is said to signify "he who speaks." The old form Rimac is still on a
Peruvian river.[14]

In Wisconsin there is a village named Lima Center in Rock County
and another named West Lima in Richland County, both unincorporated. The village of Lima is in Pepin County. Civil towns named Lima
are in Grant, Pepin, Rock, and Sheboygan counties. The town in Sheboygan County, where the now vanished village of Lima was founded in
1849, was named by Hiram Humphrey for his old home town of Lima,
New York. It is alleged that the town of Lima in Grant County was
named for lime kilns. This is not verified, but even if true it was probably suggested by the Peruvian name.

Peru, a town in Dunn County, is named for the South American
country. This name was adopted for towns, cities, and other places in
twelve states. Although some may have been inspired by the appearance
of William H. Prescott's book, *History of the Conquest of Peru* (1847),
most of them were named before that event. The earliest, Peru, Maine,
was named in 1821, the year that Peru won its independence from
Spain. Settlers from Peru, Illinois, carried the name to Kansas and
Nebraska. The particular reason for the presence of the name in Wisconsin has not been found.[15]

The name Peru is a corruption by the Spanish from the Quechuan
word *pelu.* Garcilaso de la Vega, Inca historian, said *pelu* was the word
for "river" and was given by a native in reply to a question from the
Spanish, who mistook it for the name of the country. The name Peru
was unknown to the inhabitants, who called their country Tavantin-
suyu, "the four corners of the world."[16]

It may seem strange that an article of clothing worn by Peruvian Indians should give a name to a Wisconsin place, but that is the story of
Poncho Creek in New Hope Township, Portage County.

A poncho is "a blanket-like cloak worn by Indians and Spanish-
Americans with a slit in the middle for the head to pass through." The
Inca word passed into North American English as a name for sleeveless
raincoats with an opening for the head, and later to any article of clothing so constructed.[17]

Potosi, a village and town in Grant County, were named in 1845. The
name was borrowed from that of the city and department of Potosí in

Bolivia, from which locality the Spanish obtained so much silver that the word *potosí* entered the Spanish language as a term for untold riches. The name was first adopted in the United States in 1814 as a name for the place which is now the seat of Washington County, Missouri. At that time, this was a lead mining district, and the presence of rich lead mines doubtless inspired the name in both that place and in Grant County, Wisconsin.

Potosi is reportedly taken from the Aymara Indian word *potosci*, "he who makes a noise." The reference is to a mountain which, when the Incas commanded that it be dug into for silver, made a tremendous noise, as if to say, "this silver is reserved for others."[18]

21

Potpourri

Good names, once bestowed, are among the most lasting
of things earthly. They may change in form, but they
rarely perish. They outlast dynasties, they outlive
generations and ages of men—they are in a word,
perennial.

Ainsworth R. Spofford,
"American Historical Nomenclature" (1893)

A number of Indian names do not fit into the classifications chosen
for chapter headings for this book. Still others are of doubtful origin and interpretation. Examples of both are listed here. Some names on
the map which "look Indian" are not included because no information
is available to give any conclusion about them.

Ahnapee River begins in Door County and flows south into Green
Bay at Algoma in Kewaunee County. From the river came the names of
Ahnapee State Trail, Ahnapee Trail State Park, and the town of Ahnapee
in Kewaunee County.

This name has been connected to the Ojibwa term *anapi,* or *anipi,*
signifying "When?" It hardly seems credible as a place name, but it may
have been chosen by whites for its pleasing sound.[1]

Anninan Lake in Langlade County has a name which, from its location, ought to be of Ojibwa origin. The term closest approaching it in
Baraga's dictionary is *Ininan* (*nind*), "I present or put it." The term *nin*
or *nind* is a pronoun identifying the speaker.[2] Although this name, like
several others, being a verb, does not seem to be a likely place name,
verbal Indian place names do exist.

Ashwaubenon, the name of a suburb of the city of Green Bay, of a
town, and of a creek in Brown County, is derived, according to Father
Verwyst, from Ojibwa *ashiwabiwining,* "place where they watch, or

keep a lookout,—as for enemies."[3] The difficulty of this explanation is that the place is not in Ojibwa territory.

The village of **Bibon,** Bibon Lake, and Bibon Marsh in Bayfield County are named from the Ojibwa word for "winter." It is here spelled exactly as in Baraga's dictionary,[4] but it is slightly different in *Hiawatha:*

> Mighty Peboan the winter
> Breathing on the lakes and rivers,
> Into stone had changed their waters . . .[5]

The name of **Bisanabi** Lake in Racine County is quite obviously a contraction of the Ojibwa word *bisânabiwin,* meaning "silence, tranquillity, quietude."[6]

In the *Hiawatha* poem, two spirits entered the hero's lodge to claim the life of the ailing Minnehaha:

> And the foremost said "Behold me!
> I am Famine, Bukadawin!"
> And the other said: "Behold me!
> I am Fever, Ahkosewin!"[7]

The Ojibwa name for "hunger" or "fever," given by Baraga as *bakada'win,* is the apparent source of the name of Upper and Lower **Buckatabon** Lakes in Vilas County.[8]

Kaubeshine Lakes (Upper and Lower), Oneida County, have an obscure name. According to Baraga, *Kabe,* in compositions, signifies "all, the whole."[9] This might explain the first part of the name, but the meaning of "shine" is not apparent.

Keesus Lake in Morton township, Waukesha County, has the Potawatomi name of the sun. It is spelled *Kises* in Gailland's English-Potawatomi dictionary, *Gisiss* in Baraga's *Otchipwe Language,* and *Ke'-so* in Hoffman's Menominee vocabulary.[10]

Kekoskee is the name of a village in Dodge County. A fanciful explanation of it holds that it is a Winnebago term meaning "friendly village."[11] It is in former Winnebago territory, but if from their language, the name is much corrupted. "Keesh-ko" is defined as a "Winnebago name of a people" by John Kinzie.[12] Whether that is related to Kekoskee I cannot determine.

Manawa is the name of a city and pond in Waupaca County, and should be, from its location, a Potawatomi term. The only other occurrence of this name in the United States is on Lake Manawa at Council Bluffs, Pottawattamie County, Iowa. It was created by a shift in the Missouri River during the 1870s. However, the Potawatomi Indians left that location for Kansas in 1848.

This name does not closely resemble any Potawatomi term in Gailland's dictionary. It does, however, closely approximate the Ojibwa word *minawa*, meaning "again, more, anew."[13] (Minawa Beach is a place in Fond du Lac County.) At present this affords the best guess as to the origin and meaning of this name, which could have been given by whites.

The city of **Mequon,** in Ozaukee County, has a name which is considered to be from Ojibwa *miquan*, "feather."[14] The name is apparently taken from that of a tributary of Milwaukee River shown as Micwon River on Cram's map in 1839. Today it is called Cedar Creek.

An unverified local story claims that Mequon is named for White Feather, a daughter of "Chief Waubaka."[15] Since the name was first on the river, it was used by the Indians before whites adopted it, and it was not customary for Indians to name places for individuals.

The Potawatomi form of this name is the same as the Ojibwa, and was applied to a writing pen because pens were made of feathers.[16] It was the same among the Delawares, who called William Penn by the name Mequon or Miquan. Today Miquan is the name of a village on the Schuylkill River, Montgomery County, Pennsylvania, just outside the city of Philadelphia.[17]

The name of Lake **Metonga,** in Forest County, does not appear to be from a Wisconsin language. It could be a corruption by whites from the Santee Sioux term *matanka*, "large, great in any way."[18]

The name of **Nawago** Creek on the Bad River Indian Reservation in Ashland County is very similar to Newaygo, the name of a town and county in Michigan. The latter are named for an Ottawa chief, whose name, spelled Ningwegon and in other ways, is translated "The Wing." Father Baraga's Ojibwa word for "wing," *ninwigan*, is a close approximation of the chief's name. The Wisconsin stream, of course, is not named for the Indian in Michigan, but its meaning is apparently the same as that of his name.[19]

Pemene Falls in the Menominee River, Marinette County, are said to be named from *biminik*, the Ojibwa word for "elbow," on account of a bend in the river.[20] The name is also attached to a creek on the Michigan side. The place name more closely approximates *pe·min*, the Menominee term for "sweat bath," but there is no evidence for this etymological origin.[21]

In Taylor County is **Rib** Lake, on the shore of which is a village of the same name. From the lake flows Big Rib River which flows to the Wisconsin River at Wausau, Marathon County. Along the way, a cataract called Rib Falls gives its name to a village and town. Just before reaching its outlet, Big Rib receives the waters of Little Rib River. Above the river west of Wausau rises Rib Mountain, 1,940 feet above sea level, which is enclosed by Rib Mountain State Park.

All these places are named for Rib River. According to Hiram Calkins, a resident of Wausau in 1854, the name of Rib River was a translation from the Ojibwa name *O-pik-wun-a Se-be*.[22] No reason for the name is given. Calkins, like many early recorders of Indian names, gave a crude reproduction of this one. Father Baraga lists the Ojibwa term for "rib" as *opigeganama*.[23]

Shioc River flows from Shawano County to join the Wolf River above Shiocton in Outagamie County. Several unlikely opinions about this name are in print, and it is perhaps better that they not be repeated. One possible explanation for Shiocton is Skinner's view that the name is from *Mä'no'mäne Sai'ak*, "wild rice along the banks," the name of a former Menominee village site. It may be, however, that this name is a derivation from the Menominee term *Shi' awaqui*, "bend in the river," also used as a personal name. Swanton also lists, but does not locate, a Menominee village named for its chief, Shakitok.[24]

Lake **Wandawega** in La Grange Township, Walworth County, is in former Potawatomi territory, but this name does not approximate anything in their language. One guess that can be made is that it is a corruption, and perhaps the residue of a longer name, related to the Winnebago term *wah-wen-da*, "she-bear." There is also a Dakota term, *wa-na-we-ga*, "to break with the foot." The Dakota (Sioux) did not occupy this area, but whites sometimes adopted their place names from other states, as in the case of Mendota.[25]

Wanoka Lake, Bayfield County, has a name of uncertain origin. One can only speculate that this name comes from Ojibwa *wanikan*, "a hole in the ground."[26]

A highway sign at each end of the willage of **Waunakee,** on state route 19 in Dane County, reads: "Welcome to the only Waunakee in the world." Indeed, the name is found nowhere else, except on a nearby marsh. The name is from Ojibwa *wanaki*, "peace," or *nin wanaki*, "I inhabit a place in peace."[27]

Waupun is the name of a city and town in Dodge County. As a word it is sometimes spelled *waubun* or *waban*, *wapan*, etc., and means "dawn" as well as "east" in several Algonquian languages.[28] Mrs. John H. Kinzie named her famous book *Wau Bun; or, The Early Day in the Northwest* (1858). In the *Hiawatha* epic, *Wabun* is both the morning star and the east wind. In that spelling it is the name of rail stops in Ontario and Virginia.

The village of **Wiota** in Lafayette County, for which a town is also named, received its name in the 1830s from Col. William Hamilton, youngest son of Alexander Hamilton. Colonel Hamilton had a trading post at this location. Reportedly, he changed the spelling of the name from *Wyota* to *Wiota* in 1847. The older spelling is in a street name in Madison. *Wiota* is widely assumed to be an Indian name, but its origin and meaning are shrouded in mystery. There is no substance to the belief that *wiota* is "an Indian word meaning crossroads." From the surface appearance, it could be called a Dakota word meaning "many moons" or a corruption from Dakota *niota*, meaning "much water."

There is, however, some cause to suspect that this may be an artificial name of obscure literary origin. *Wiota* is the name of a village in Cass County, Iowa, and was formerly the name of a village in Valley County, Montana.[29]

Names of Doubtful Origin

There is a list of place names which have not yielded their secrets to research. Neither has local inquiry brought credible answers to questions about them. The names that follow might or might not be of American Indian origin. They are not explainable at this time for one or more reasons. Some may be of Indian origin but are too corrupted to trace. Some may be artificial or pseudo-Indian names, perhaps taken, in some cases, from obscure literary works. Some may be from Old World languages, including garbled French. A few may be obscure Indian names borrowed from another state. I do not believe that any of them represent extinct languages, because very ancient names of that sort have not been found to survive in this region. I list the doubtful names here as problems for future study.

> **Chippanazie** Lake and Creek, Washburn County. An inquiry to the county historical society brought an unsigned reply, September 12, 1985, that the name means "crooked bark," in an unspecified language. Indian names in this area are Chippewa, but the above definition is not reconcilable with Chippewa vocabularies. Another preferred definition, "crooked water," likewise has no foundation in fact. A folk etymology holds that the name arose from lumbermen's practice of notching a tree to determine the direction of its fall. This was called to "chip-in-a-zee."[30]
>
> **Koshawago** Spring, Sauk County.
>
> **Mackaysee** Lake, on Chambers Island in Green Bay, Door County.[31]
>
> **Muskesin** Lake, Vilas County.
>
> **Noboken** Lake, Langlade County.
>
> **Nonoken** Lake, Forest County.
>
> **Pauto** Lake, Vilas County. Pahto is the Yakima name for Mt. Adams, in Washington, but there is no evidence of alteration or transfer of the name.
>
> **Paya** Lake, Oconto County.
>
> **Pesabic** Lake, Lincoln County.
>
> **Sapokesick** Lake, Menominee County. *Kesick* is Menominee for "sky," but *Sapo* cannot be explained in that language.[32]
>
> **Sheosh** Creek, tributary of St. Croix River, Douglas County. The name is not recognized by St. Croix Chippewa informants.
>
> Lake **Tahkodah,** Bayfield County. According to Stephen R. Riggs, *takodaku* is one form, in both Teton and Santee Dakota, for the particular friend of a Dakota man. However, there is no evidence to connect the name in Bayfield County to the Dakotas.[33]
>
> **Wautoma,** city, town, pond, swamp, lake, Waushara County. A local informant says that this name is composed of parts of two words.

"Wau" from "Waugh" and "Tom" from "Tomah," the name of a famous Menominee. "The two united are supposed to mean 'good earth' or 'good life' or 'where to spend a good life.'" However, there is no word written as "waugh" in any local language, and terms for "good earth" or "good life" cannot be matched with Wautoma in any Wisconsin Indian language.[34]

Weeting Lake, Sauk County.

Weso Creek and Lake, Menominee County. Possibly related to *wâseo*, "catfish" (Menominee).[35]

Wiscobee Lake, Oconto County.

Wyandock Lake, Vilas County. Possibly a corruption from the tribal name Wyandot.

22

Artificial Names

Pseudo-Indian names occur . . . the forms of which
approximate so closely real Indian words that the
historical records alone can settle the question of their
real origin.
    A. F. Chamberlain, introduction to W. W. Tooker,
    Indian Place Names of Long Island (*1962*)

L ike most states, Wisconsin has a number of artificial or semiar-
tificial "Indian" names. Some of them have been mentioned under
literary names; the others are examined here. The coinage of names, in
the view of the late George R. Stewart, "is the most distinctive feature
of American place-naming. Nowhere has it so flourished."[1] Coined or
artificial names may be generally defined as contrived names which do
not constitute recognizable words in any language. Artificial names
may not normally be explained by linguistic analysis. Although they
may sometimes be explained from their locations, it is often necessary
to seek their origin in records or interviews. However, in going that
route, one is likely to run into a welter of fanciful stories or folk ety-
mologies. The task of documentation of these names is often difficult.
At times a namesmith such as Henry R. Schoolcraft records the manner
of his name inventions, but often gives conflicting explanations in different places. A measure of sleuthing is called in order to track down the
truth.

    One of the more picturesque of the coined names in Wisconsin is **Al-
goma,** given to a city in Kewaunee County and to a town in Winnebago
County. Algoma is also the name of villages, towns, or townships in Virginia, West Virginia, Michigan, Mississippi, Minnesota, and Oregon. It
is the name of a village and district of Ontario, and of a railroad in that
region, the Algoma Central. Schoolcraft unsuccessfully tried to fasten

the name to Lake Superior. In variant spelling, the name occurs as Algona in Iowa and Washington, and Algonac in Michigan.

Algoma in Kewaunee County was named in 1899, probably as a borrowing from Michigan. A local tourist brochure gives a purely fanciful explanation of the name, "Indian for Park of Flowers." Alanson Skinner, an ethnologist, tried to tie the name to *Agoma* representing *agim*, Ojibwa for "snowshoes."[2]

Schoolcraft, who coined this name, earned the epithet of "picturesque liar,"[3] by giving four different interpretations of the name: *Algonquin* plus *maig*, "waters"; "Lake of Algons"; *al*, from Algonquin, plus *goma*, "collected waters"; and finally, from the same roots, "Sea of Algonquins."[4] The fact is that Algoma, in its present form, is meaningless, since no part of it can stand alone, nor can the whole of it convey any meaning. However, the pleasing sound has won it acceptance.

Chiwaukee Prairie in Kenosha County is one of a common variety of names fashioned from parts of the names of adjoining places. The Chiwaukee Prairie is located halfway between Chicago and Milwaukee, and so the name givers joined the first three letters of Chicago to the last six letters of Milwaukee to form the name. (The names of Chicago and Milwaukee are discussed elsewhere.)

Irogami Lake in Waushara County has a name formed from part of the names of two Indian tribes. Formerly it was called Fish Lake. The story of the origin of the present name was told in a letter of June 10, 1985, by Phillip Poulette of Wautoma, secretary-treasurer of the Waushara County Historical Society:

> A friend of mine decided that Fish Lake was too common a
> name for the lake so he started a campaign to have it named
> "Indian Battle Lake," after a story written by Hjalmar Holand
> who wrote semi-historical stories.[5] He claimed that the Iroquois were coming from the East on foot to avenge a defeat by
> the Illinois Indians. According to his story they (the Iroquois)
> were spotted by a small Chippewa Indian party who informed
> the Outagamie tribe at their village at Fish and Silver Lakes.
> The Iroquois were surrounded and destroyed in the isthmus
> between the two lakes.
>
> However, the residents did not like "Indian Battle Lake" so

they [took] "Iro" from Iroquois and "gami" from Outagamie to make Irogami Lake.

The authenticity of the battle story is arguable, but the tribal names are real, although the Iroquois were a New York tribe. The meaning of Iroquois is disputed. Hewitt and Swanton held it to mean "adders."[6] It has also been held to mean "bear" and "tobacco people," among other explanations.[7] Outagamie, from which a county is named, is the Chippewa name for the Fox or Mesquakie tribe, and signifies "people on the other side."[8]

Itasca is a neighborhood in the city of Superior, Douglas County. It has a branch post office and is a stop on the Northwestern railroad. Itasca is one of several places about the country which are named for Lake Itasca, in Clearwater County, Minnesota, which is the source of the Mississippi River. In the Gopher State, the name is also attached to a village and township in Clearwater County, to a state park which surrounds the lake, to a glacial moraine, to a county situated many miles to the east of the lake, and to a tiny lake in Freeborn County. Itasca is also the name of towns in Du Page County, Illinois, and Hill County, Texas. In the variant spelling Itaska, this name also occurs in Broome County, New York.

Henry R. Schoolcraft, a prolific name craftsman, who led the expedition which reached the source of the Mississippi on July 13, 1832, claimed authorship of the name Itasca, but gave irreconcilable accounts of its etymology. It is claimed that Schoolcraft devised the name "from the Latin words *veritas*, truth, and *caput*, head, supplied to him by [Rev. William T.] Boutwell, the name being made by writing the words together and cutting off . . . the first the last syllables." In 1872, forty years after, Boutwell publicly claimed authorship of the name.[9]

In their journals of the expedition, neither Schoolcraft, Boutwell, Lieut. James Allen, nor anyone else mentioned *veritas caput*. In 1936, however, William J. Peterson discovered an obscure published letter by Schoolcraft which supported the above explanation, although he did not credit it to Boutwell.[10] It was dated July 25, 1832, only twelve days after the discovery of Lake Itasca, and addressed to Dr. Addison Philleo. It was published in the *Galenian*, of Galena, Illinois, August 22, 1832, and reads ". . . we made a portage of six miles, with our canoes, into La Biche or Itasca Lake (from a derivation of the phrase *veritas caput*) which is the true source of this celebrated stream, being at the same time its most northern and western head."[11]

Not only did the letter to the *Galenian* differ in details from versions published in two other papers, it differed radically from Schoolcraft's version, published in 1851, of a letter he claims to have written on the same date, July 25, 1832, from St. Peters to the "editors of a western newspaper" (probably the *Galenian*): ". . . a portage was made over difficult ascents . . . for about six miles, when we reached the banks of Itasca Lake, the source of the other and longer branch (of the Mississippi)."[12] Not a word was said about *veritas caput*, but perhaps he was reconstructing the letter from memory.

Philip Mason, editor of *Schoolcraft's Expedition* (1958), held that the newspaper accounts, originating with Schoolcraft, are "conclusive evidence that Schoolcraft derived the name 'Itasca' from the Latin words 'veritas caput.'"[13] However, it seems more correct to say that they merely prove that Schoolcraft contradicted himself.

O. D. Von Engeln and Jane Urquhart, who erroneously attributed the authorship of the name to Lieut. James Allen, scoffed that "the proper way to say 'true head' in Latin is *caput verum*, so the name should have been *Putver*, not Itasca."[14]

So far, the *veritas caput* explanation has won general acceptance. It was endorsed by Warren Upham, Minnesota's place name scholar,[15] and by the state, which has placed this explanation on signs at the entrance to Itasca State Park. It also appears in several source books. Yet the fact is ignored that Schoolcraft in five places alleged Indian origin for the name and that none of his companions made any reference to the Latin story before Boutwell did so forty years after.

In Schoolcraft's first full account of his expedition, published in 1834, he made no mention of the source of Itasca.[16] In a letter addressed to the mayor of New York, October 28, 1844, Schoolcraft included Itasca in a list of Indian names suggested for the streets of that city. Elsewhere, he inveighed against Latin or Greek place name borrowings.[17]

In a short account of his expedition, published in 1851, Schoolcraft wrote that upon arriving at the source of the Mississippi, "It was declared by our guide to be Itasca Lake—the source of the main, or South fork of the Mississippi."[18] Since the guide was an Indian, this made it appear that Itasca was the aboriginal name of the lake, which it was not.

In a list of "Anglo-Indian Words" Schoolcraft listed "Itascan" as an adjective "relative to the summit bearing Itasca Lake, in which the Mississippi River rises."[19]

In his second full account of his expedition, published in 1855, Schoolcraft wrote that upon arriving at the source of the Mississippi, "I inquired of *Ozawindib* [his Indian guide] the Indian name of this lake; he replied *Omushkös*, which is the Chippewa name of the Elk.[20] Having previously got an inkling of some of their mythological and necromantic notions of the origin and mutations of the country, I denominated it ITASCA."[21] That is a bit obscure, but in another place, Schoolcraft was more explicit: "I-TAS-CA, from *Ia*, to be, *totosh*, the female breast or origin, and *ka*, a terminal subs [sic] inflection. . . . This name has been applied to the lake in which the Mississippi River originates."[22] To confuse matters further, Schoolcraft had published, in his 1834 *Narrative*, a short verse about an Indian maiden named Itasca, whose tears for a lost lover, according to legend, formed the lake. The tale was expanded and popularized by Mary Eastman in 1853.[23]

Theodore C. Blegen, a Minnesota historian, citing Stephen Riggs and Charles H. Baker, speculated that Itasca might be of Dakota origin, signifying "white face" or "white nose."[24]

In 1958 the journals and letters of three of Schoolcraft's companions, Lieut. James Allen, Douglass Houghton, and William Boutwell, were published for the first time, along with Schoolcraft's previously published reports and the known newspaper accounts.[25] Allen merely mentioned their arrival at "Lac la Biche," which they were sure was the "true source" of the great river. Houghton, a geologist, mentioned "Elk Lake" or "Lac la Beiche." Boutwell, a missionary referred to their arrival at "Omoshkos Sagaiigan (Elk Lake)," adding that "the lake is very irregular in shape and from this reason, the Indians gave it the name."[26] Since Boutwell claimed forty years later that he was the author of the name Itasca, derived from two Latin words, it is strange that his journal of 1832 made no mention of this.

Despite the inconclusive evidence, John G. Shea mentioned the supposed Latin derivation of Itasca in his edition of Charlevoix's *History of New France* (1868), and called it preposterous, but did not indicate where he obtained his information or who originated the name. That explanation was repeated in varying forms in later years.[27]

Schoolcraft was for twenty years the government agent to the Ojibwa at the Sault and Mackinac, was married to an Ojibwa woman, and officiated at several treaties. He knew the Ojibwa language and could conceivably, as he says, have fashioned Itasca from the Ojibwa word for a woman's breast, *totosh*. It occurs in other place names, such as Tadoussac, Quebec, said to be from "Totoshak, (Breasts), the place is so called from its landmark, two dome-shaped mountains."[28]

Historian Irving Hart decided that the origin and meaning of Itasca must "remain one of the unsolved problems of history," and added that "the conflicting evidence . . . cannot be reconciled without sacrificing somewhat the reputation of one or more of the men involved in the discovery of Lake Itasca."[29]

The question remains as to why Schoolcraft told conflicting stories. We might guess that he shared the prudery of his time in reference to feminine anatomy. Mentor Williams, editor of a volume of Schoolcraft's Indian legends, observed that "his own religious bias . . . was evident in the exclusion of the more off-color legends."[30] Even in several assertions of Indian origin of the name, only once does Schoolcraft explicitly link it with the female breast.

Perhaps Schoolcraft believed that an aboriginal name connected with female anatomy was appropriate for a lake which was the "source" of the Mississippi, but decided to veil the term in fractured Latin. This would be consistent with his penchant for language mixture in names.

Konsin Beach, an unincorporated community in Calumet County, was named by clipping *Wis* from Wiskonsin, which is one of the older spellings of the state name, used in Cram's map of 1839.

Mohawksin Lake in Lincoln County, an artificial lake formed by a dam, is so named for the three rivers which meet at that place: the So*mo*, the Toma*hawk*, and the Wiscon*sin*, according to information furnished in a letter dated June 19, 1985, from Mr. Graham Foster, editor of the *Tomahawk Leader*. This name, like most artificial names, could easily be mistaken for something else were it not for the facts provided by local informants.

Shoto Lake and the village of Shoto in Manitowoc County received their name by shortening *Neshoto*, Ojibwa for "twin." Shoto is located on West Twin River, called **Neshoto** in its upper course, which joins its sister stream, East Twin River, at Two Rivers, where they enter Lake Michigan. Neshoto (also Nashota, Nashotah) was the aboriginal name of the Twin Rivers. In Waukesha County a village is called **Nashotah,** near Upper and Lower Nashotah Lakes.[31]

Clipping syllables from two state names produced the name of Lake **Wissota** and the village bearing the same name in Chippewa County. The lake is enclosed by Lake Wissota State Park. The name is taken from parts of the names of Wisconsin and Minnesota, for the Minnesota-Wisconsin Power Company which built Wissota Dam on the Chippewa River in 1915. The name was chosen by the engineer, Louis G. Arnold of Eau Claire.[32]

Notes

Bibliography

Index

Notes

Abbreviations

BAE   Bureau of American Ethnology
FWP   Federal Writers Program
GPO   Government Printing Office
SHSW   State Historical Society of Wisconsin

Preface

1 Charles J. Kappler, *Indian Affairs: Laws and Treaties*, 4 vols. (Washington, D.C.: GPO, 1904), 1:1021.
2 Frederick Webb Hodge, ed., *Handbook of American Indians North of Mexico*, BAE Bulletin 30, 2 vols. (Washington, D.C.: GPO, 1907–10).

Introduction

1 Robert Louis Stevenson, *Across the Plains* (New York: Charles Scribner's Sons, 1930), 13–14.
2 Alfred H. Meyer, "Toponomy in Sequent Occupance Geography: Calumet Region, Indiana-Illinois," *Proceedings of the Indiana Academy of Science* 14 (1944): 142–59.
3 Morris Swadesh, "Linguistics as an Instrument of Prehistory" (Paper read at the annual meeting of the American Anthropological Association, Chicago, December 29, 1957), 1, 15.

1. Wisconsin's Name

1 Information in this chapter is taken from Virgil J. Vogel, "Wisconsin's Name: A Linguistic Puzzle," *Wisconsin Magazine of History* 48 (Spring 1965): 181–86, reprinted as the pamphlet *Wisconsin's Name* (Madison: SHSW, 1980). See also H. W. Kuhm, "Indian Place-Names in Wisconsin," *Wisconsin Archeologist*, n.s., 33 (March and June 1962): 144–48.
2 Reuben G. Thwaites, ed., *Jesuit Relations and Allied Documents*, 73 vols. (Cleveland: Burrows Bros., 1896–1901) 59: 105, 107.

3 Alice E. Smith, "Stephen H. Long and the Naming of Wisconsin," *Wisconsin Magazine of History* 26 (September 1942): 69.
4 Caleb Atwater, *The Indians of the Northwest, Their Manners, Customs, &c.* (Columbus, 1850), 71; August Derleth, *The Wisconsin* (New York: Farrar and Rinehart, 1942; rpt., Madison: University of Wisconsin Press, 1985), 34–36.
5 Frederick Marryat, *A Diary in America* (New York: Knopf, 1962), 181; Alfred Brunson, "Wisconsin Geographical Names," *Collections SHSW* 1 (1855, rpt. 1903): 112; Frederic Baraga, *A Dictionary of the Otchipwe Language,* 2 vols. in 1 (rpt., Minneapolis: Ross and Haines, 1966), 2: 421; B. W. Brisbois, "Recollections of Prairie du Chien," *Collections SHSW* 9 (1882): 301; Chrysostom Verwyst, "Geographical Names in Wisconsin, Minnesota, and Michigan Having a Chippewa Origin," *Collections SHSW* 12 (1892): 398; Alanson Skinner, *Material Culture of the Menomini* (New York: Museum of the American Indian, 1921), 321; Henry E. Legler, "Origin and Meaning of Wisconsin Place Names . . . ," *Transactions of the Wisconsin Academy of Sciences, Arts, and Letters* 14, pt. 1 (1902): 22; Huron H. Smith, "Indian Place Names in Wisconsin," *Milwaukee Public Museum Yearbook* 10 (1930): 266; Albert O. Barton, "Where Wisconsin Names Originated," *Wisconsin Archeologist,* n.s., 26 (December 1945): 84; Charles F. Hockett, "Potawatomi: Part I," *International Journal of American Linguistics* 14, no. 1 (1948): 10; Phebe Jewell Nichols, "What Does Wisconsin Mean?" *American Indigena* 8 (July 1948): 171–76; John P. Harrington, *Our State Names* (Washington, D.C.: Smithsonian Institution, 1955), 387; Edward Taube, "The Name Wisconsin," *Names* 15 (September 1967): 173–81.
6 John H. Kinzie, "Sketch of Hoo-wan-nee-kaw," annotated by Nellie Kinzie Gordon, Newberry Library, Chicago.
7 Louise P. Kellogg, *Early Narratives of the Northwest, 1634–1699* (rpt., New York: Barnes and Noble, 1967, 345.
8 [John Beach], "Sac and Fox Indian Council of 1841," *Annals of Iowa,* 3d ser., 12 (July 1920): 329.

2. Tribal Names

1 A list of all tribes recorded as having lived in Wisconsin is contained in John G. Shea, "The Indian Tribes of Wisconsin," in *Collections SHSW* 3 (1856): 125–38. A more recent treatment is in Nancy Lurie, *Wisconsin Indians* (Madison: SHSW, 1980).
2 Henry R. Schoolcraft, *Information Respecting the History, Condition, and Prospects of the Indian Tribes of the United States,* 6 vols. (Philadelphia: Lippincott Grambo, 1851–56), 5: 40, 6: 483.
3 William Keating, *Narrative of an Expedition to the Sources of St. Peter's River . . . ,* 2 vols. in 1 (rpt., Minneapolis: Ross and Haines, 1959), 2: 147.

4 William W. Warren, *History of the Ojibway Nation* (rpt., Minneapolis: Ross and Haines, 1970), 33, 37, 43, 56; Hodge, *Handbook of American Indians* 1: 28.

5 Nicolas Perrot, "Memoir on . . . the Savages of North America," in Emma H. Blair, *The Indian Tribes of the Upper Mississippi Valley and Region of the Great Lakes,* 2 vols. in 1 (rpt., New York: Kraus Reprint, 1969), 1: 173, 191n; Alfred Brunson, "Wisconsin Geographical Names," 114; Warren, *Ojibway Nation,* 193; Louise P. Kellogg, *The French Regime in Wisconsin and the Northwest* (Madison: SHSW, 1925), 99.

6 Virgil J. Vogel, "The Missionary as Acculturation Agent: Rev. Peter Dougherty and the Indians of Grand Traverse," *Michigan History* 51 (Fall 1967): 197–200.

7 Warren, *Ojibway Nation,* 82. See also Schoolcraft, *Indian Tribes* 5: 50; Hodge, *Handbook of American Indians* 2: 167, 169; Verwyst, "Geographical Names Having a Chippewa Origin," 395–96. Alternate explanations include "his ear" or "bullrushes" in Baraga, *Otchipwe Language* 1: 300; and "it is boiling," referring to Chaudiere Falls in Ottawa River, Canada, in George Lemoine, *Dictionnaire Français-Montagnais* (Boston: W. B. Cabot and P. Cabot, 1901), 280.

8 On the Potawatomi, see *Native American Directory* (San Carlos, Ariz.: National Native American Cooperative, 1982), 159, and Robert E. Ritzenthaler, *The Potawatomi Indians of Wisconsin,* Milwaukee Public Museum Bulletin 19 (Milwaukee, January 1953), 1, 6, 13.

9 Warren, *Ojibway Nation,* 82.

10 Keating, *Narrative of an Expedition* 1: 87–89.

11 Kuhm, "Indian Place-Names in Wisconsin," 106.

12 Blair, *Indian Tribes* 2: 142.

13 J. Mooney and C. Toomey in Hodge, *Handbook of American Indians* 1: 472.

14 William Jones, "Algonquian (Fox)," in *Handbook of American Indian Languages,* ed. Franz Boas, BAE Bulletin 40 (Washington, D.C.: GPO, 1911), pt. 1, p. 10n. Verwyst, "Geographical Names," 396; Warren, *Ojibway Nation,* 33; Joseph Jouvency in *Jesuit Relations* (1710), reprinted in Edna Kenton, *Black Gown and Redskins* (London: Longmans, Green, 1956), 7; John R. Swanton, *Indian Tribes of North America,* BAE Bulletin 145 (Washington, D.C.: GPO, 1952), 250. See also the synonymy in Hodge, *Handbook of American Indians* 1: 474.

15 Virgil J. Vogel, "Research Report on the Fox or Mesquakie Indians" (MS prepared for Native American Rights Fund, May 26, 1976), Newberry Library, Chicago; idem, *Iowa Place Names of Indian Origin* (Iowa City: University of Iowa Press, 1983), 42–43.

16 Virgil J. Vogel, *Indian Place Names in Illinois* (Springfield: Illinois State Historical Society, 1963), 3, 113; Swanton, *Indian Tribes,* 252; Henry R. Schoolcraft, quoted in Philip P. Mason, ed., *Schoolcraft's Expedition to Lake Itasca* (East Lansing: Michigan State University Press, 1958), 82.

17 Joshua Hathaway, "Indian Names," *First Annual Report and Collections SHSW for 1854* (Madison, 1855; rpt. 1903), 116–18.

18 Swanton, *Indian Tribes*, 256–57; William Jones in Hodge, *Handbook of American Indians* 2: 471–80.

19 Jonathan Carver, *Travels through the Interior Parts of North America* (Minneapolis: Ross and Haines, 1956; rpt. of 3d ed. [1781]), 45–48.

20 Donald Jackson, ed., *Black Hawk: An Autobiography* (Urbana: University of Illinois Press, 1955), 47.

21 William T. Hagan, *The Sac and Fox Indians* (Norman: University of Oklahoma Press, 1958).

22 Hodge, *Handbook of American Indians* 2: 480; Keating, *Narrative of an Expedition* 1: 223–24; Blair, *Indian Tribes* 2: 141, n. 39.

23 Schoolcraft, *Indian Tribes* 6: 484; Milo M. Quaife, *The Western Country in the Seventeenth Century* (New York: Citadel Press, 1962), 65. Forsyth quoted in Blair, *Indian Tribes* 2: 183.

24 Kellogg, *Early Narratives of the Northwest*, 156–57.

25 The standard history of the Kickapoo is A. M. Gibson, *The Kickapoos* (Norman: University of Oklahoma Press, 1963). Also used in this sketch are Frederick A. Peterson and Robert E. Ritzenthaler, "The Kickapoos Are Still Kicking," *Natural History* 54 (April 1955): 200–206, 224; Hiram W. Beckwith, *The Illinois and Indiana Indians* (rpt., New York: Arno Press, 1975, 117–37; and contemporary newspaper clippings.

26 Mooney in Hodge, *Handbook of American Indians* 1: 684; Schoolcraft, *Indian Tribes* 4: 246.

27 This historical sketch is based on Walter J. Hoffman, "The Menomini Indians," in *Fourteenth Annual Report, Bureau of American Ethnology, 1892–93*, pt. 1 (Washington, D.C.: GPO, 1896): 11–328; Patricia Ourada, *The Menominee Indians* (Norman: University of Oklahoma Press, 1979); Malcolm Rosholt and John B. Gehl, *Florimond J. Bonduel, Missionary to Wisconsin Territory* (Rosholt, Wis.: Rosholt House, 1976); and news clippings.

28 Kellogg, *Early Narratives of the Northwest*, 158, 230–31.

29 Warren, *Ojibway Nation*, 33; Chief Simon Pokagon, *Ogimawkwe Mitigwaki (Queen of the Woods)* (Hartford, Mich.: C. H. Engle, 1899), 124; Hoffman, "Menomini Indians" 1: 12–14; Hodge, *Handbook of American Indians* 1: 842.

30 Keating, *Narrative of an Expedition* 1: 77; Hagan, *Sac and Fox Indians*, 117, 134–35; William K. Ackerman, *Early Illinois Railroads* (Chicago: Fergus Printing, 1844), 139.

31 Kellogg, *Early Narratives of the Northwest*, 344; Carver, *Travels through the Interior*, 29.

32 Augustin Grignon, "Seventy-Two Years' Recollections of Wisconsin," *Collections SHSW* 3 (1856): 265; Shea, "Indian Tribes of Wisconsin," 134–35; Warren, *Ojibway Nation*, 49.

33 Verwyst, "Geographical Names," 395; Swanton, *Indian Tribes*, 243–44; William F. Gagnieur, "Indian Place-Names in the Upper Peninsula and Their Interpretation," *Michigan History* 2 (July 1918): 548–49; Hodge, *Handbook of American Indians* 2: 82–83.

34 Charles J. Kappler, ed., *Indian Treaties, 1778–1880* (New York: Interland Publishing, 1972), 493–94.

35 Carver, *Travels through the Interior*, 103; Warren, *Ojibway Nation*, 304–5.

36 Warren, *Ojibway Nation*, 101–4.

37 Ibid., 72; Philander Prescott in Schoolcraft, *Indian Tribes* 2: 170; See also "Sioux Indian: Nadowessi," in Baraga, *Otchipwe Language*, 1: 231.

38 Keating, *Narrative of an Expedition* 1: 336–37.

39 Bartelemy Vimont in Kellogg, *Narratives of the Northwest*, 15–16.

40 Paul Radin, *The Winnebago Tribe* (rpt. Lincoln: University of Nebraska Press, 1970), 5; Sebastian Rasles in Thwaites, *Jesuit Relations* 67: 151.

41 E.g., François Xavier de Charlevoix, *Journal of a Voyage to North America*, ed. Louise P. Kellogg, 2 vols. (Chicago: Caxton Club, 1923), 2: 57–58; Thwaites, *Jesuit Relations* 16: 252–53; Reuben G. Thwaites, ed., *Early Western Travels, 1748–1846*, 32 vols. (Cleveland: Arthur H. Clark, 1904–7), 2: 186–87; Louis Hennepin, *A New Discovery of a Vast Country in America*, ed. Reuben G. Thwaites, 2 vols. (Chicago: A. C. McClurg, 1903), 1: 308; Schoolcraft, *Indian Tribes* 3: 277, 566; Marryat, *A Diary in America*, 193.

42 Raguenau in Thwaites, *Jesuit Relations* 33: 149–51.

43 Thwaites, *Jesuit Relations* 59: 238; Quaife, *Western Country*, 66–67.

44 Alexander Mackenzie, *Alexander Mackenzie's Voyage to the Pacific Ocean in 1793*, ed. Milo M. Quaife (Chicago: Lakeside Press, 1931), 111; Baraga, *Otchipwe Language* 1: 300. The Cree word for "sea" is given as *we-nipak* in E. A. Watkins, *A Dictionary of the Cree Language* (rpt., Toronto: Anglican Book Centre, 1981), 163, and in Montagnais as *Uenepek* (Wenepek) in Lemoine, *Dictionnaire Français-Montagnais*, 377.

45 La Potherie in Blair *Indian Tribes* 1: 289–90. Hennepin, *New Discovery* 1: 308.

46 Information on the Winnebago is derived from communications with Frances Perry of Black River Falls, Wis., June 14 and July 5, 1985; and from Lurie, *Wisconsin Indians*, 12–14.

47 Barbara Graymont, *The Iroquois in the American Revolution* (Syracuse: Syracuse University Press, 1972), 65, 69–70, 86, 111–12.

48 On the Oneida, see Robert E. Ritzenthaler, *The Oneida Indians of Wisconsin*, Milwaukee Public Museum Bulletin 19 (Milwaukee, November 1950), 9–15; U.S. Department of Commerce, Economic Development Administration, *Federal and State Reservations: An EDA Handbook* (Washington, D.C.: U.S. Department of Commerce, 1971), 403–4; William Skenandore, "To the Oneida Indian Council" (a three-part, 13-page mimeographed report, dated April 5, May 22, and July 10, 1954, dealing with the Oneida land

problem); "Attorney Says Suit Against Oneidas Is Fatally Flawed," *Green Bay Press-Gazette,* July 23, 1986, A-1.

49 William M. Beauchamp, *Aboriginal Place Names of New York* (1907; rpt., Detroit Grand River Books, 1971), 139–40; Henry R. Schoolcraft, *Notes on the Iroquois* (Albany: Erastus H. Pease, 1847), 47, 210; idem, *Indian Tribes* 4: 384. Cf. Lewis H. Morgan, *League of the Ho-de-no-sau-nee or Iroquois,* 2 vols. (New Haven: Human Relations Area Files, 1954), 1: 49.

50 Sarah C. Sedgwick and Christine Sedgwick Marquand, *Stockbridge, 1739–1974* (Stockbridge, Mass.: Berkshire Traveller Press, 1974), ch. 1.

51 Jeremy Belknap and Jedidiah Morse, *Report on the Oneida, Stockbridge, and Brotherton Indians, 1796* (New York: Museum of the American Indian, 1955).

52 Lurie, *Wisconsin Indians,* 12; Henry R. Schoolcraft, *Personal Memoirs of a Residence of Thirty Years with the Indian Tribes . . .* (rpt., New York: Arno Press, 1975), 555; Alanson Skinner, *Notes on Mahikan Ethnology,* Milwaukee Public Museum Bulletin 2 (Milwaukee, January 1925), 91–92.

53 Federal Writers Program, *Wisconsin: A Guide to the Badger State* (New York: Hastings House, 1954), 349–50.

54 Ibid., 369, 473–74.

55 Hewitt in Hodge, *Handbook of American Indians* 1: 385–86, 957; George P. Donehoo, *Indian Villages and Place Names in Pennsylvania* (Baltimore: Gateway Press, 1977), 101; Jacob P. Dunn, *True Indian Stories, with Glossary of Indiana Indian Names* (Indianapolis: Sentinel Printing, 1909), 285–86; John G. Heckewelder, *History, Manners and Customs of the Indian Nations . . .* (rpt., New York: Arno Press, 1971), 51–52.

56 Skinner, *Mahikan Ethnology,* 98.

57 Morgan, *League of the Iroquois* 1: 49; 2: 129; see also Beauchamp, *Aboriginal Place Names,* 34, citing A. Cusack.

58 Robert E. Gard and L. G. Sorden, *The Romance of Wisconsin Place Names* (New York: October House, 1968), 20.

59 Hewitt in Hodge, *Handbook of American Indians* 1: 921; Cotton Mather, "Decennium Luctuosum," in Charles H. Lincoln, ed., *Narratives of the Indian Wars, 1675–1699* (New York: Scribner's, 1952), 249. On Hewitt's interpretation cf. A. F. Chamberlain, "they eat them," in "Algonkian Words in American English," *Journal of American Folklore* 15 (October–December, 1902): 248–49.

60 Schoolcraft, *Notes of the Iroquois,* 44.

61 Hodge, *Handbook of American Indians* 2: 502; Morgan, *League of the Iroquois* 1: 48–49; 2:130; Beauchamp, *Aboriginal Place Names,* 204–8; E. M. Ruttenber, *Footprints of the Red Man: Indian Geographical Names . . .* (Albany: New York State Historical Association, 1906), 211.

62 Gard and Sorden, *Wisconsin Place Names,* 115.

63 James Adair, *Adair's History of the Indians,* ed. Samuel C. Williams (rpt., New York: Promontory Press, n.d.), 226; James Mooney in Hodge, *Hand-*

book of American Indians 1: 245–46; Swanton, *Indian Tribes*, 215; Grace S. Woodward, *The Cherokees* (Norman: University of Oklahoma Press, 1963), 21–22.

64 Morris Bishop, *Champlain: Life of Fortitude* (New York: Alfred Knopf, 1940), 140.

65 Thwaites, *Jesuit Relations* 8: 177, 294, 307; 16: 229-31; 38: 249;Charlevoix, *History* 2: 71.

66 Hodge, *Handbook of American Indians* I: 584.

67 Thwaites, Jesuit Relations 6: 229–31, 38: 249; Pierre F. X. de Charlevoix, *History and General Description of New France*, ed. John G. Shea, 6 vols. (New York: John G. Shea, 1872), 2: 71.

68 Russell Errett, "Indian Geographical Names, Part 2," *Magazine of Western History* 2 (July 1885): 238–40. On the French *h* before vowels see Jean de Brebeuf in Kenton, *Blackgown and Redskins*, 116.

69 Morgan, *League of the Iroquois* 1: 39n; Charlevoix, *History of New France* 2: 266.

70 Beauchamp, *Aboriginal Place Names*, 242.

71 W. Vernon Kinietz, *The Indians of the Western Great Lakes, 1615–1760* (Ann Arbor: University of Michigan Press, 1965), 2–3.

72 Canada, Department of Indian and Northern Affairs, *Linguistic and Cultural Affiliations of Canadian Indian Bands* (Ottawa, 1980), 49.

73 Thwaites, *Jesuit Relations* 59: 127; 66: 107.

74 Henry R. Schoolcraft, *The American Indians, Their History, Condition, and Prospects*, rev. ed., in one vol. (Rochester: Wanzer, Foot, 1851), 254; idem, *Indian Tribes* 1: 305–6, 2: 358; Errett, "Indian Geographical Names, Part 1," *Magazine of Western History* 2 (May 1885): 52; Warren, in Schoolcraft, *Indian Tribes* 2: 139; Hewitt in Hodge, *Handbook of American Indians* 1: 38–39.

75 Gard and Sorden, *Wisconsin Place Names*, 20.

76 William A. Read, *Florida Place-Names of Indian Origin* (Baton Rouge: Louisiana State University Press, 1934), 56.

77 John R. Swanton, *The Indians of the Southeastern United States*, BAE Bulletin 137 (Washington, D.C.: GPO, 1946), 217.

78 Mari Sandoz, *Cheyenne Autumn* (New York: McGraw-Hill, 1953).

79 Peter Powell, *Sweet Medicine*, 2 vols. (Norman: University of Oklahoma Press, 1969), 1: xviii and note; Swanton, *Indian Tribes*, 278–80; Hodge, *Handbook of American Indians* 1: 250–57.

3. Personal Names

1 Robert E. Gard and Elaine Reetz, *The Trail of the Serpent* (Madison: Wisconsin House, 1973), 151–54.

2 Kappler, *Indian Treaties*, 282, 386, 465, 756. Amendments to the 1854

treaty are in George E. Fay, "Treaties between the Menominee Indians and the United States of America," *Journal of the Wisconsin Indians Research Institute* 1 (March 1965): 100.

3 Phebe Jewell Nichols, "I Knew Chief Oshkosh," *Journal of the Wisconsin Indians Research Institute* 1 (March 1965): 24–32, and idem, *Oshkosh the Brave, Chief of the Wisconsin Menominees, and His Family* (Oshkosh: Castle Pierce, 1954).

4 Lyman C. Draper, cited in Kuhm, "Indian Place-Names," 95; Grignon, "Recollections," 285; Nichols, "I Knew Chief Oshkosh," 24.

5 Leonard Bloomfield, *The Menomini Language* (New Haven: Yale University Press, 1966), 22; Hoffman, "Menomini Indians," 46–48, 309; Frederick J. Dockstader, *Great North American Indians* (New York: Van Nostrand Reinhold, 1977), 200; Cyrus Toomey and William Jones in Hodge, *Handbook of American Indians* 2: 160.

6 Hoffman, "Menomini Indians," 321; Kappler, *Indian Treaties,* 756.

7 Hoffman, "Menomini Indians," 302; Kappler, *Indian Treaties,* 756; Felix M. Keesing, *The Menomini Indians of Wisconsin* (1939; rpt., Madison: University of Wisconsin Press, 1987), 149, 151.

8 Leonard Bloomfield, *Menominee Lexicon,* ed. Charles F. Hockett (Milwaukee: Milwaukee Public Museum Press, 1973), 137; Skinner, *Material Culture of the Menominee,* 383.

9 Larry Fields, "Poverty of the Menominees," *Milwaukee Sentinel,* March 22, 1965, 4.

10 Kappler, *Indian Treaties,* 282, 323–24.

11 Ourada, *Menomini Indians,* 92.

12 Bloomfield, *Menominee Lexicon,* 155; Ourada, *Menomini Indians,* 198.

13 Hoffman, "Menomini Indians," 48, 306; Gard and Sorden, *Wisconsin Place Names,* 97.

14 Bloomfield, *Menominee Lexicon,* 205; Kappler, *Indian Treaties,* 283.

15 Hoffman, "Menomini Indians," 44; Henry Gannett, *American Names* (rpt., Washington, D.C.: Public Affairs Press, 1947), 243; Swanton, *Indian Tribes,* 254–55.

16 Hoffman, "Menomini Indians," 45.

17 Ibid., 325.

18 Kappler, *Indian Treaties,* 323–24, 574.

19 On Tomah, see Hoffman, "Menomini Indians," 45, 50–58, and Dockstader, *Great North American Indians,* 302.

20 Jedidiah Morse, *Report to the Secretary of War on Indian Affairs* (New Haven: S. Converse, 1822), appendix, 53n.

21 Grignon, "Recollections," 95–96, 269.

22 Greater Tomah Area Chamber of Commerce, *Tomah* (information folder, 1985).

23 Kappler, *Indian Treaties,* 574, 627, 756; Fay, "Treaties," 100.

24 Bloomfield, *Menominee Lexicon,* 368.

25 M. J. Smith, Omro, Wis., letter to author, August 26, 1986, citing Ruth Westover, *Waukau: A History* (1979); Bloomfield, *Menominee Lexicon,* 268.

26 Beauford Marceil and Kathleen Marceil, *Legends and Tales of She-she-Pe-ko-Naw* (Neopit: the authors, 1973), 17–18; Charles F. Carr, *Some Indian Chiefs Who Reigned over New London, Wisconsin Territory* (n.p., 1911), not paginated; Kappler, *Indian Treaties,* 465, 574, 627, 756; Gard and Sorden, *Wisconsin Place Names,* 134; Hoffman, "Menomini Indians," 314, 318; Bloomfield, *Menominee Lexicon,* 259; Ourada, *Menominee Indians,* 137.

27 Keesing, *Menomini Indians,* 151; J. S. Slotkin, *The Menomini Powwow,* Publications in Anthropology no. 4 (Milwaukee: Milwaukee Public Museum, 1957), 157–58; Hoffman, "Menomini Indians," 314.

28 Elijah Haines, *The American Indian* (1888; rpt., Evansville: Unigraphic, 1977), 335; Bloomfield, *Menominee Lexicon,* 279; Henry E. Legler, "Origin and Meaning of Wisconsin Place Names, with Special Reference to Indian Nomenclature," *Transactions of the Wisconsin Academy of Sciences, Arts, and Letters* 14, pt. 1 (1902): 35.

29 FWP, *Wisconsin,* 461.

30 Maxine Schmitz, *Lake of the Torch, Past and Present* (Lac du Flambeau: published by author, 1988), n.p.; telephone conversation with Ms. Schmitz, September 17, 1990; Baraga, *Otchipwe Dictionary* 2: 312.

31 Ethel E. Chapelle, *The "Why of Names" in Washburn County* (Birchwood, Wis.: the author, 1965), 60. See also Michel Curot, "A Wisconsin Fur Trader's Journal, 1803–1804," *Collections SHSW* 20 (1911): 467n.

32 Warren, *Ojibway Nation,* 318; Gard and Sorden, *Wisconsin Place Names,* 84.

33 Interview with Ben Skinaway, September 7, 1985; Baraga, *Otchipwe Language* 1: 295.

34 Albert C. Beckwith, *History of Walworth County,* 2 vols. (Indianapolis: B. F. Bowen, 1912), 1: 39; William Hickling and Gurdon S. Hubbard, "Sketches of Billy Caldwell and Shabonee," in *Addresses Delivered at the Annual Meeting of the Chicago Historical Society, November 19, 1868* (Chicago: Fergus Printing, 1877), 41–46.

35 Mrs. John H. [Juliette] Kinzie, *Wau-Bun; or, The Early Day in the Northwest* (Chicago: Rand McNally, 1901), 249–50.

36 Charles Brown and Theodore T. Brown, "Lake Geneva and Lake Como," *Wisconsin Archeologist,* n.s., 7 (April 1928): 139–41; report of subagent Stephen Cooper, Council Bluffs, October 12, 1840, in *Report of Commissioner of Indian Affairs, 1838–40* (Washington, D.C., 1841[?]), 321, 504.

37 Kappler, *Indian Treaties,* 294, 299, 404.

38 Dorothy M. Brown, *Wisconsin Indian Place-Name Legends* (n.p.: the authors, 1948), 11.

39 Radin, *Winnebago Tribe,* 51; Publius V. Lawson, "The Potawatomi," *Wisconsin Archeologist* 19 (April 1920): 58; Hoffman, "Menomini Indians,"

299; Alanson Skinner, *The Mascoutens or Prairie Potawatomi Indians, Part III: Mythology and Folklore,* Bulletin of the Public Museum of the City of Milwaukee (January 22, 1927), 399; Huron H. Smith, "Indian Place Names in Wisconsin," *Milwaukee Public Museum Yearbook* 10 (1930), 257.

40 Lawson, "Potawatomi," 51–53; Gard and Sorden, *Wisconsin Place Names,* 81; Kuhm, "Indian Place-Names," 69, citing Louis Falge; Skinner, *Material Culture of the Menomini,* 383.

41 Information on John Shabbodock is drawn from a clipping, "John Shopodick [*sic*] Was a Colorful Part of Local History," *Iron River* (Mich.) *Reporter,* April 21, 1976, in the possession of Mark Bruhy, archaeologist of Nicolet and Chequamegon National Forests, Rhinelander, Wis., who kindly furnished photocopies.

42 Huron H. Smith, "Indian Place Names," 265; Maurice Gailland, "English-Potawatomi Dictionary" (BAE MS 1761, n.d.), 421; James A. Clifton, *The Prairie People* (Lawrence: Regents Press of Kansas, 1971), 171. See the discussion of Waupee, the White Hawk, in the "Celestial Sisters" legend, in Mentor Williams, *Schoolcraft's Indian Legends* (East Lansing: Michigan State University Press, 1956), 31–33.

43 Kuhm, "Indian Place-Names," 130; Lawson, "Potawatomi," 57; Gailland, "English-Potawatomi Dictionary," 49.

44 A. J. Lawson, "New London and Neighborhood," *Collections SHSW* 3 (1857; rpt. 1904), 487; Gailland, "English-Potawatomi Dictionary," 299.

45 *Wisconsin Historical Markers* (Verona, Wis.: Guide Press, 1985), 109; Skinner, *Mascoutens, Part III,* 399.

46 Cecil Eby, *"That Disgraceful Affair": The Black Hawk War* (New York: W. W. Norton, 1973), 238.

47 Donald Jackson, ed., *Black Hawk,* 33, 182.

48 Kappler, *Indian Treaties,* 128.

49 Schoolcraft, *Personal Memoirs,* 390.

50 Warren Upham, *Minnesota Geographic Names* (rpt., St. Paul: Minnesota Historical Society, 1969), 209.

51 Keating, *Narrative of an Expedition* 1: 269–70.

52 Kappler, *Indian Treaties,* 129, 308.

53 Sandra Ebert to author, June 19, 1985, citing Biggs and Falconer, *Illustrated Atlas of the Counties of Buffalo and Pepin, Wisconsin* (1878).

54 Stephen R. Riggs, *A Dakota-English Dictionary* (rpt., Minneapolis: Ross and Haines, 1968), 518–26; John P. Williamson, *An English-Dakota Dictionary* (rpt., Minneapolis: Ross and Haines, 1970), 56.

55 Keating, *Narrative of an Expedition* 1: 459–60; Kappler, *Indian Treaties,* 254, 784.

56 Kappler, *Indian Treaties,* 229.

57 Other biographical information may be found in Dockstader, *Great North American Indians,* 321–22, and Jack Swisher, "War Eagle," *Palimpsest* 19 (February 1949): 33–41.

58 Schoolcraft, *Personal Memoirs*, 555.

59 Kappler, *Indian Treaties*, 39, 382, 530–31, 577–78, 582, 747–50.

60 Ibid., 530, 578.

61 Skinner, *Mahikan Ethnology*, 93–94.

62 Kappler, *Indian Treaties*, 382, 576–77.

63 Dockstader, *Great North American Indians*, 227–28; Gard and Sorden, *Wisconsin Place Names*, 105.

64 Grignon, "Recollections," 388; Norton W. Jipson, "General History of the Winnebago Indians," MS, (Chicago Historical Society (1924), 239; Radin, *Winnebago Tribe*, 3.

65 Kinzie, *Wau-Bun*, 73–74.

66 Jipson, "General History," 277.

67 Kappler, *Indian Treaties*, 283, 293, 302.

68 Kinzie, *Wau-Bun*, 75–76. Note that Kinzie errs in referring to Dandy as "young Four-Legs." Dandy's uncle was Four Legs (not his father).

69 Jipson, "General History," 270.

70 Information on Dandy drawn from ibid., 239–40; Derleth quotation from *Wisconsin*, 93.

71 Cyrus Toomey in Hodge, *Handbook of American Indians* 1: 384–85; Kellogg, *French Regime*, 15, 435.

72 Radin, *Winnebago Tribe*, 20–21.

73 Milo M. Quaife, *Lake Michigan* (Indianapolis: Bobbs-Merrill, 1944), 317–18.

74 Gannett, *American Names*, 102.

75 *Niles Weekly Register* 43 (September 29, 1832): 78–79; Jackson, *Black Hawk*, 162. Walking Cloud told Thwaites that One-Eyed (Big Canoe) Decorah was not a captor of Black Hawk; see Reuben G. Thwaites, ed., "Walking Cloud's Version of Black Hawk's Surrender," *Collections SHSW* 13 (1895): 464–65.

76 Charles P. Hexom, *Indian History of Winneshiek County* (Decorah, Iowa: A. K. Bailey, 1913), not paginated; Thomas Hughes, *Indian Chiefs of Southern Minnesota* (rpt., Minneapolis: Ross and Haines, 1969, 159–65; Upham, *Minnesota Geographic Names*, 59.

77 Kappler, *Indian Treaties*, 293, 302, 345, 358, 500, 565; James A. Horan, *The McKenney-Hall Portrait Gallery of American Indians* (New York: Crown Publishers, 1972), 286; Virgil J. Vogel, *Iowa Place Names of Indian Origin* (Iowa City: University of Iowa Press, 1983), 16, 103–4.

78 Other facts on the Decorahs are from Louise S. Houghton, *Our Debt to the Red Man* (Boston: Stratford, 1918), 184–85, and Reuben G. Thwaites, ed., "Narrative of Spoon Decorah," *Collections SHSW* 13 (1895): 448–62.

79 Frances R. Perry to author, June 15 and July 5, 1985; personal interview with Perry and visits to sites mentioned, August 28, 1985.

80 Jipson, "General History," 274.

81 Upham, *Minnesota Geographic Names*, 59–60; Hughes, *Indian Chiefs of Southern Minnesota*, 187–89; Kappler, *Indian Treaties*, 500, 567, 693.

82 Radin, *Winnebago Tribe*, 3.

83 Jipson, "General History," 278.

84 Ibid., 237.

85 Frederic G. Cassidy, *Dane County Place Names* (Madison: University of Wisconsin Press, 1968), 103–4; Jipson, "Winnebago-English Vocabulary" (MS, Chicago Historical Society, ca. 1924), 365.

86 Hughes, *Indian Chiefs of Southern Minnesota*, 65–70; Kappler, *Indian Treaties*, 308, 788.

87 Mitchell Red Cloud, "Chief Black Hawk," *Wisconsin Archeologist*, n.s., 26 (December 1945): 80–82.

88 Nancy Lurie, "Trends of Change in Patterns of Child Care and Rearing among the Wisconsin Winnebago," *Wisconsin Archeologist*, n.s., 29 (September–October 1948): 40–156.

89 Additional information on Red Cloud is from documents and letters furnished by David L. Henke, president of the La Crosse County Historical Society, September 1985; information from Frances Perry, Black River Falls, Wisconsin, August 27, 1985, and a personal visit to Decorah Cemetery and Red Cloud Memorial Park at the powwow grounds; and Jackson County Historical Society, *Jackson County: A History* (Black River Falls: printed by Taylor Publishing, Dallas, 1984), 236.

90 Jipson, "General History," 274.

91 Radin, *Winnebago Tribe*, 3; Jipson, "General History," 346–47, 387; idem, "Winnebago Place Names" (MS, Chicago Historical Society, n.d.), 1.

92 Atwater, *Indians of the Northwest*, 109.

93 Kappler, *Indian Treaties*, 293, 693.

94 Virgil J. Vogel, *Indian Place Names in Illinois* (Springfield: Illinois State Historical Society, 1963), 171–72.

95 Biographical data in this section are from W. E. Alexander, *History of Winneshiek and Allamakee Counties, Iowa* (Sioux City: Western Publishing, 1882), 141; Hexom, *Indian History of Winneshiek County* (not paginated); Hughes, *Indian Chiefs of Southern Minnesota*, 171–84; Jipson, "General History," 211–33; idem, "Winnebago Villages and Chieftains of the Lower Rock River Region," *Wisconsin Archeologist* 2 (July 1923): 126–39; Schoolcraft, *Indian Tribes*, 3: 281, 4: 223–24; Upham, *Minnesota Geographic Names*, 58, 592.

96 Swanton, *Indian Tribes*, 258; Radin, *Winnebago Tribe*, 3, map.

97 Jipson, "General History," 268.

98 Kinzie, *Wau-Bun*, 83.

99 Kappler, *Indian Treaties*, 202, 500.

100 Derleth, *Wisconsin*, 150–51.

101 Jipson, "General History," 252.

102 *Sauk County Weekly News*, March 3, 1987, p. 7.

103 My account is based on Florida Historical Society, "The Complete Story of Osceola," *Florida Historical Quarterly* 23 (January–April 1955), entire

issue; C. Toomey in Hodge, *Handbook of American Indians* 2:159; and
E. C. McReynolds, *The Seminoles* (Norman: University of Oklahoma Press,
1957).
104 William Bradford, *Of Plymouth Plantation*, ed. Harvey Wish (New York:
Capricorn Books, 1962), 72–73.
105 Hodge, *Handbook of American Indians* 2:424–25.

4. Women's Names

1 Carver, *Travels through the Interior*, 32.
2 Radin, *Winnebago Tribe*, 20, 21, 145.
3 FWP, *Wisconsin*, 327; Thomas H. Dickinson, ed., *Wisconsin Plays* (New
York: B. W. Huebsch, 1914), 115–87.
4 Frances Perry, letter to the author, September 20, 1987.
5 Rhoda R. Gilman, *Historic Chequamegon* (n.p.: the author, 1971). 4; Warren, *Ojibway Nation*, 32; *Wisconsin's Historical Markers* (Madison: Guide
Press, 1985), 85.
6 Quotations from fragment of E. S. Ingalls, "Centennial History of Menominee County [Michigan]," *Michigan Pioneer and Historical Society
Collections* 1 (1874–76): 265–66; Gard and Sorden, *Wisconsin Place
Names*, 75.
7 FWP, *Wisconsin*, 419.
8 Frances Perry, letter to the author, September 20, 1987.
9 Biographical data from Charlevoix, *History of New France* 4:283–96;
Evelyn Brown, *Kateri Tekakwitha* (New York: Farrar-Straus, 1958); Hewitt
in Hodge, *Handbook of American Indians* 2:725–26; *Kateri* (magazine
published at Caughnawaga, Quebec), various issues; *Chicago Tribune*,
January 11, 1956; *Time*, September 6, 1969.
10 Marion Gridley, *America's Indian Statues* (Chicago: Towertown Press,
1966), 58, 65.
11 For this information I am indebted to Rev. C. Luke Leiterman, of Pickerel,
Wis., a friend of Fathers Hogan and LeClair. Then president of the Langlade
County Historical Society, Father Leiterman escorted me about Lake
Tekakwitha on August 10, 1980.
12 Information from Sue Herges, postmistress of Sisseton, S.D., replying to my
inquiries of September 11 and November 4, 1980; other data from Sister
Mary Claudia Duratschek, *Crusading along Sioux Trails* (Yankton, S.D.:
Bernardine Convent of the Sacred Heart, 1947), 260, 264–65.

5. French-Indian Personal Names

1 Mitford Mathews, *Dictionary of Americanisms* (Chicago: University of
Chicago Press, 1956), 1048–49; Magnus Mörner, *Race Mixture in the History of Latin America* (Boston: Little, Brown, 1967), 1.

2 Ourada, *Menominee Indians,* 41.

3 Warren, *Ojibway Nation,* 132.

4 Radin, *Winnebago Tribe,* 20–21.

5 I have not included in this chapter some names which evolved from French, such as Decorah and Tomah, because they have been "Indianized."

6 Information for this section from Warren, *Ojibway Nation,* 9–11, 372, 451, 464; Houghton, *Our Debt to the Red Man,* 71–75; Gard and Sorden, *Wisconsin Place Names,* 18.

7 Merton E. Krug, *Du Bay, Son-in-Law of Oshkosh* (Appleton: C. C. Nelson Publishing, 1946), 13, 39.

8 Ibid., 62. The term *half-breed* is today considered derogatory.

9 Kappler, *Indian Treaties,* 493, 574.

10 Houghton, *Our Debt to the Red Man,* 65–66, 114–16; Kappler, *Indian Treaties,* 324.

11 Grignon, "Recollections," 197–296.

12 Kappler, *Indian Treaties,* 574, 627, 756.

13 On Langlade, see Houghton, *Our Debt to the Red Man,* 60–65; Warren, *Ojibway Nation,* 437; *Antigo Herald,* December 5, 1918, reproduced in Gard and Sorden, *Wisconsin Place Names,* 68–69; and *Dictionary of American Biography* 5: 216–17.

14 Alanson Skinner, "Some Menomini Indian Place Names in Wisconsin," *Wisconsin Archeologists* 18 (August 1919): 102.

15 Maxine Schmitz, *Lake of the Torch, Past and Present* Lac du Flambeau: the author, 1988).

16 Information in this section is derived from Warren, *Ojibway Nation,* 381; Gard and Sorden, *Wisconsin Place Names,* 112; and Tom Hollatz, *Louis No. 1: The Life and Legend of Louis St. Germaine* (Neshkoro, Wis.: Laranmark Press, 1984), 110.

6. Literary and Legendary Names

1 Vogel, *Iowa Place Names of Indian Origin,* 20–21.

2 Henry Whiting, *Sannilac: A Poem by Henry Whiting, with Notes by Lewis Cass and Henry R. Schoolcraft* (Boston: Carter, Hendee and Babcock, 1831).

3 Lewis H. Morgan, *Indian Journals, 1859–62,* ed. Leslie A. White (Ann Arbor: University of Michigan Press, 1959), 53; Mooney in Hodge, *Handbook of American Indians* 1: 867–68; A. R. Dunlap and C. A. Weslager, *Indian Place Names in Delaware* (Wilmington: Archaeological Society of Delaware, 1950), 27; Daniel Brinton and Albert S. Anthony, *A Lenape-English Dictionary* (Philadelphia: Historical Society of Pennsylvania, 1888), 81.

4 Gard and Sorden, *Wisconsin Place Names,* 57.

5 James Fenimore Cooper, *The Last of the Mohicans* (New York: Grosset and Dunlap, n.d.), vi.

6 Hodge, *Handbook of American Indians* 1: 569; Beauchamp, *Aboriginal Place Names,* 238.

7 Ruttenber, *Footprints of the Red Men*, 71n; Shea, in Hodge, *Handbook of American Indians* 1: 569; Cooper, *Last of the Mohicans*, 8n.

8 H. R. Schoolcraft, *Algic Researches* (New York: Harper's, 1839), reprinted with explanatory notes by Mentor L. Williams in *Schoolcraft's Indian Legends* (East Lansing: Michigan State University Press, 1956); Mary Eastman, *Dahcotah; or, Life and Legends of the Sioux around Fort Snelling* (New York: John Wiley, 1849). Eastman's book was Longfellow's source for the names Wenonah and Minnehaha, the mother and wife, respectively, of Hiawatha.

9 Morgan, *League of the Iroquois* 1: 60, 64; 2: 215, 254; idem, *Ancient Society* (rpt., Chicago: Charles H. Kerr, 1910), 129–39, 132; Hewitt in Hodge, *Handbook of American Indians* 1: 546; Schoolcraft, *Indian Tribes* 3: 315, 5: 157.

10 *Nókomiss* in Baraga, *Otchipwe Language* 1: 120.

11 Henry W. Longfellow, *The Song of Hiawatha* (New York: Cupples and Leon, n.d.), 41; hereafter cited as *Hiawatha*.

12 *Hiawatha*, 13.

13 Ibid., 107.

14 Baraga, *Otchipwe Language*, 1: 20.

15 *Hiawatha*, 112.

16 Gard and Sorden, *Wisconsin Place Names*, 57; Upham, *Minnesota Geographic Names*, 226.

17 Baraga, *Otchipwe Language* 1: 37; Schoolcraft, *Indian Tribes* 5: 624.

18 Kuhm, "Indian Place-Names," 95–96.

19 *Hiawatha*, 8. Cf. *pakwéne*, "smoke," in Baraga, *Otchipwe Language* 1: 235.

20 *Hiawatha*, 27; Baraga, *Otchipwe Language* 1: 205.

21 Hoffman, "Menomini Indians," 314.

22 *Hiawatha*, 120.

23 Ibid., 38.

24 *The Works of Henry Wadsworth Longfellow* (New York: National Library Co., 1909), 3: 207; Baraga, *Otchipwe Language* 1: 214.

25 Keating, *Narrative of an Expedition* 1: 290–95.

26 Eastman, *Dahcotah*, 165–76. See also Hodge, *Handbook of American Indians* 2: 963.

27 Upham, *Minnesota Geographic Names*, 581, 584–85; Gard and Sorden, *Wisconsin Place Names*, 73.

28 Cassidy, *Dane County Place Names*, 59–60, 88; idem, "The Naming of the Four Lakes," *Wisconsin Magazine of History* 29 (September 1945): 17.

29 *History of Clayton County, Iowa* (Chicago: Interstate Publishing, 1882), 1027; *History of Monona County, Iowa* (Chicago: National Publishing, 1890), 166. The story has been repeated in at least four other places.

30 Albert Keiser, *The Indian in American Literature* (New York: Oxford University Press, 1933), 89–90.

31 Keating, *Narrative of an Expedition* 1: 290–95. Mary Eastman also told the story, in 1849 *Dahcotah*, 165–78).

32 J. C. Beltrami, *A Pilgrimage in Europe and America*, 2 vols. (London: Hunt

and Clarke, 1828), 2: 183—84. Neither Oholaitha nor Oolaita is an authentic Dakota or Ojibwa name. The sound of *l* is not found either in Ojibwa or in the Santee Sioux dialect of this region. *Tallula* is a word which has been attributed to both the Choctaw and Cherokee. Vogel, *Indian Place Names in Illinois,* 145.

33 Alanson Skinner guessed that Monona was from Potawatomi *Monaman,* "wild rice" *Mascoutens, Part III,* 399). One of Cassidy's informants said Monona was the name of a female deity of the Sauk and Foxes (Cassidy, "Naming of the Four Lakes," 18—19). This story was repeated by George R. Stewart, *American Place Names* (New York: Oxford University Press, 1970), 303, and by H. W. Kuhm, in "Indian Place Names in Wisconsin," 73. Gard and Sorden reported that Monona "is said" to be Winnebago for "lost" or "stolen" or "tepee lake," but that "most authorities" claim it meant "beautiful" (*Romance of Wisconsin Place Names,* 82). There is no evidence to support any of these guesses.

34 Thomas Campbell, *The Poetical Works of Thomas Campbell* . . . (Philadelphia: Lea and Blanchard, 1845), 29; Mary R. Miller, *Thomas Campbell* (Boston: Twayne Publishers, 1978), 29.

35 Gard and Sorden, *Wisconsin Place Names,* 96; James W. Phillips, *Washington State Place Names* (Seattle: University of Washington Press, 1972), 101.

36 Donald J. Orth, *Dictionary of Alaska Place Names* (Washington, D.C.: GPO, 1967; rpt. 1971), 1006—9; James W. Phillips, *Alaska-Yukon Place Names* (Seattle: University of Washington Press, 1973), 136.

37 Gannett, *American Names,* 311; Gard and Sorden, *Wisconsin Place Names,* 131.

38 Robert Beasacker, "Ten Notable Michigan Novels," *Chronicle* 21 (Spring 1985): 26.

39 Francis Parkman, *The Conspiracy of Pontiac,* 2 vols. (Boston: Little, Brown, 1922) 1: 227—28; Howard Peckham, *Pontiac and the Indian Uprising* (Chicago: University of Chicago Press, 1961), 121—25.

40 Pedro de Cieza de Leon, *The Incas* (Norman: University of Oklahoma Press, 1959), 208—21; William Prescott, *History of the Conquest of Mexico and History of the Conquest of Peru* (New York: Modern Library, n.d.), 778 and note.

41 John Richardson, *Wacousta; or, The Prophesy,* 2 vols. (New York: DeWitt and Davenport, 1832).

42 Louise Barnett, *The Ignoble Savage* (Westport, Conn.: Greenwood Press, 1975), 110.

43 Upham, *Minnesota Geographic Names,* 209.

44 Hodge, *Handbook of American Indians* 2: 978; John Heckewelder, *A Narrative of the Mission of the United Brethren among the Delaware and Mohegan Indians* (rpt., Cleveland: Burrows Bros. 1907, 449; Donehoo, *Indian Villages,* 259—63.

45 Campbell, "Gertrude of Wyoming," pt. 1, verse 1, in *Poetical Works.*

46 Frances R. Perry, letter to author, December 29, 1986. In further remarks to

the author on September 11, 1987, Frances Perry wrote: "A correction on *Sand Pillow* by a Winnebago friend who remembers the incident—It was the Nebraska band who had come up just as guests—not a hunting party. I just learned this last week. And it happened just some time before WW I—1912?" The corrected version of the story by an unnamed Winnebago must be viewed as a disagreement with the earlier version set forth by named individuals who appear well qualified. This is an example of how quickly the facts fall into dispute even when the events concerned are recent. I prefer to publish the original story with the altered version recorded as a postscript.

7. The Spirit World

1 In Ojibwa, *manito* (Baraga, *Otchipwe Language* 1: 240); in Ottawa, *mau-ne-to* (Andrew J. Blackbird, *History of the Ottawa and Chippewa Indians of Michigan* [rpt., Petoskey: Little Traverse Regional Historical Society, 1977], 112); in Potawatomi, *manito* (Pokagon, *Queen of the Woods*, 122).
2 Kenton, *Blackgown and Redskins*, 321.
3 Mason, *Schoolcraft's Expedition*, 187, 315.
4 Dorothy M. Brown, "Myths and Legends of Wisconsin Waterfalls," *Wisconsin Archeologist*, n.s., 18 (July 1938): 112–13.
5 Baraga, *Otchipwe Language* 1: 220; John Tanner, *Narrative of the Captivity and Adventures of John Tanner* . . . ed. Edwin James (rpt., Minneapolis: Ross and Haines, 1956), 224; Gard and Sorden, *Wisconsin Place Names*, 74.
6 Grignon, "Recollections," 290, 337; Hoffman, "Menomini Indians," 301, Hathaway, "Indian Names," 117.
7 Riggs, *Dakota-English Dictionary*, 314, 316, 508.
8 Ibid., 508.
9 Jipson, "Winnebago Place Names."
10 Ruth Landes, *Ojibwa Religion and the Midewiwin* (Madison: University of Wisconsin Press, 1968), 21.
11 Ruth Worthington lists this feature as Devil's Pond, "a low spot in Section 30 of Empire [town]" and adds that "it was once thought to be a bottomless pond in which a farmer's wagon and team of horses disappeared" (*History of Fond du Lac County*, 26). This story may explain the name.
12 Virgil J. Vogel, *American Indian Medicine* (Norman: University of Oklahoma Press, 1970), 25.
13 Hodge, *Handbook of American Indians* 2: 930. Baraga, *Otchipwe Language* 1: 41, records *windigo* as meaning "cannibal, eater of human flesh." In Potawatomi *win-di-go* means "giant" (Pokagon, *Queen of the Woods*, 27).
14 Keating, *Narrative of an Expedition* 2: 128. The lake's location is 52°N, 92°W.
15 Williams, *Schoolcraft's Indian Legends*, 169–74; see also Herbert T. Schwarz, *Windigo and Other Tales of the Ojibways* (Toronto: McClelland Stewart, 1972).

16 *Hiawatha*, 42.
17 Williams, *Schoolcraft's Indian Legends*, 65–67, 224–27; Brown, *Wisconsin Indian Place-Name Legends*, 28.

8. Material Culture

1 Schoolcraft, *Personal Memoirs*, 368.
2 Phillipe Regis Denis de Keredern de Trobriand, *Army Life in Dakota*, ed. Milo M. Quaife (Chicago: Lakeside Press, 1941), 72.
3 Roger Williams, *A Key into the Language of America* (rpt., Ann Arbor: Gryphon Press, 1971), 127.
4 A. F. Chamberlain in Hodge, *Handbook of American Indians* 2: 303; idem, "Algonkian Words," 71–72; Mathews, *Dictionary of Americanisms*, 1297–98; Eric Partridge, *Origins: A Short Etymological Dictionary of the English Language* (London: Routledge and Kegan Paul, 1958), 517; Georg Friederici, *Amerikanistisches Wörterbuch* (Hamburg: Cram, de Gruyter, 1960), 484.
5 Lawson, "Potawatomi," 68; Beckwith, *History of Walworth County* 1: 418.
6 Marcel Barbeau, "Maple Sugar: Its Native Origin," *Transactions of the Royal Society of Canada*, 3d ser., 40, sec. 2 (1946): 75–86.
7 Baraga, *Otchipwe Language* 2: 216.
8 The notable Wisconsin historian of the frontier, Frederick Jackson Turner, wrote his doctoral dissertation at the University of Wisconsin on this subject. Entitled "The Character and Influence of the Indian Trade in Wisconsin: A Study of the Trading Post as an Institution," it was published at Baltimore by Johns Hopkins Press in 1891.
9 J. N. Nicollet, *The Journals of Joseph N. Nicollet* (St. Paul: Minnesota Historical Society, 1970), 143 (entry for August 4, 1837); Nicollet's maps of 1836, 1837, and 1843; see *Journals*, 239.
10 Baraga, *Otchipwe Language* 1: 267.
11 Ibid., 1: 28, 2: 325.
12 Ibid. 2: 327.
13 Walter Romig, *Michigan Place Names* (Grosse Pointe, Mich.: the author, n.d.), 317; Mason, *Schoolcraft's Expedition*, 312; Verwyst, "Geographical Names," 395; Gannett, *American Place Names*, 238.
14 Frank Werner, letter to the author, August 3, 1985.
15 Baraga, *Otchipwe Language* 2: 262.
16 John P. Harrington, ed., *The Original Strachey Vocabulary of the Virginia Indian Language*, extract from BAE Bulletin 157 (Washington, D.C.: GPO, 1955), sheet 13; J. H. Trumbull, *Natick Dictionary*, BAE Bulletin 25 (Washington, D.C.: GPO, 1903), 321; Baraga, *Otchipwe Language* 1: 227. See also William R. Gerard, "Virginia's Indian Contributions to English," *American Anthropologist*, n.s., 9 (1907): 97.

17 Baraga, *Otchipwe Language* 2: 326.
18 Carver, *Travels through the Interior*, 358–59.
19 Verwyst, "Geographical Names," 396. See also Baraga, *Otchipwe Language* 1: 194.
20 Bloomfield, *Menomini Language*, 32.
21 Pokagon, *Queen of the Woods*, 137.
22 Albert E. Jenks, *Wild Rice Gatherers of the Upper Lakes*, extract from *Nineteenth Annual Report, Bureau of American Ethnology* (Washington, D.C.: GPO, 1901), 1095.
23 Phillip T. Poulette, letter to the author, June 10, 1985.
24 Huron H. Smith, "Indian Place Names," 262.
25 Verwyst, "Geographical Names," 396.
26 Ibid., 397; B. F. H. Witherell, "Reminiscences of the North-West," *Collections SHSW* 3 (1856): 337.
27 Baraga, *Otchipwe Language* 1: 120, 194.
28 *Chicago Tribune*, "Line O' Type or Two," January 1, 1959; Fred Dustin, "Some Indian Place-Names around Saginaw," *Michigan History* 12 (October 1928): 734.
29 Hathaway, "Indian Names," 117.
30 Frank Werner, letter to the author, August 3, 1985.
31 Robert A. Murray, "Some Notes on Pipe-Making Stone and Place Names in and around the Plains," *Minnesota Archeologist* 25 (October 1963): 156–59.
32 Baraga, *Otchipwe Language* 1: 236.
33 Andrew White and Cecil Calvert, *A Relation of Maryland, 1635* (Ann Arbor: University Microfilms, 1966), 30.
34 William H. Holmes, "The Tomahawk," *American Anthropologist*, n.s., 10 (1908): 264–76.
35 Information furnished by Graham Foster, editor of the *Tomahawk Leader*, June 19, 1985.
36 [W. H. Stennett], *A History of the Origin of the Place Names Connected with the Chicago and Northwestern . . .* , 2d ed. (Chicago: n.p., 1908), 131.
37 Chrysostom Verwyst, "A Glossary of Chippewa Indian Names of Rivers, Lakes, and Villages," *Acta et Dicta* 4 (July 1916): 255.
38 Gard and Sorden, *Wisconsin Place Names*, 40.
39 H. W. Kuhm, "Wisconsin Indian Fishing," *Wisconsin Archeologist*, n.s., 7 (January 1928): 74.
40 Gerard in Hodge, *Handbook of American Indians* 2: 910; Watkins, *Dictionary of the Cree Language*, 206; Mathews, *Dictionary of Americanisms*, 1829. "Our kitchen—the 'wanigan'—was a whirl of people and dishes around meal times" (William Gray Purcell, *St. Croix Trail Country* [Minneapolis: University of Minnesota Press, 1967], 55).
41 Chamberlain, "Algonkian Words," 265; Ramon Adams, *Western Words: A Dictionary of the American West* (Norman: University of Oklahoma Press,

1968), 340, 354; Walter McCulloch, *Woods Words: A Comprehensive Dictionary of Loggers' Terms* (rpt., Corvallis, Ore.: Oregon Historical Society, 1977), 207; John C. Huden, *Indian Place Names of New England* (New York: Museum of the American Indian, 1962), 267; Baraga, *Otchipwe Language* 2: 400, 419.

42 Allouez in Kellogg, *Early Narratives of the Northwest,* 150. See also Bacqueville de la Potherie, "History of the Savage Peoples," in Blair, *Indian Tribes* 1: 305.

43 Baraga, *Otchipwe Language* 1: 94.

44 Verwyst, "Glossary of Chippewa Indian Names," 259.

45 Nicollet, *Journals,* 145n.

46 "*Tipi*: a tent, house, dwelling, abode" (Riggs, *Dakota-English Dictionary,* 470).

47 A. C. Myers, ed., *Narratives of Early Pennsylvania* (New York: Barnes and Noble, 1959), 232. Cf. "Wigwam, house," in Brinton and Anthony, *Lenape-English Dictionary,* 158.

48 Baraga, *Otchipwe Language* 1: 136; Gailland, "English-Potawatomi Dictionary," 160; Blackbird, *History of the Ottawa,* 124.

49 Baraga, *Otchipwe Language* 1: 267, 2: 314.

50 Skinner, "Some Menomini Indian Place Names," 99. Cf. "*meni-ka·n:* settlement, village, city," in Bloomfield, *Menominee Lexicon,* 123.

51 Smith, "Indian Place Names in Wisconsin," 264.

52 Jipson, "Winnebago Place Names,"; idem, "Winnebago-English Vocabulary" (MS, ca. 1924, Chicago Historical Society), 343, 346.

53 Jipson, "Winnebago-English Vocabulary," 343, 373.

54 On prehistoric sites, see Paul Martin, George I. Quimby, and Donald Collier, *Indians Before Columbus* (Chicago: University of Chicago Press, 1947); Robert E. Ritzenthaler, *Prehistoric Indians of Wisconsin* (Milwaukee: Milwaukee Public Museum, 1953); and *Wisconsin's Historical Markers,* 49, 88, 110, 112. I also obtained information along with mimeographed and printed literature, from Dennis Konkol, chief of the Administrative Services Section of the Bureau of Parks and Recreation, Department of Natural Resources, Madison, May 21, 1986.

9. Ethnicity, Gender, Rank, Occupation, and Age

1 FWP, *Wisconsin,* 387; William F. Stark, *Along the Black Hawk Trail* (Sheboygan: Zimmerman Press, 1984), 187.

2 FWP, *Wisconsin,* 437.

3 Cassidy, *Dane County Place Names,* 78.

4 Heckewelder, *History, Manners and Customs of the Indian Nations,* 77n.

5 Marquis de Chastellux, *Travels in North America* 2 vols. (Chapel Hill: University of North Carolina Press, 1963), 1: 262n; see also Gannett, *American Names,* 332.

6 Dunn, *True Indian Stories*, 192.

7 Eric Partridge, *A Dictionary of Slang and Unconventional English* (New York: Macmillan, 1961), 968; Walter W. Skeat, *Etymological Dictionary of the English Language*, 4th ed. (London: Oxford University Press, 1961), 726–27; Mathews, *Dictionary of Americanisms*, 1896; *Webster's New World Dictionary of the American Language*, 2d college ed. (n.p.: Walter Collins and World, 1976), 1646.

8 Haines, *American Indian*, 740; William L. Jenks, "History and Meaning of the County Names of Michigan," *Michigan Pioneer and Historical Society Collections* 38 (1912): 452.

9 William A. Galloway, *Old Chillicothe* (Xenia, Ohio: Buckeye Press, 1934), 316; C. C. Trowbridge, "Shawnese Traditions," *Occasional Contributions, University of Michigan Museum of Anthropology* 9 (1939): 16; Ebenezer Denny, *Military Journal, 1781–95* (Philadelphia: J. B. Lippincott, 1860), 276; Brinton and Anthony, *Lenape-English Dictionary*, 63.

10 Baraga, *Otchipwe Language* 1: 166.

11 Williams, *Key into the Language of America*, 134; Trumbull, *Natick Dictionary*, 154, 344, 346.

12 Brinton and Anthony, *Lenape-English Dictionary*, 103; Vogel, *Indian Place Names in Illinois*, 142, n. 920.

13 Edward Everett Hale, Introduction to Trumbull, *Natick Dictionary*, x.

14 Baraga, *Otchipwe Language* 1: 46; Verwyst, "Geographical Names," 395.

15 Baraga, *Otchipwe Language* 1: 204.

16 Williams, *Key into the Language of America*, 26.

17 Baraga, *Otchipwe Language* 1: 48.

10. Trails and Portages

1 A general treatment of Indian trails and place names is in Virgil J. Vogel, "Indian Trails and Place Names," *Names* 33 (March–June 1985): 39–50.

2 Baraga, *Otchipwe Language* 1: 214; Kuhm, "Indian Place Names," 58.

3 Baraga, *Otchipwe Language* 2: 187.

4 Radin, *Winnebago Tribe*, 176; information, Frances Perry of Black River Falls, personal communication, August 20, 1985.

5 Information, Dennis Konkol, chief, administrative services, Wisconsin Bureau of Parks and Recreation, letter of March 21, 1986.

6 Schoolcraft, "warrior prairie," in *Indian Tribes* 3: 506; Tuscola, from *"dusinagon,* a level, and *cola,* lands"; idem, in *Indian Tribes* 5: 624.

7 William A. Read, *Indian Place-Names in Alabama* (Baton Rouge: Louisiana State University Press, 1937), 72.

8 Frances Perry, personal communication, citing Bernard Eagle, August 20, 1985.

9 Thwaites, *Jesuit Relations* 59: 101.

10 Frederica H. Kleist, *Portage Heritage at Fort Winnebago Area* (Portage, Wis.: the author, 1984), not paginated.

11 *Wa-wa-āa*, "portage" Jipson, "Winnebago-English Dictionary," 388. Kleist spells it *Wau-wau-ah-na*, "carry on the shoulder."

12 According to Joshua Hathaway (1854), the Chippewa called this portage *Wah-bau-ga Oning-ah-ning*, "Eastern portage" "Indian Names," 122).

11. Descriptive Names

1 Jipson's "English-Winnebago Dictionary," has "black-*saip*," and "water-*nee*" (pp. 371, 377). In Winnebago, adjectives follow nouns.

2 Frances Perry to Gene Gallo of Elmhurst, Illinois, October 13, 1978.

3 Blackbird, *History of the Ottawa*, 113.

4 Baraga, *Otchipwe Language* 1: 207.

5 Ibid. 1: 252, 287; 2: 392.

6 J. A. Leonard, "Sketch of Whitewater, Walworth County," *Collections SHSW* for the year 1856 3 (1857): 427–34, n. 488.

7 Nicollet, *Journals*, 241.

8 Jipson, "Winnebago-English Vocabulary," 371, 396, 346.

9 Baraga, *Otchipwe Language* 2: 148; Upham, *Minnesota Geographic Names*, 15.

10 Baraga's word for "left hand" is *namandji* (*Otchipwe Language* 2: 269; Nicollet, *Journals*, 241). See also Upham, *Minnesota Geographic Names*, 75, 505; Verwyst, "Geographical Names," 394–95.

11 Baraga, *Otchipwe Language* 1: 213, 2: 321.

12 Skinner, *Mascoutens, Part III*, 399.

13 Baraga, *Otchipwe Language* 1: 154, 326; Skinner, *Mascoutens, Part III*, 399; Verwyst, "Geographical Names," 396.

14 Nicollet, *Journals*, 149; Baraga, *Otchipwe Language* 2: 56.

15 Verwyst, "Geographical Names," 396.

16 Baraga, *Otchipwe Language* 2: 66; Verwyst, "Geographical Names," 391.

17 Upham, *Minnesota Geographic Names*, 18, 156, citing Gilfillan.

18 Paul Foster, president, Racine County Historical Society and Museum, letter to the author, July 12, 1985; W. F. Moore, *Indian Place Names in Ontario* (Toronto: Macmillan of Canada, 1930), 29; Mason, *Schoolcraft's Expedition to Lake Itasca*, 63–64.

19 Verwyst, "Geographical Names," 390.

20 Baraga, *Otchipwe Language* 2: 40; Bloomfield, *Menominee Lexicon*, 21.

21 Tanner, *Narrative of Captivity*, 37; J. B. Tyrell, "Algonquian Indian Names in Northern Canada," *Transactions of the Royal Canadian Institute* 10 (May 1914): 228.

22 Charles L. Emerson, *Wisconsin Scenic and Historic Trails* (Madison: Straus Publishing, 1933), 39.

23 Baraga, *Otchipwe Language* 1: 300; Charles Hockett, note, *American Name Society Bulletin* 76 (February 15, 1985), 13.

24 Witherell, "Reminiscences," 337; Grignon, "Recollections," 290, 337.

25 Kuhm, "Indian Place-Names," 63–66.

26 William S. Powell, *North Carolina Gazetteer* (Chapel Hill: University of North Carolina Press, 1968), 327; Donehoo, *Indian Villages*, 107; Sneve, *South Dakota Geographic Names*, 348; Virgil J. Vogel, *Indian Names in Michigan* (Ann Arbor: University of Michigan Press, 1986), 147; Lewis A. McArthur, *Oregon Geographic Names* (Portland: Oregon Historical Society, 1974), 494.

27 Thwaites, *Jesuit Relations* 59: 154, Haines, *American Indian*, 753.

28 Sipe, *Indian Wars of Pennsylvania*, 11; Donehoo, *Indian Villages*, 110.

29 Brinton and Anthony, *Lenape-English Dictionary*, 47, 170.

30 Blackbird, *History of the Ottawa*, 113.

31 Baraga, *Otchipwe Language* 2: 266.

32 Ibid. 1: 219; Kuhm, "Indian Place Names," 79.

33 Baraga, *Otchipwe Language* 2: 283, 285.

34 Ibid. 2: 287; Vogel, *Indian Names in Michigan*, 148–49.

35 Jipson, "English-Winnebago Vocabulary," 324–25; idem, "Winnebago-English Vocabulary," 371.

36 Hathaway, "Indian Names," 117; Baraga, *Otchipwe Language* 2: 289; Skinner, *Mascoutens, Part III*, 399; Gailland, "English-Potawatomi Dictionary," 385; Bloomfield, *Menominee Lexicon*, 162.

37 Keating, *Narrative of an Expedition* 1: 191–92.

38 Hennepin, *New Discovery* 2: 656; Thwaites, *Jesuit Relations* 59: 141; 56: 225; S. Augustus Mitchell, *Illinois in 1837* (Philadelphia: Grigg and Elliott, 1837). Other recorded spellings of this name include Pecha-tan-oke, Peeka-tonakie, Peckitanoni, Peekatonokee, Pee-kee-tan-no, Peekatolika, Peek-tano, Pekatolika, Pekatonica, Pickatonick, and Pickotonokee. Vogel, *Indian Place Names in Illinois*, 107–8.

39 Gagnieur, "Indian Place Names," 544; Kelton, *Indian Names of Places*, 47–48.

40 Baraga, *Otchipwe Language* 1: 106, 181, 235.

41 Ibid. 1: 154, 181; 2: 23, 24, 198.

42 Ibid. 2: 364.

43 Gard and Sorden, *Wisconsin Place Names*, 135.

44 Baraga, *Otchipwe Language* 2: 401.

45 Hoffman, "Menomini Indians," 377–78.

46 Kappler, *Indian Treaties*, 187.

47 Read, *Florida Place-Names*, 66.

48 Huron H. Smith, "Indian Place Names," 265.

49 Bloomfield, *Menominee Language*, 129.

50 Skinner, *Material Culture of the Menominee*, 388.

51 Verwyst, "Geographical Names," 398.

52 M. J. Smith, letter to the author, August 25, 1986; punctuation edited. The nineteenth-century writer Publius Lawson also thought that *Winneconne* was named for a Menominee chief called Wau-nau-ko, who engaged in McKay's capture of Prairie du Chien in 1814, and also took to the warpath against the Sauk and Foxes in 1832 (Lawson, *The Story of Oshkosh* [n.p., n.d.], 19). There is no supporting evidence for his claim.

12. Names from Fauna

1 Charlevoix, *Voyage to North America* 1: 180.
2 Swanton, *Indian Tribes*, 247; Verwyst, "Geographical Names," 394
3 Pokagon, *Queen of the Woods*, 108, 140; Baraga, *Otchipwe Language* 1: 24.
4 Baraga, *Otchipwe Language* 1: 24.
5 Nicollet, *Journals*, 150.
6 Verwyst, "Geographical Names," 394.
7 Baraga, *Otchipwe Language* 1: 24, 2: 283–84.
8 Robert Blodgett, county clerk of Boone County, Illinois, and Bessie C. Bowley of the Boone County Historical Society tried unsuccessfully to trace this name in response to my inquiries. On Piscasaw, see Kappler, *Indian Treaties*, 174, 354, 355, 404; Baraga, *Otchipwe Dictionary* 1: 206.
9 Lewis H. Morgan, *The American Beaver and His Works* (Philadelphia: J. B. Lippincott, 1868).
10 Baraga, *Otchipwe Language* 1: 65.
11 Baraga, *Otchipwe Language* 2: 27.
12 Verwyst, "Geographical Names," 393.
13 Verwyst, "Glossary of Chippewa Indian Names," 256.
14 Chamberlain, "Algonkian Words," 241–242; cf. *Kwekwuhakao*, "wolverine," in Watkins, *Dictionary of the Cree Language*, 228; Schoolcraft, *Personal Memoir*, 499; Baraga, *Otchipwe Language* 1: 291.
15 Mathews, *Dictionary of Americanisms*, 308.
16 Henry D. Thoreau, *The Maine Woods* (New York: W. W. Norton, 1950), 108.
17 Friederici, *Amerikanistisches Wörterbuch*, 171.
18 Chamberlain, "Algonkian Words," 243; Baraga, *Otchipwe Language* 1: 242.
19 Longfellow, *Hiawatha*, 75.
20 Chamberlain, "Algonkian Words," 243.
21 Lewis C. Beck, *Gazetteer of the States of Illinois and Missouri* (Albany: Charles R. and George Webster, 1823), 115; Kinzie, *Wau-Bun*, 254; Jackson, *Black Hawk*, 22.
22 Isaac T. Smith, "Journal of Isaac T. Smith, 1835–36," in "Early Rock County," *Collections SHSW* 6 (1872): 424.
23 Verwyst, "Geographical Names," 392; Kuhm, "Indian Place-Names, 47–49.
24 Frederic G. Cassidy, "Koshkonong: A Misunderstood Place Name," *Wisconsin Magazine of History* 31 (June 1948): 429–40; see also idem, *Dane County Place Names*, 87–88.

25 Baraga, *Otchipwe Language* 1: 106; Gailland, "English-Potawatomi Dictionary," 118.

26 Cassidy, "Koshkonong," 430.

27 Baraga, *Otchipwe Language* 1: 134; Gailland, "English-Potawatomi Dictionary," 148.

28 Heckewelder, *Mission of the United Brethren*, 106; Donehoo, *Indian Village*, 85–87; C. Hale Sipe, *A Supplement to the First Edition of Indian Wars of Pennsylvania* (Harrisburg: Telegraph Press, 1931), 10.

29 Hoffman, "Menomini Indians," 320; Romig, *Michigan Place Names*, 268; A. F. Butler, "Rediscovering Michigan's Prairies," *Michigan History* 32 (March 1948): 20.

30 Alexander Henry, *Travels and Adventures* (Ann Arbor: University Microfilms, 1966), 262.

31 Carver, *Travels through the Interior*, 448–49.

32 Trumbull, *Natick Dictionary*, 66.

33 Baraga, *Otchipwe Language* 1: 173.

34 Mon-so-nee, "Moose Tail," was a chief at Courte Oreilles; Warren, *Ojibway Nation*, 318; Mosinee (q.v.) in Marathon County is named for him. The Ojibwa phratry, Monsonis, is mentioned by Perrot, and La Potherie said the lakes tribes called October the moose-rutting moon (in Blair, *Indian Tribes* 1: 224; 2: 126).

35 Wa-pos, "jackrabbit," also man's name, now family name, "Waupoose," in Bloomfield, *Menominee Lexicon*, 266; "Wa-bose, The Rabbit," Treaty of Green Bay, October 27, 1832. Kappler, *Indian Treaties*, 381.

36 Baraga, *Otchipwe Language* 1: 205.

37 Lyon G. Tyler, ed., *Narratives of Early Virginia, 1606–1625* (rpt., New York: Barnes and Noble, 1959), 95; William Strachey, *The Historie of Travaile into Virginia Britannia* (London: printed for the Hakluyt Society, 1845), 183, 187, 195; see also Chamberlain, "Algonkian Words," 255–56; *Webster's New World Dictionary*, 1197.

38 Skinner, *Mascoutens, Part III*, 399; Hoffman, "Menomini Indians," 297.

39 Carver, *Travels through the Interior*, 431; Trumbull, *Natick Dictionary*, 155, 323; Friederici, *Amerikanistisches Wörterbuch*, 568; Partridge, *Origins*, 629; John R. Bartlett, *Dictionary of Americanisms*, 3d ed. (Boston: Little, Brown, 1860), 410; Hodge, *Handbook of American Indians* 2: 596.

40 Tanner, *Narrative of Captivity*, 303; Baraga, *Otchipwe Language* 1: 196; Watkins, *Dictionary of the Cree Language*, 173; A. F. Chamberlain, "The Significance of Certain Algonquian Animal Names," *American Anthropologist*, n.s., 3 (1901): 669–83.

41 Tanner, *Narrative of Captivity*, 298.

42 Curot, "Wisconsin Fur Trader's Journal," 467n. See also Chapelle, *The "Why of Names,"* 60.

43 Vogel, *Indian Place-Names in Illinois*, 23–25.

44 Skinner, "Some Menomini Indian Place Names," 101; Hoffman, "Menomini Indians," 328.

45 Verwyst, "Geographical Names," 398; Baraga, *Otchipwe Language* 1: 291; 2: 422.

46 Baraga, *Otchipwe Language* 1: 62; Haines, *The American Indian*, 698.

47 Charles Brown, "Lake Wingra," *Wisconsin Archeologist*, o.s. 14 (1915): 78.

48 Cassidy, *Dane County*, 90–91; Jipson, "English-Winnebago Vocabulary," 301.

49 Baraga, *Otchipwe Language* 1: 83.

50 Ibid. 2: 189–90.

51 Ibid., 2: 291, 285.

52 Jipson, "Winnebago-English Vocabulary," 374; Emma Heiple and Bob Heiple of Green Lake, personal communication, July 2, 1985.

53 Baraga, *Otchipwe Language* 2: 86.

54 Schoolcraft, *Personal Memoirs*, 380; Kuhm, "Indian Place-Names," 20; Swanton, *Indian Tribes*, 261; Warren, *Ojibway Nation*, 309.

55 Verwyst, "Geographical Names," 393; Baraga, *Otchipwe Language* 1: 193, 2: 231; Kuhm, "Indian Place-Names," 58–59.

56 Blackbird, *History of the Ottawa*, 121; Tanner, *Narrative of Captivity*, 308; Dunn, *True Indian Stories*, 269.

57 Kappler, *Indian Treaties*, 276, 368, 458.

58 Verwyst, "Geographical Names," 392. Supporting the "prairie chicken or hen" interpretation are, among others, Joshua Hathaway, in "Indian Names," 117, and Skinner, in *Mascoutens, Part III*, 399.

59 Cassidy, *Dane County*, 90; idem, "Naming of the Four Lakes," 19–20; Verwyst, "Geographical Names," 397. See "swan": *wâbisi*, in Baraga, *Otchipwe Language* 1: 252.

60 Baraga, *Otchipwe Language* 1: 103. *Keego* is used in *Hiawatha*, and *Kegoi* by Schoolcraft in *Indian Tribes* 6: 676.

61 Baraga, *Otchipwe Language* 2: 183.

62 Cassidy, *Dane County*, 86.

63 Baraga, *Otchipwe Language* 1: 49.

64 Kappler, *Indian Treaties*, 78; Hodge, *Handbook of American Indians* 1: 803; Vogel, *Indian Place Names in Illinois*, 69–70.

65 Cassidy, *Dane County*, 194.

66 Jipson, "Winnebago-English Vocabulary," 339; letter, Frances Perry to Gene Gallo, October 15, 1975, copy furnished by Mr. Gallo.

67 Chamberlain, "Algonkian Words," 243; Verwyst, "Geographical Names," 397; Gerard in Hodge, *Handbook of American Indians* 2: 580; Mathews, *Dictionary of Americanisms*, 1550.

68 Nicollet, *Journals*, 152.

69 Henry, *Travels and Aventures*, 30.

70 Baraga, *Otchipwe Language* 1: 299.

71 M. Frank, "Early History of Kenosha," *Collections SHSW* 3 (1853): 374. In Baraga's *Otchipwe Language* 2: 190, the word for "pike" is *kinoje*, as Baraga uses *j* to express the *sh* sound. In Potawatomi there is no difference. One

source claims that Kenosha was named for a white settler named Pike, but the name was in use before that person arrived.

72 Swanton, *Indian Tribes*, 255; Bloomfield, *Menominee Lexicon*, 172; Hoffman, "Menomini Indians," 308, 324.

73 In Kellogg, *Early Narratives of the Northwest*, 150.

74 Verwyst, "Geographical Names," 392; Hoffman, "Menomini Indians," 308, 321.

75 Verwyst, "Geographical Names," 394; Baraga, *Otchipwe Language* 1: 248.

76 Nicollet, *Journals* (August 8, 1837), 146; Schoolcraft called this place *Namai Kowagon*.

77 Hoffman, "Menomini Indians," 307; Swanton, *Indian Tribes*, 254; Skinner, "Some Menominee Indian Place Names," 99.

78 Baraga, *Otchipwe Language* 1: 42, 249.

79 Vogel, *Indian Names in Michigan*, 108.

80 Baraga, *Otchipwe Language* 2: 401.

81 Frank Werner, letter to the author, August 3, 1985.

82 Baraga, *Otchipwe Language* 2: 269.

83 Verwyst, "Geographical Names," 390; Brown, "Myths and Legends," 114–15.

84 Nicollet, *Journals*, 228.

85 Upham, *Minnesota Place Names*, 265; Baraga, *Otchipwe Language* 1: 235; Schoolcraft, *Indian Tribes* 1: 94; Henry, *Travels and Aventures*, 178.

86 Myron Eells, "Aboriginal Geographic Names in the State of Washington," *American Anthropologist* 5 (January 1892): 27; Edmond Meany, *Origin of Washington Geographical Names* (rpt., Detroit: Gale Research, 1968), 45.

87 Baraga, *Otchipwe Language* 1: 272.

88 George H. Cannon, "Michigan's Land Boundary," *Michigan Pioneer and Historical Collections* 38 (1912): 166.

89 Thoreau, *Maine Woods*, 145.

90 Adams, *Western Words*, 208; McCulloch, *Woods Words*, 122.

91 Baraga, *Otchipwe Language* 2: 312.

92 Kappler, *Indian Treaties*, 496; Gard and Sorden, *Wisconsin Place Names*, 136.

93 Skinner, *Mascoutens, Part III*, 339.

94 Verwyst, "Geographical Names," 398.

95 Baraga, *Otchipwe Language* 2: 404; Tanner, *Narrative of Captivity*, 309; Upham, *Minnesota Geographical Names*, 235, 786.

13. Names from Flora

1 Mason, *Schoolcraft's Expedition*, 275, 314, 341–42.

2 Stennett, *Place Names*, 21; Kuhm, "Indian Place Names," 7; Baraga, *Otchipwe Language* 1: 22; Robert M. Dessureau, *History of Langlade*

County (Antigo, Wis.: Barnes Bros., 1922), 99; Huron H. Smith, "Indian Place Names," 254.

3 J. N. Nicollet, *Report Intended to Illustrate a Map of the Hydrographic Basin of the Upper Mississippi River*, Senate Document 237, February 16, 1841 (Washington, D.C.: Blair and Rives, 1843), map.

4 Tyler, *Narratives of Early Virginia*, 91; Chamberlain in Hodge, *Handbook of American Indians* 1: 547.

5 H. A. Schuette and Sybil C. Schuette, "Maple Sugar: A Bibliography of Early Records," *Transactions of the Wisconsin Academy of Science* 29 (1935): 209–36.

6 Baraga, *Otchipwe Language* 2: 216.

7 Ibid., 1: 269.

8 Increase Lapham, *Wisconsin* (Milwaukee: P. C. Hall, 1844), quoted in Kuhm, "Indian Place Names," 15.

9 Baraga, *Otchipwe Language* 1: 193; Gailland, "English-Potawatomi Dictionary," 246.

10 Radin *Winnebago Tribe* 67, 176.

11 Kuhm, "Indian Place Names," 131–32; Jipson, "Winnebago-English Vocabulary," 312, 389.

12 Vide: *a-ja*, "place," in Jipson, "Winnebago-English Vocabulary," 320; Upham, *Minnesota Geographic Names*, 174.

13 Bartlett, *Dictionary of Americanisms*, 186; Chamberlain, "Algonkian Words," 244, 260; Mathews, *Dictionary of Americanisms*, 1702; Beauchamp, *Aboriginal Place Names*, 241.

14 Smith, "Indian Place Names," 259; see: *Min*, "whortleberry" (i.e., blueberry or berry) + *ong* "place." Baraga, *Otchipwe Language* 2: 239.

15 Verwyst, "Geographical Names," 394; Baraga, *Otchipwe Language* 1: 119; Tanner, *Narrative of Captivity*, 296.

16 Tanner, *Narrative of Captivity*, 294–96; cf. Nikiminika Creek in northwestern Ontario, said to have a name shortened from the Ojibwa word for "gooseberry"; Tyrrell, "Algonquian Indian Names," 228–29.

17 Schoolcraft, *Personal Memoirs*, 223.

18 Nicollet, *Journals*, 152, 228.

19 Baraga, *Otchipwe Language* 1: 300; Nicollet, *Journals*, 100–101 and n. 38; Keating, *Narrative of an Expedition*, 2, appendix, 38; Friederici, *Amerikanistisches Wörterbuch*, 489; Chamberlain, "Algonkian Words," 252; Tanner, *Narrative of Captivity*, 63.

20 Gard and Sorden, *Wisconsin Place Names*, 99.

21 Dwight H. Kelton, *Indian Names and History of the Sault Ste. Marie Canal* (Detroit: the author, 1889), 29; Gilman, *Historic Chequamegon*, 11.

22 Nicollet, *Journals*, 236; Baraga, *Otchipwe Language* 2: 239, 250–55.

23 Tanner, *Narrative of Captivity*, 296; Baraga, *Otchipwe Language* 2: 239.

24 Walter J. Hoffman, "Menomini Indians," 316, 320; Ruth S. Worthing, *The History of Fond Du Lac County as Told by Its Place Names*, 2d ed. (Oshkosh: Globe Printing, 1976), 64.

25 Baraga, *Otchipwe Language* 2: 331.

26 Chamberlain in Hodge, *Handbook of American Indians* 1: 692.

27 Kinzie, *Wau-Bun*, 76.

28 Jenks, *Wild Rice Gatherers*, 1115–26; Carver, *Travels through the Interior*, 523.

29 Skinner, "Some Menomini Indian Place Names," 101.

30 Warren, *Ojibway Nation*, 308.

31 Nicollet, *Journals*, 142.

32 George Gibbs, *A Dictionary of the Chinook Jargon; or, Trade Language of Oregon* (New York: Cramoisy Press, 1863), 28; Elliott Coues, ed., *The History of the Lewis and Clark Expedition*, 3 vols. (1893; rpt., New York: Dover Publications, n.d., 2: 691 and 693n; Mathews, *Dictionary of Americanisms*, 1829.

33 Bloomfield, *Menominee Lexicon*, 265.

34 Smith, "Indian Place Names," 265; Kuhm, "Indian Place Names," 127–28.

35 Partridge, *Origins*, 519; W. R. Gerard, "Plant Names of Indian Origin," *Garden and Forest* 9 (1896), 292; Friederici, *Amerikanistisches Wörterbuch*, 81–82; Skeat, *Etymological Dictionary*, 468.

36 Verwyst, "Geographical Names," 396.

37 Kinzie, *Wau-Bun*, 64–65.

38 Schoolcraft, *Personal Memoirs*, 223.

39 Bloomfield, *Menominee Lexicon*, 158.

40 Nicollet, *Journals*, 152.

41 Cf. Baraga: *apakwei*, "mat, lodge mat" (*Otchipwe Language* 2: 44); and Tanner, "puk-kwi, or mats, which had belonged to the Ojibbeway Lodges" (*Narrative of Captivity*, 171).

42 Chamberlain, "Algonkian Words," 257; Gerard in Hodge, *Handbook of American Indians* 2: 493; Powell, *North Carolina Gazetteer*, 270, 444.

43 Williams, *Key into the Language of America*, 101.

44 Carver, *Travels through the Interior*, 526.

45 Baraga, *Otchipwe Language* 1: 105; 2: 392; J. A. Rayburn, "Geographical Names of Amerindian Origin in Canada, Part II," *Names* 17 (June 1969): 151; Kuhm, "Indian Place Names," 124.

46 Gustav William Buchen, *Historic Sheboygan County* (n.p.: the author, 1944), 267, 337.

47 Huden, *Indian Place Names*, 290; Kuhm, "Indian Place Names," 144, citing Gerend; Marryat, *Diary in America*, 269.

48 Pierre Margry, *Découvertes et Établissements des Français dans . . . L'Amerique Septentrionale, 1614–1698* 3 vols. (Paris: Maisonneuve et Cie, Libraires-Editeurs, 1879) 3: 485 (my translation).

49 Albert Gatschet, "Lexicon of the Peoria Language," an unnumbered card file, BAE cat. no. 2481, Smithsonian Institution, 1904.

14. Water Names

1 Beltrami, *A Pilgrimage in Europe and America* 2: 519.
2 Friederici, *Amerikanistisches Wörterbuch*, 84–85; Partridge, *Origins*, 42; *Webster's New World Dictionary*, 121; William A. Read, *Louisiana Place Names of Indian Origin*, Bulletin 19 (Baton Rouge: Louisiana State University, 1927), xii.
3 Cyrus Byington, *A Dictionary of the Choctaw Language*, BAE Bulletin 46 (Washington, D.C.: GPO, 1915), 94–95.
4 Vogel, *Indian Place Names in Illinois*, 72–73.
5 Pokagon, *Queen of the Woods*, 211; Baraga, *Otchipwe Language* 2: 383; Lemoine, *Montagnais*, 282.
6 Baraga, *Otchipwe Language* 1: 300.
7 William Bartram, *Travels of William Bartram* (rpt., New York: Dover Publications, 1955), 341.
8 Binneteau in Thwaites, *Jesuit Relations* 15: 71; Hennepin, *New Discovery* 1: 141.
9 Vogel, *Indian Place Names in Illinois*, 75–76; idem, *Iowa Place Names of Indian Origin*, 44–45.
10 "Water" *nibi, nibish* (Baraga, *Otchipwe Language* 2: 282).
11 J. H. Trumbull, "The Composition of Indian Geographical Names, Illustrated from the Algonkin Languages," *Collections of the Connecticut Historical Society* 2 (1870): 14–15.
12 Jipson, "Winnebago-English Vocabulary," 371. According to Frances Perry, "Water is *Ni* but *the* water or stream isn't nee-ra but Nee-nah. . . . The story is told that, when in the early days, a map maker wanted to put the lower Fox R. on the map he dipped his hand in it and asked a Hochunk Wunsheegra [Winnebago] 'What do you call this?' The Wunksheek said 'Ni Na,' meaning water, wondering at the stupidity of the Ma'-hee-xe-te-ra [Big Knife]. So the city on the lower Fox R. is Neenah. The lower Fox to the Wunksheegra is Ne o x te [? illegible]: Stream-where-big-the, since 'white man talks backward,'" Letter to the author, September 20, 1987.
13 Stennett, *Place Names*, 106.
14 Huron H. Smith, "Indian Place Names," 260.
15 Kappler, *Indian Treaties*, 131.
16 Jipson, "Winnebago-English Vocabulary," 371; idem, "Winnebago Place Names," 2.
17 Huron H. Smith, "Indian Place Names," 260.
18 Francis La Flesche, *A Dictionary of the Osage Language*, BAE Bulletin 189 (Washington, D.C.: GPO, 1932), 109, 294; John Rydjord, *Kansas Place Names* (Norman: University of Oklahoma Press, 1972), 113, 435–36.
19 Charlevoix, *Voyage to North America* 2: 209.
20 Marston to Morse, November 1820, in Blair, *Indian Tribes* 2: 147.
21 Keating, *Narrative of an Expedition* 1: 184.

22 "Plan for the Temporary Government of the Western Territory," in *The Complete Jefferson*, ed. Saul K. Padover (New York: Duell, Sloan and Pearce, 1943), 238.

23 E.g., Nils M. Holmer, *Indian Place Names in North America* (Cambridge: Harvard University Press, 1948), 41–42.

24 See *assen*, "rock," and *neppe*, "water," in Thomas Forsyth's "Memoirs of the Sauks and Foxes," in Blair, *Indian Tribes* 2: 241. There is no truth in the claim that this name signifies "lead ore."

15. Topography

1 Carver, *Travels through the Interior*, 138.

2 Gilman, *Historic Chequamegon* (n.p.: the author, 1971).

3 Verwyst, "Geographical Names," 391; Walter J. Hoffman, "The Midewiwin or 'Grand Medicine Society' of the Ojibwas," *Seventh Annual Report, Bureau of American Ethnology, 1885–86* (Washington, D.C.: GPO, 1891), 180; Warren, *Ojibway Nation*, 403n. See also Baraga, *Otchipwe Language* 1: 178.

4 Virgil J. Vogel, *Indian Names in Michigan* (Ann Arbor: University of Michigan Press, 1986), 124; Baraga, *Otchipwe Language* 1: 214.

5 Skinner, "Some Menomini Indian Place Names," 100; idem, *Material Culture of the Menomini*, 387. Cf. also Bloomfield, *Menominee Lexicon*, 123.

6 Cassidy, *Dane County*, 103, 119.

7 Jipson, "Winnebago-English Vocabulary," 366.

8 Gailland, "English-Potawatomi Dictionary," 177.

9 Baraga, *Otchipwe Language* 1: 147.

10 Ibid. 1: 198.

11 Gard and Sorden, *Wisconsin Place Names*, 85; "Editorial Comment," *Wisconsin Magazine of History* 7 (1923–24): 240–41.

12 Nicollet, *Report on the Hydrographic Basin*, 14.

13 Baraga, *Otchipwe Language* 1: 167, 252; Watkins, *Dictionary of the Cree Language*, 193; Tanner, *Narrative of Captivity*, 45; Pokagon, *Queen of the Woods*, 93; Chamberlain, "Algonkian Words," 250; Partridge, *Origins*, 422.

14 Tanner, *Narrative of Captivity*, 24; Warren, *Ojibway Nation*, 33.

15 Jesuit map in Sarah Jones Tucker, *Indian Villages of the Illinois Country* (Springfield: Illinois State Museum, 1942), pl. 1; Warren, *Ojibway Nation*, 243, 262; Baraga, *Otchipwe Language* 1: 22.

16 Verwyst, "Geographical Names," 394; Kappler, *Indian Treaties*, 454–55.

17 Bloomfield, *Menominee Lexicon*, 8; Baraga, *Otchipwe Language* 1: 84; Gailland, "English-Potawatomi Dictionary," 91; Verwyst, "Geographical Names," 395; Blackbird, *History of the Ottawa*, 123.

18 Verwyst, "Geographical Names," 396; Witherell, "Reminiscences," 337.

19 R. G. Thwaites, ed., "The Story of the Black Hawk War," *Collections SHSW* 12 (1892): 244; Vogel, *Indian Place Names in Illinois*, 139–40.

20 Truman Michelson, *Contributions to Fox Ethnology*, BAE Bulletin 85, (Washington, D.C.: 1927), 58, line 29; 30, lines 40–41 (phonetic symbols omitted).

21 Kuhm, "Indian Place Names," 115; H. F. Kett, *History of Jo Daviess County* (Illinois) (Chicago, 1878), 226, says "home of the eagle." Thanks to Sister M. Amato, O.P., archivist of the Dominican Motherhouse, Santa Clara Convent, Sinsinawa, Wisconsin, for information in her letter on August 11, 1962.

22 Swanton, *Indian Tribes*, 254; Skinner, "Some Menominee Indian Place Names," 99.

23 Verwyst, "Geographical Names," 397.

24 Ibid.; Baraga, *Otchipwe Language* 1: 122.

25 Schoolcraft, *Personal Memoirs*, 370.

26 Baraga, *Otchipwe Language* 1:24, 154.

16. Commemorative Names

1 Stark, *Along the Black Hawk Trail*, 139–53; Jackson, *Black Hawk*, 157–62.

2 Stark, *Along the Black Hawk Trail*, 81–85; Eby, *"That Disgraceful Affair,"* 183–87.

3 Letter to author, May 21, 1986, from Dennis Konkol, chief, Administrative Services Section, Wisconsin Bureau of Parks and Recreation, and brochure of Wisconsin Department of Natural Resources.

4 Lawson, "Potawatomi," 49–50; Brown, *Wisconsin Indian Place-Name Legends*, 8.

5 Stark, *Along the Black Hawk Trail*, 192.

6 Gard and Sorden, *Wisconsin Place Names*, 118.

7 Hauberg, "Black Hawk War," 125–29; Milo M. Quaife, *Chicago's Highways Old and New* (rpt., Ann Arbor: University Microfilms, 1968), 235.

17. French-Indian Place Names

1 Peter Pond, "Journal of Peter Pond," in R. G. Thwaites, ed., *Collections SHSW* 18 (1908): 331.

2 Kinzie, *Wau-Bun*, 62. See also Polly Brody, *Discovering Wisconsin* (Madison: Wisconsin House, 1973), 119.

3 Brunson, "Wisconsin Geographical Names," 114; Gard and Sorden, *Wisconsin Place Names*, 26; Kellogg, *French Regime*, 99; Warren, *Ojibway Nation*, 193.

4 Nicollet, *Report on the Hydrographic Basin*, 22–23.

5 Dunn, *Indiana and Indianans* 1: 86.

6 Morgan, *Ancient Society*, 169–71.

7 Theodore Pease and Raymond C. Werner, eds., *The French Foundations, 1680–1693* (Springfield: Illinois State Historical Library, 1934), 307.

8 Hermon Dunlap Smith, *The Des Plaines River, 1673–1940* (Lake Forest, Ill.: privately printed, 1940).

9 Keating, *Narrative of an Expedition* 1: 176.

10 "River aux Plaines, named by the French, signifies soft maple" (Hathaway, "Indian Names," 118). "Plaines" is the name for maple trees in the De Gannes memoir, in Pease and Werner, *French Foundations*, 394.

11 Hiram Calkins, "Indian Nomenclature of Northern Wisconsin," *First Annual Report and Collections SHSW for 1854* (Madison, 1855; rpt. 1903): 120.

12 Nicollet, *Journals*, 230; Calkins, "Indian Nomenclature," 120.

13 Skinner, "Some Menominee Indian Place Names," 100.

14 Warren, *Ojibway Nation*, 130; Baraga, *Otchipwe Language* 1: 106; 2: 396.

15 Worthing, *History of Fond du Lac County*, 33–38.

16 Zebulon Pike, *An Account of an Expedition to the Sources of the Mississippi River . . .* (Philadelphia: C. A. Conrad, 1810), entry for September 12, 1805.

17 This should be *croix.*

18 Keating, *Narrative of an Expedition* 1: 279.

19 Henry, *Travels and Adventures*, 78; Warren, *Ojibway Nation*, 202; Stuart Culin, *Games of the North American Indians* (rpt., New York: Dover Publications, 1975), 561–616.

20 Jipson, "Winnebago Place Names"; Thwaites, "Narrative of Spoon Decorah," 454.

21 Warren, *Ojibway Nation*, 192.

22 William F. Gagnieur, "Ketekitiganing (Lac Vieux Desert)," *Michigan History* 12 (October 1928): 776–77 (the USGS calls this place Katakitekon); Brody, *Discovering Wisconsin*, 286.

23 Nicollet, *Journals*, 129; square brackets are by editor, Martha C. Bray. Ground nut is *Apios tuberosa.* From the limited description, this plant could also be *Convolvulus pandurata (Ipomoea pandurata).*

24 Dorothy M. Brown, *Wisconsin Indian Place-Name Legends*, 8; Lawson, "Potawatomi," 49–50.

25 Leaflet published locally, "Crossing Death's Door to Washington Island" (no publication data).

26 Carver, *Travels through the Interior*, 50.

27 Keating, *Narrative of an Expedition*, 1: 245, 250.

28 Louise P. Kellogg, ed., *The British Regime in Wisconsin and the Northwest* (Madison: SHSW, 1935), 69; B. W. Brisbois, narrator, "Recollections of Prairie du Chien," noted down and annotated by Lyman C. Draper, *Collections SHSW* 9 (1882): 282–83.

29 Carver, *Travels through the Interior,* 46–47.
30 Lawson, "Potawatomi," 67; Gailland, "English-Potawatomi Dictionary," 303.
31 Kellogg, *Early Narratives of the Northwest,* 345.
32 Carver, *Travels through the Interior,* 56.
33 Keating, *Narrative of an Expedition* 1: 280–81.

18. State Names

1 Frank Werner, president Polk County Historical Society, letter to the author, August 3, 1985; Swanton, *Indian Tribes,* 153–56; Hodge, *Handbook of American Indians* 1: 43–44; Read, *Indian Place Names in Alabama,* 4; Byington, *Choctaw Language,* 144, 404; Harrington, *Our State Names,* 375.
2 Gard and Sorden, *Wisconsin Place Names,* 3; Orth, *Alaska Place Names,* 60; Stewart, *Names on the Land,* 388–89, 398–99; J. Ellis Ransom, "Derivation of the Name Alaska," *American Anthropologist,* n.s., 42 (1940): 550–51.
3 Gard and Sorden, *Wisconsin Place Names,* 5.
4 Muriel Wright, *A Guide to the Indian Tribes of Oklahoma* (Norman: University of Oklahoma Press, 1951), 218–19; W. David Baird, *The Quapaws* (Norman: University of Oklahoma Press, 1980), 5; Harrington, *Our State Names,* 376, 379–80.
5 Albert Lea, *Notes on the Wisconsin Territory* (Philadelphia: H. S. Tanner, 1836), 8.
6 Tucker, *Indian Villages,* pl. XXIX; Hodge, ed., *Handbook of American Indians* 1: 612–15; Martha R. Blaine, *The Ioway Indians* (Norman: University of Oklahoma Press, 1979), 3–4; Edwin James, *Account of an Expedition from Pittsburgh to the Rocky Mountains...* (2 vols.; Ann Arbor: University Microfilms, 1966), 1: 339.
7 Riggs, *Dakota-English Dictionary,* 60, 202; Swanton, *Indian Tribes,* 265–66; Vogel, *Iowa Place Names,* 26–29.
8 Gard and Sorden, *Wisconsin Place Names,* 63; Robert Hay, "Kaw and Kansas," *Collections Kansas State Historical Society* 2 (1905–6), 521–26; William Hamilton, "Names Derived from the Indian Languages," *Transactions and Reports, Nebraska State Historical Society* 1 (1885): 73–75; Floyd Streeter, *The Kaw* (New York: Rinehart, 1941), 4; Rydjord, *Kansas Place Names,* 104–6; William Unrau, *The Kansa Indians* (Norman: University of Oklahoma Press, 1971), 6–12.
9 William D. Palmer, ed., *Calendar of Virginia State Papers,* 9 vols. (Richmond: R. F. Walker, Supt. of Public Prints, 1875–92), 1: 282–85. The same information was given in an address on June 1, 1892, at a celebration of the

Filson Club of Louisville, and published by the speaker, Reuben T. Durrett, in *The Centenary of Kentucky* . . . (Louisville: J. P. Morton, 1892), 38.

10 Thomas Filson, *Discovery of Kentucke* (Ann Arbor: University Microfilms, 1966), 8, 10; Andre Michaux, "Journal of Travels into Kentucky . . ." in Thwaites, *Early Western Travels* 3: 224; Charles F. Hoffman, *A Winter in the West* (Ann Arbor: University Microfilms, 1966), 2: 164.

11 Stennett, *Place Names*, 103; Upham, *Minnesota Geographic Names*, 3; Carver, *Travels through the Interior*, 65; Keating, *Narrative of an Expedition* 1: 326, 336; Riggs, *Dakota-English Dictionary*, 316, 540.

12 Marquette in Thwaites, *Jesuit Relations* 59: 143; Joseph Ignatius Le Boulanger, "French-Illinois Dictionary," MS (1720), 58; Gatschet, "Lexicon of the Peoria Language"; unsigned note, "The Word 'Missouri'," *Missouri Historical Review* 34 (October 1939), 87–92; Blair, *Indian Tribes* 1: 171n, quoting Forsyth; Swanton, *Indian Tribes*, 269; Harrington, *Our State Names*, 382; Virgil J. Vogel, "The Origin and Meaning of 'Missouri'," *Bulletin Missouri Historical Society* 16 (April 1960): 213–22.

13 Hamilton, "Names from Indian Languages," 73; James, *Account of an Expedition* 1: 203; Lilian Fitzpatrick, *Nebraska Place Names* (Lincoln: University of Nebraska Press, 1960), 63; Francis La Flesche, "Linguistic Notes," ed. A. S. Gatschet, *American Antiquarian* 11 (1889): 129; Henry Fontanelle, "History of the Omaha Indians," *Transactions and Reports, Nebraska State Historical Society* 1 (1885): 76.

14 Cassidy, *Dane County*, 128; Gard and Sorden, *Wisconsin Place Names*, 91.

15 T. C. Elliott, "The Origin of the Name Oregon," *Oregon Historical Quarterly* 22 (June 1921): 101; Carver, *Travels through the Interior*, ix, 76.

16 Coues, *Lewis and Clark Expedition* 1: xxxi; John Wyeth, *Oregon* (Ann Arbor: University Microfilms, 1966), 47.

17 Elliott, "Origin of the Name Oregon," 99–100.

18 George R. Stewart, "The Source of the Name 'Oregon'," *American Speech* 19 (April 1944): 15–17; this article was reprinted by Stewart in *Names* 15 (September 1967): 169–72, and vigorously defended, in an article entitled "Ouaricon Revisited" in the same issue, 166–68. My reply to Stewart, "Oregon: A Rejoinder," was published in *Names* 16 (June 1968): 136–40. Stewart's view was also summarized in his book *Names on the Land*, rev. ed. (Boston: Houghton Mifflin, 1958), 154–55. It was adopted by McArthur in *Oregon Geographic Names* (1974), 556–59, by Mathews in *Dictionary of Americanisms*, 1166, and by several other authors.

19 Elliott, "Origin of the Name Oregon," 108.

20 Watkins, *Dictionary of the Cree Language*, 401; Baraga, *Otchipwe Language* 1: 300.

21 Vernon F. Snow, "From Ouragon to Oregon," *Oregon Historical Quarterly* 60 (December 1959): 439–47.

22 Kellogg, *Early Narratives of the Northwest*, 91; Lahontan, *New Voyages* 2: 737.

23 Kinietz, *Indians of the Western Great Lakes*, 375.

24 Thwaites, *Jesuit Relations* 65: 43–47; see also comments of Le Jeune and others in 5: 97 and 6: 287.

25 Malcolm H. Clark, "Oregon Revisited," *Oregon Historical Quarterly* 61 (June 1960): 211–19.

26 Coues, *Lewis and Clark Expedition* 2: 691n.

27 Gibbs, *Dictionary of the Chinook Jargon*, 17, 23, 26, 28.

28 Herbert Eugene Bolton, *Spanish Exploration in the Southwest, 1542–1706* (New York: Charles Scribner's, 1930), 359.

29 On Texas as a name, see Hodge, *Handbook of American Indians* 2: 738–41; Harrington, *Our State Names*, 356; H. B. Staples, "Origin of the Names of the States of the Union," *Proceedings of the American Antiquarian Society*, n.s., 1 (1880–81): 366–83.

19 Transfer Names

1 Thoreau, *Maine Woods* (1906), 338–39.

2 Lucius L. Hubbard, *Some Indian Place Names in Northern Maine* (Boston: James R. Osgood, 1884), 194.

3 J. G. Heckewelder to Peter S. DuPonceau, September 3, 1816, in Heckewelder, *History . . . of the Indian Nations*, 422.

4 Henry S. Burrage, ed., *Early English and French Voyages, 1534–1608* (1906; rpt., New York: Dover Publications, n.d.), 45–47, 60, 86–88, 99; see also Kellogg, *French Regime*, 18.

5 Gard and Sorden, *Wisconsin Place Names*, 20.

6 Fannie Eckstorm, *Indian Place-Names of the Penobscot Valley and Maine Coast* (Orono, Maine: University Press, 1941), 168–69.

7 Erwin Gudde, *1000 California Place Names* (Berkeley: University of California Press, 1959), 18; Stephen Powers, *Tribes of California* (rpt., Berkeley: University of California Press, 1976), 315.

8 Baraga, *Otchipwe Language* 1: 104, 214.

9 Bernard C. Peters, ed., *Lake Superior Journal: Bela Hubbard's Account of the 1840 Houghton Expedition* (Marquette: Northern Michigan University Press, 1983), 45, map 5; idem, "The Origin and Meaning of Chippewa Indian Place Names along the Lake Superior Shoreline," *Names* 32 (September 1984): 239, 242.

10 Baraga, *Otchipwe Language* 2: 114.

11 Verwyst, "Geographical Names," 391; for his other guesses, see idem, "Glossary of Chippewa Indian Names," 46.

12 Gard and Sorden, *Wisconsin Place Names*, 46.

13 Morgan, *League of the Iroquois* 2: 91–92; cf. *jone shi:yoh* in Wallace L. Chafe, *Seneca Morphology and Dictionary* (Washington, D.C.: Smithsonian Institution Press, 1967), 68, item 1118.

14 Donehoo, *Indian Villages*, 87.

15 Riggs, *Dakota-English Dictionary*, 313–14; Cassidy, *Dane County*, 88.

16 Gard and Sorden, *Wisconsin Place Names*, 79; Vogel, *Indian Place Names in Illinois*, 63–64 and n. 326; 69–70 and n. 378.

17 "Deep place" in Huden, *New England*, 112; "place of noises," in W. W. Tooker, "The Original Significance of 'Merrimac'," *American Antiquarian and Oriental Journal* 21 (January–November 1899): 14–16.

18 Montague Chamberlain, *Maliseet Vocabulary* (Cambridge: Harvard Cooperative Society, 1899), 17; Trumbull, *Natick Dictionary*, 63, 259; Baron Armand de Lahontan, *New Voyages to North-America*, ed. Reuben G. Thwaites, 2 vols. (Chicago: A. C. McClurg, 1905) 2: 742; see *Manumaig* in Hodge, *Handbook of American Indians* 1: 103.

19 Donehoo, *Indian Villages*, 127–28; Heckewelder, *Narrative Mission of United Brethren*, 547.

20 FWP, *Wisconsin*, 332: communication to author, Rita Sorkness, archives assistant, William D. McIntyre Library, University of Wisconsin–Eau Claire, May 27, 1987.

21 Schoolcraft, *Notes on the Iroquois*, 453–54.

22 Hewitt in Hodge, *Handbook of American Indians* 2: 68.

23 Beauchamp, *Aboriginal Place Names*, 134–35; Morgan, *League of the Iroquois* 2: 97–98.

24 Stennett, *Place Names*, 108.

25 Franklin B. Dexter, "The History of Connecticut as Illustrated by the Names of Her Towns," *Proceedings of the American Antiquarian Society*, n.s., 3 (October 1883–April 1885): 428.

26 J. Hammond Trumbull, *Indian Names in Connecticut* (rpt., Hamden, Conn.: Archon Books, 1974), 40–41.

27 Beauchamp, *Aboriginal Place Names*, 173; Schoolcraft, *Notes on the Iroquois*, 396.

28 Gard and Sorden, *Wisconsin Place Names*, 96.

29 Hennepin, *A New Discovery* 2: 559.

30 Morgan, *League of the Iroquois* 2: 132.

31 J. A. Rayburn, "Geographical Names of Amerindian Origin II," 149.

32 Beauchamp, *Aboriginal Place Names*, 39, 155, 169. Cf. Handsome Lake: *Kanyotaiyo*, "A Seneca chief's title and name of the prophet." Chafe, *Seneca Morphology and Dictionary*, 74, item 1352.

33 Horatio Hale, *The Iroquois Book of Rites* (Toronto: University of Toronto Press, 1963), 176.

34 Beauchamp, *Aboriginal Place Names*, 171; Morgan, *League of the Iroquois* 2, table facing p. 61.

35 Gard and Sorden, *Wisconsin Place Names*, 97.

36 Morgan, *League of the Iroquois* 2: 138; Beauchamp, *Aboriginal Place Names*, 148–49, 174.

37 Paul Bailey, *The Thirteen Tribes of Long Island* (Amityville, N.Y.: Long Is-

land Forum, 1956), 5–6; F. H. Douglas, *Long Island Indian Tribes,* leaflet 99 (Denver: Denver Art Museum, 1932); Robert F. Grumet, *Native American Place Names in New York City* (New York: Museum of the City of New York, 1981), 46–48.

38 Blackbird, *History of the Ottawa,* 94.

39 Quaife, *Western Country,* 65.

40 Blair, *Indian Tribes* 2: 183.

41 Verwyst, "Geographical Names," 397; idem, "Glossary of Chippewa Names," 270.

42 Trumbull, "Indian Geographical Names," 31.

43 Gard and Sorden, *Wisconsin Place Names,* 113.

44 Ludy E. Keeler, "Old Fort Sandoski of 1715 and the 'Sandusky Country'," *Ohio Archaeological and Historical Quarterly* 17 (October 1908): 357–429; Hodge, *Handbook of American Indians* 2: 421; Vogel, *Indian Place Names in Illinois,* 122–23 and nn. 791–95.

45 Ruttenber, *Footprints of the Red Men,* 180–84. Other views are in Beauchamp, *Aboriginal Place Names,* 196–97; Hodge, *Handbook of American Indians* 2: 466; and Schoolcraft, *Indian Tribes* 3: 328.

46 A. L. Kroeber, *Handbook of the Indians of California* (rpt., New York: Dover Publications, 1976), 897; Helen S. Carlson, *Nevada Place Names* (Reno: University of Nevada Press, 1974), 228.

47 Hodge, *Handbook of American Indians* 2: 670; Byington, *Dictionary of the Choctaw Language,* 346; Henry S. Halbert, "Choctaw Names in Alabama and Mississippi," *Transactions of the Alabama Historical Society* 3 (1898–99): 76; Read, *Indian Place Names in Alabama,* 59.

48 Morgan, *League of the Iroquois* 2: 102, 133; Heckewelder, *Mission of the United Brethren,* 555–56; Donehoo, *Indian Villages,* 226–27; Beauchamp, *Aboriginal Place Names,* 230; Mooney and Dunn in Hodge, *Handbook of American Indians* 2: 755.

49 Dunn, *True Indian Stories,* 307.

50 Heckewelder, *Mission of the United Brethren,* 556.

51 Brinton and Anthony, *Lenape-English Dictionary,* 139.

52 Donehoo, *Indian Villages,* 232.

53 Swanton, *Indian Tribes,* 447; Livingston Farrand in Hodge, *Handbook of American Indians* 2: 900; McArthur, *Oregon Geographic Names,* 373; Edmond S. Meany, *Origin of Washington Geographic Names* (Seattle: University of Washington Press, 1923), 332; Myron Eells, "Aboriginal Geographic Names in the State of Washington" *American Anthropologist* 5 (1892): 34–35.

54 Donehoo, *Indian Villages,* 257; Sipe, *Supplement to the Indian Wars,* 15; Hodge, *Handbook of American Indians* 2: 977.

55 Gard and Sorden, *Wisconsin Place Names,* 142.

56 Kroeber, *Handbook of Indians of California,* 897.

57 Gudde, *1000 California Place Names,* 96; Kroeber, *Handbook of Indians of California,* 897.

58 Orth, *Dictionary of Alaska Place Names*, 1069; Phillips, *Alaska-Yukon Place Names*, 145.
59 Hodge, *Handbook of American Indians*, I, 714–15, Mathews, *Dictionary of Americanisms*, p. 934, James W. Phillips, *Alaska-Yukon Place Names* (Seattle: University of Washington Press, 1973), pp. 75–76; W. B. Hamilton, *The Macmillan Book of Canadian Place Names* (Toronto: Macmillan of Canada, 1978), p. 322.

20. Names from South of the Border

1 Wilfred Funk, *Word Origins and Their Romantic Stories* (New York: Wilfred Funk, 1950), 346; Friederici, *Amerkanistisches Wörterbuch*, 127–28.
2 Nils M. Holmer, "Indian Place Names in South America and the Antilles," part 2, *Names* 8 (December 1960): 219; Gard and Sorden, *Wisconsin Place Names*, 26–27.
3 Mathews, *Dictionary of Americanisms*, 853.
4 Read, *Louisiana Place Names*, 32; Bartlett, *Dictionary of Americanisms*, 209.
5 Daniel G. Brinton, *Myths of the New World*, 2d ed. (New York: Henry Holt, 1876), 52.
6 Walter W. Skeat, *The Language of Mexico, and Words of West Indian Origin* (London: Philological Society, 1890), 145.
7 Lake Mills–Aztalan Historical Society, *The Aztalan Story* (Lake Mills, 1952); Kuhm, "Indian Place-Names," 10.
8 Fred Tarpley, *1001 Texas Place Names* (Austin: University of Texas Press, 1980), 10; Gannett, *American Place Names*, 34.
9 Rudolfo Acuña, *Occupied America* (San Francisco: Canfield Press, 1972), 229.
10 Byrd Granger, *Will C. Barnes' Arizona Place Names* (Tucson: University of Arizona Press, 1960), 332.
11 Haines, *American Indian*, 717.
12 Gutierre Tibon, "Mexico, the Name," *Onomastica* 17 (1959): 5–10; "Mexican Place Names," *Amigos* 1 (August 1942): 37; T. M. Pearce, *New Mexico Place Names* (Albuquerque: University of New Mexico Press, 1965), 108.
13 Friederici, *Amerikanistiches Wörterbuch*, 174; Skeat, *Etymological Dictionary*, 775; Myron J. Quimby, *Scratch Ankle, USA: American Place Names and Their Derivation* (New York: A. S. Barnes, 1969), 83; Gard and Sorden, *Wisconsin Place Names*, 22; Nils M. Holmer, "Indian Place Names of South America and the Antilles," part 3, *Names* 9 (March 1960): 40.
14 Brinton, *Myths of the New World*, 321; William Prescott, *History*, 1006–7.
15 Buchen, *Historic Sheboygan County*, 339; Gard and Sorden, *Wisconsin Place Names*, 71.
16 Prescott, *History*, 752 and n.
17 Friederici, *Amerikanistisches Wörterbuch*, 520–21.

18 Gard and Sorden, *Wisconsin Place Names,* 103; O. D. Von Engeln and Jane M. Urquhart, *Story Key to Geographic Names* (rpt., Port Washington, N.Y.: Kennikat Press, 1970) 142–43.

21. Potpourri

1 Verwyst, "Geographical Names," 390; Baraga, *Otchipwe Language* 1: 287.
2 Baraga, *Otchipwe Language* 2: 156, 293–94.
3 Verwyst, "Geographical Names," 391.
4 Baraga, *Otchipwe Language* 1: 290, 2: 73.
5 Longfellow, *Hiawatha,* 181.
6 Baraga, *Otchipwe Language* 2: 87.
7 Longfellow, *Hiawatha,* 190.
8 Baraga, *Otchipwe Language* 2: 96, 137.
9 Ibid., 2: 178.
10 Skinner, *Mascoutens, Part III,* 399, Gailland, "English-Potawatomi Dictionary," 358; Baraga, *Otchipwe Language* 1: 250; Walter J. Hoffman, "Menomini Indians," 326.
11 Gard and Sorden, *Wisconsin Place Names,* 63.
12 Annuity List (MS), November 8, 1832 (Chicago Historical Society), 275.
13 Vogel, *Iowa Place Names,* 39; Baraga, *Otchipwe Language* 2: 240; Verwyst, "Geographical Names," 392.
14 Verwyst, "Geographical Names," 393.
15 Gard and Sorden, *Wisconsin Place Names,* 79.
16 Gailland, "English-Potawatomi Dictionary," 111.
17 Brinton and Anthony, *Lenape-English Dictionary,* 84; Dunn, *True Indian Stories,* 188.
18 Riggs, *Dakota-English Dictionary,* 457.
19 Vogel, *Indian Names in Michigan,* 43–44; Baraga, *Otchipwe Language* 1: 290.
20 Kuhm, "Indian Place Names," 101; cf. Baraga, *Otchipwe Language* 1: 85.
21 Walter J. Hoffman, "Menominee Indians," 310.
22 Calkins, "Indian Nomenclature," 120.
23 Baraga, *Otchipwe Language* 1: 213.
24 Skinner, *Material Culture of the Menominee,* 388; Walter J. Hoffman, "Menomini Indians," 311; Swanton, *Indian Tribes,* 255.
25 Jipson, "Winnebago-English Vocabulary," 382, Riggs, *Dakota-English Dictionary,* 523.
26 Baraga, *Otchipwe Language* 2: 400.
27 Ibid., 1: 191; 2: 398.
28 *Wa-pan,* "dawn," in Bloomfield, *Menominee Lexicon,* 264; *waban,* Ojibwa, "east," in Verwyst, "Geographical Names," 398; and Baraga, *Otchipwe Language* 2: 190.

29 Mrs. Marion Howard, director of the Darlington Public Library, letter to the author, September 26, 1986; W. Davidson, "Personal Narrative of the Black Hawk War," *Collections SHSW* 5 (1868; rpt. 1907), 318; *The Lafayette County Centennial Book,* 1976 (Madison: Straus Printing & Publishing, 1976), 187; Riggs, *Dakota-English Dictionary,* 387, 564.

30 Gard and Sorden, *Wisconsin Place Names,* 23.

31 The following are listed as Indian names, without definition or language identification, by Kuhm in "Indian Place-Names in Wisconsin": Mackay-see, Muskesin, Noboken, Nonoken, Pauto, and Tahkodah.

32 Bloomfield, *Menominee Lexicon,* 91.

33 Riggs, *Dakota-English Dictionary,* 293, 454.

34 Philip Poulette, Waushara County Historical Society, letter to author, June 10, 1985. Variations of this story, and other details, are in Gard and Sorden, *Wisconsin Place Names,* 135–36.

35 Skinner, *Material Culture of the Menomini,* 207.

22. Artificial Names

1 Stewart, *American Place Names,* xxxi.

2 Skinner, *Mascoutens, Part III,* 399.

3 Erwin H. Ackerknecht, "White Indians . . . ," *Bulletin of the History of Medicine* 4 (January 1944): 21.

4 Schoolcraft, *Indian Tribes* 3: 509; 5: 624; Chase Osborn and Stellanova Osborn, *Schoolcraft, Longfellow and Hiawatha* (Lancaster, Pa.: Jacques Cattell Press, 1942), 260; Schoolcraft, *Personal Memoirs,* 115.

5 Hjalmar P. Holand, "A Historic Spot near Wautoma, Wisconsin," *Wisconsin Magazine of History* 33 (March 1950): 310–17.

6 Hodge, *Handbook of American Indians* 1: 617; Swanton, *Indian Tribes,* 33.

7 Beauchamp, *Aboriginal Place Names,* 191; Schoolcraft, *Indian Tribes* 2: 488; M. A. Armstrong, *The Origin and Meaning of Place Names in Canada* (Toronto: Macmillan, 1930), 142, citing Horatio Hale.

8 Swanton, *Indian Tribes,* 252.

9 Upham, *Minnesota Geographic Names,* 126; B. A. Botkin, *Treasury of Mississippi River Folk Lore* (New York: Crown Publishers, 1955), 517–18. Boutwell's claim was published in the *St. Paul Pioneer,* June 16, 1872, and reprinted in Edward C. Gale, "The Legend of Lake Itasca," *Minnesota History* 12 (September 1931): 215–25; see also Mason, *Schoolcraft's Expedition,* 350–51.

10 William J. Peterson, "Veritas Caput, Itasca," *Minnesota History* 18 (June 1937): 180–85.

11 Published also in differing details in the *Niles Weekly Register* 43 (December 1, 1832), 227, and the *Democratic Free Press and Michigan Intelli-*

gencer (Detroit), October 25, 1832; reprinted in Mason, *Schoolcraft's Expedition*, 357–58. The *Galenian* and *Niles Weekly Register* accounts were examined and compared at the Chicago Historical Society.

12 Schoolcraft, *Personal Memoirs*, 420–21.

13 Mason, *Schoolcraft's Expedition*, 352.

14 Von Engeln and Urquhart, *Story Key to Geographic Names*, 49.

15 Upham, *Minnesota Geographic Names*, 126.

16 Schoolcraft, *Narrative of an Expedition*.

17 Schoolcraft, *Indian Tribes* 5: 621–23; idem, *Notes on the Iroquois* (New York: Bartlett and Welford, 1846), 225.

18 Schoolcraft, *Personal Memoirs*, 413.

19 Schoolcraft, *Indian Tribes* 5: 533.

20 This agrees with Boutwell's diary entry for July 13, saying that "the lake is very irregular in shape and from this reason, the Indians gave it the name Moshkos, an Elk" (Mason, *Schoolcraft's Expedition*, 330).

21 Henry R. Schoolcraft, *Summary Narrative of an Exploratory Expedition to the Sources of the Mississippi River . . .* (Philadelphia: Lippincott Grambo, 1855), 243.

22 Schoolcraft, *Indian Tribes* 5: 624.

23 Mary H. Eastman, *The American Aboriginal Portfolio* (Philadelphia: Lippincott Grambo, 1853), 14–18.

24 Theodore C. Blegen, "That Name Itasca," *Minnesota History* 13 (June 1932): 163–74.

25 Mason, *Schoolcraft's Expedition*.

26 Ibid., 204–5, 255–56, 330.

27 Charlevoix, *History of New France* 3: 207n; Mason, *Schoolcraft's Expedition*, 350–51.

28 Dwight H. Kelton, *Indian Names of Places near the Great Lakes* (Detroit: Detroit Free Press, 1888), 51. On *Totosh*, see Baraga, *Otchipwe Language* II: 388.

29 Irving H. Hart, "The Origin and Meaning of the Name 'Itasca'," *Minnesota History* 12 (September 1931): 220.

30 Williams, *Schoolcraft's Indian Legends*, xviii.

31 Twin: *nijôde'*. Baraga, *Otchipwe Language* I: 272.

32 Gard and Sorden, *Wisconsin Place Names*, 141.

Bibliography

Books

Ackerman, William K. *Early Illinois Railroads*. Chicago: Fergus Printing, 1884.

Acuña, Rudolfo. *Occupied America*. San Francisco: Canfield Press, 1972.

Adair, James. *Adair's History of the Indians*. Reprint. New York: Promontory Press, n.d.

Adams, Ramon. *Western Words: A Dictionary of the American West*. Norman: University of Oklahoma Press, 1968.

Alexander, W. E. *History of Winneshiek and Allamakee Counties, Iowa*. Sioux City: Western Publishing, 1882.

Alsberg, H. G., ed. *The American Guide*. New York: Hastings House, 1949.

Alvord, Clarence W., ed. *Kaskaskia Records, 1778–1790*. Springfield: Illinois State Historical Library, 1909.

Armour, David A., ed. *Attack at Michilimackinac, 1763*. Mackinac Island: Mackinac Island State Park Commission, 1971.

Armstrong, M. A. *The Origin and Meaning of Place Names in Canada*. Toronto: Macmillan, 1930.

Asimov, Isaac. *Words on the Map*. Boston: Houghton-Mifflin, 1962.

Assiniwi, Bernard. *Lexique des Noms Indiens en Amérique*. Ottawa: Editions Lemeac, 1973.

Atwater, Caleb. *The Indians of the Northwest, Their Manners, Customs, &c., or Remarks Made on a Tour to Prairie du Chien . . .* Columbus, 1850.

Bailey, Paul. *The Thirteen Tribes of Long Island*. Amityville, N.Y.: Long Island Forum, 1956.

Baird, W. David. *The Quapaws*. Norman: University of Oklahoma Press, 1980.

Baraga, Bishop Frederic. *A Dictionary of the Otchipwe Language*. 1878. Reprint (2 vols. in 1). Minneapolis: Ross and Haines, 1966.

Barnett, Louise. *The Ignoble Savage*. Westport, Conn.: Greenwood Press, 1975.

Bartlett, John R. *Dictionary of Americanisms: A Glossary of Words and Phrases Usually Regarded as Peculiar to the United States*. 3d ed. Boston: Little, Brown, 1860.

Bartram, William. *Travels of William Bartram*. Reprint. New York: Dover Publications, 1955.

Beauchamp, William. *Aboriginal Place Names of New York*. 1907. Reprint. Detroit: Grand River Books, 1971.

283

Beck, Lewis C. *Gazetteer of the States of Illinois and Missouri.* Albany: Charles R. and George Webster, 1823.

Becker, Donald W. *Indian Place-Names in New Jersey.* Cedar Grove, N.J.: Phillips-Campbell Publishing, 1964.

Beckwith, Albert C. *History of Walworth County.* 2 vols. Indianapolis: B. F. Bowen, 1912.

Beckwith, Hiram W. *The Illinois and Indiana Indians.* New York: Arno Press, 1975.

Belknap, Jeremy, and Jedidiah Morse. *Report on the Oneida, Stockbridge and Brothertown Indians,* 1796. New York: Museum of the American Indian, 1955.

Beltrami, J. C. *A Pilgrimage in Europe and America.* 2 vols. London: Hunt and Clarke, 1828.

Bishop, Morris. *Champlain: Life of Fortitude.* New York: Alfred Knopf, 1940.

Bissell, Benjamin. *The American Indian in English Literature of the Eighteenth Century.* New Haven: Yale University Press, 1925; rpt. Archon, 1968.

Blackbird, Andrew J. *History of the Ottawa and Chippewa Indians of Michigan.* 1887. Reprint. Petoskey: Little Traverse Regional Historical Society, 1977.

Blaine, Martha R. *The Ioway Indians.* Norman: University of Oklahoma Press, 1979.

Blair, Emma H. *The Indian Tribes of the Upper Mississippi Valley and Region of the Great Lakes.* 1911. Reprint (2 vols. in one). New York: Kraus Reprint, 1969.

Bloomfield, Leonard. *The Menomini Language.* New Haven: Yale University Press, 1962.

Bloomfield, Leonard. *Menominee Lexicon.* Ed. Charles F. Hockett, Milwaukee: Milwaukee Public Museum Press, 1975.

Bolton, Herbert Eugene. *Spanish Exploration in the Southwest, 1542–1706.* New York: Charles Scribner's, 1930.

Botkin, B. A. *Treasury of Mississippi River Folk Lore.* New York: Crown Publishers, 1955.

Brinton, Daniel G. *Myths of the New World.* 2d ed. New York: Henry Holt, 1876.

Brinton, Daniel G., and Albert S. Anthony. *A Lenape-English Dictionary.* Philadelphia: Historical Society of Pennsylvania, 1888.

Brody, Polly. *Discovering Wisconsin.* Madison: Wisconsin House, 1973.

Brown, Dorothy Moulding. *Wisconsin Indian Place-Name Legends.* N.p.: the author, 1948.

Brown, Douglas S. *The Catawba Indians.* Columbia: University of South Carolina Press, 1966.

Brown, Evelyn. *Kateri Tekakwitha.* New York: Farrar-Strauss, 1958.

Buchen, Gustav William. *Historic Sheboygan County.* N.p.: the author, 1944.

Burnett, Reuben T. *The Centenary of Kentucky.* Louisville: J. P. Morton, 1892.

Burrage, Henry S., ed. *Early English and French Voyages, 1534–1608.* 1906. Reprint. New York: Dover Publications, n.d.

Byington, Cyrus. *A Dictionary of the Choctaw Language.* Bureau of American Ethnology Bulletin 46; Washington, D.C.: Government Printing Office, 1915.

Campbell, Thomas. *The Poetical Works of Thomas Campbell.* Philadelphia: Lea and Blanchard, 1845.

Canada Department of Indian and Northern Affairs, *Linguistic and Cultural Affiliations of Canadian Indian Bands.* Ottawa, 1980.

Carlson, Helen S. *Nevada Place Names.* Reno: University of Nevada Press, 1974.

Carr, Charles F. *Some Indian Chiefs Who Reigned over New London, Wisconsin Territory.* N.p., 1911.

Carra, Emma. *Virginia; or, The Flower of the Ottawas, a Tale of the West.* Boston: F. Gleason, 1848.

Carver, Jonathan. *Travels through the Interior Parts of North America.* 3d ed. 1781. Reprint. Minneapolis: Ross and Haines, 1956.

Cassidy, Frederic G. *Dane County Place Names.* Madison: University of Wisconsin Press, 1968.

Chafe, Wallace L. *Seneca Morphology and Dictionary.* Washington, D.C.: Smithsonian Institution Press, 1967.

Chamberlain, Montague. *Maliseet Vocabulary.* Cambridge: Harvard Cooperative Society, 1899.

Chapelle, Ethel Elliott. *The "Why of Names" in Washburn County, Wisconsin.* Birchwood, Wis.: the author, 1965.

Charlevoix, Pierre François Xavier de. *History and General Description of New France.* Ed. John G. Shea. 6 vols. New York: John G. Shea, 1872.

Charlevoix, Pierre François Xavier de. *Journal of a Voyage to North America.* Ed. Louise P. Kellogg. 2 vols. Chicago: Caxton Club, 1923.

Chastellux, Marquis de. *Travels in North America.* 2 vols. Chapel Hill: University of North Carolina Press, 1963.

Cheney, Roberta C. *Names on the Face of Montana.* Missoula: Mountain Press Publishing, 1983.

Clifton, James A. *The Prairie People.* Lawrence: Regents Press of Kansas, 1971.

Cooper, James Fenimore. *The Last of the Mohicans.* New York: Grosset and Dunlap, n.d.

Coues, Elliott, ed. *The History of the Lewis and Clark Expedition.* 3 vols. 1893. Reprint. New York: Dover Publications, n.d.

Crévecoeur, Michel-Guillaume St. Jean de. *Journey into Northern Pennsylvania and the State of New York.* Ann Arbor: University of Michigan Press, 1964.

Culin, Stewart. *Games of the North American Indians.* 1907. Reprint. New York: Dover Publications, 1975.

Cuoq, J. A. *Lexique de la Langue Algonquine.* Montreal: J. Chapleau et Fils, 1886.

Danziger, Edmund J. *The Chippewas of Lake Superior.* Norman: University of Oklahoma Press, 1978.

De Leon, Pedro de Cieza. *The Incas.* Norman: University of Oklahoma Press, 1959.

Denny, Maj. Ebenezer. *Military Journal, 1781–95.* Memoirs of the Pennsylvania Historical Society. Philadelphia: J. B. Lippincott, 1860.

Derleth, August. *The Wisconsin: River of a Thousand Isles.* New York: Farrar and Rinehart, 1942. Reprint. Madison: University of Wisconsin Press, 1985.

Dessereau, Robert M. *History of Langlade County, Wisconsin.* Antigo: Barnes Bros., 1922.

Dickinson, Thomas H., ed. *Wisconsin Plays.* New York: B. W. Huebsch, 1914.

Dockstader, Frederick J. *Great North American Indians.* New York: Van Nostrand Reinhold, 1977.

Dolbier, John, and Joan Dolbier. *From Sawmills to Sunfish: A History of Onalaska, Wisconsin,* 1985.

Donehoo, George P. *Indian Villages and Place Names in Pennsylvania.* 1928. Reprint. Baltimore: Gateway Press, 1977.

Douglas, F. H. *Long Island Indian Tribes.* Leaflet 99. Denver: Denver Art Museum, 1932.

Douglass, John M. *The Indians in Wisconsin's History.* Milwaukee: Milwaukee Public Museum, 1954.

Dunlap, A. R., and C. A. Weslager. *Indian Place Names in Delaware.* Wilmington: Archaeological Society of Delaware, 1950.

Dunn, Jacob P. *True Indian Stories, with Glossary of Indiana Indian Names.* Indianapolis: Sentinel Printing, 1909.

Duratschek, Sister Mary Claudia. *Crusading along Sioux Trails.* Yankton, S.D.: Bernardine Convent of the Sacred Heart, 1947.

Durrett, Reuben T. *The Centenary of Kentucky . . .* Louisville: J. P. Morton, 1892.

Eastman, Charles A. *Indian Boyhood.* 1902. Reprint. New York: Dover Publications, 1971.

Eastman, Mary H. *Dahcotah; or, Life and Legends of the Sioux around Fort Snelling.* New York: John Wiley, 1849.

Eastman, Mary H. *The American Aboriginal Portfolio.* Philadelphia: Lippincott Grambo: 1853.

Eby, Cecil. *"That Disgraceful Affair": The Black Hawk War.* New York: W. W. Norton, 1973.

Eckstorm, Fannie. *Indian Place-Names of the Penobscot Valley and Maine Coast.* Orono, Maine: University Press, 1941.

Edmunds, R. David. *The Potawatomi Indians: Keepers of the Fire.* Norman: University of Oklahoma Press, 1978.

Emerson, Charles L. *Wisconsin Scenic and Historic Trails.* Madison: Straus Publishing, 1933.

Federal Writers Program, *North Dakota: A Guide to the Northern Prairie State.* Fargo: Knight Printing, 1938.

Federal Writers Program. *Wisconsin: A Guide to the Badger State.* New York: Hastings House, 1954.

Filson, Thomas. *The History of Kentucke.* Ann Arbor: University Microfilms, 1966.

Fitzpatrick, Lilian. *Nebraska Place Names.* Lincoln: University of Nebraska Press, 1960.

Friederici, Georg. *Amerikanistisches Wörterbuch . . .* Hamburg: Cram, De Gruyter, 1960.

Funk, Wilfred. *Word Origins and Their Romantic Stories.* New York: Wilfred Funk, 1950.

Galloway, William A. *Old Chillicothe.* Xenia, Ohio: Buckeye Press, 1934.

Gannett, Henry. *American Names.* 1905. Reprint. Washington, D.C.: Public Affairs Press, 1947.

Gard, Robert E. *This Is Wisconsin.* Spring Green: Wisconsin House, 1969.

Gard, Robert E., and Elaine Reetz. *The Trail of the Serpent: The Fox River Valley, Lore and Legend.* Madison: Wisconsin House, 1973.

Gard, Robert E., and L. G. Sorden. *The Romance of Wisconsin Place Names.* New York: October House, 1968.

Gibbs, George. *A Dictionary of the Chinook Jargon; or, Trade Language of Oregon.* New York: Cramoisy Press, 1863.

Gibson, A. N. *The Kickapoos: Lords of the Middle Border.* Norman: University of Oklahoma Press, 1963.

Gilman, Rhoda R. *Historic Chequamegon.* N.p.: the author, 1971.

Goff, John H. *Place Names of Georgia.* Athens: University of Georgia Press, 1975.

Granger, Byrd. *Will C. Barnes' Arizona Place Names.* Tucson: University of Arizona Press, 1960.

Graymont, Barbara. *The Iroquois in the American Revolution.* Syracuse: Syracuse University Press, 1972.

Gridley, Marion. *America's Indian Statues.* Chicago: Towertown Press, 1966.

Grumet, Robert S. *Native American Place Names in New York City.* New York: Museum of the City of New York, 1981.

Gudde, Erwin. *1000 California Place Names.* Berkeley: University of California Press, 1959.

Hagan, William T. *The Sac and Fox Indians.* Norman: University of Oklahoma Press, 1958.

Haines, Elijah M. *The American Indian.* 1888. Reprint. Evansville, Ind.: Unigraphic, 1977.

Hale, Horatio. *The Iroquois Book of Rites.* Toronto: University of Toronto Press, 1963.

Hamilton, William B. *The Macmillan Book of Canadian Place Names.* Toronto: Macmillan of Canada, 1978.

Harder, Kelsie. *Illustrated Dictionary of Place Names.* New York: Van Nostrand Reinhold, 1974.

Harrington, John P., ed. *The Original Strachey Vocabulary of the Virginia Indian Language.* Extract from Bureau of American Ethnology Bulletin #157. Washington, D.C.: Government Printing Office, 1955.

Harrington, John P., ed. *Our State Names.* Reprint from Smithsonian Institution Report, 1954. Washington, D.C.: Smithsonian Institution, 1955.

Heckewelder, John. *A Narrative of the Mission of the United Brethren among the Delaware and Mohegan Indians.* Reprint. Cleveland: Burrows Bros., 1907.

Heckewelder, John. *History, Manners and Customs of the Indian Nations Who Once Inhabited Pennsylvania and the Neighboring States.* Reprint. New York: Arno Press, 1971.

Hennepin, Louis. *A New Discovery of a Vast Country in America.* Ed. Reuben G. Thwaites. 2 vols. Chicago: A. C. McClurg, 1903.

Henry, Alexander. *Travels and Adventures.* Ann Arbor: University Microfilms, 1966.

Hexom, Charles P. *Indian History of Winneshiek County.* Decorah, Iowa: A. K. Bailey and Sons, 1913.

History of Clayton County, Iowa. Chicago: Interstate Publishing, 1882.

History of Monona County, Iowa. Chicago: National Publishing, 1890.

Hodge, Frederick Webb, ed., *Handbook of American Indians North of Mexico.* Bureau of American Ethnology Bulletin 30. 2 vols. Washington, D.C.: Government Printing Office, 1907–10.

Hoffman, Charles F. *A Winter in the West.* 2 vols. Ann Arbor: University Microfilms, 1966.

Hollatz, Tom. *Louis No. 1: The Life and Legend of Louis St. Germaine.* Neshkoro, Wis.: Laranmark Press, 1984.

Horan, James D. *The McKenney-Hall Portrait Gallery of American Indians.* New York: Crown Publishers, 1972.

Houghton, Louise Seymour. *Our Debt to the Red Man: The French-Indians in the Development of the United States.* Boston: Stratford, 1918.

Hubbard, Lucius L. *Some Indian Place Names in Northern Maine.* Boston: James R. Osgood, 1884.

Huden, John C. *Indian Place Names of New England.* New York: Museum of the American Indian, 1962.

Hudson, Charles M. *The Catawba Nation.* Athens: University of Georgia Press, 1970.

Hughes, Thomas. *Indian Chiefs of Southern Minnesota.* Reprint. Minneapolis: Ross and Haines, 1969.

Hulbert, Archer B. *Portage Paths: The Keys to the Continent.* Cleveland: Arthur H. Clark, 1903.

Hunt, John W. *Wisconsin Gazetteer.* Madison: Begiah Brown, 1853.

International Colportage Mission. *A Cheap and Concise Dictionary of the Ojibwa and English Languages.* 2d ed. Toronto, 1912.

Jackson, Donald, ed. *Black Hawk: An Autobiography.* Urbana: University of Illinois Press, 1955.

Jackson County Historical Society. *Jackson County: A History.* Black River Falls, Wis.: printed by Taylor Publishing, Dallas, 1984.

James, Edwin. *Account of an Expedition from Pittsburgh to the Rocky Mountains.* 2 vols. Reprint. Ann Arbor: University Microfilms, 1966.

Jenks, Albert E. *The Wild Rice Gatherers of the Upper Lakes.* Extract from *Nineteenth Annual Report,* Bureau of American Ethnology, Part 2. Washington, D.C.: Government Printing Office, 1901.

Kane, Joseph N. *The American Counties.* 3d ed. Metuchen, N.J.: Scarecrow Press, 1972.

Kappler, Charles J., ed. *Indian Affairs: Laws and Treaties,* vol. 1. Washington, D.C.: GPO, 1904.

Kappler, Charles J., ed. *Indian Treaties, 1778–1883.* Reprint. New York: Interland Publishing, 1972.

Kaukauna—Glimpses of Its History. Kaukauna: n.p., 1985.

Keating, William H. *Narrative of an Expedition to the Source of St. Peters River* . . . Reprint (2 vols. in 1). Minneapolis: Ross and Haines, 1959.

Keesing, Felix M. *The Menomini Indians of Wisconsin.* 1939. Reprint. Madison: University of Wisconsin Press, 1987.

Keiser, Albert. *The Indian in American Literature.* New York: Oxford University Press, 1933.

Kellogg, Louise P., ed. *The French Regime in Wisconsin and the Northwest.* Madison: State Historical Society of Wisconsin, 1925.

Kellogg, Louise P., ed. *The British Regime in Wisconsin and the Northwest.* Madison: State Historical Society of Wisconsin, 1935.

Kellogg, Louise P., ed. *Early Narratives of the Northwest, 1634–1699.* New York: Barnes and Noble, 1967.

Kelton, Dwight H. *Indian Names of Places Near the Great Lakes.* Detroit: Detroit Free Press, 1888.

Kelton, Dwight H. *Indian Names and History of the Sault Ste. Marie Canal.* Detroit: the author, 1889.

Kenton, Edna, ed. *Black Gown and Redskins.* London: Longmans, Green, 1956.

Kett, H. F. *History of Jo Daviess County* (Illinois). Chicago, 1878.

Kinietz, W. Vernon. *The Indians of the Western Great Lakes, 1615–1760.* Ann Arbor: University of Michigan Press, 1965.

Kinzie, Mrs. John H. [Juliette]. *Wau-Bun; or, The Early Days in the Northwest.* Chicago: Rand McNally, 1901.

Kleist, Frederica H. *Portage Heritage at Fort Winnebago Area.* Portage, Wis.: the author, 1984.

Kohl, Johann George. *Kitchi-Gami: Life Among the Lake Superior Ojibway.* Reprint. St. Paul: Minnesota Historical Society Press, 1985.

Kort, Ellen. *The Fox Heritage—A History of Wisconsin's Fox Cities.* Northridge, Calif.: Windsor Publications, [1984?]

Kroeber, A. L. *Handbook of the Indians of California.* Reprint. New York: Dover Publications, 1976.

Krug, Merton E. *DuBay, Son-in-Law of Oshkosh.* Appleton: C. C. Nelson Publishing, 1946.

La Flesche, Francis. *A Dictionary of the Osage Language.* Bureau of American Ethnology Bulletin 109. Washington, D.C.: Government Printing Office, 1932.

Lafayette County Bicentennial Book 1976, The. Madison: Straus Printing and Publishing, 1976.

Lahontan, Baron Armand de. *New Voyages to North-America.* Ed. Reuben G. Thwaites. 2 vols. Chicago: A. A. McClurg, 1905.

Lake Mills–Aztalan Historical Society. *The Aztalan Story.* Lake Mills, Wis., 1952.

Landes, Ruth. *Ojibwa Religion and the Midewiwin.* Madison: University of Wisconsin Press, 1968.

Lawson, Publius V. *The Story of Oshkosh, His Tribe and Fellow Chiefs.* N.p., n.d.

Lea, Albert M. *Notes on the Wisconsin Territory.* Philadelphia: H. S. Tanner, 1836.

Lemoine, George. *Dictionnaire Français-Montagnais.* Boston: W. B. Cabot and P. Cabot, 1901.

Lincoln, Charles H., ed. *Narratives of the Indian Wars, 1675–1699.* Reprint. New York: Charles Scribner's Sons, 1952.

Longfellow, Henry W. *The Song of Hiawatha.* New York: Cupples and Leon, n.d.

Loughridge, R. M. *English and Muskokee Dictionary.* Reprint. Okmulgee, Okla.: Baptist Home Mission Board, 1964.

Lurie, Nancy O. *Wisconsin Indians.* Madison: State Historical Society of Wisconsin, 1980.

McArthur, Lewis A. *Oregon Geographic Names.* 4th ed. rev. Portland: Oregon Historical Society, 1974.

McCulloch, Walter F. *Woods Words: A Comprehensive Dictionary of Loggers Terms.* Reprint. Corvallis: Oregon Historical Society, 1977.

McKenney, Thomas L. *Sketches of a Tour to the Lakes.* Barre, Mass.: Imprint Society, 1972.

Mackenzie, Alexander. *Alexander Mackenzie's Voyage to the Pacific Ocean in 1793.* Ed. Milo M. Quaife. Chicago: Lakeside Press, 1931.

McReynolds, E. C. *The Seminoles.* Norman: University of Oklahoma Press, 1957.

Marceil, Beauford, and Kathleen Marceil. *Legends and Tales of She-she-Pe-ko-Naw.* Reprint. Neopit(?): the authors, 1973.

Margry, Pierre. *Découvertes et Établissements des Français dans L'ouest et dans le sud de L'Amérique Septentrionale, 1614–1698.* 3 vols. Paris: Maisoneuve et Cie, Libraires-Editeurs, 1879.

Marryat, Frederick. *A Diary in America.* New York: Alfred Knopf, 1962.

Martin, Paul, George I. Quimby, and Donald Collier. *Indians before Columbus.* Chicago: University of Chicago Press, 1947.

Mason, Philip P., ed. *Schoolcraft's Expedition to Lake Itasca.* East Lansing: Michigan State University Press, 1958.

Mathews, Mitford W. *Dictionary of Americanisms.* Chicago: University of Chicago Press, 1956.

Meany, Edmond S. *Origin of Washington Geographic Names.* Seattle: University of Washington Press, 1923.

Menominee Indian Centennial Committee. *Menominee Indian Centennial, 1854–1954.* N.p., 1954.

Michelson, Gunther. *A Thousand Words of Mohawk.* Ottawa: National Museum of Man, National Museums of Canada, 1973.

Michelson, Truman. *Contributions to Fox Ethnology.* Bureau of American Ethnology Bulletin 85. Washington, D.C.: Government Printing Office, 1927.

Miller, Mary R. *Thomas Campbell.* Boston: Twayne Publishers, 1978.

Minnesota Department of Economic Development. *Tales of Great Spirit: Minnesota Indian Legends.* St. Paul, n.d.

Mitchell, S. Augustus. *Illinois in 1837.* Philadelphia: Grigg and Elliott, 1837.

Moore, W. F. *Indian Place Names in Ontario.* Toronto: Macmillan of Canada, 1930.

Morgan, Lewis H. *The American Beaver and His Works.* Philadelphia: J. B. Lippincott, 1868.

Morgan, Lewis H. *Ancient Society.* Reprint. Chicago: Charles H. Kerr, 1910.

Morgan, Lewis H. *League of the Ho-de-no-sau-nee or Iroquois.* 2 vols. New Haven: Human Relations Area Files, 1954.

Morgan, Lewis H. *Indian Journals, 1859–62.* Ed. Leslie A. White. Ann Arbor: University of Michigan Press, 1959.

Mörner, Magnus. *Race Mixture in the History of Latin America.* Boston: Little, Brown, 1967.

Morse, Jedidiah. *Report to the Secretary of War on Indian Affairs.* New Haven: S. Converse, 1822.

Murray, Robert A. *A History of Pipestone National Monument, Minnesota.* Pipestone, Minn.: Pipestone Indian Shrine Association, n.d.

Myers, A. C., ed. *Narratives of Early Pennsylvania.* Reprint. New York: Barnes and Noble, 1959.

Native American Directory. San Carlos, Ariz.: National Native American Cooperative, 1982.

Nichols, Phebe Jewell. *Oshkosh the Brave, Chief of the Wisconsin Menominees, and His Family.* Oshkosh: Castle Pierce, 1954.

Nicollet, J. N. *Report Intended to Illustrate a Map of the Hydrographic Basin of the Upper Mississippi River.* Washington, D.C.: Blair and Rives, 1843.

Nicollet, J. N. *The Journals of Joseph N. Nicollet.* St. Paul: Minnesota Historical Society, 1970.

Orth, Donald J. *Dictionary of Alaska Place Names.* Washington, D.C.: Government Printing Office, 1967.

Osborn, Chase S. and Stellanova Osborn. *Schoolcraft, Longfellow and Hiawatha.* Lancaster, Pa.: Jacques Cattell Press, 1942.

Ourada, Patricia. *The Menominee Indians.* Norman: University of Oklahoma Press, 1979.

Padover, Saul K., ed. *The Complete Jefferson.* New York: Duell, Sloan and Pearce, 1943.

Palmer, William D., ed. *Calendar of Virginia State Papers.* 9 vols. Richmond: R. F. Walker, Supt. of Public Prints, 1875–92. (Vol. 1).

Parkman, Francis. *The Conspiracy of Pontiac.* 2 vols. Boston: Little, Brown, 1922.

Partridge, Eric. *Origins: A Short Etymological Dictionary of Modern English.* London: Routledge and Kegan Paul, 1958.

Partridge, Eric. *A Dictionary of Slang and Unconventional English.* New York: Macmillan, 1961.

Pearce, T. M. *New Mexico Place Names.* Albuquerque: University of New Mexico Press, 1965.

Pease, Theodore, and Raymond C. Werner, eds. *The French Foundations, 1680–1693.* Springfield: Illinois State Historical Library, 1934.

Peckham, Howard H. *Pontiac and the Indian Uprising.* Reprint. Chicago: University of Chicago Press, 1961.

Peters, Bernard C., ed. *Lake Superior Journal: Bela Hubbard's Account of the 1840 Houghton Expedition.* Marquette: Northern Michigan University Press, 1983.

Phillips, James W. *Washington State Place Names.* Seattle: University of Washington Press, 1972.

Phillips, James W. *Alaska-Yukon Place Names.* Seattle: University of Washington Press, 1973.

Pike, Zebulon M. *An Account of an Expedition to the Sources of the Mississippi River and through the Western Parts of Louisiana . . .* Philadelphia: C. A. Conrad, 1810.

Pokagon, Chief [Simon]. *O-gi-maw-kwe Mit-i-gwa-ki, Queen of the Woods . . .* Hartford, Mich.: C. H. Engle, 1899.

Powell, Peter J. *Sweet Medicine.* 2 vols. Norman: University of Oklahoma Press, 1969.

Powell, William S. *North Carolina Gazetteer.* Chapel Hill: University of North Carolina Press, 1968.

Powers, Stephen. *Tribes of California.* Reprint. Berkeley: University of California Press, 1976.

Prescott, William. *History of the Conquest of Mexico and History of the Conquest of Peru.* New York: Modern Library, n.d.

Purcell, William G. *St. Croix Trail Country.* Minneapolis: University of Minnesota Press, 1967.

Quaife, Milo M. *Chicago and the Old Northwest, 1673–1835.* Chicago: University of Chicago Press, 1913.

Quaife, Milo M. *Lake Michigan.* Indianapolis: Bobbs-Merrill, 1944.

Quaife, Milo M., ed. *The Western Country in the Seventeenth Century.* New York: Citadel Press, 1962.

Quaife, Milo M. *Chicago's Highways Old and New: From Indian Trail to Motor Road.* Reprint. Ann Arbor: University Microfilms, 1968.

Quimby, Myron J. *Scratch Ankle, USA: American Place Names and Their Derivation.* New York: A. S. Barnes, 1969.

Radin, Paul. *The Winnebago Tribe.* Reprint. Lincoln: University of Nebraska Press, 1970.

Read, William A. *Louisiana Place Names of Indian Origin.* Bulletin 19. Baton Rouge: Louisiana State University, 1927.

Read, William A. *Florida Place Names of Indian Origin.* Baton Rouge: Louisiana State University Press, 1934.

Read, William A. *Indian Place-Names in Alabama.* Baton Rouge: Louisiana State University Press, 1937.

Richardson, John. *Wacousta; or, The Prophesy.* 2 vols. New York: Dewitt and Davenport, 1832.

Riggs, Stephen R. *A Dakota-English Dictionary.* Reprint. Minneapolis: Ross and Haines, 1968.

Ritzenthaler, Robert E. *The Oneida Indians of Wisconsin.* Milwaukee: Milwaukee Public Museum Bulletin 19, no. 1, November 1950.

Ritzenthaler, Robert E. *Prehistoric Indians of Wisconsin.* Milwaukee: Milwaukee Public Museum, 1953.

Ritzenthaler, Robert E. *The Potawatomi Indians of Wisconsin.* Milwaukee: Milwaukee Public Museum Bulletin 19, no. 3, January 1953.

Rogers, Robert. *Journals of Major Robert Rogers.* London: J. Miller, Bookseller, 1765 (1775).

Romig, Walter, *Michigan Place Names.* Grosse Pointe, Mich.: Walter Romig, n.d.

Rosholt, Malcolm, and John B. Gehl. *Florimond J. Bonduel, Missionary to Wisconsin Territory.* Rosholt, Wis.: Rosholt House, 1976.

Rudolph, Robert S. *Wood County Place Names.* Madison: University of Wisconsin Press, 1970.

Ruttenber, E. M. *Footprints of the Red Men: Indian Geographical Names . . .* Albany: New York State Historical Association, 1906.

Rydjord, John. *Kansas Place Names.* Norman: University of Oklahoma Press, 1972.

Schmitz, Maxine O. *Lake of the Torch, Past and Present.* Lac du Flambeau, Wis.: the author, 1987.

Schoolcraft, Henry R. *Narrative of an Expedition through the Upper Mississippi to Itasca Lake . . .* New York: Harper and Bros., 1834.

Schoolcraft, Henry R. *Algic Researches.* See Williams, Mentor.

Schoolcraft, Henry R. *Notes on the Iroquois.* Albany: Erastus H. Pease, 1847.

Schoolcraft, Henry R. *The American Indians, Their History, Condition and Prospects.* Rev. ed. Rochester: Wanzer Foot, 1851.

Schoolcraft, Henry R. *Information Respecting the History, Condition and Prospects of the Indian Tribes of the United States.* 6 vols. Philadelphia: Lippincott Grambo, 1851–56.

Schoolcraft, Henry R. *Summary Narrative of an Exploratory Expedition to the Sources of the Mississippi River in 1820 . . .* Philadelphia: Lippincott Grambo, 1855.

Schoolcraft, Henry R. *Personal Memoirs of a Residence of Thirty Years with the Indian Tribes . . .* Reprint. New York: Arno Press, 1975.

Schoolcraft, Henry R. *Legends of the American Indians.* New York: Crescent Books, 1980.

Schwarz, Herbert T. *Windigo and Other Tales of the Ojibways.* Toronto: McClelland Stewart, 1972.

Sedgwick, Sarah Cabot, and Christina Sedgwick Marquand. *Stockbridge, 1739–1974.* Stockbridge, Mass.: Berkshire Traveller Press, 1974.

Shawano County Historical Society and Shawano Area Writers. *The Shawano Story, 1874–1974.* Shawano, 1974.

Sipe, C. Hale. *A Supplement to the First Edition of Indian Wars of Pennsylvania.* Harrisburg: Telegraph Press, 1931.

Skeat, Walter W. *Notes on English Etymology and on Words of Brazilian and Peruvian Origin.* London: Reprint from Transactions of the Philological Society, 1885–87.

Skeat, Walter W. *The Language of Mexico, and Words of West Indian Origin.* London: Philological Society, 1890.

Skeat, Walter W. *Etymological Dictionary of the English Language.* 4th ed. London: Oxford University Press, 1961.

Skinner, Alanson. *Material Culture of the Menomini.* New York: Museum of the American Indian, 1921.

Skinner, Alanson. *Notes on Mahikan Ethnology.* Milwaukee: Bulletin of Public Museum of Milwaukee, January 1925.

Skinner, Alanson. *The Mascoutens or Prairie Potawatomi Indians, Part III: Mythology and Folklore.* Milwaukee: Bulletin of the Public Museum of the City of Milwaukee, 6: 5 January 22, 1927.

Slotkin, J. S. *The Menomini Powwow.* Milwaukee: Milwaukee Public Museum Publications in Anthropology, no. 4, 1957.

Smith, Hermon Dunlap. *The Des Plaines River, 1673–1940.* n.p.: printed for author by Wisconsin Cuneo Press, 1940.

Smith, Huron H. *Ethnobotany of the Menomini Indians.* Westport, Conn.: Greenwood Press, 1970.

Sneve, Virginia Driving Hawk. *South Dakota Geographic Names.* Sioux Falls: Brevet Press, 1973.

Stark, William F. *Along the Black Hawk Trail.* Sheboygan: Zimmerman Press, 1984.

[Stennett, W. H.] *A History of the Origin of the Place Names Connected with the Chicago and Northwestern . . .* 2d ed. Chicago, 1908.

Stewart, George R. *Names on the Land.* Rev. ed. Boston: Houghton Mifflin, 1958.

Stewart, George R. *American Place Names.* New York: Oxford University Place, 1971.

Strachey, William. *The Historie of Travaile into Virginia Britannia.* London: printed for the Hakluyt Society, 1845.

Streeter, Floyd. *The Kaw.* New York: Rinehart, 1941.

Swanton, John R., ed. *The Indians of the Southeastern United States.* Bureau of

American Ethnology Bulletin 137. Washington, D.C.: Government Printing Office, 1946.

Swanton, John R., ed. *The Indian Tribes of North America.* Bureau of American Ethnology Bulletin 145. Washington, D.C.: Government Printing Office, 1952.

Tanner, H. B. *History of the Streets of Kaukauna.* Kaukana: Kaukauna Times Publishing, n.d. Updated in 1985 by Andrew Kailhofer.

Tanner, Helen Hornbeck. *Atlas of Great Lakes Indian History.* Norman: University of Oklahoma Press, 1986.

Tanner, John. *Narrative of the Captivity and Adventures of John Tanner . . .* Ed. Edwin James. Reprint. Minneapolis: Ross and Haines, 1956.

Tarpley, Fred. *1001 Texas Place Names.* Austin: University of Texas Press, 1980.

Taylor, Lolita. *The Native American: Ojibwa, the Wild Rice People, and Native American Contributions to Progress.* Shell Lake, Wis.: Wisconsin Indianhead Vocational, Technical and Adult Education District Office, 1976.

Taylor, Theodore. *The States and their Indian Citizens.* Washington, D.C.: Bureau of Indian Affairs, 1972.

Thoreau, Henry D. *The Maine Woods.* New York: W. W. Norton, 1950.

Thwaites, Reuben G., ed. *Jesuit Relations and Allied Documents, 1610–1791.* 73 vols. Cleveland: Burrows Bros., 1896–1901.

Thwaites, Reuben G., ed. *The French Regime in Washington, 1634–1760.* 3 vols. Madison: Collections State Historical Society of Wisconsin, 1902–8.

Thwaites, Reuben G., ed. *Early Western Travels.* 32 vols. Cleveland: Arthur H. Clark, 1904–7.

Tibbles, Thomas H. *Buckskin and Blanket Days.* Reprint. Lincoln: University of Nebraska Press, 1969.

Tooker, William W. *The Indian Place Names on Long Island.* Reprint. Port Washington, N.Y.: Ira H. Friedman, 1962.

Trobriand, Philippe Regis Denis de Keredern de. *Army Life in Dakota.* Ed. Milo M. Quaife. Chicago: Lakeside Press, 1941.

Trumbull, J. Hammond. *Natick Dictionary.* Bureau of American Ethnology Bulletin 25. Washington, D.C.: Government Printing Office, 1903.

Trumbull, J. Hammond. *Indian Names in Connecticut.* Reprint. Hamden, Conn.: Archon Books, 1974.

Tyler, Lyon G., ed. *Narratives of Early Virginia, 1606–1625.* Reprint. New York: Barnes and Noble, 1959.

United States Department of Commerce, Economic Development Administration. *Federal and State Indian Reservations: An EDA Handbook.* Washington, D.C.: U.S. Department of Commerce, 1971.

United States Geological Survey. National Mapping Division. Office of Geographic Research, National Center. *Wisconsin Geographic Names, Alphabetical Finding List.* 2 vols. Reston, Va.: n.d. Computer printout, spiral bound.

United States House of Representatives. *Report with Respect of the House Reso-*

lution Authorizing the . . . Investigation of the Bureau of Indian Affairs. Washington, D.C.: Government Printing Office, 1953.

Unrau, William E. *The Kansa Indians.* Norman: University of Oklahoma Press, 1971.

Upham, Warren. *Minnesota Geographic Names.* Reprint. St. Paul: Minnesota Historical Society, 1969.

Urbanek, Mae. *Wyoming Place Names.* Boulder, Colo.: Johnson Publishing, 1974.

Vogel, Virgil J. *American Indian Medicine.* Norman: University of Oklahoma Press, 1970.

Vogel, Virgil J. *Indian Place Names in Illinois.* Springfield: Illinois State Historical Society, 1963.

Vogel, Virgil J. *Iowa Place Names of Indian Origin.* Iowa City: University of Iowa Press, 1983.

Vogel, Virgil J. *Indian Names in Michigan.* Ann Arbor: University of Michigan Press, 1986.

Von Engeln, O. D., and Jane M. Urquhart. *Story Key to Geographic Names.* Reprint. Port Washington, N.Y.: Kennikat Press, 1970.

Ware, John M. *History of Waupaca County.* 2 vols. Chicago: Lewis Publishing, 1917.

Warren, William W. *History of the Ojibway Nation.* Reprint. Minneapolis: Ross and Haines, 1970.

Watkins, E. A. *A Dictionary of the Cree Language.* Reprint. Toronto: Anglican Book Centre, 1981.

Webster's New World Dictionary of the American Language. 2d college ed. N.p.: William Collins and World, 1976.

White, Andrew, and Cecil Calvert. *A Relation of Maryland, 1685.* Ann Arbor: University Microfilms, 1966.

Whiting, Henry. *Sannilac: A Poem by Henry Whiting, with Notes by Lewis Cass and Henry R. Schoolcraft.* Boston: Carter, Hendee and Babcock, 1831.

Williams, Mentor L. *Schoolcraft's Indian Legends.* East Lansing: Michigan State University Press, 1956. (Contains a reprint of Schoolcraft's *Algic Researches.*)

Williams, Roger. *A Key into the Language of America.* Reprint. Ann Arbor: Gryphon Press, 1971.

Williamson, John P. *An English-Dakota Dictionary.* Reprint. Minneapolis: Ross and Haines, 1970.

Winter, Nevin Otto. *A History of Northwest Ohio.* Chicago: Lewis Publishing, 1917.

Wisconsin Department of Administration. Demographic Services Center. *Official Population Estimates for 1984.* Madison, 1984.

Wisconsin State Gazetteer and Business Directory. Milwaukee: Hogg and Wright, 1882.

Wisconsin's Historical Markers: A Tourist Guide. Madison: Guide Press, 1988.

Woodward, Grace S. *The Cherokees*. Norman: University of Oklahoma Press, 1963.

Worthing, Ruth S. *The History of Fond du Lac County as Told by Its Place Names*. 2d ed. Fond du Lac: Globe Printing, 1976.

Wright, Muriel. *A Guide to the Indian Tribes of Oklahoma*. Norman: University of Oklahoma Press, 1951.

Wyeth. John B. *Oregon*. Ann Arbor: University Microfilms, 1966.

Zeisberger, David. *Indian Dictionary. English, German, Iroquois—the Onondaga, and Algonquin—the Delaware*. Cambridge: John Wilson and Son, University Press, 1887.

Articles

Ackerknecht, Erwin H. "White Indians . . . ," *Bulletin of the History of Medicine* 15 (January 1944): 15–36.

Barbeau, Marcel. "Maple Sugar: Its Native Origin." *Transactions Royal Society of Canada*, 3d ser., 40, sec. 2 (1946): 75–86.

Barton, Albert O. "Where Wisconsin Names Originated." *Wisconsin Archeologist*, n.s., 26 (December 1945): 84–85.

[Beach, John]. "Sac and Fox Indian Council of 1841." *Annals of Iowa*, 3d ser., 12 (July 1920): 325–45.

Beasacker, Robert. "Ten Notable Michigan Novels." *Chronicle* 21 (Spring 1985): 26–17.

Blegen, Theodore G. "That Name Itasca." *Minnesota History* 13 (June 1932): 163–74.

Brisbois, B. W., narrator. "Recollections of Prairie du Chien." Noted down and annotated by Lyman C. Draper, *Collections SHSW* 9 (1882): 282–302.

Brown, Charles. "Lake Wingra." *Wisconsin Archeologist*, o.s., 14 (September 1915): 75–117.

Brown, Charles, and Theodore T. Brown. "Lake Geneva and Lake Como." *Wisconsin Archeologist*, n.s., 7 (April 1928): 129–41.

Brown, Charles, and L. E. Drexel. "Fox Lake." *Wisconsin Archeologist*, o.s., 20 (1921): 112–13.

Brown, Dorothy M. "Indian Lovers Leaps in Wisconsin." *Wisconsin Archeologist*, n.s., 17 (September 1937): 84–87.

Brown, Dorothy M. "Legends of the Wisconsin Hills." *Wisconsin Archeologist*, n.s., 18 (December 1937): 17–24.

Brown, Dorothy M. "Myths and Legends of Wisconsin Waterfalls." *Wisconsin Archeologist*, n.s., 18 (July 1939): 114–15.

Brown, Dorothy M. "Indian Tree Myths and Legends." *Wisconsin Archeologist*, n.s., 19 (February 1939): 30–36.

Brunson, Alfred. "Wisconsin Geographical Names." *First Annual Report and Collections SHSW* 1 (1855; reprint 1903): 110–15.

Butler, A. F. "Rediscovering Michigan's Prairies." *Michigan History* 32 (March 1948): 15–36.

Butler, James D. "Taychoperah: The Four Lakes Country." *Collections SHSW* 10 (1888; reprint 1909): 63–89.

Calkins, Hiram. "Indian Nomenclature of Northern Wisconsin . . ." *First Annual Report and Collections SHSW for 1854* (reprint 1903): 119–26.

Cannon, George H. "Michigan's Land Boundary." *Michigan Pioneer and Historical Collections* 38 (1912): 163–68.

Cassidy, Frederic G. "The Naming of the Four Lakes." *Wisconsin Magazine of History* 29 (September 1945): 7–24.

Cassidy, Frederic G. "Koshkonong: A Misunderstood Place Name." *Wisconsin Magazine of History* 31 (June 1948): 429–40.

Cassidy, Frederic G. "From Indian to French to English—Some Wisconsin Place Names." *Names* 33 (1985): 51–57.

Chamberlain, A. F. "The Significance of Certain Algonquian Animal Names." *American Anthropogist,* 3 (1901): 669–83.

Chamberlain, A. F. "Algonkian Words in American English." *Journal of American Folk Lore* 15 (October–December 1902): 240–67.

Clark, Malcolm H. "Oregon Revisited." *Oregon Historical Quarterly* 61 (June 1960): 211–19.

Cruzat, Don Francisco. "Lieut. Gov. Cruzat's Message to the Sauks and Foxes." *Collections SHSW* 3 (1856): 504–5.

Curot, Michel. "A Wisconsin Fur Trader's Journal, 1803–1804." *Collections SHSW* 20 (1911): 396–471.

Davidson, W. "Personal Narrative of the Black Hawk War." *Collections SHSW* 5 (1868; rpt., 1907): 317–20.

De la Ronde, John T. "Personal Narrative." *Collections SHSW* 7 (1876; reprint 1908): 345–65.

Dexter, Franklin B. "The History of Connecticut as Illustrated by the Names of Her Towns." *Proceedings of the American Antiquarian Society,* n.s., 3 (October 1883–April 1885): 421–45.

Dorsey, J. Owen. "Indian Personal Names." *American Anthropologist* 3 (July 1890): 263–68.

Doty, James Duane. "Northern Wisconsin in 1820." *Collections SHSW* 7 (1876): 195–206.

Dustin, Fred. "Some Indian Place-Names around Saginaw." *Michigan History* 12 (October 1928): 729–39.

Eells, Myron. "Aboriginal Geographic Names in the State of Washington." *American Anthropologist* 5 (1892): 27–35.

Elliott, T. C. "The Strange Case of Jonathan Carver." *Oregon Historical Quarterly* 21 (December 1920): 341–68.

Elliott, T. C. "The Origin of the Name Oregon." *Oregon Historical Quarterly* 22 (June 1921): 91–115.

Elliott, T. C. "Jonathan Carver's Case for the Name Oregon." *Oregon Historical Quarterly* 23 (March 1922): 53–69.

Elliott, T. C. "The Mysterious Oregon." *Washington Historical Quarterly* 22 (October 1931): 289–92.

Ellis, Albert G. "Advent of the New York Indians into Wisconsin." *Collections SHSW* 2 (1856; reprint 1903): 415–49.

Ellis, Albert G. "Fifty-Four Years Recollections of Men and Events in Wisconsin." *Collections SHSW* 7 (1876; reprint 1908): 206–68.

Errett, Russell. "Indian Geographical Names." Part 1, *Magazine of Western History* 1 (May 1885): 51–59; part 2, *Magazine of Western History* 2 (July 1885): 238–46.

Fay, George E. "Bibliography on the Indians of Wisconsin." *Journal of the Wisconsin Indians Research Institute* 1 (March 1965): 107–32.

Fay, George E. "Treaties between the Menominee Indians and the United States of America." *Journal of the Wisconsin Indians Research Institute* 1 (March 1965): 67–106.

Florida Historical Society. "The Complete Story of Osceola." *Florida Historical Quarterly* 33 (January–April 1955): entire issue.

Fontanelle, Henry. "History of the Omaha Indians." *Transactions and Reports, Nebraska State Historical Society* 1 (1885): 76–83.

Forbes, Abbé J. W. Note. *Kateri* 122 (Winter 1979): 27–28.

Frank, M. "Early History of Kenosha." *Collections SHSW* 3 (1853): 370–94.

Gagnieur, William F. "Indian Place-Names of the Upper Peninsula and Their Interpretation." *Michigan History* 2 (July 1918): 526–55; *Michigan History* 3 (July 1919): 412–19.

Gagnieur, William F. "Ketekitiganing (Lac Vieux Desert)." *Michigan History* 12 (October 1928): 776–77.

Gale, Edward C. "The Legend of Lake Itasca." *Minnesota History* 12 (September 1951): 215–25.

Gerard, William R. "Plant Names of Indian Origin." *Garden and Forest* 9 (1896): 252–53, 262–63, 282–83, 292–93, 302–3.

Gerard, William R. "Virginia's Indian Contributions to English." *American Anthropologist*, n.s., 9 (1907): 87–112.

Grignon, Augustin. "Seventy-Two Years' Recollections of Wisconsin." *Collections SHSW* 3 (1856): 197–296.

Halbert, Henry S. "Choctaw Names in Alabama and Mississippi." *Transactions of the Alabama Historical Society* 3 (1898–99): 64–77.

Hamilton, William. "Names Derived from the Indian Language." *Transactions and Reports, Nebraska State Historical Society* 1 (1885): 73–75.

Hart, Irving H. "The Origin and Meaning of the Name 'Itasca'." *Minnesota History* 12 (September 1931): 225–29.

Hartley, Alan H. "The Expansion of Ojibway and French Place Names . . ." *Names* 28 (March 1980): 43–68.

Hathaway, Joshua. "Indian Names." *First Annual Report and Collections, SHSW for 1854* (reprint 1903): 116–18.

Hauberg, John H. "The Black Hawk War, 1831–1832." *Transactions Illinois State Historical Society for 1932* (Springfield, 1932): 91–134.

Hay, Robert. "Kaw and Kansas." *Collections Kansas State Historical Society* 9 (1905–6): 521–26.

Hickling, William, and Gurdon S. Hubbard. "Sketches of Billy Caldwell and Shabonee." In *Addresses Delivered at Annual Meeting, Chicago Historical Society, November 19, 1868* (Chicago: Fergus Printing, 1877).

Hockett, Charles F. "Potawatomi: Part I." *International Journal of American Linguistics* 14, no. 1 (1948): 1–80.

Hockett, Charles F. Note (untitled) in *American Name Society Bulletin* 76 (February 13, 1985); 13.

Hoffman, Walter J. "The Midewiwin or 'Grand Medicine Society' of the Ojibwa." In *Seventh Annual Report Bureau of American Ethnology, 1885–86*, pp. 149–300. Washington, D.C.: Government Printing Office, 1891.

Hoffman, Walter J. "The Menomini Indians." In *Fourteenth Annual Report, Bureau of American Ethnology, 1892–93*, pt. 1, pp. 11–328. Washington, D.C.: Government Printing Office, 1896.

Holand, Hjalmar R. "A Historic Spot near Wautoma, Wisconsin." *Wisconsin Magazine of History* 33 (March 1950): 310–17.

Holmer, Nils M. "Indian Place Names in South America and the Antilles." Part 2, *Names* 8 (December 1960): 197–219; part 3, *Names* 9 (March 1961): 37–52.

Holmes, William H. "The Tomahawk." *American Anthropologist*, n.s., 9 (1908): 264–76.

Hubbard, Gurdon S. "Narrative." In *Addresses Delivered at the Annual Meeting, Chicago Historical Society, November 19, 1868*, pp. 41–46. Chicago: Fergus Printing, 1877.

Ingalls, E. S. "Centennial History of Menominee County [Michigan]," a fragment. *Michigan Pioneer and Historical Society Collections* 1 (1874–76): 265–66.

Jenks, William L. "History and Meaning of the County Names in Michigan." *Michigan Pioneer and Historical Society Collections* 38 (1912): 439–78.

Jipson, Norton W. "Winnebago Villages and Chieftains of the Lower Rock River Region." *Wisconsin Archeologist* 2 (July 1923): 126–39.

Jones, William. "Algonquian (Fox)." ("Fox Texts") in *Handbook of American Indian Languages*, ed. Franz Boas, part 1, BAE. Bulletin 40 Washington, D.C.: Government Printing Office, 1911.

Kahquados, Simon. "The Nation of the Three Fires." *Wisconsin Archeologist* 18 (1919): 109–10.

Keeler, Lucy Elliott. "Old Fort Sandoski of 1745 and the Sandusky Country." *Ohio Archaeological and Historical Quarterly* 17 (1908): 357–429.

Kingston, John T. "Early Western Days." *Collections SHSW* 7 (1876: reprint 1908): 297–344.

Kuhm, Herbert W. "Wisconsin Indian Fishing." *Wisconsin Archeologist*, n.s., 7 (January 1928): 61–114.

Kuhm, Herbert W. "Indian Place-Names in Wisconsin." *Wisconsin Archeologist*, n.s. 33 (March and June 1952): entire issue.

La Flesche, Francis. "Linguistic Notes." Ed. A. S. Gatschet. *American Antiquarian 11* (1889): 129.

Lawson, A. J. "New London and Neighborhood." *Collections SHSW* 3 (1857; reprint 1904): 477–88.

Lawson, Publius V. "The Potawatomi." *Wisconsin Archeologist* 19 (April 1920): 43–116.

Legler, Henry E. "Origin and Meaning of Wisconsin Place Names, with Special Reference to Indian Nomenclature." *Transactions of the Wisconsin Academy of Sciences, Arts and Letters*, part 1, 14 (1902): 16–39.

Leonard, J. A. "Sketch of Whitewater, Walworth County." *Collections SHSW* 3 (1857): 427–34.

Lockwood, James H. "Early Times and Events in Wisconsin." *Collections SHSW* 2 (1856; reprint 1903): 98–196.

Lookaround, Mrs. Angus F. "In the Moon of Sugar Making." *Wisconsin Magazine of History* 32 (March 1949): 321–27.

Lookaround, Phebe Nichols. "Wisconsin's People of the Wild Rice." *Journal of the Wisconsin Indians Research Institute* 2 (December 1966): 61–63.

McArthur, Lewis. "Oregon Geographic Names." *Oregon Historical Quarterly* 27 (January 1926): 431–35.

Mahr, August C. "Indian River and Place Names in Ohio." *Ohio Historical Quarterly* 66 (1957): 137–58.

Martin, Maria E. "Origin of Ohio Place Names." *Ohio Archaeological and Historical Publications* 14 (1905): 272–290.

"Mexican Place Names." *Amigos* 1 (August 1942): 33–39.

Meyer, Alfred H. "Toponomy in Sequent Occupance Geography: Calumet Region, Indiana-Illinois." *Proceedings of the Indiana Academy of Sciences* 54 (1945): 142–59.

Murray, Robert A. "Some Notes on Pipe-Making Stone and Place Names in and around the Plains." *Minnesota Archaeologist* 25 (October 1963): 156–59.

Nichols, Phebe Jewell. "What Does Wisconsin Mean?" *American Indigena* 8 (July 1948): 171–76.

Nichols, Phebe Jewel. "I Knew Chief Oshkosh." *Journal of the Wisconsin Indians Research Institute* 1 (March 1965): 24–32.

Nichols, Phebe Jewel. [Lookaround], Phebe J. "A Letter about the Menominee Indians." *Journal of the Wisconsin Indians Research Institute* 2 (December 1966): 64–67.

Oestreich (Lurie), Nancy. "Trends of Change in Patterns of Child Care and Training among the Wisconsin Winnebago." *Wisconsin Archeologist* 29, n.s., (September–December 1948): 40–136.

Perry, Frances R. "The Meaning of Ocooch." *Ocooch Mountain News* (Richland Center, Wis.), Summer 1978, pp. 3–5.

Peters, Bernard C. "The Origin and Meaning of Chippewa Indian Place Names along the Lake Superior Shoreline." *Names* 32 (September 1984): 234–51.

Peterson, Frederick A., and Ritzenthaler, Robert E. "The Kickapoo Are Still Kicking." *Natural History* 54 (April 1955): 200–206, 224.

Peterson, William J. "Veritas Caput, Itasca." *Minnesota History* 18 (June 1937): 180–85.

Pond, Peter. "Journal of Peter Pond." In "British Regime in Wisconsin," ed. R. G. Thwaites, *Collections SHSW* 18 (1908): 314–54.

Ransom, J. Ellis. "Derivation of the Word 'Alaska'." *American Anthropologist,* n.s., 42 (1940): 550–51.

Rayburn, J. A. "Geographical Names of Amerindian Origin in Canada, Part II." *Names* 17 (June 1969): 49–58.

Robertson, Melvin L. "A Brief History of the Menominee Indians." *Wisconsin Indians Research Institute* 1 (March 1965): 4–19.

Schuette, H. A., and Sybil C. Schuette. "Maple Sugar: A Bibliography of Early Records." *Transactions of the Wisconsin Academy of Science* 29 (1935): 209–36.

Shaw, John. "Indian Chiefs and Pioneers of the Northwest," *Collections SHSW* 10 (1885; reprint 1909): 213–22.

Shea, John G. "The Indian Tribes of Wisconsin." *Collections SHSW* 3 (1856): 125–38.

Skinner, Alanson. "Some Menomini Indian Place Names in Wisconsin." *Wisconsin Archeologist* 18 (August 1919): 97–102.

Smith, Alice E. "Stephen Long and the Naming of Wisconsin." *Wisconsin Magazine of History* 26 (September 1942): 67–71.

Smith, Huron H. "Indian Place Names in Wisconsin." *Milwaukee Public Museum Yearbook* 10 (1930): 252–66.

Smith, Isaac T. "Journal of Isaac T. Smith, 1835–36." In "Early Rock County." *Collections SHSW* 6 (1872): 416–25.

Snow, Vernon F. "From Ouragon to Oregon." *Oregon Historical Quarterly* 60 (December 1959): 439–47.

Staples, H. B. "Origin of the Names of the States of the Union." *Proceedings of the American Antiquarian Society,* n.s., 1 (1880–81): 366–83.

Stewart, George R. "The Source of the Name 'Oregon'." *American Speech* 19 (April 1944): 115–17.

Stewart, George R. "Ouaricon Revisited." *Names* 15 (September 1967): 166–68.

"Stockbridge Indian, A." "Death of John W. Quinney." *Collections SHSW* 4 (1859; reprint 1906): 309–11.

Swisher, Jacob. "War Eagle." *Palimpsest* 19 (February 1949): 33–41.

Taube, Edward. "The Name Wisconsin." *Names* 15 (September 1967): 173–81.

Thwaites, Reuben G., ed. "The Story of the Black Hawk War." *Collections SHSW* 12 (1892): 217–75.

Thwaites, Reuben G., ed. "Walking Cloud's Version of Black Hawk's Surrender." *Collections SHSW* 13 (1895): 463–67.

Thwaites, Reuben G., ed. "Narrative of Spoon Decorah." *Collections SHSW* 13 (1895): 448–62.

Tibon, Gutierre. "Mexio, the Name." *Onomastica* 17 (1959): 5–18.

Tooker, W. W. "The Original Significance of 'Merrimac'." *American Antiquarian and Oriental Journal* 21 (January–November 1899): 14–16.

Trowbridge, C. C. "Shawnese Traditions." *Occasional Contributions, University of Michigan Museum of Anthropology* 9 (1939): 1–71.

Trumbull, J. H. "The Composition of Indian Geographical Names, Illustrated from the Algonkin Languages." *Collections Connecticut Historical Society* 2 (1870): 3–50.

Tyrrell, Joseph B. "Algonquian Indian Names in Northern Canada." *Transactions of the Royal Canadian Institute* 10 (May 1914): 213–31.

Verwyst, Chrysostom. "Geographical Names in Wisconsin, Minnesota and Michigan Having a Chippewa Origin." *Collections SHSW* 12 (1892): 390–98.

Verwyst, Chrysostom. "A Glossary of Chippewa Indian Names of Rivers, Lakes, and Villages." *Acta et Dicta* 4 (July 1916): 253–74.

Vieau, Peter J. "Narrative of Peter J. Vieau." *Collections SHSW* 15 (1900): 458–69.

Vogel, Virgil J. "The Origin and Meaning of 'Missouri'." *Bulletin Missouri Historical Society* 16 (April 1960): 213–22.

Vogel, Virgil J. "Wisconsin's Name: A Linguistic Puzzle." *Wisconsin Magazine of History* 48 (Spring 1965): 181–86. Reprinted as the pamphlet *Wisconsin's Name*. SHSW, 1980.

Vogel, Virgil J. "The Missionary as Acculturation Agent: Peter Dougherty and the Indians of Grand Traverse." *Michigan History* 51 (Fall 1967): 185–201.

Vogel, Virgil J. "Oregon: A Rejoinder." *Names* 16 (June 1968): 136–40.

Vogel, Virgil J. "Indian Trails and Place Names." *Names* 33 (March–June 1985): 39–50.

Whittlesey, Charles. "The Cass Manuscripts." *Collections SHSW* 3 (1856): 141–77.

"Winneboujou." *Wisconsin Archeologist* 9 (January 1930): 130.

Witherell, B. F. H. "Reminiscences of the Northwest." *Collections SHSW* 3 (1857; reprint 1904): 297–337.

Zeisberger, David. "A History of the Indians." Ed. A. B. Hulbert and W. N. Schwarze. *Ohio Archaeological and Historical Quarterly* 19 (January and April 1910): 12–153.

Newspapers and Magazines

Galenian (Galena, Illinois), August 22, 1832. Schoolcraft letter.

Green Bay Press Gazette, July 23, 1986, p. A1. Oneidas.

Iron River Reporter (Michigan), April 21, 1976. Shabbodock.

Kateri (magazine), various issues (Caughnawaga, Quebec).

Milwaukee Sentinel, November 20 and December 13, 1972; June 22, 1985. Indian stories.

Niles Weekly Register, no. 43 (December 1, 1832). Itasca.

Racine Journal-Times, October 30, 1973, p. 80. Oneidas.

Sauk County Weekly News, March 3, 1987, p. 9. Chief Yellow Thunder.

Time, September 6, 1969. Lily of the Mohawks (Kateri Tekakwitha).

Chicago Tribune, January 18, 1956. Kateri Tekakwitha.

Unpublished Material

Chouteau, August. "Notes on the Indians of North America," from "Ancient and Miscellaneous Surveys," 4. St. Louis, February 21, 1816. National Archives.

Gailland, Maurice, S. J. "English-Potawatomi Dictionary." Bureau of American Ethnology MS 1761, n.d.

Gatschet, Albert. "Lexicon of the Peoria Language." A card file, 5 boxes. Bureau of American Ethnology, cat. no. 2481. 1904.

Hartley, Alan H. "Preliminary Observations on Ojibwa Place Names." From author, Duluth, Minn., April 1981.

Jipson, Norton W. "The Story of the Winnebagoes," and "Winnebago Vocabulary." Chicago Historical Society, 1923.

Jipson, Norton W. "Winnebago Place Names," with information from Lyman Draper, John Blackhawk, and Oliver Lamere. Chicago Historical Society, n.d. [1923].

Jipson, Norton W. "Winnebago-English Vocabulary" and "English-Winnebago Vocabulary." Chicago Historical Society, ca. 1924.

Kinzie, John H. "Vocabulary and Grammar of the Winnebago Language." Chicago Historical Society, 1825.

Kinzie, John H. "Sketch of Hoo-wan-nee-kaw," annotated by Nellie Kinzie Gordon. Newberry Library, Chicago, 1831.

Le Boulanger, Joseph Ignatius, S. J. "French-Illinois Dictionary." Photocopy of MS in John Carter Brown Library. Newberry Library, Chicago, 1720.

National Archives. "Letters Received by the Office of Indian Affairs, 1824–81. Chicago Agency, 1824–1834." Microcopy M 234, Roll no. 132.

Skenandore, William. "To the Oneida Indian Council." A three-part report, 13 pages, mimeo dated April 5, May 22, and July 10, 1954. History of the Oneida land problem in Wisconsin. Copy obtained from author, 1954.

Swadesh, Morris. "Linguistics as an Instrument of Prehistory." Paper delivered at meeting of Association of American Anthropologists, Chicago, December 29, 1957.

Vogel, Virgil J. "Research Report on the Fox or Mesquakie Indians." Prepared for Native American Rights Fund in case of Sac and Fox tribe vs. Lacklider, May 26, 1976.

Zindel, Elmer. "Amerindian Loan Words in American English." M.A. thesis, Columbia University, 1955. From Columbia University Library.

Maps

Bradford, T. G. Engraved by G. W. Boynton. *Iowa and Wisconsin.* 1838.

Cram, George F. *Map of Wiskonsin Territory.* 1939.

Farmer, John. *Map of Ouisconsin.* 1830.

Farmer, John. *Farmer's Map of Michigan and Ouisconsin.* New York: J. E. Colton, 1836.

Farmer, John. *Map of the Territories of Michigan and Ouisconsin.* 1851.

Kroeber, A. L. *Distribution of Indian Tribes of North America.* Los Angeles: Southwest Museum, n.d.

Lapham, I. A. *Wisconsin Sectional Map, with the Most Recent Surveys.* Milwaukee: P. C. Hale, 1846.

Polk County Historical Society. *Polk County Wisconsin Road Map, with Directory of Historical Sites.*

Robinson, Arthur, and Jerry Colver. *The Atlas of Wisconsin: General Maps and Gazetteer.* Madison: University of Wisconsin Press, 1974.

Roark, Gene, ed. *Wisconsin Water Trails.* Madison: Wisconsin Conservation Department, n.d.

Tax, Sol, director. *The North American Indians.* 5th printing. Chicago: Department of Anthropology, University of Chicago, 1960.

Tucker, Sarah Jones. *Indian Villages of the Illinois Country.* Vol. 2, Scientific Papers, Illinois State Museum, part 1, atlas. Springfield: Illinois State Museum, 1942.

U.S. Forest Service. *Chequamegon National Forest.* Park Falls, Wisconsin, n.d.

U.S. Geological Survey. *Wisconsin Topographic Map.* Washington, D.C., 1968.

U.S. Geological Survey. Wisconsin local maps, selected quadrangles.

U.S. National Park Service. *Recreational Areas of the U.S.* Washington, D.C.

Wisconsin Department of Transportation. 72 county maps, corrected for January 1984.

Wisconsin Department of Transportation. *Townships and Civil Towns.*

Wisconsin Department of Transportation. Enlarged map, state of Wisconsin.

Wood., W. Raymond, compiler. *An Atlas of Early Maps of the Midwest.* Scientific Papers, vol. 18. Springfield: Illinois State Museum, 1983.

Correspondence

Note: Titles and affiliations are those in effect when correspondence took place.

Amato, Sister Mary, O. P. St. Clara Convent, Sinsiniwa, Wis. August 11 and 21, 1962.

Bruhy, Mark. Archaeologist, Nicolet and Chequamegon National Forests, Rhinelander, Wis. June 12, 1985.

Cassidy, Frederic G. Editor, *Dictionary of American Regional English,* Madison, Wis. January 13, 1984; April 3 and July 25, 1986; February 12, March 13, May 22, and November 27, 1987.

County clerk, Bayfield County, Washburn, Wis. June 20, 1985.

Ebert, Sandra. Deputy county clerk, Buffalo County, Alma, Wis. June 19, 1985.

Foster, Graham. Editor, *Tomahawk Leader,* Tomahawk, Wis. June 19, 1985.

Foster, Paul. President, Racine County Historical Society, Racine, Wis. June 19, 1985.

Hart, William O. Prairie du Sac, Wis. November 18, 1986.

Heiple, Emma, and Robert Heiple. Green Lake, Wis. June 29, 1985.

Hemshrot, Stephen A. Resource agent, Waupaca County Extension, University of Wisconsin, Cooperative Extension Service, Waupaca, Wis. September 10, 1985.

Henke, David L. Executive director, La Crosse County Historical Society, La Crosse, Wis. September 19, 1985.

Herges, Sue. Postmistress, Sissetonn, S.D. September 11 and November 4, 1980.

Howard, Mrs. Marion. Director, Darlington Public Library, Darlington, Wis. September 26, 1986.

Irvin, Mrs. John M. Green County Historical Society, Monroe, Wis. September 3, 1986; January 30 and February 4, 1987.

Kalman, Steve. Milwaukee Post Office. June 10, 1985.

Kleist, Frederica H. Portage Canal Society, Portage, Wis. June 12, 1985.

Konkel, Dennis. Chief, Administrative Services, Wisconsin Bureau of Parks and Recreation, Madison, Wis. May 21, 1986.

Leiterman, Rev. Luke. President, Langlade County Historical Society, Pickerel, Wis. September 9, 1985.

Marsh, Dale E. Executive secretary, Geographic Names Council, Department of Natural Resources, Madison, Wis. July 29, 1987.

Mathias, Harold. Deputy clerk, Buffalo County, Alma, Wis. June 19, 1985.

Miller, Mrs. Dolores J. Appleton, Wis. June 15, 1985.

Munroe, Mara. Historical and genealogy librarian, Oshkosh, Wis. July 27, 1985.

Naylor, Robert K. Demographic Services Center, Madison, Wis. March 31, 1985.

Orth, Donald J. United States Board on Geographic Names, Reston, Va. August 6, 1987.

Payne, Roger L. Manager, Geographic Names Information Service, Reston, Va. October 15, 1986.

Pederson, Paul. Recreation forester, Chequamegon National Forest, Park Falls, Wis. June 19, 1985.

Perry, Frances R. Jackson County Historical Society, scholar of the Winnebago language, Black River Falls, Wis. June 15 and July 5, 1985; December 29, 1986; September 11, 1987.

Poulette, Philip T. Secretary-treasurer, Waushara County Historical Society, Wautoma, Wis. June 10, 1985; May 28, 1986.

Radloff, Eugene. Vilas County Cooperative Extension Resource agent, University of Wisconsin, Eagle River, Wis. August 28, 1986.

Schmitz, Maxine. Lac du Flambeau, Wis. April 12, 1988.

Schweigert, Gerald. President, Rusk County Historical Society, Brule, Wis. July 25, 1985.

Smith, M. J. Omro Area Historical Society, Omro, Wis. August 25, 1986.

Sorkness, Rita. Archives assistant, McIntyre Public Library, University of Wisconsin–Eau Claire, Eau Claire, Wis. May 27, 1987.

Turner, Clara M. Beaver Dam, Wis. June 11 and 23, 1985.

Vallier, Jacque D. Menominee Indian Historical Foundation, Mequon, Wis. June 13, 1985.

Waidlilich, Ann. Librarian, Municipal Reference Service, Madison, Wis. May 1, 1987.
Werner, Frank. President, Polk County Historical Society, Balsam Lake, Wis. August 3, 1985; September 3, 1986.
Williams, Griff. Prairie du Chien, Wis. August 5, 1984; June 12, 1985.
Zeidler, Frank P. Former mayor, Milwaukee, Wis. October 11, 1985.

Interviews

Note: Titles and affiliations are those in effect at the time of interview.

Connor, Gene. Historic preservation officer, St. Croix band of Chippewa Indians, Webster, Wis. September 7, 1985.
Gallo, Gene. Elmhurst, Ill. October 15, 1978; August 2, 1979.
Guthrie, Ben. Lac du Flambeau, Wis. August 28, 1982.
Johnson, Robinson (Whirling Thunder). Winnebago Indian, Chicago, Ill. September 10, 1955.
Leiterman, Rev. R. Luke. Pickerel, Wis. August 10, 1980.
Matrious, Larry. Potawatomi language teacher, Nah-Tah-Wahsh Indian School, Hannahville Reservation, Wilson, Mich. August 22, 1984.
Perry, Frances. Black River Falls, Wis. August 27, 1985.
Schmitz, Maxine. Lac du Flambeau, Wis. September 17, 1990 (by telephone).
Skenandore, William. Oneida Indian, Chicago, Ill. April 7, 1955.
Skinaway, Bennie. Vice-chairman, St. Croix band of Chippewa Indians, Luck, Wis. September 7, 1985.
Taylor, Eugene. Chairman, St. Croix band of Chippewa Indians, Webster, Wis. September 7, 1985.
Taylor, Lolita. Author, member St. Croix band of Chippewa Indians, Webster, Wis. September 7, 1985.
Wagosh, Agnes. Teacher of Ojibwa, NAES College, Chicago. November 8, 1990.

Index